The 21st Century Webster's
Family Encyclopedia

The 21st Century
Webster's
Family Encyclopedia

Volume 2
Blai - Const

1999 Edition

IMPORTED BY/IMPORTE PAR
DS-MAX CANADA
RICHMOND HILL, ONTARIO
L4B 1H7

MALAYSIA
PRO ENTERPRISE SDN BHD
LOT 605, SS13/1K, OFF JLN.
KEWAJIPAN, 47500 SUBANG JAYA
SELANGOR D.E., MALAYSIA

ENGLAND
WENTWALK LTD.
278A ABBEYDALE ROAD, WEMBLEY
MIDDLESEX, HA0 1NT

DS-MAX
IRVINE, CA 92618
IMPORTER: #16-1241510
949-587-9207

TRIDENT PRESS INTERNATIONAL

Copyright © 1999, Uitgeverij Het Spectrum BV, Utrecht

ISBN 1-55280-457-7

Printed in Peru

The 21st Century Webster's Family Encyclopedia
is based on the Spectrum Database

editors:
Bart Drubbel
Tjeerd van der Velde
Saskia van Iperen

Blaine, James Gillespie (1830-93), U.S. politician. He served as U.S. rep-
resentative (1863-76) and senator (1876-81) from Maine, and as secretary
of state under Presidents James A. Garfield (1881) and Benjamin Harrison
(1889-92). He was the Republican candidate for president in 1884, losing to
Grover Cleveland in a campaign in which he refused to repudiate a sup-
porter's description of the Democrats of New York as the party of "rum,
Romanism, and rebellion."

Blair, U.S. family influential in 19th-century politics and the formation of
the Republican Party. **Francis Preston Blair** (1791-1876) of Abington, Va.
founded the *Washington Globe* and was a member of President Andrew
Jackson's Kitchen Cabinet. He later helped to found the new Republican
Party. His eldest son, **Montgomery Blair** (1813-83), was the lawyer who
defended Dred Scott before the Supreme Court in 1857 and was postmaster
general under Lincoln (1861-64). Another son, **Francis Preston Blair, Jr.**
(1821-75), was instrumental in keeping Missouri from seceding when the
Civil War broke out. He was a general in the Union army and was a senator
from Missouri in 1871-73.
See also: Republican Party.

Blair, Eric *See:* Orwell, George.

Blair, Henry (19th-century), U.S. slave and inventor. He became the first
black to hold a patent when he obtained patents for a corn harvester (1835)
and a cotton planter (1836). In 1858, however, it was ruled that slaves could
not hold federal patents; this situation prevailed until after the Civil War.

Blair, John (1732-1800), U.S. jurist who served on the committee that
drafted Virginia's constitution (1776). A delegate to the Constitutional
Convention (1787), Blair sat on the general court and the first court of appeals
and was an associate justice of the U.S. Supreme Court (1789-96).
See also: Supreme Court of the United States.

Blair House, official guest house of the U.S. government, on Pennsylvania
Ave. in Washington, D.C. It was used as a temporary White House by
President Truman (1948-52). The house, built in 1824, was named for its
second owner, Francis Preston Blair, whose family sold it to the government
in 1942.

Blake, Eubie (James Hubert Blake; 1883-1983), African-American ragtime
pianist and composer of the Broadway musical *Shuffle Along* (1921) and the
songs "I'm Just Wild About Harry" and "Memories of You." He was still
performing publicly in his 90s.

Blake, William (1757-1827), English poet and painter. With the help of his
wife, Catherine Boucher, he developed a printing process that he used to
illustrate and publish his own works, including *Songs of Innocence* (1789)
and *Songs of Experience* (1794), collections of lyrics that contrast natural
beauty with humanity's material world. Blake was a revolutionary in both
politics and religion, which is reflected in his art, particularly in the powerful
"Prophetic Books," in which he created a mythology of his own. The most
famous of his Prophetic Books are *The Marriage of Heaven and Hell*

(c.1790) and the epic *Jerusalem* (1804-20). Blake's work was largely ignored by his contemporaries, and his reputation grew significantly after his death.

Blakelock, Ralph Albert (1847-1919), U.S. painter associated with the Hudson River School and known for his moonlit landscapes (*Brook by Moonlight*). Distressed by poverty, Blakelock suffered a mental breakdown (1899); his paintings increased in value and popularity in the early years of the twentieth century.
See also: Hudson River School.

Blanc, Mont, highest peak (15,771 ft/4,807 m) in the European Alps, in southeastern France on the border with Italy. One of the world's longest vehicular tunnels (7.5 mi/12 km), exceeded in Europe only by the 10.2 mi (16.4 km) St. Gotthard (1980), was constructed through Mont Blanc's base in 1965.

Blanchard, Jean Pierre François (1753-1809), French balloonist who made the first aeronautical crossing of the English Channel (1785) and the first balloon ascent in America (1793). He also invented the parachute (1785).
See also: Parachute.

Bland, James A. (1854-1911), African-American composer. In the late 1800s he helped popularize "minstrel music" and was an accomplished banjo player. Among the songs he wrote were "Carry Me Back to Old Virginny" (1878), "Oh, Dem Golden Slippers" (1879), and "In the Evening by the Moonlight" (1879).

Blank verse, unrhymed verse in iambic pentameter (lines consisting of 5 short-long feet, totaling 10 syllables). The most common English meter, it was used to great effect by Marlowe, Shakespeare, and Milton.

Blarney stone, stone of Blarney Castle, Ireland. In legend it has the magical power to confer the gift of eloquence on those who kiss it.

Blasco Ibáñez, Vicente (1867-1928), Spanish antimonarchist politician and novelist. His naturalistic novels include *Reeds and Mud* (1902), *Blood and Sand* (1909), and the World War I novel *The Four Horsemen of the Apocalypse* (1916). He was imprisoned dozens of times for his political activities.

Blatch, Harriot Eaton Stanton (1856-1940), U.S. suffragist; daughter of Elizabeth Cady Stanton and Henry B. Stanton. Blatch formed the Equality League of Self-Supporting Women (1907) and was a member of the National Woman's Party. Her books include *Mobilizing Woman Power* (1918), *A Woman's Point of View* (1920), a biography of her mother (1921), and *Challenging Years* (1940).
See also: Woman suffrage.

Blazing star, or gay feather, any of about 30 species of perennial North American wildflowers of the family Asteraceae, found in prairies and woodlands. The blazing star grows 1 to 6 ft (30 to 180 cm) high, with clusters of purple or pink blossoms surrounded by bracts (leaflike structures the same color as the flowers).

Bleaching, the process of whitening materials, usually with chemicals that reduce or oxidize color. Textiles, flour, oil, and sugar are often bleached.

Bleeding heart, garden plant (*Dicentra spectabilis*) with drooping, heart-shaped flowers, native to China and Japan. The bleeding heart vine of the verbena family is from West Africa.

Blenheim, Battle of, decisive battle in the War of Spanish Succession. On Aug. 13, 1704, troops of the Grand Alliance (England, Austria, and the United Provinces), commanded by the Duke of Marlborough and Prince Eugene of Savoy, triumphed over the Franco-Bavarian soldiers under Marshall Tallard. Fought on the Danube between the Bavarian villages of Blindheim and Hochstadt, Blenheim saved Vienna from the forces of King Louis XIV, consolidated the Grand Alliance, and ended French occupation of Germany.
See also: Spanish Succession, War of the.

Blériot, Louis (1872-1936), French pioneer aviator and inventor. In 1909 he became the first to fly a heavier-than-air machine across the English Channel.

Bligh, William (1754-1817), reputedly cruel British naval officer, captain of the *Bounty* at the time of the now-famous mutiny (1789). In 1805 he became governor of New South Wales and was subsequently imprisoned by mutinous soldiers (1808-10).

Blindness, partial or complete loss of vision, caused by injury to the eyes, congenital defects, or diseases such as cataracts, diabetes, glaucoma, and hypertension. Infant blindness can result if the mother had rubella (German measles) early in pregnancy; malnutrition (especially vitamin A deficiency) may cause blindness in children. There are many ways for blind people to overcome their disability, including Braille (a method of reading with the fingers by touching raised dots), books on tape, and optical scanners generating speech. The use of a cane, guide dog, and sonar devices on glasses all contribute in assisting the blind. The first U.S. school for the blind was the Perkins School for the Blind (1832) in Boston.

Blindworm, legless European lizard (*Anguis fragilis*), found in meadows and woodlands. The adult is about 1 ft (30 cm) long, brownish in color, with smooth scales. The blindworm eats snails and slugs. It is believed to be blind.

Blitzkrieg (German, "lightning war"), originally used to describe the sudden German mechanized warfare attacks on Poland and France in World War II, now applied to any rapid, forceful military advance, such as the 1944 sweep through France by the U.S. Army under Patton.
See also: World War II.

Blitzstein, Marc (1905-64), U.S. composer and librettist. He wrote the texts and music for the operas *The Cradle Will Rock* (1937) and *Regina* (1949). His greatest achievement was his translation and adaption of the English text for the 1954 New York state production of *The Threepenny Opera*, by Kurt Weil and Berthold Brecht.

Blixen-Finecke, Karen *See:* Dinesen, Isak.

Blizzard, snowstorm with high velocity winds, temperatures well below freezing, and visibility less than 500 ft (152.4 m). Such storms are common on the Great Plains east of the Rockies in the United States and Canada, in polar regions, and in parts of Europe and Asia.
See also: Snow.

Bloch, Ernest (1880-1959), Swiss-American classical composer. He was greatly influenced by traditional Jewish music, as evidenced in his symphonic poem *Israel* (1916), *Sacred Service* (1930-33), and *Three Jewish Poems* (1913). He also wrote concertos, chamber music, and suites for piano and strings.

Bloch, Konrad Emil (1912-   ), U.S. biochemist. His studies of animal cells resulted in the discovery of cholesterol, a fatty substance produced from acetic acid. In 1964 he shared the Nobel Prize for physiology or medicine.
See also: Biochemistry; Cholesterol.

Blockade, maneuver normally imposed by means of seapower, designed to cut an enemy's supply routes and force a surrender. The objective may also be to capture an enemy port.

Block, Herbert Lawrence (1909-   ), U.S. political cartoonist. His dry and witty cartoons have been appearing under the signature Herblock in the *Washington Post* since 1943. He was awarded the Pulitzer Prize in 1942 and 1954.

Blockhouse, small log or stone fortification, usually temporary and built to defend newly won territory. Common in frontier America, blockhouses were used by settlers as a gathering place to protect themselves from Native American attacks.
See also: Pioneer life in America.

Bloemfontein, capital of the Orange Free State and judicial capital of South Africa. First settled by Dutch farmers in 1846, it is now a rail and industrial center. Harvard University and the University of Michigan maintain astronomical observatories in the city.
See also: South Africa.

Blood, thick red fluid pumped by the heart and flowing throughout the body in the blood vessels of the circulatory system. The blood serves many functions in the body, but principally it carries nutrients to and waste away from individual cells and helps regulate the body's metabolism. It carries oxygen from the lungs to the tissues, and carbon dioxide from the tissues to the lungs. It transports hormones to tissues that need them, carries nutrients absorbed from the intestine, and bears away the waste products of metabolism to the organs of excretion—the lungs, the kidneys, the intestines, and the skin. Blood also defends the body against infection, and the clotting mechanism minimizes the loss of blood after an injury.

Seen with the naked eye, the blood appears opaque and homogeneous, but upon microscopic examination it is seen to consist of cells. The most numerous are red corpuscles (erythrocytes), which normally outnumber white cells (leucocytes) by 500 to 1. Also present in the blood are minute circular bodies known as platelets, or thrombocytes, necessary for clotting. The blood cells subsist in an intercellular liquid called plasma. The volume of cells and plasma is approximately equal. Blood plasma itself is a complex fluid; 90% of it is water, but the balance consists of proteins, electrolytes, other minerals, and nutrients needed by the body's cells.

Common blood disorders are leukemia (excess white blood cells or leucocytes) and anemia (a lack of red blood cells). For medical purposes, principally transfusion, blood is usually categorized into one of 4 groups, A, B, AB, and O.

See also: Blood transfusion; Blood type, Circulatory system.

Blood count, number of blood cells found in a standard volume of blood; also, the test used to determine that number.
See also: Blood; Hemoglobin.

Bloodhound, breed of dog of European origin, often used for tracking because of its acute sense of smell. Full-grown bloodhounds stand about 2 ft (0.61 m) high at the shoulder and weigh up to 110 lb (50 kg).

Bloodless Revolution *See:* Glorious Revolution.

Blood poisoning, or septicemia, invasion of the bloodstream by toxic microorganisms from a local infection. Symptoms include chills, fever, and prostration.
See also: Blood.

Blood pressure, pressure of the blood upon the walls of the arteries as it is pumped from the heart. The pressure is strongest at the left ventricle of the heart but can be felt pulsing at various points on the body. The pulsing corresponds to the force and rhythm of the heart's pumping action, and it can be measured to determine blood pressure. An instrument called a sphygmomanometer is used to ascertain the pressure at the brachial artery of the forearm, just above the elbow.

Blood pressure is recorded by 2 figures written as a fraction. The numerator indicates the systolic, or maximum, pressure produced by the heart; the denominator indicates the diastolic, or lower, pressure produced by the heart, which results in the least pressure upon the artery. "130/90," for example, is read as "130 over 90." Hypertension and stroke are disorders accompanied by high blood pressure.
See also: Blood.

Bloodroot (*Sanguinaria canadensis*), spring-flowering North American perennial. The blossom is white with 8 to 12 petals and is about 2 in (5 cm) across on a reddish stalk. Native Americans used the red sap as a paint and dye.

Bloodsucker *See:* Leech.

Blood transfusion, transfer of blood or components of blood from one person or animal to another. Transfusions are used to replace blood loss due to hemorrhaging, severe burns, or shock, and in such disorders as hemophilia. They are also used regularly in surgical procedures. Blood must be tested for compatible classification (blood group and Rh factor) to prevent rejection reactions by the recipient. Plasma, the fluid part of blood, is often given when whole blood is not needed or is unavailable.
See also: Blood; Plasma.

Blood type, classification of an individual's blood by group—A, B, AB, or O—and Rh-factor (negative or positive). People with blood group AB can receive blood from all other groups; those with group O can donate to all other groups.
See also: Blood.

Blood vessel *See:* Artery; Blood; Capillary; Vein.

Bloody Sunday *See:* Lenin, V.I.; Union of Soviet Socialist Republics.

Bloomer, Amelia Jenks (1818-94), U.S. social reformer. She edited (1848-54) *The Lily*, a journal advocating temperance and women's rights. In a search for more practical clothes for women, she introduced the baggy pantaloons that came to be known as bloomers.
See also: Woman suffrage.

Bloomfield, Leonard (1887-1949), U.S. linguist whose book *Language* (1933) was the chief text of the structuralist school of linguistics, the scientific study of the form and pattern of language. Bloomfield taught at Illinois and Ohio State universities and was Sterling professor of linguistics at Yale after 1940.
See also: Linguistics.

Bloomsbury group, influential coterie of writers and artists who met in Bloomsbury Square, London, in the early 20th century. Influenced by G. E. Moore, the group included Virginia Woolf, Leonard Woolf, Clive Bell, Vanessa Bell, E. M. Forster, V. Sackville-West, Roger Fry, Duncan Grant, J. M. Keynes, and Lytton Strachey.

Bloor, Mother (Ella Reeve Bloor; 1862-1951), U.S. radical activist. She participated in the temperance and women's suffrage movements and was a Socialist Party organizer (1902-19) before cofounding the U.S. Communist Party (1919). Called the "Matron Saint" of the party, she served on its national committee (1932-48).
See also: Woman suffrage.

Blount, William (1749-1800), U.S. politician and a signer of the Constitution. President Washington appointed him governor of the Tennessee territory, and in 1796 he was elected to the Senate from the new state. Blount was expelled from the Senate the next year for aiding the British in their plot to seize Spanish Florida.

Blow fly, any of various flies of the family Calliphoridae. The best known of these 2-winged flies is the bluebottle (*Calliphora vicina*). Blowflies lay eggs in carrion, excrement, or open wounds.

Blücher, Gebhard Leberecht von (1742-1819), Prussian general, made a field marshal after helping to defeat Napoleon in the Battle of Leipzig (1813). A year later he led Prussian troops into Paris, and in 1815 the timely intervention of his troops was important in Wellington's victory over Napoleon at Waterloo.
See also: Napoleonic Wars.

Blue baby, infant with a blueness of skin usually caused by a congenital heart defect leading to a mixture of venous and arterial blood.
See also: Cyanosis.

Bluebeard, villain of a traditional tale in which a rich man's seventh wife disobeys him and finds the murdered bodies of former wives. She is saved by her brothers. Maeterlinck based a play on the legend.

Bluebell, any of various wild perennial plants with blue bell-shaped flowers. The term also refers to the Scottish bluebell or harebell of the bellflower family, most commonly the English bluebell, California bluebell, and Virginia bluebell.

Blueberry, any of several hardy deciduous shrubs (genus *Vaccinium*) bearing a blue-black fruit, many species of which are found in North America. The high-bush blueberry (*V. cerymbosum*), which may reach 15 ft (4.6 m) in height, and the low-bush blueberry (*V. augustifolium*) are the two most commonly cultivated. A popular component of jellies, jams, and pastry fillings, blueberries are frequently canned and frozen.

Bluebird, any of several species (genus *Sialia*) of migratory songbirds of the thrush family, related to the robin but with blue above a red breast. Bluebirds often nest near human habitations.

Bluebonnet (*Lupinus subcarnosus*), annually blooming, low-growing lupine (with edible, bean-like seeds). It is the state flower of Texas.

Blue crab, any of several edible, soft-shell crabs (*Callinectes sapidus* and *C. hastatus*) that inhabit Atlantic coastal shores and estuaries. The shell is green-brown and about 6 in (15 cm) wide; the legs are bluish. The blue crab is a scavenger, feeding on dead animals.

Bluefish (*Pomatomus saltatrix*), voracious fish of the family Pomatomidae, found in the Atlantic and Indian oceans and the Mediterranean Sea. It can grow to a length of about 4 ft (1.22 m) and attain a weight up to 30 lb (13.6 kg), though it normally averages 30 in (.75 m) in length and 10-12 lb (4.5-5.5 kg) in weight. A popular game fish resembling the pompano and related to the sea bass, the bluefish is caught commercially for food.

Bluegrass, traditional, instrumental country music, played on unamplified string instruments (banjo, fiddle, mandolin, and guitar). The style, highly improvisational with close harmonies, was developed in the late 1930s by Bill Monroe and his Blue Grass Boys and by the banjo player Earl Scruggs.

Bluegrass State *See:* Kentucky.

Blue jay, crested bird (*Cyanocitta cristata*) widespread in the eastern half of the United States and Canada. The adult is 1 ft (30 cm) long with pale gray underparts and a black necklace. Upperparts are blue with black and white markings.

Blue law, U.S. state law regulating public and private behavior in accordance with criteria of "public morality." The term, derived from the blue paper on which some were printed, was first used to describe 17th-century laws of the New Haven Colony that prohibited dancing, card playing, and drunkenness and were particularly restrictive concerning activities that could be engaged in on Sundays. The most famous blue law (ultimately repealed) was the 18th amendment to the Constitution (1919), which made the manufacture, transport, and sale of alcoholic beverages illegal. Some states still enforce blue laws today, mostly those which regulate business and public events on Sunday. Some laws have been found to be unconstitutional under the First Amendment.

Blue Nile *See:* Nile River.

Blue Ridge Mountains, eastern range of the Appalachians extending southwest 600 mi (960 km) from Pennsylvania to northern Georgia. Grandfather Mountain, at 5,964 ft (1,818 m), is the tallest peak. The Blue Ridge Mountains are pre-Cambrian metamorphic rock with igneous intrusions. Constituent ranges include the Great Smoky Mountains and the Black Mountains. *See also:* Appalachian Mountains.

Blues, U.S. musical form derived from the work songs, spirituals, and "field hollers" of African Americans of the South, characterized by the use of flattened "blue notes." The blues, which came to be the principal basis of the jazz idiom, has the characteristic pattern of a 12-bar structure, with distinctive harmonies, most probably of African origin. What began as songs, many about despair and cynicism, accompanied by guitar, harmonica, or piano, has expanded to include a purely instrumental form. The blues were first popularized by W.C. Handy ("Memphis Blues" and "St. Louis Blues"); early blues artists include Ma Rainey, Bessie Smith, and Blind Lemon Jefferson.

Bluet, North American wildfower (*Houstonia caerula*) having 4 bluish lobes with a yellow center.

Blue thistle *See:* Viper's bugloss.

Blue vitriol *See:* Sulfate.

Blue whale, member (*Balaenoptera musculus*) of the rorqual family of baleen whales. The blue whale is the largest animal that has ever lived—up to 100 ft (30 m) in length and 220 tons (200 metric tons) in weight. Baleen whales have no teeth. Instead, thin plates in their mouths (called baleen) strain out tiny organisms, called plankton, on which the whales feed. Blue whales live in all oceans, but breed in warm waters. Like other whales, they are mammals; they bear live young and suckle them on milk. A newborn blue whale may be over 20 ft (6.1 m) long and weigh 3 tons (2.7 metric tons). Today, the blue whale is an endangered species because of excessive whaling.

Bluford, Guion Stewart, Jr. (1942-   ), U.S. astronaut. In 1983, Bluford made a 6-day voyage on the space shuttle *Challenger*, becoming the first African American to travel in space.

Blum, Léon (1872-1950), creator of the modern French Socialist party, and the first socialist and the first Jewish person to become premier of France. As premier in 1936-37, he led the Popular Front, a coalition of Socialists and Radicals opposed to fascism. Blum was imprisoned by the Germans, 1940-45. He became premier again in 1946-47.

Blume, Judy (1938-   ), U.S. author. Her best-known works are in the "young adult" genre and deal with experiences of teenagers and preteens as they grow toward maturity. Her books in this vein include *Are You There, God? It's Me, Margaret* (1970), *Then Again, Maybe I Won't* (1971), and *Forever* (1975). Adult novels include *Wifey* (1978) and *Smart Woman* (1983).

Blushing, sudden, brief redness to the face and neck that occurs when capillaries, tiny blood vessels in the skin, swell with blood.

Bly, Nellie (Elizabeth Cochrane; 1867-1922), U.S. reporter. She pretended to be insane to gain entry to an insane ward to report on treatment of the insane (1888). In 1889 she beat the record of the Jules Verne character Phileas Fogg (*Around the World in Eighty Days*), traveling around the world in 72 days, 6 hours, 11 minutes, and 14 seconds.

Bly, Robert (1926-   ), U.S. poet and translator whose works deal with American themes. *Silence in a Snowy Field* (1962) explores his native state of Minnesota and concepts of solitude and silence. *The Light Around the Body* (1967) is an anti-Vietnam War statement. He has also translated and printed works of foreign poets including Rilke. He was the recipient of the National Book Award in 1968.

B'nai B'rith, Jewish service organization founded in New York in 1843. B'nai B'rith supports hospitals and orphanages and offers vocational guidance and disaster relief. Branch organizations include the Hillel Foundation, for Jewish university students and faculty; B'nai B'rith Youth; and the Anti-Defamation League (founded 1913) to combat discrimination.

Boa constrictor (*Constrictor constrictor*), nonpoisonous snake of the family Boidae (which includes pythons and anacondas), mostly found in the tropics of the Americas. The live-bearing boa constrictor, 10-18 ft (3-5 m) in length, suffocates its prey (birds and mammals) by squeezing.

Boadicea, or Boudicca (d. A.D. 61), British queen of the Iceni of Norfolk. In A.D. 60 she led a revolt against the Romans, sacking Camulodunum (Colchester), Londinium (London), and Verulamium (St. Albans) before being defeated. She took poison to avoid capture.

Boar, wild, either of 2 species of wild pig, the Eurasian *Sus scrofa* and the Indian *S. cristatus*. The wild boar stands about 3 ft (91 cm) at the shoulder and has stiff bristles over a short gray-black undercoat. It has 2 tusks in the lower jaw and broad feet, adaptations to the marshy areas it inhabits. The wild boar is omnivorous.
See also: Peccary.

Boas, Franz (1858-1942), German-born U.S. anthropologist and ethnologist, leader in establishing the cultural-relativist school of anthropology in the English-speaking world. One of the earliest to use statistical methods in his field, he was an authority on Native American languages, the first professor of anthropology at Columbia University (1899-1936), and the author of more than 30 books, including *The Mind of Primitive Man* (1911) and *Anthropology and Modern Life* (1928).
See also: Anthropology; Ethnography.

Boat *See:* Boating; Ship.

Boating, popular pastime using waterborne craft for pleasure. Boats can be propelled by small motors, sails, or paddles (oars). They vary from 1- and 2-person kayaks, canoes, and rowboats to yachts ranging from 30 to 120 ft (9 to 36.5 m). There are more than 14 million pleasure boats in the United States, used primarily for sports fishing and cruising inland waterways.

Bobcat (*Lynx rufus*), ferocious North American spotted lynx (wild cat), named for its short (6 in/15.2 cm) tail. A nocturnal animal, the bobcat grows to a length of about 3 ft (0.9 m) and has a brown and white coat with black spots and stripes.

Bobolink (*Dolichonyx oryzivorus*), North American migratory songbird. Also called ricebird (for feeding on rice crops during southern migration), it has a dull plumage, except in spring, when the male acquires white and yellow patches. Once hunted but now protected, the bobolink breeds in the United States and southern Canada, migrating to South America for the winter.

Bobsledding, winter sport pitting 2- or 4-person sleds against each other down a steep incline. Capable of traveling at 90 mph (145 kmph), bobsleds negotiate a twisting course with steep embankments ranging from 1,312 yards (1,200 m) to 1,640 yards (1,500 m) long. The team posting the fastest times after 4 runs is the winner. Bobsledding was invented in Switzerland around 1890.

Bobwhite, any of several North American gamebirds (genus *Colinus*)of the pheasant family, often called quail or partridge. About 10 in (25 cm) long and reddish-brown in color, the bobwhite is named for the sound of its mating call and feeds on insects and seeds. Bobwhites travel and sleep in groups, called coveys.

Boccaccio, Giovanni (1313-75), Italian writer and humanist, whose work had a lasting influence on European literature and was used as a source by such writers as Chaucer and Shakespeare. A classical scholar and friend and admirer of Petrarch, he is the author of *Amorous Fiammetta* (1343-44), the first modern psychological novel, and the *Decameron* (1348-53), a collection of 100 short and often ribald tales set against the background of a plague epidemic in Florence. The latter work was the first literary expression of Renaissance humanist realism. He also produced important works in mythology, anthropology, and biography.
See also: Renaissance.

Boccherini, Luigi (1743-1805), Italian composer and cellist, noted for his chamber music. His more than 400 works, including string quartets and quintets and cello concertos, have been compared to those of Haydn, his contemporary.
See also: Chamber music.

Boccioni, Umberto (1882-1916), Italian painter and sculptor. A pioneer of futurism, he tried to capture the movement, speed, and sensations of modern life by using dynamic forms.
See also: Futurism.

Bode's law, or Titius-Bode law, a statement of the relative mean distances of the planets from the sun. The formula begins with the numbers of the series, 0, 3, 6, 12, 24 (each new number being twice the previous one). If each number is increased by 4 and divided by 10, the series becomes 0.4, 0.7, 1.0, 1.6, 2.8, 5.2, 10.0, 19.6, 38.8. The law holds that these numbers express the relative mean distances of the planets from the sun, the earth's distance being the standard: 1.0. The German mathematician Johann Titius discovered this relationship in 1766; the German astronomer Johann Bode published it in 1772. It holds fairly well for the planets known at the time and for Uranus and the asteroid belt (both discovered later), but not for Neptune and Pluto.
See also: Astronomy.

Bodhisattva, in Mahayana Buddhism, spiritual being on the path to enlightenment. A bodhisattva delays entrance into the state of nirvana until all others have entered the same state. Bodhisattvas are worshiped and can respond to prayer; their exemplary lives are the subject of many Buddhist legends.
See also: Buddha, Gautama; Buddhism.

Bodhi tree *See:* Bo tree; Buddha, Gautama.

Bodin, Jean (1530?-96), French political philosopher who argued that stable government required a moderate absolutism founded on divine right but subject to divine and natural law. He advocated religious toleration as necessary in a just state.
See also: Philosophy.

Bodleian Library, the library of Oxford University in Britain. It was established in 1602 by the English diplomat Sir Thomas Bodley to replace an earlier library, dating back to the 14th century, that had been destroyed. Its collection includes 2.5 million books, including many Oriental manuscripts.
See also: Oxford University.

Bodoni, Giambattista (1740-1813), Italian printer. The Bodoni typeface, with its sharp contrast between thick and thin strokes, has been widely used in modern printing.
See also: Printing.

Boehmeria, any of about 100 species of perennial plants of the nettle family. One variety, called *false nettle*, grows as a wild flower in the Eastern United States. Another kind, *ramie*, native to China and Japan, has been cultivated for fiber since prehistoric times. Ramie is used in industrial sewing thread, packing materials, and fishnet.
See also: Ramie.

Boeing, William Edward (1881-1956), U.S. industrialist and founder of the Boeing Aircraft Company, a firm specializing in large commercial and military aircraft. Boeing helped carry the world's first international airmail in one of his planes in 1919. In the post-World War I and World War II periods, his company gained worldwide importance with the development of various kinds of military aircraft. The company currently produces some of the most widely used jet aircraft in commercial aviation, including the Boeing 707 and the famous jumbo jet, the Boeing 747.

Boeotia, region of ancient Greece, north of the Gulf of Corinth in central Greece. The area of 1,100 sq mi (2,850 km) was rich farmland. The chief city, Thebes, dominated the Boeotian League, formed to protect the area from encroachment by other city-states. The home of the poets Hesiod and Pindar, Boeotia later became part of the modern Greek state.
See also: Thebes.

Boers (Dutch, "farmers"), term applied to South African inhabitants of Dutch, German, and French Huguenot descent who settled in the region beginning in 1652. Now called Afrikaners, they speak their own language (Afrikaans). Their racial attitudes were responsible for the rise of apartheid.

Boer War, or South African War, fought between the British and the Boers (settlers of Dutch descent) from 1899 to 1902. The Boers resented British territorial expansion from their Cape of Good Hope colony, while the British aimed at a united South Africa and complained of the harsh treatment of immigrant British gold prospectors by Boers. Well-equipped by Germany, the more numerous Boer forces took the offensive in 1899, but the arrival of British reinforcements turned the tide, and by late 1900 the Boers had to resort to guerrilla tactics. The war ended with the Treaty of Vereeniging in 1902, a British victory that shifted the conflict into the political arena.
See also: South Africa.

Boethius, Anicius Manlius Severinus (c.480-525), Roman philosopher and statesman whose works profoundly influenced medieval thought. A high official under Theodoric the Great, he was accused of treason and executed. While in prison, he wrote his great work, *The Consolation of Philosophy*. *See also:* Philosophy.

Bog, spongy, waterlogged ground composed chiefly of decaying vegetation. Often formed in stagnant lakes, bogs are mainly produced by sphagnum (bog moss), from which peat is formed. Their acidity makes bogs good natural preservers, and in Europe and America they have yielded plant and animal remains from earlier ages.

Bogart, Humphrey DeForest (1899-1957), U.S. film actor, famous for his screen image as the cool, tough anti-hero. Among his most notable films are *The Maltese Falcon* (1941), *Casablanca* (1942), and *The African Queen* (1951), for which he won an Academy Award as best actor.

Bogotá (pop. 5,026,000), capital and largest city of Colombia. Founded by the Spanish in 1538 on the site of Chibcha settlement, it is a commercial and cultural center, with several universities (the oldest from 1573). Its climate is mild because of its altitude of over 8,500 ft (2,591 m), at the edge of an Andean plateau.
See also: Colombia.

Bohemia, historic region in central Europe. It was once part of the Austro-Hungarian Empire. In 1918, after a war-torn history, it became a province in the republic of Czechoslovakia, of which its chief city, Prague, became the capital. In 1949 it lost its separate provincial status. The area is rich in minerals and fine agricultural land.

Bohr, Niels Henrik David (1885-1962), Danish physicist who proposed a model of the atom in 1913, suggesting that the hydrogen atom consisted of a single electron orbiting around a central proton (the nucleus), and that the electron could carry only certain well-defined quantities of energy. This theory accounted both for the atom's stability and for its characteristic radiation and absorption of energy. In 1927 Bohr proposed the complementarity principle to account for apparent paradoxes in the wave and particle approaches to describing sub-atomic particles. Although he helped develop the atomic bomb, he was always deeply concerned about implications for humanity. In 1922 he received the Nobel Prize in physics.
See also: Atom; Physics.

Boileau-Despréaux, Nicolas (1636-1711), French poet, satirist, and critic. His insistence on classical standards, expressed in the didactic poem *L'Art poétique* (1674), influenced literary taste in France and England in the 18th century.

Boiler, device for heating water to produce steam. The 2 main types of boiler are the fire-tube, in which hot gases are passed through tubes surrounded by water, and the water-tube, in which water is passed through tubes surrounded by hot gases. Fuels include coal, oil, gas, and nuclear energy.

Boise (pop. 205,775), largest city and capital of the state of Idaho, located in the lower Boise River valley. Named by French-Canadian settlers Boisé

(meaning wooded), it provided a resting place for travelers from the heat of the Snake River Plains. The modern city was founded in 1863. The influx of Basque shepherds in the early 20th century turned the area into a center for wool production. Products today include the famous Idaho potatoes, sugar beets, alfalfa, fruits, and dairy products, as well as steel products, furniture, and electrical equipment. The city is a center for the insurance and construction trades. There are several hot springs nearby, and the region is a vacation area.
See also: Idaho.

Boito, Arrigo (1842-1918), Italian poet and composer. His own operas include *Mefistofele* (1868; revised 1875) and *Nerone* (1918), though he is best known as the librettist of Verdi's *Otello* (1887) and *Falstaff* (1893) and of Ponchielli's *La Gioconda* (1876).
See also: Opera.

Bok, Edward William (1863-1930), Dutch-born U.S. editor. As editor of *The Ladies' Home Journal* (1889-1919), he used the magazine to campaign for good causes. In his retirement he wrote the Pulitzer Prize-winning *The Americanization of Edward Bok* (1920).

Bola (Spanish, "ball"), weapon used for hunting by native South American tribes. It consists of round leather-covered stone or iron weights connected by cords or leather thongs up to 8 ft (2.4 m) long. There may be 2 or 3 such covered balls, each with its own cord connected to a common center. The bolas are whirled overhead to gain momentum and then hurled at quarry. On contact the balls wind around the animal's legs and prevent it from fleeing. Argentinean gauchos still use bolas for catching cattle, and Eskimos in the Arctic hunt with a similar weapon.

Bolero, type of Spanish folk dance and the music that accompanies it. The bolero is performed in 3/4 time. It is often accompanied by castanets, guitars, and tambourines. Dancers perform solo or as couples. *Bolero* (1928), a 1-act ballet composed by Maurice Ravel, helped popularize the dance and musical form.

Boleyn, Anne (1507-36), second wife of Henry VIII and mother of Elizabeth I. Henry's first queen, Catherine of Aragon, had failed to produce a son, and he divorced her to marry Anne in 1533. Elizabeth was born later that year, but Anne bore no living son either. She was beheaded after being convicted of dubious charges of adultery and incest.
See also: Henry (England).

Bolingbroke, Henry St. John, 1st Viscount (1678-1751), English statesman and historian. A Tory, as secretary of state he successfully handled the negotiations for the Treaty of Utrecht (1713). He lost office on the death of Queen Anne, and sought exile in France (1715-25).
See also: Utrecht, Peace of.

Bolívar, Simón (1783-1830), South American soldier and statesman responsible for several liberation movements against Spanish authority. After several abortive attempts during the 1810s, he led the liberation of Venezuela in 1821 and created the federal state of Greater Colombia, including what is now Venezuela, Colombia, and Ecuador. He went on to liberate Peru (1824) and to form the republic of Bolivia (1825). Bolívar envisaged a united South America, but secessionist movements arose, and Peru and Bolivia turned against him in the 1820s. Venezuela and Ecuador seceded from Greater Colombia in 1829, and in the following year Bolívar resigned as president. Today he is regarded as the liberator of South America, one of the great heroes of its history.

See also: Venezuela.

Bolivia, landlocked South American republic, bordered by Brazil in the north and east, Paraguay in the southeast, Argentina in the south, and Peru and Chile in the west.

Land and climate. The 3 distinct regions of Bolivia are the Oriente (east), the Montañas (center), and the Altiplano (west). The Oriente is a low alluvial plain containing tropical forest and extensive swamps. The Montañas consists of the Cordillera Oriental mountain range, whose eastern slopes shelter fertile valleys. It is Bolivia's largest cultivated area with peaks over 21,000 ft (6,400 m) high and valleys that fall to 6,000 ft (1,929 m). The windswept Altiplano, a broad plain between 2 high Andes ranges, is the most populous area and the highest inhabited area in the world, most of it over 12,000 ft (3,658 m). It is home to more than half the population. Lake Titicaca on the Peruvian border is the highest navigable lake in the world (12,507 ft/3,812 m). The climate varies from the steady cold of the Altiplano to jungle heat in the Oriente.

People. More than 40% of Bolivians are Native Americans, with another one-third being mestizo (Native American and Caucasian) and about 15% Caucasians of Spanish descent. Spain's colonial policy prevented Native Americans from learning Spanish, so less than 40% of the population speak it. Most Caucasians speak at least 1 Native American language. About 95% of the people are Roman Catholic. Sucre is Bolivia's capital, but La Paz is its major city.

Economy. About two-fifths of Bolivians work subsistence farms and wheat and rice must be imported to meet basic needs. The animals of the highlands

---

Bolivia

Capital:	Sucre (official), La Paz (actual)
Area:	424,164 sq mi (1,098,581 sq km)
Population:	7,826,352
Language:	Spanish, Aymara, Quechua
Government:	Presidential republic
Independent:	1825
Head of gov.:	President
Per capita:	U.S. $800

(llamas, alpacas, and vicuñas) furnish high-grade wool, a leading source of income in certain areas. Bolivia is leading world producer of tin and antimony. Oil has been a major export since 1967. Despite its mineral wealth Bolivia remains a comparatively poor country.

History. Before being conquered by Gonzalo and Hernando Pizarro (1538), Bolivia was home to an advanced Ayamará civilization around Lake Titicaca that was subjugated by the Incas. The Spanish exploited Bolivia's wealth with forced Indian labor. The country won its independence in 1825 after long campaigns led by José de Sucre, but over the next 100 years Bolivia lost much valuable territory in wars with Brazil, Chile, and Paraguay. The Nationalist Revolutionary Movement (MNR), a pro-miner organization, came to power in 1952 but was overthrown by the military in 1964. In 1980, after nearly 20 years of unstable military regimes, a civilian government came to power under President Hernán Siles Zuazo. Zuazo resigned in 1985 and was succeeded by Paz Estenssoro. Jaime Paz Zamora was elected president in 1989 and left his seat to Gonzalo Sanchez de Lozada in 1993. The latter was succeeded by Hugo Bánzer Suárez in 1997.

Böll, Heinrich (1917-85), German author and winner of the Nobel Prize for literature in 1972. His books are bitterly satiric, exploring themes of despair and love in post-World War II Europe. Important among his works are *Billiards at Half Past Nine* (1959) and *The Clown* (1965).

Boll weevil (*Anthonomus grandis*), most damaging cotton pest in the United States. The beetle, 1/4 in (6 mm) long, lays eggs in cotton buds and fruit and feeds on the bolls and blossoms, causing estimated losses of $200 million a year.

Bologna (pop. 401,300), Italian city 51 mi (82 km) north of Florence at the foot of the Apennines. It is an ancient Etruscan and Roman city, with a university founded in 1088, many medieval buildings, and Renaissance paintings and sculptures. Capital of the Emilia Romagna region, it is an agricultural and industrial center.
See also: Italy.

Bolometer, in physics, instrument used to measure minute differences of radiant energy by changes in the electrical resistance of a *thermistor*, a form of conductor exposed to the energy. Biometers can measure the radiation from stars.
See also: Physics.

Bolsheviks, proponents of the wing of the Russian Social Democratic Labor Party (RSDLP) led by Lenin. The name originated in 1903 when the Central Committee of the RSDLP split over the criteria of party membership. Lenin called his followers *Bolsheviks* (from the Russian word for *majority*) and his opponents *Menshevik* (from the word for *minority*). The party seized state power in the revolution of Oct. 1917. In March 1918 the name was changed to Russian Communist Party. The Bolsheviks later founded the Third (Communist) International, while the Mensheviks remained affiliated to the Second (Socialist) International.
See also: Communism; Mensheviks; Lenin, V.I.

Bolshoi Ballet, the foremost ballet company of the former USSR. The Moscow company (established 1825) was overshadowed by the more traditional St. Petersburg companies until the early 20th century, when it was taken over by Alexander Gorsky, who reshaped the Bolshoi. It has been one of the world's leading companies since the late 1950s.
See also: Ballet.

Bolshoi Theater, Russian theater, ballet, and opera house, with one of the largest stages in the world. It is the home of the Bolshoi Ballet, and its productions have a worldwide reputation.
See also: Bolshoi Ballet.

Boltzmann, Ludwig (1844-1906), Austrian physicist who made fundamental contributions to thermodynamics, classical statistical mechanics, and kinetic theory. His Stefan-Boltzmann Law states that the total energy radiated from a body is proportional to the fourth power of the temperature.
See also: Thermodynamics.

Bomb, in computer technology, major failure in a program. A computer system is said to be "bombed" when it is significantly disrupted by a faulty program.
See also: Computer.

Bomb, explosive weapon that injures and kills on detonation. World War I bombs dropped by aircraft weighed as much as 660 lb (300 kg). During the late 1960s, the United States built bombs weighing 15,000 lb (6,800 kg) for use in the Vietnam War. The development of the atomic bomb enormously increased explosive power. In 1952, the United States exploded an even more destructive (10.4 megaton) hydrogen bomb, with an explosive force equivalent to 10.4 million tons of TNT. Hydrogen bombs with an explosive power of up to 100 million tons of TNT have been built since then. The so-called "smart bomb" was developed in the 1980s and used extensively in the Persian Gulf War of 1991. These bombs contain electronic mechanisms that guide the trajectory and have remarkable pinpoint accuracy. The use of cameras located in the "nose" of the bombs have provided excellent photographs of such hits.
See also: Explosive.

Bombay (pop. 9,925,900), large seaport in western India, capital of Maharashtra state, on the Arabian Sea. Bombay was built on several small islands, now joined to each other and to the mainland, forming an area of 25 sq mi (65 sq km). Its large harbor deals with the bulk of India's imports, notably wheat and machinery, and exports such as cotton, rice, and manganese. Local industries include textiles, leather goods, and printing. Bombay is an important cultural center, with a university founded in 1857. The city is overcrowded, with a fast-growing, mainly Hindu population. The site was ceded to the Portuguese in 1534 and passed to Great Britain in 1661. The city was headquarters of the British East India Company (1668-1856).
See also: India.

Bonaparte, family name of the Emperor **Napoleon I**. The Italian spelling, Buonaparte, was general until Napoleon adopted the French form in 1796.

The family emigrated to the island of Corsica in the 16th century, and Napoleon was born there in 1769. His older brother, **Joseph** (1768-1844), was king of Naples (1806-08) and of Spain (1808-13); his youngest brother, **Jérôme** (1784-1860), held the throne of Westphalia (1807-13). Napoleon's son by Empress Marie Louise of Austria was hailed by supporters as **Napoleon II** (1811-32) and king of Rome (1811-14), but he never reigned in France. **Napoleon III** (Louis Napoleon Bonaparte; 1808-73), the son of Napoleon I's brother Louis, became emperor of France after a coup in 1852, establishing the Second Empire. He was deposed in 1870.
See also: Napoleon I; Napoleon II; Napoleon III.

Bonaparte, Napoleon *See:* Napoleon I.

Bonaventure, Saint (1221-74), Italian medieval scholastic philosopher and theologian. He taught at Paris and later became Master General of the Franciscan order. He distinguished between philosophy, based on humanity's natural knowledge, and theology, which attempts to understand the Christian mysteries.
See also: Scholasticism.

Bond, chemical, link that holds atoms together in compounds. The theory that atoms consist of electrons orbiting in shells around the nucleus led to an explanation of chemical bonding, which had first been noted in the nineteenth century. Atoms combine to achieve highly stable filled outer shells containing 2, 8, or 18 electrons, either by transfer of electrons from one atom to the other (ionic bond) or by the sharing of one electron from each atom such that both electrons orbit around both nuclei (covalent bond). The energy and length of chemical bonds, as well as the angles between them, may be investigated by spectroscopy and X-ray diffraction.
See also: Atom; Chemistry.

Bond, Julian (1940-   ), U.S. civil rights leader, Democratic member of the Georgia House of Representatives 1965-75, and state senator 1975-87. In 1965, after Bond's election to the Georgia state legislature, fellow members refused him his seat because they objected to his opposition to U.S. involvement in the Vietnam War. In December, 1966, the U.S. Supreme Court ruled in Bond's favor. At the 1968 Democratic National Convention, Bond became the first African American to have his name placed in nomination for Vice-President, but he was too young to qualify. In 1971 Bond helped found the Southern Poverty Law Center, which helps protect the legal rights of poor people of all races.
See also: Civil rights.

Bone, hard tissue that forms the skeleton. Bone supports the body, protects its organs, acts as an anchor for muscles and as a lever for the movement of limbs, and is the main reserve of calcium and phosphate in the body. Bones have a compact, hard shell surrounding a porous, spongy bone inner layer. Human bones are classified as long bones (mostly in the arms and legs) and short bones (e.g., the skull, pelvis, and vertebrae). A hollow cavity in long bones contains marrow, which helps to form blood cells. Broken bones (fractures) mend by the production of new cartilage and its gradual replacement by new bone. Insufficient calcium, phosphate, or vitamin D causes soft

bones (rickets). Other disorders include osteoporosis (loss of bone density, common in old age) and osteoarthritis.
See also: Skeleton.

Bonefish, or ladyfish, herringlike fish (*Elops saurus*) named for the large numbers of fine bones that make it tedious to eat. A popular game fish nonetheless, the bonefish is found in the West Indies and along the coast of Mexico.

Boneset, perennial plant (*Eupatorium perfoliatum*) with hairy leaves, native to wet areas of the United States. This bitter herb grows from 2 ft to 6 ft (.5 m to 2 m) high and bears small white flowers in numerous heads. Tea made from the leaves makes people sweat and is used as a tonic.

Bonheur, Rosa (1822-99), French artist famous for paintings of animals. She made her reputation with *The Horse Fair* (1853), a scene full of vigor and grace. Much of her work can be seen in England and America.

Bonhoeffer, Dietrich (1906-45), German Lutheran pastor and theologian, author of many books on Christianity in a secular world. A prominent anti-Nazi, he was arrested in 1943 and executed two years later.
See also: Theology.

Bonhomme Richard *See:* Jones, John Paul.

Boniface VIII (1235-1303), pope 1294-1303. He asserted papal authority over the political leaders of Europe. His bull (decree) *Unam Sanctam*, which called for the subjugation of political leaders to the pope, led to a clash with Philip IV of France. In 1303 the king's emissaries attacked Boniface in his palace at Anagni, Italy. He died three weeks later in Rome and was succeeded as pope by Benedict XI.

Boniface, Saint (c.672-754?), English missionary, called the Apostle of Germany. Backed by the Frankish rulers Charles Martel and Pepin the Short, he organized the German church, reformed the Frankish clergy, and advanced the conversion of the Saxons.

Bonifácio, José *See:* Andrada é Silva, José Bonifácio de.

Bonington, Richard Parkes (1802-28), English artist noted for his watercolor landscapes and genre subjects. He spent most of his brief career in France; among those he influenced were Delacroix and Corot.

Bonin Islands, group of volcanic islands about 500 mi (802 km) southeast of Japan. In all there are 27 islands with some 200 inhabitants. They were administered by the United States from 1945 to 1968, when they were returned to Japan.

Bonito, 3 types of fish resembling bluefin tuna, but rarely more than 30 in (76 cm) long. The striped bonito is found in all warm oceanic waters. The Atlantic bonito flourishes in the Mediterranean and warm sections of the Atlantic. The Pacific bonito is found in and near the Indian Ocean. They are strong swimmers and congregate in schools. Bonito, which average 6 lbs (2.7 kg), are valuable food fish.

Bonn (pop. 294,300), historic city on the Rhine River in North Rhine-West-phalia, founded in the 1st century A.D. by the Romans. It was the birthplace of Beethoven and from 1238 to 1794 served as the residence of the electors of Cologne. In 1949 it became the de facto capital of West Germany (Berlin was always considered the de jure capital). As such it served as the administrative center of the German Federal Republic. With the unification of the Federal Republic and the East German communist People's Democratic Republic in October 1990 into a single German state, Bonn lost it's status as capital to Berlin in 1991. The full transition to Berlin will take until the early 2000s.
See also: Germany.

Bonnard, Pierre (1867-1947), French artist whose style gave sparkling life and color to the sunny interiors he favored (*The Breakfast Room*). With Maurice Denis and Jean Vuillard, he formed the group known as the Nabis.

Bonneville, Benjamin Louis Eulalie de (1796-1878), French-American soldier and pioneer. He explored the far west (1832-35) and fought in the Mexican War (1846-48). He is remembered largely because of Washington Irving's romanticized *The Adventures of Captain Bonneville* (1837).
See also: Pioneer life in America.

Bonneville Dam, large hydroelectric dam spanning the Columbia River between Oregon and Washington. It is 2,690 ft (820 m) long, 197 ft (60 m) high, and 1,250 ft (177 m) wide. Built 1933-43 as part of the New Deal Program, it is used for navigation, flood control, and power production.
See also: Water power.

Bonney, William H. *See:* Billy the Kid.

Bonsai, ancient Oriental art of growing dwarf trees. Trees are kept small by pruning roots and branches and by restricting growth in trays or pots. The modern enthusiast may spend many years cultivating a miniature tree. Plants that can be dwarfed include the cedars, myrtles, junipers, oaks, cypresses, pyracanthas, and pines.

Bontemps, Arna Wendell (1902-73), African-American author of more than 30 books on black culture, including biographies, children's stories, history, literary criticism, novels, and poetry. He and Countee Cullen, a novelist and poet, adapted his *God Sends Sunday* (1931) into a musical comedy, *St. Louis Woman* (1946). An earlier novel, *Black Thunder* (1936) describes a slave revolt in Virginia. *Drums at Dusk* (1938) deals with a slave revolt in Haiti. Bontemps was a public school teacher and principal 1924-38. From 1943 until his death, he was a college professor and librarian.

Bonus Army March *See:* Hoover, Herbert Clark.

Booby, large fish-eating bird of the Sulidae family, so named because it is unwary and easily captured. Boobies have straight, sharp bills, long wedge-shaped tails, short, stout legs, and long tapered wings. Excellent fliers, boobies live mainly in tropical and subtropical regions.

Boogie-woogie *See:* Jazz.

Book, medium of communication consisting of written, printed, or blank sheets of a material, usually paper, bound together into a volume. Ancient Assyrian and Babylonian clay tablets, incised when wet, then baked until hard, are the earliest form of books. The Egyptians further developed books by changing their materials. From papyrus they made paper, which they inscribed with reed pens and ink. The ancient world adopted the Egyptian innovations, and portable rolls of sheets joined together to form scrolls were at one time the most common form of books. But animal skins were also used and eventually led to a new form. Sheets of animal skin were much stronger than papyrus; they could be sewn together and folded to form rectangular pages. Pressed tightly between wooden boards to make up a book or "codex," these were prototypes of modern books. The Chinese discovered the art of making paper in the 2nd century. Paper reached Europe in the 12th century, and by the 15th century it had almost entirely replaced all kinds of parchment in the making of books. Then, around 1436 or 1437, Johann Gutenberg of Mainz perfected movable type and produced the first mechanically printed books. The history of books since the 15th century is the story of innovations and advances in materials, techniques, and technology, which continues with today's computerized type setting, automated presses, and a wide variety of photographic and other reproduction processes.

Bookbinding, craft of gathering the pages of a book into a volume with a protective cover. Bookbinding began after papyrus gave way to parchment, sheets of which could be sewn together, glued, and secured with leather thongs and protective boards. Leather was used for bookbinding for many centuries but is now reserved for special editions. Printing and the use of paper made the production of smaller books possible. During the 19th century, new cover materials were introduced.
See also: Book.

Bookkeeping, systematic recording of financial transactions. The single-entry system consists of a single account that shows the debts owed to and by the firm. The double-entry system, more detailed, enters debit and credit items in a journal and then classifies them in a ledger. In the monthly system, a number of separate daybooks are kept, and monthly totals are posted to the ledger accounts.
See also: Accounting.

Book of Changes *See:* I Ching.

Book of Common Prayer, name of the official liturgy of the Church of England, including the services of Morning and Evening Prayer and of Holy Communion, and the Psalter, Gospels, and Epistles.
See also: Church of England.

Book of Hours, collection of prayers to be said at canonical hours, widely used by laymen during the late Middle Ages. Illuminated editions were often masterpieces of the miniaturist's art. Ffamous are the Rohan and the de Berry Hours.

Book of Kells, illuminated manuscript of the Gospels dating from the late 8th or early 9th century, probably produced by monks of Kells in County Meath, Ireland. Its rich decoration makes it one of the finest examples of medieval manuscript decoration. It is exhibited in the library of Trinity College, Dublin.

Book of Mormon *See:* Mormons; Smith, Joseph.

Book of the Dead, collection of prayers, hymns, and spells brought into the object-laden tombs of the ancient Egyptians, the earliest of which dates to the 16th century B.C. These writings, which were either inscribed on the walls of the tomb or collected in a text, served as a guide for the soul's journey in the afterlife and a protection against evil.

Book of the Dead,

Boomerang, throwing weapon developed in Australia. Precisely bent and balanced, it follows a curved path when thrown, such that it comes back to the thrower.

Boone, Daniel (1734-1820), American pioneer and hunter. Beginning in 1767 he made a series of trips into what is now Kentucky and in 1775 built a fort there, called Boonesboro. In 1778 he was captured by the Shawnee, who were allied with the British against the American revolutionaries. Boone escaped to warn settlers at Boonesboro of a planned attack, which they successfully resisted. He moved to Missouri in 1799, after his land titles in Kentucky were overturned.
See also: Pioneer life in America; Wilderness Road.

Boorstin, Daniel Joseph (1914-   ), U.S. historian, 12th Librarian of Congress (1975-87). He was, by virtue of an Act of Congress (July 1987), designated Librarian of Congress Emeritus. Dr. Boorstin's tenure was characterized by greater public visibility for the library. He is responsible for the establishment of the Center for the Book in the Library of Congress (1977) and the Council of Scholars (1980). A significant highlight of his era was the passage of the revision of the Copyright Law (1976), of which he was a strong supporter. Boorstin is known for his insightful interpretations of U.S. history. He is the author of *The Genius of American Politics* (1958); the widely acclaimed trilogy *The Americans* (1958, 1965,1973), for which he received the Bancroft Prize and the Francis Parkman Prize; and *The Discovers* (1983).

Boötes, constellation of the Northern Hemisphere, easily recognizable because it contains Arcturus, one of the brightest orange stars in the sky. Boötes is also known as The Huntsman or the Bear Driver.
See also: Arcturus.

Booth, Edwin Thomas (1833-92), U.S. actor, famous on the New York and London stage. His Shakespearean roles, particularly Hamlet, were considered theatrical landmarks. He retired briefly in 1865, because of the scandal surrounding his brother, John Wilkes Booth, who assassinated President Lincoln.

Booth, John Wilkes (1838-65), U.S. actor who assassinated Abraham Lincoln. A son of the actor Junius Brutus Booth, he was a Confederate sympathizer; eager to avenge the South's defeat, he shot President Lincoln during a performance at Ford's Theater, Washington, D.C., on April 14, 1865. Booth, breaking a leg, escaped but was finally trapped in a barn near Bowling Green, Va., where he either was shot or shot himself.

Bop, or bebop, style of jazz developed toward the end of World War II, so named in imitation of its basic rhythmic feature. Under the inspiration of musicians like Dizzy Gillespie and Charlie Parker, bop broke with the blues tradition, and carried jazz forward into new harmonic and rhythmic fields, opening the way for a more intellectual kind of jazz.

Boracic acid *See:* Boric acid.

Borax, common name for a hydrated form of sodium borate or sodium tetraborate, a white powder that becomes transparent and glasslike when heated. Borax is used in glazes and in the manufacture of ceramics and heat-resistant glass. In metallurgy it is used to remove oxide slags. Borax "beads" are used as a test for metals in chemical analysis. Large quantities of borax in the form of the mineral tincal come from Searle's Lake, Ca.
See also: Boric acid; Boron.

Bordeaux (pop. 213,300), city in southwestern France and capital of Gironde department, on the Garonne River. It is France's third-largest port and chief center for the French wine trade. Bordeaux also has canning and shipbuilding industries. The city dates from Roman times.
See also: France.

Borden, Lizzie Andrew (1860-1927), U.S. woman accused of murdering her father and stepmother with an ax on Aug. 4, 1892. She was acquitted but remained popularly condemned. The murder became part of American folklore.

Borden, Sir Robert Laird (1854-1937), Canadian prime minister (1911-20) who helped his country gain an independent voice in world affairs. Borden became Conservative leader in 1901. He was a vigorous World War I prime minister, forming a Union Party government with pro-conscription Liberals in 1917, and securing separate representation for Canada at the peace conference and in the League of Nations.
See also: Canada.

Border Patrol, United States, uniformed enforcement agency of the Immigration and Naturalization Service, which attempts to prevent the unlawful entry of non-citizens into the United States through coastal areas of Florida and the Gulf of Mexico.

Borg, Björn (1956-   ), Swedish tennis player and the only player in modern tennis history to win the men's singles title at the Wimbeldon Championships in five consecutive years, 1976-80. Earlier, as a 19-year-old, he led Sweden to its first Davis Cup victory. Borg retired from tournament tennis in 1983 and made a comeback in 1991.

Borges, Jorge Luis (1899-1986), Argentine poet and prose writer. At first influenced by the metaphorical style of Spanish *ultráismo*, he later developed a unique form between short story and essay, the "fiction." Some of the best examples are in his *Ficciones* (1944) and *El Aleph* (1949).

Borgia, powerful Italian family descended from the Borjan of Valencia in Spain. **Alfonso de Borja** (1378-1458) became Pope Calixtus III. By bribery, his nephew **Rodrigo Borgia** (1431-1503) became Pope Alexander VI in 1492 and worked to enrich his family by crushing the Italian princes. His son, **Cesare Borgia** (1476-1507), used war, duplicity, and murder to seize much of central Italy. Alexander's notorious daughter, **Lucrezia Borgia** (1480-1519), was probably a pawn in her family's schemes. As duchess of Ferrara, she generously patronized the arts and learning.

Borglum, Gutzon (1867-1941), U.S. sculptor best remembered for Mt. Rushmore National Memorial in South Dakota, with its enormous portrait heads of Washington, Jefferson, Lincoln, and Theodore Roosevelt carved on mountainsides. Begun in 1927, the project was completed by his son after Borglum's death.
See also: Rushmore, Mount.

Boric acid, white crystalline acid (H_3BO_3) occurring in nature or prepared from borax and used as a weak antiseptic.

Borlaug, Norman Ernest (1914-   ), U.S. agricultural scientist who was awarded the 1970 Nobel Peace Prize for his part in the development of improved varieties of cereal crops that are important in the green revolution in the developing nations of the Third World.

Borman, Frank (1928-   ), U.S. astronaut. After joining the Manned Space-craft Center of NASA in 1962, Borman became command pilot on the 14-day orbital *Gemini 7* flight in December 1965. Along with James Lovell and William Anders, Borman participated in the *Apollo 8* flight, the first humans to voyage around the moon. In 1970, Borman retired from NASA and entered commercial aviation.
See also: Astronaut.

Bormann, Martin Ludwig (1900-45), German Nazi politician, Hitler's deputy from 1941. Though he vanished in 1945, he was sentenced to death for war crimes at the Nuremberg Trials in 1946. It is now thought he was killed as Berlin fell.
See also: Nazism; Nuremberg Trials.

Born-again Christians, fundamentalist Christians who feel themselves re-generated through the experience of being "born again" (John 3:3). Related to the Calvinist doctrine of election, the experience today assumes a revivalist character. In the late 1970s, citing a decline in morality, Born-again Christians became active in U.S. politics through such organizations as the Moral Majority, led by Rev. Jerry Falwell.

Born, Max (1882-1970), German theoretical physicist active in the development of quantum physics. His probabilistic interpretation of the Schrödinger wave equation provided a link between wave mechanics and the quantum theory. Sharing the Nobel Prize for physics with W. Bothe in 1954, he devoted his later years to the philosophy of physics.

Borneo, largest island of the Malay Archipelago and third largest in the world (280,100 sq mi/725,459 sq km). It contains the Indonesian province of Kalimantan, the sultanate of Brunei, and the Malaysian states of Sabah and Sarawak. Borneo is a mountainous equatorial island largely clad in tropical rain forest, and drained by several major rivers. Its highest point is Mt. Kinabalu (13,455 ft/4,101 m). The island suffered severely because of the forest fires in 1997-98, which spread easily due to the fact that the rain held off.
See also: Brunei; Indonesia; Malaysia.

Borodin, Aleksandr Porfirevich (1833-87), Russian chemist and composer of the group known as the Five. His musical works include the opera *Prince Igor*, completed after his death by Aleksandr Glazunov and Nikolai Rimsky-Korsakov.

Boron, chemical element, symbol B; for physical constants see Periodic Table. Boron is not found free in nature, but its compounds have been known for thousands of years. The most important source of boron is the mineral *kernite* (sodium borate). A nonmetal, boron is prepared by the vapor phase reduction of boron trichloride with hydrogen on electrically heated filaments. It is similar to carbon in that it forms stable, covalently bonded molecular networks. Compounds of boron are used in the manufacture of fiberglass, bleach, laundry products, flame retardants, antiseptics, and borosilicate glasses. Boron-10 is used as a control in nuclear reactors. Filaments of boron are lightweight and strong and are used for aerospace structures.

Bosch, Hieronymus (c.1450-1516), Dutch painter whose work features grotesque fantasy. In paintings like the *Haywain* (1485) and *The Garden of Earthly Delights* (1500) he used part-human, part-animal, part-vegetable forms to express symbolically his obsessive vision of worldly sin and eternal damnation.

Bosch, Juan *See:* Dominican Republic.

Bosnia and Hercegovina (Republic of), independent country in southeastern Europe, bordering Croatia and   the Federal Republic of Yugoslavia, formerly one of the 6 states of Yugoslavia. The population of over 4,300,000 consists of Serbian Orthodox, Croatian Roman Catholics, and Turkish Muslims. Before the war that ensued independence, the economy was largely based on agriculture, with wheat, maize, sugar, meat and milk the most important products. However, the war caused an economic standstill in the early 1990s, and the population became almost completely dependent on

Bosnia and Hercegovina

Capital:	Sarajevo
Area:	20,452 sq mi
	(51,129 sq km)
Population:	4,383,000
Language:	Serbo-Croatian
Government:	Republic
Independent:	1991
Head of gov.:	2 (co)Prime ministers
Per capita:	U.S. $765
Mon. unit:	1 Bosnian dinar = 100
	para

foreign-relief aid. When Yugoslavia disintegrated, Bosnia Hercegovina became an independent state. The Bosnian Serbs opposed independence from Serbian-dominated Yugoslavia and started to expand the area under their control. Despite international intervention, the war between the Muslims, Croatians and Serbs continued into the mid-1990s. In 1995 Bosnia was partitioned into two autonomous states: the Muslim-Croatic Federation Bosnia-Hercegovina and the Bosnian Serbian Republic (Republika Srpska). In 1997 the first federal Bosnian government was formed.
See also: Yugoslavia.

Boson, one of the 4 major classes of elementary particles (the others being the leptons, mesons, and baryons). The bosons have no mass. They include photons, gluons, and, hypothetically, the graviton. Bosons were named for the Indian physicist Satyendranath Bose, who with Albert Einstein developed a statistical theory of the behavior of these particles in the 1920s.
See also: Particle physics.

Bosporus, Turkish strait 19 mi (30.6 km) long and about 0.5-2.5 mi (0.8-3.6 km) wide connecting the Black Sea and the Sea of Marmara (which is connected to the Aegean arm of the Mediterranean by the Dardanelles strait). Historically important as the sole sea link between the Black Sea and the Mediterranean, it was bridged in 1973.
See also: Turkey.

Bossuet, Jacques Bénigne (1627-1704), French prelate and historian renowned for his eloquence as an orator, especially his *Funeral Orations* (1689). He was bishop of Condom (1669-71) and of Meaux (from 1681). He wrote the famous *Discourse on Universal History* (1681) and *Treatise of the Knowledge of God and One's Self* (1722).

Boston (pop. 3,200,000), capital and largest city of Massachusetts, seaport on Massachusetts Bay. It is the most populous state capital, New England's largest city, and the nearest major U.S. seaport to Europe. It is also a major commercial, financial, manufacturing, and cultural center. Boston's industries include shipbuilding, electronics, chemicals, plastics, rubber products,

and printing. The city's wool market is the nation's largest. Historic buildings include the Old State House, Paul Revere House, Christ Church, and Faneuil Hall. Boston has many notable educational institutions, and nearby Cambridge has Harvard University and the Massachusetts Institute of Technology. Settled by English Puritans in 1630, Boston became the capital of Massachusetts Bay Colony. In the Boston Massacre and Boston Tea Party the city led colonial unrest that erupted into the Revolutionary War. Modern Boston shares the acute urban problems of most large U.S. cities.
See also: Massachusetts.

Boston Massacre, incident March 5, 1770, in which some 60 Bostonians, enraged by the presence of British soldiers in Boston, harassed a British sentry, and British troops fired on the mob, killing 5 people.

Boston Tea Party, incident at Boston on Dec. 16, 1773, in protest against the tea tax and British import restrictions. A party of colonial patriots disguised in Native American dress boarded three British East India Company ships and dumped their cargo of tea into the harbor.
See also: Intolerable Acts; Revolutionary War in America.

Boswell, James (1740-95), Scottish writer and lawyer, most famous for his *Life of Samuel Johnson* (1791). In his journals he recorded his life and times with great zest. From them he culled the accounts of his travels in Corsica and elsewhere, and the brilliant conversations that distinguish the portrait of his friend Samuel Johnson.
See also: Johnson, Samuel.

Botany, the study of plants. Botany has several closely related branches. *Plant morphology*, the study of plant structure, has 2 subdisciplines: (1) plant anatomy deals with the gross structure of the plant—the shapes of the roots, stems, and leaves and the organization of the flowers; (2) plant histology deals with the structure and arrangement of the cells and tissues inside the plant. *Plant physiology* is concerned with how the plant works—how it gets its water from the soil, how the water passes up the stem, how the plant grows and moves, how its flowers open, and so on. *Biochemistry* deals with the chemical reactions going on in the plant. *Cytology* is the study of the cell protoplasm and its contents, including the nucleus. *Plant breeding* helps to produce bigger and better crops. Plants have been bred for thousands of years, but it was not until the present century, when Gregor Mendel's work in the 19th century was rediscovered, that scientists understood how characteristics are passed on from parent to offspring. By cross-pollinating selected plants, 2 or more desirable features can be combined into 1 variety. *Plant pathology* deals with plant diseases and their control. *Plant ecology* deals with the relationships between plants and their surroundings and is concerned especially with why plants grow where they do. *Plant taxonomy* deals with the naming and classification of plants. The Swedish naturalist Carolus Linnaeus (1707-78) put forward the idea of the species as the smallest unit and the genus as a group of closely related species, giving species a generic name and a specific name. For example, the plant whose common name is ragwort is scientifically known as *Senecio jacobaea*. Taxonomy is designed to show the relationships between living things, drawing information from morphology, physiology, and other branches of botany. Species with many features in common are grouped into a genus, genera with common features are grouped into a family, and families with common features are grouped into an order. If relationships exist, they may be discovered by specialists in *paleobotany*, the study of fossil plants.

Botfly, family of flies (order Diptera) whose larvae are parasitic in the tissues and cavities of humans and other mammals. The name is generally given in the United States to the horse botfly, a yellowish-brown insect about 1/2 in (13 mm) long. It lays eggs in the mane and on the legs and belly of horses. When these are licked off and swallowed, they are carried to the stomach, where they hatch. The larvae attach themselves to the lining of the stomach. Within a year, the mature larvae are discharged in the feces; they pupate in the ground and change into flies. The flies have virtually no mouth parts and do not feed during their short adult life.

Botha, Pieter Willem (1916-   ), South African politician who became the first executive president under a new constitution (1984-89). He entered Parliament in 1948, becoming defense minister in 1966 and prime minister in 1978. He came to recognize the importance of political change and the need to win over the loyalty and cooperation of the country's black majority. In 1984 he became president of South Africa. He reformed apartheid policy, although not enough for the black majority of the population. In 1989 he abdicated and was succeeded by F. W. de Klerk.
See also: South Africa.

Bothwell, James Hepburn, 4th Earl of (1536-78), Scottish nobleman who married Mary Queen of Scots in May 1567, after helping to murder her husband, Lord Darnley. In June he fled Scotland, and later died in a Danish prison.

Bo tree, or bodhi tree, Asian fig (*Ficus religiosa*), sacred to Buddhists as the tree under which Buddha received enlightenment. The Bo tree grows to 100 ft (30 m).
See also: Buddha, Gautama.

Botswana (formerly Bechuanaland), landlocked republic in southern Africa, enclosed by Namibia, Zimbabwe, and the Republic of South Africa. Its capital is Gabarone.
Land and climate. Botswana is divided into 3 main regions: the Okavango Swamp to the north, the Kalahari Desert in the south and southwest, and the mountainous areas to the east. Most of Botswana is an arid plateau some 3,000 ft (914 m) above sea level, and lack of water makes farming difficult.
People. The majority of the people are Iswana. Both English and Iswana are the official languages. Most of the people adhere to traditional African religions. About three-quarters of the population is literate.
Economy. Botswana is rich in mineral resources, principally diamonds, but also manganese, asbestos, copper, nickel, and coal. Because Botswana is landlocked, it is dependent upon its neighbors, South Africa, Namibia and Zimbabwe. Diamonds are the principal export. Botswana also exports its labor: considerable numbers of men move into South Africa for at least part of each year to work in the larger mines.

Botswana

Capital:	Gaborone
Area:	224,607 sq mi
	(582,000 sq km)
Population:	1,448,000
Language:	English
Government:	Presidential republic
Independent:	1966
Head of gov.:	President
Per capita:	U.S. $3,020
Mon. unit:	1 Pula = 100 thebe

History. The San Bushmen, original inhabitants of Bechuanaland, were replaced by the Iswana in the 19th century. Under the leadership of King Khama in the early 1800s, the Iswana maintained their independence against invasions by Zulu and Ndebele warriors. By the mid-19th century Boers of the Transvaal sought to annex portions of Bechuanaland for its gold deposits. Bechuana sought British protection and by 1885 had become a British protectorate. On Sept. 30, 1966, the country was given complete independence as Botswana. Sir Seretse M. Khama, grandson of King Khama, was president from 1965 until his death in 1980. Khama was succeeded by Sir Ketumile Joni Masire, who abdicated in 1998.

Botticelli, Sandro (Alessandro di Mariano Filipepi; c.1444-1510), Florentine Renaissance painter. His work is noted for superb draftsmanship, the use of sharp yet graceful and rhythmic line, and exquisite coloring. Among his most famous works are the allegorical tableaux on mythological subjects, *Spring* and *The Birth of Venus.*
See also: Renaissance.

Bottle tree, Australian tree (*Brachychiton rupestris*) of the chocolate family, with a trunk resembling a round bottle. Although the main trunk is short and thick, the trees may grow to 60 ft (18 m). A related tree, the baobab of Africa, is also sometimes called a bottle tree.

Botulism, acute type of food poisoning, often fatal, caused by a toxin produced by the anaerobic bacteria *Clostridium botulinum* and *C. parabotulinum*, which normally live in soil but may infect poorly canned food. The toxin paralyzes the nervous system. Thorough cooking destroys both bacteria and toxin.
See also: Toxin.

Boucicault, Dion (1822?-90), Irish-born actor and playwright active in London and New York. The 150 plays that he wrote or adapted, including *London Assurance* (1841) and *The Shaughraun* (1874), ranged from light social drama to melodrama.

Boudicca *See:* Boadicea.

Bougainville, largest of the Solomon Islands, a part of the independent nation of Papua-New Guinea. Bougainville produces cacao, copra, and gold. *See also:* Solomon Islands.

Bougainvillea, ornamental tropical and subtropical flowering vine (genus *Bougainvillaea*) named for the French navigator and explorer, Louis Antoine de Bougainville. The flower clusters are white or creamy-colored, each surrounded by three large floral bracts that may range from crimson or purple to yellow or white.

Boulder, city in north-central Colorado, 30 mi (48 km) northwest of Denver and the seat of Boulder County. The University of Colorado is located in the city. Glaciers, forests, and Rocky Mountain National Park make Boulder a popular resort. Local industries include space and research. *See also:* Colorado.

Boulder Dam *See:* Hoover Dam.

Boulding, Kenneth Ewart (1910-   ), British-born U.S. economist who proposes a social science unifying economics, politics, and sociology. He is the author of more than 15 books, including *A Reconstruction of Economics* (1950), *Economics as a Science* (1970), and *A Primer on Social Dynamics* (1970).

Boulez, Pierre (1925-   ), French composer and conductor, noted for his extension of 12-tone techniques to rhythm and dynamics in such works as *Le Marteau sans maître* (1951) and *Pli selon pli* (1960). He was music director of the New York Philharmonic (1971-77), and has conducted many of the world's leading orchestras.

Bounty, Mutiny on the *See:* Bligh, William; Nordhoff and Hall.

Bourbon, powerful family that for generations ruled France, Naples and Sicily (the Two Sicilies), Parma, and Spain; named for the castle of Bourbon northwest of Moulins. Bourbons became part of the French ruling house when a Bourbon heiress married **Duke Robert**, Louis IX's sixth son, in 1272. In 1589 their descendant, **Henry of Navarre**, founded France's Bourbon dynasty as Henry IV. Bourbon rule in France was interrupted with Louis XVI's execution in 1793, was restored in 1814 under **Louis XVIII**, and finally ended with the deposition of **Charles X** in 1830. In Spain, Louis XIV's grandson came to the throne in 1700 as **Philip V**. In Italy, cadet branches of his family ruled Parma (1748- 1860) and Naples and Sicily (1759-1861). Bourbons ruled Spain until 1931, when Alfonso XIII abdicated. In 1947 Spain was again declared a monarchy, and in 1975 **Prince Juan Carlos** of Bourbon succeeded the head of state, General Franco.

Bourgeoisie *See:* Communism.

Bourguiba, Habib Ben Ali (1903-   ), Tunisian nationalist politician and Tunisia's first president (1957-87). He led the campaign for independence

from the 1930s onwards and was imprisoned by the French several times. He was ousted in 1987.
See also: Tunisia.

Bourke-White, Margaret (1906-71), U.S. photographer and war correspondent who covered World War II and the Korean War for Time-Life, Inc. Her coverage of India's independence movement and its leader, Mohandas Gandhi, is famous.

Bowditch, Nathaniel (1773-1838), self-taught U.S. mathematician and astronomer remembered for his *New American Practical Navigator* (1802), "the seaman's bible," later made standard in the U.S. navy. He also translated and annotated Laplace's *Celestial Mechanics* (1829-38).

Bowdoin, James (1726-90), U.S. revolutionary leader. Bowdoin served in the Massachusetts legislature (1753-76) and supported the patriots' cause. A conservative, as governor of Massachusetts (1785-87), he suppressed Shays' Rebellion. He was first president of the American Academy of Arts and Sciences.
See also: Shays' Rebellion.

Bowell, Sir Mackenzie (1823-1917), Canadian prime minister (1894-96). Elected to the House of Commons from Ontario in 1867, he held 3 cabinet-level positions under 3 successive prime ministers. On December 21, 1894, he was chosen prime minister following the death of Sir John Thompson, but his refusal to act decisively in several provincial disputes cost him the support of Parliament and his cabinet. He resigned on April 27, 1896 and remained in the Senate until 1906.
See also: Canada.

Bowen, Elizabeth (1899-1973), English-Irish novelist, whose works are distinguished by their meticulous style and emotional sensitivity. They include *The Death of the Heart* (1938), *The Heat of the Day* (1949), and *Eva Trout* (1969).

Bowerbird, forest-dwelling bird (family Ptilonorhynchidae) native to Australia and New Guinea that builds "bowers" of sticks decorated with bones, shells, berries, and flowers. Males fight and court in the bowers; the birds mate in the bower, but nest in a nearby tree. The largest of these birds, the great or red-crested bowerbird, may grow 14 in (36 cm) long.

Bowfin, large freshwater fish (*Amia calva*) of eastern North America, also known as the grindle, mudfish, or freshwater dogfish. It is sometimes referred to as a "living fossil" because it resembles a type of fish that can be traced back 130 million years. Its body may reach a length of 30 in (76 cm). Because it eats large numbers of valuable food fish, it is sometimes regarded as a pest.

Bowie, James (1796-1836), Kentucky-born frontier hero who reputedly invented the bowie hunting knife. He grew rich by land speculation and slave trading. Bowie joined the Texan fight for independence from Mexico and was one of the leaders at the Alamo, where he died.
See also: Alamo.

Bowles, Paul (1910-   ), U.S. author and composer living in Morocco. He is known for his exotic novels and short stories of alienation, despair, and psychological horror. His works include *The Sheltering Sky* (1949) and *Collected Stories: 1939-1976* (1979). His wife, **Jane Auer Bowles** (1917-73), was also a writer. Her works include the novel *Two Serious Ladies* (1943) and the play *In the Summer House* (1954).

Bowles, Samuel (1826-78), U.S. newspaper editor and political leader. Born in Springfield, Mass., Bowles inherited the *Springfield Republican* at age 25 and made it one of the most influential papers in the United States. He assisted the antislavery movement and helped found the Republican Party in New England.

Bowling, indoor sport that involves rolling a ball to knock down wooden pins. In tenpin bowling, the most popular form in the United States, players aim a large heavy ball down a long wooden lane at 10 pins set in a triangle. The number of pins felled determines the score. Bowling became popular in 14th-century Europe, and was brought to America by the Dutch in the 17th century. Tenpin bowling was standardized by the American Bowling Congress, founded in 1895.

Boxelder, or ash-leaf maple (*Acer negundo*), deciduous tree native to North America. It grows up to 70 ft (20 m) high and has compound leaves and grooved bark. The greenish-yellow flowers are unisexual and are borne on separate trees. The sap is sometimes tapped for its sugar.

Boxer, medium-sized dog first bred in Germany in the 1800s. The stocky, muscular dog has been used as a guide dog for the blind. Its short, shiny coat is sometimes striped or caramel-colored. It measures 21-24 in (53-61 cm) in height at the shoulder and weighs about 60-75 lb (27-34 kg).

Boxer Rebellion, violent uprising in China in 1900 directed against foreigners and instigated by the secret society "Harmonious Fists" (called Boxers by the Europeans). Encouraged by the Dowager Empress Tz'u Hsi, the Boxers showed their dislike of growing European influence and commercial exploitation in China, attacking missionaries and Chinese converts to Christianity. Troops sent to protect European nationals at Peking were repulsed. The German minister in Peking was murdered and foreign legations were besieged for nearly 2 months until relieved by an international force. Boxer violence was the pretext for Russian occupation of South Manchuria. On Sept. 7, 1901, China was forced to sign the humiliating Boxer Protocol, in which it promised to pay a huge indemnity to the United States and the European powers concerned.
See also: China; Open-Door Policy.

Boxing, sport of skilled fist-fighting. Two contestants wearing padded gloves attack each other by punching prescribed parts of the body, while avoiding or blocking their opponent's punches. Boxing contests are arranged between opponents in the same weight division or class; there are 10 classes ranging from flyweight to heavyweight. Fights take place in a square roped-off ring and consist of a number of 2- or 3-minute rounds. Scoring is usually made by a referee and 2 judges. A win can occur by a knockout, if a boxer legitimately knocks down his opponent and the man cannot regain his feet in 10 sec. A fight may also end in a technical knockout if the referee decides that a boxer is physically unfit to go on fighting. If a contest goes its full length, the contestant awarded the most points or rounds wins by a decision. Boxing can be traced back to the Olympic Games of ancient Greece, and to Roman gladiatorial contests. Modern boxing has its roots in 18th-century English fairground fights between bare-knuckled pugilists, who battered each other for bets until one could no longer continue.

Boxwood, or box, several species of evergreen shrubs and trees (genus *Buxus*), native to tropical and subtropical parts of the Old World and Central America, but widely introduced elsewhere. They have small glossy leaves and are excellent hedge plants, rarely exceeding 12 ft (4 m) in height. Boxwood grows slowly. Its yellow, finely grained wood is used for musical instruments and wood engraving.

Boyd, Belle (1843-1900), Confederate spy in the American Civil War. An actress, she lived in Virginia and passed military information to the South. Caught in 1862, she was released for lack of evidence in 1863. She wrote *Belle Boyd in Camp and Prison* (1865).
See also: Civil War, U.S.

Boyle, Robert (1627-91), British natural philosopher, often called the father of modern chemistry for his rejection of the theories of the alchemists and his espousal of atomism. He discovered what is called Boyle's Law for Gases: At a constant temperature the volume of a given quantity of gas varies inversely to the pressure to which the gas is subjected.
See also: Chemistry; Philosophy.

Boyne, Battle of the, battle on the River Boyne in East Ireland on July 12, 1690, which ended James II's attempt to regain the English throne. William III's 35,000 troops decisively defeated the Catholic Jacobites' 21,000. Northern Ireland's Protestants celebrate the victory to this day.

Boy Scouts, international boys' organization founded in 1908 by Sir Robert Baden- Powell to develop character, initiative, and good citizenship. The organization is nonsectarian, nonpolitical, and nonmilitary. The Boy Scouts are organized in about 100 countries, and worldwide membership is approximately 8 million. Scouting emphasizes outdoor knowledge and skills, including nature lore and woodcraft. The Boy Scout program includes Cubs (8-10 years old), Scouts (11-13), and Explorers (14 years and older). Other senior scout groups are the Sea Scouts and Air Scouts. To achieve higher ranks, Scouts must pass tests for merit badges in various fields. In the United States, where the movement was incorporated in 1910, the scouting program is administered by a National Council, with headquarters in New Brunswick, NJ. The standard troop, led by a volunteer adult scoutmaster, has 32 members and is divided into 4 patrols of 8 Scouts. Boy Scouts have been active in safety campaigns, and conservation programs, and other community service.
See also: Baden-Powell, Robert Stephenson Smyth, Lord.

Boysenberry, variety of blackberry (*Rubus ursinus*) that grows on a trailing plant. The tart, dark-red to black fruits are made up of clusters of drupelets.

Boysenberries grow best in mild climates and can be eaten fresh or in pies, jams, and jellies.

Boys Town, village near Omaha, Neb., founded in 1917 as a community for homeless and abandoned boys by Father Edward J. Flanagan and governed by the boys.
See also: Flanagan, Edward Joseph.

Bozeman Trail, route between Wyoming, and Montana used as a short-cut during the 1860s to reach gold fields in Montana and Idaho. The trail, named for John M. Bozeman, covered 600 mi (970 km). Native American attacks, protesting rampant European immigration, closed the trail in the late 1860s.
See also: Gold Rush.

Brace, Charles Loring (1826-90), U.S. social reformer who worked to improve conditions for poor children and helped organize the Children's Aid Society in New York City in 1853.

Braces *See:* Orthodontics.

Bradbury, Ray (1920-), U.S. science-fiction writer, whose short stories deal with moral dilemmas. Among his best-known science fiction works are *The Martian Chronicles* (1950) and *Fahrenheit 451* (1953).

Braddock, Edward (1695-1755), commander-in-chief of British forces in North America, who was disastrously defeated in the French and Indian Wars. His 1755 expedition against Fort Duquesne (on the site of present-day Pittsburgh), ran into a French and Indian ambush. Braddock was fatally wounded and his men were routed. Among the survivors was a Virginian officer, George Washington.
See also: French and Indian Wars.

Bradford, family name of prominent U.S. printers and editors. **William Bradford** (1663-1752) set up Philadelphia's first printing press and began New York's first newspaper, the *Gazette*, in 1725. His son, **Andrew Bradford** (1686-1742), started the first newspaper in Philadelphia, the *American Weekly Mercury*, in 1719. **William Bradford, III** (1722-91), grandson of William Bradford and nephew of Andrew Bradford, established the *Pennsylvania Journal* in 1742. Through this newspaper he fought for freedom of the press and became printer to the First Continental Congress.
See also: Printing.

Bradford (pop. 477,500), city and parliamentary borough of Yorkshire, England, in the Aire valley, 9 mi (14 km) from Leeds. It was concerned with the wool trade during the Middle Ages, and by the end of the 15th century had become an important center of the industry. The Bradford Exchange is a major international wool market, and the Bradford Institute of Technology is world famous for its textile design.
See also: England.

Bradford, William (1590-1657), Pilgrim Father who helped to establish Plymouth Colony and governed it most of his life (reelected 30 times from

1621). He described the *Mayflower's* voyage and the colony's first years in his *History of Plymouth Plantation*.
See also: Pilgrims.

Bradley, James (1693-1762), British astronomer. His 2 great discoveries were the aberration of light (1729) and the nutation (nodding motion) of the earth's axis (1748). Just before his death he published a catalog listing more han 60,000 stars.
See also: Astronomy.

Bradley, Omar Nelson (1893-1981), U.S. general. In 1944-45 he led the 12th Army Group (1 million men in 4 armies) in Europe. He was chief of staff of the U.S. Army (1948-49) and first chairman of the joint chiefs of staff (1949-53).
See also: World War II

Bradley, Thomas (1917-   ), U.S. public official, mayor of Los Angeles. A former college track star and Los Angeles policeman who was admitted to the bar in 1956, he was elected to the Los Angeles city council in 1963. In 1973 Bradley became the city's first black mayor. He was California's Democratic gubernatorial candidate in 1982 but lost in a close race; he continued as mayor.

Bradstreet, Anne Dudley (c.1612-72), English-American colonial poet. She began writing after her emigration to Massachusetts in 1630. Her poems deal with personal reflections on the Puritan ethic. Her collection, *The Tenth Muse Lately Sprung Up in America*, was published in England in 1650.

Brady, Mathew B. (1823-96), U.S. photographer of historic events and eminent people, including 18 U.S. presidents. He spent his fortune in hiring 20 teams of photographers to take over 3,500 shots covering almost every big battle of the Civil War, a project that bankrupted him. His most famous photographs are those of Lincoln and of the battles of Bull Run and Gettysburg.

Bragg, Braxton (1817-76), Confederate Civil War general. He led the Army of Tennessee to defeat William S. Rosencrans at Chickamauga (1863), but soon lost to Ulysses S. Grant at Chattanooga, after which he forfeited his command.
See also: Fort Bragg; Civil War, U.S.

Bragg, Sir William Henry (1862-1942), British physicist who shared the 1915 Nobel Prize in physics with his son, **Sir William Lawrence Bragg** (1890-1971), for the deduction of the atomic structure of crystals from their X-ray diffraction patterns (1912).
See also: Physics.

Brahe, Tycho (1546-1601), Danish astronomer, the greatest exponent of naked-eye positional astronomy. Johannes Kepler, who became his assistant in 1601, postulated an elliptical orbit for Mars based on his confidence in Brahe's data. Brahe's "Tychonic system," in which the planets circled the sun, which in turn orbited a stationary earth, was the principal 17th-century

rival of the Copernican hypothesis. Brahe observed a supernova with the naked eye in 1872.
See also: Astronomy.

Brahmanism, Indian religion based on belief in Brahma. It developed about 500 B.C. from Dravidian and Aryan beliefs. Its ritual, symbolism, and theosophy came from the *Brahmanas*, sacred writings of the priestly caste, and from the Upanishads. It developed the "divinely ordered" caste system and gave rise to modern Hinduism.
See also: Hinduism.

Brahmans *See:* Hinduism.

Brahmaputra River, river that rises in the Himalayas and flows about 1,800 mi (2,897 km) through Tibet, northeastern India, Bangladesh, and south to the Ganges, forming the Ganges-Brahmaputra delta on the Bay of Bengal. A holy river to the Indians, its name means "son of Brahma."

Brahms, Johannes (1833-97), major German Romantic composer. Though strongly influenced by Beethoven and the Romantic movement, he developed his own rhythmic originality and emotional intensity, while using classical forms. He lived largely in Vienna from 1863. His major works include four symphonies, two piano concertos, a violin concerto, a double concerto for violin and cello, piano and chamber works, songs, part-songs, and choral works—notably, *A German Requiem* (1868) and the *Alto Rhapsody* (1869).
See also: Schumann, Clara.

Braille, system of writing for the blind developed by Louis Braille, employing patterns of raised dots that can be read by touch. Braille typewriters and printing presses allow the mass production of books for the blind.
See also: Braille, Louis.

Braille, Louis (1809-52), French inventor of braille. Accidentally blinded at the age of 3, he conceived his raised-dot system at 15, while at the National Institute for the Blind in Paris. In 1829 he published a book explaining how his system could be used, not only for reading but also for writing and musical notation.
See also: Braille.

Brain, complex organ coordinating nerve activity and responsible for thought in higher animal forms. Invertebrates have only a rudimentary brain, most highly developed in the octopus. Vertebrates have brains more fully differentiated, consisting of forebrain, midbrain, and hindbrain. In highly developed vertebrate animals, the forebrain has developed into a large and highly differentiated *cerebrum*. The human brain is composed of some billions of interconnecting nerve cells and many more supporting cells (neuroglia). Together with the spinal cord, the brain makes up the central nervous system (CNS), which governs and coordinates the operations of all tissues and organs and is the physical basis of all mental activities: consciousness, sensation, thought, speech, memory, emotion, character, and skill.

The nervous system carries information in the form of electric signals. All the outlying nervous pathways—the peripheral nervous system, or PNS—converge on the CNS. Nerve fibers conduct in 1 direction only: Those that carry information from the sensory organs to the CNS are called afferent, or sensory pathways; those that carry impulses outward from the CNS to the muscles and glands are called efferent, or motor, pathways. Nervous pathways are made up of separate units—nerve cells known as neurons. The main parts of the neuron are the cell body, the axon, and the dendrites. Dendrites generally carry an impulse toward the cell body, and the axon carries it away from the cell body to another cell. The ends of the axon lie adjacent to, but not quite touching, the dendrites or cell bodies of other neurons; the region where the 2 nearly touch is called a synapse. Electrical impulses cannot cross synapses; the transfer is made by chemical substances called neurotransmitters. These substances have become extremely important because of the part they play in the pharmacological treatment of some psychiatric and neurological conditions. The full-grown brain is described as having 3 parts.

(1) The *brain stem* is chiefly a relay station for nervous pathways between the higher parts of the brain and the rest of the body; if it is damaged, sensory and motor functions are greatly impaired. It is also responsible for subvoluntary activities like digestion and respiration.

(2) The *cerebellum*, divided into hemispheres, each controlling a side of the body, is responsible for the coordination of voluntary muscular movements and for posture.

(3) The *cerebrum*, the highest center of the brain and the latest in evolutionary development, is responsible for sensation, thought, and the initiation of voluntary motor activity. It, too, is divided into hemispheres, each consisting of 2 main parts: (1) the *basal ganglia*, made up of a complicated collection of bunches of gray matter that clusters about the top of the brain stem, and (2) the *cerebral cortex*, also made of gray matter, separated from the basal ganglia by tracts of white matter. The cerebrum is customarily divided into 4 lobes: (1) The *frontal lobe (lobus frontalis)* controls voluntary motor patterns, the organization of the motor units necessary for speech, original thinking, and the evaluation of ideas. (2) The *parietal lobe (lobus parietalis)* is mainly concerned with the reception of body sensations and memory in regard to language and learning. The region also has a role in spatial organization. (3) The *temporal lobe (lobus temporalis)* receives auditory sensations (the sense of hearing), participates in speech through auditory monitoring, plays a role in spatial organization, and is a memory mechanism. The temporal lobe has also been variously claimed to be concerned with memory and dreams. (4) The *occipital lobe (lobus occipitalis)*, in the back of the head, is the primary center for vision. The limbic system contains components of the frontal, parietal, and temporal lobes, and controls behavioral reactions to the external environment, possibly influenced by the internal environment, which may alter the excitability of the nervous system. It seems to operate in preserving the individual (feeding, fleeing, or fighting) or the species (reproduction).

The *corpus callosum*, a large white bundle of fibers that connects the cerebral hemispheres, appears concerned with the transfer of learning from 1 hemisphere to another. The functions of the *corpus callosum* include (1) correlation of images in the left and right halves of the visual field, (2) integration of sensations from paired limbs or for learning that requires motor coordination of the limbs, and (3) unification of cerebral processes of attention and awareness. The absence of a *corpus callosum* slows down the rate of learning.

Brainwashing, manipulation of an individual's will, generally without his or her knowledge and against his or her wishes. Most commonly, it consists of a combination of isolation, personal humiliation, disorientation, systematic indoctrination, and alternating punishment and reward.

Brake, device for slowing or halting motion, usually by conversion of kinetic energy into heat energy via the medium of friction. Most airplane, automobile, and railroad brakes are mechanical drum or disk brakes, applying friction directly to some portion of the wheel or of a drum rotating with the wheel. Mechanically operated brakes cannot always be used, as when a single control must operate on a number of wheels simultaneously and equally. Hydraulic, vacuum, and air brakes, which use different mediums to distribute the pressure, may be used in combination with mechanical brakes.

Bramante, Donato (1444-1514), Italian architect who developed the classical principles of High Renaissance architecture. In 1499, he moved from Milan to Rome, where his major designs included the Tempietto of S. Pietro in Montorio (1502) and the Belvedere Court at the Vatican (1505). His greatest project, the reconstruction of St. Peter's, was not realized.
See also: Renaissance.

Bramble, any of a genus (*Rubus*) of prickly shrubs of the rose family. Several of the more than 300 species produce edible berrylike fruits, including blackberries, raspberries, and boysenberries.

Bran, husk of cereal grains (e.g., wheat, rye, or corn), removed from the flour during milling. Bran is ground and used as cattle fodder and is also mixed with cereals and other foods for human consumption, to add roughage and some nutritional elements to the diet. Certain bran extracts are also used in cleaning and dyeing compounds.

Brancusi, Constantin (1876-1957), Romanian sculptor famous for his simple, elemental, polished forms. Living in Paris from 1904, he rejected Rodin's influence, turning to abstract forms and the example of primitive art. Among his best-known works are *The Kiss* (1908) and *Bird in Space* (1919).

Brandeis, Louis Dembitz (1856-1941), U.S. jurist, influential in securing social, political, and economic reforms, especially while an associate justice of the Supreme Court (1916-39). As a lawyer he crusaded for organized labor against big business interests. Brandeis was an active Zionist. Brandeis University was named in his honor.
See also: Supreme Court of the United States.

Brandenburg, historic region in eastern Germany. Formerly the central province of Prussia, it was divided by the Allies at the end of World War II between Poland and East Germany. In 1952 the German state of Brandenburg was abolished and divided into the districts of Frankfurt, Potsdam, and Cottbus.
See also: Germany.

Brand name *See:* Trademark.

Brando, Marlon (1924-   ), U.S. stage and screen actor. Brando's first great success was his portrayal of Stanley Kowalski in the Broadway production of Tennessee Williams's *A Streetcar Named Desire*, the film version of which (1951) brought him international fame. Although widely acclaimed as one of the greatest actors of his time, he has appeared in relatively few parts, particularly in recent years. He won Academy Awards for *On the Waterfront* (1954) and *The Godfather* (1972).
Other films include *Last Tango in Paris* (1972), *Apocalypse Now* (1979), and *Don Juan de Marco* (1995).

Brandt, Willy (Karl Herbert Frahm; (1913-92), Social Democratic chancellor of West Germany 1969-74, whose *Ostpolitik* (Eastern policy) marked a major step towards East-West detente in Europe. He opposed Hitler, fleeing to Norway (1933) and returning after World War II to become mayor of West Berlin (1957- 66). As chancellor, he secured friendship treaties with Poland and the USSR (1970), with East Germany (1972), and with Czechoslovakia (1974). Brandt's initiative won him the 1971 Nobel Peace Prize. Forced to resign in 1974 over a spy scandal in his own administration, he returned to political life in 1975.
See also: Germany.

Brandy, alcoholic drink of distilled wine, usually matured in wood casks. Brandies include cognac, made from white grapes of the Charente district in France, kirsch (made from cherries), and slivovitz (made from plums).

Brandywine, Battle of, British victory in the American Revolutionary War. On Sept. 11, 1777, at Brandywine Creek, Pa., Gen. William Howe's 15,000 British troops surprised the right flank of Washington's 11,000 men protecting Philadelphia. Washington retreated to Germantown, and Howe went on to take Philadelphia.
See also: Revolutionary War in America.

Brant, any of several North American wild geese (genus *Branta*) which breed in the Arctic and fly southward to Eurasia and North America for the winter.

Brant, Joseph (Thayendanegea; 1742-1807), Mohawk chief, Episcopal missionary, and British army colonel. He served with the British forces in the French and Indian Wars and in the American Revolutionary War, participating in the Cherry Valley Massacre (1778).
See also: Revolutionary War in America; French and Indian Wars.

Braque, Georges (1882-1963), French painter and sculptor. From fauvism he went on, together with Pablo Picasso, to evolve cubism and to be among the first to use collage. Among his major works are *Woman with a Mandolin* (1937) and the *Birds* series (1955-63).
See also: Collage; Cubism; Fauves.

Brasília (pop. 1,596,300), federal capital of Brazil since 1960, located on the Paraná River, 600 mi (966 km) northwest of the old coastal capital, Rio de

Janeiro. It was built to help open the immense Brazilian interior. Its cross-shaped plan was designed by Lúcio Costa, while such major buildings as the presidential palace and the cathedral are the work of Oscar Niemeyer.
See also: Brazil.

Brass, alloy of copper and zinc, known since Roman times and widely used in industry and for ornament and decoration. Up to 36% zinc forms "alpha" α-brass, which can be worked cold; with more zinc a mixture of α and "beta"-brass is formed, which is less ductile but stronger. Brasses containing more than 45% zinc (white brasses) are unworkable and have few uses. Some brasses also contain other metals: lead for machinability, aluminum or tin for corrosion resistance, and nickel, manganese, or iron for strength.
See also: Alloy.

Bratislava (pop. 446,600), capital of Slovakia. Bratislava is a port city on the Danube River. Its industries include mechanical engineering, oil refining, petrolem products, and cloth.
See also: Slovakia.

Brattain, Walter Houser (1902-87), U.S. physicist who helped invent the transistor. He shared the 1956 Nobel Prize in physics with William Shockley and John Bardeen for this invention, and for the research into the electrical properties of semiconductors that made it possible. All 3 men worked at the Bell Telephone Laboratories—Brattain from 1929—where the transistor was first announced in 1948.
See also: Physics; Transistor.

Braun, Eva (1912-45), mistress (from 1930) and later wife of Adolf Hitler. On April 29, 1945, a few days before Germany's defeat in World War II, they were married. The next day both Braun and Hitler committed suicide.
See also: Hitler, Adolf.

Braun, Wernher von (1912-77), German-American rocket pioneer. He designed most of the rockets that powered the U.S. space program, including the Jupiter rocket that launched the first U.S. satellite, *Explorer 1*, in 1958. Von Braun was born in Wirsitz, Germany (now Wyrzysk, Poland). He studied engineering at Berlin and Zürich, and in 1936, became director of the Peenemünde rocket research station. During World War II he developed the V-2 rocket, more than 4,000 of which were fired against Britain. Von Braun surrendered to the U.S. forces at the end of the war, and went to work in the United States, becoming a U.S. citizen in 1955.
See also: Rocket.

Braxton, Carter (1736-97), American political leader during the Revolutionary War period. He was a signer of the Declaration of Independence and served in the House of Burgesses, the Continental Congress, and the Congress of the Confederation.

Brazil, fifth largest country in the world and largest in South America, constituting nearly half the continent's land area. Brazil shares borders with all South American countries except Ecuador and Chile. It is the only Latin American country whose official language is Portuguese.

Brazil

Capital:	Brasília
Area:	3,286,488 sq mi
	(8,511,965 sq km)
Population:	169,807,000
Language:	Portuguese
Government:	Federal presidential republic
Independent:	1822
Head of gov.:	President
Per capita:	U.S. $3,640
Mon. unit:	1 Real = 100 centavos

Land and climate. Most of Brazil falls within 2 major geographical regions: the lowlands of the Amazon River system and the plateau. Drained by the Amazon River and its tributaries, the Amazonian lowlands form the world's most extensive tropical rain forests. The climate is not excessively hot, but rainfall is as much as 80 in (203 cm) annually. The Brazilian plateau, rising to 1,000 to 3,000 ft (305 to 914 m) above sea level, is studded with occasional mountain ranges. About 40% of the population lives in the southerly part of the plateau, known as the "heartland," which contains some of the country's most productive farmland and valuable mineral deposits.

Economy. Agriculture is the traditional mainstay of Brazil's economy. Exports include cattle, coffee, cotton, sugarcane, cocoa, tobacco, soybeans, citrus fruit, and bananas. Industry has also developed; particularly iron and steel, motor vehicles, textiles, and machinery. Brazil's vast natural resources have yet to be fully developed. Rich oil deposits have been found, as well as, iron, manganese, coal, chromium, quartz, uranium, and industrial grade diamonds. The exploitation of the Amazon basin has posed a threat to the tropical rain forest, creating a major point of controversy, within Brazilan politics.

History. Portuguese colonists under Pedro lvarez Cabral claimed Brazil in 1500, and colonization began in 1532. Slaves were extensively used by plantation owners. The country remained a colony until winning its independence in 1822, as a monarchy. Slavery was abolished in 1888, and Brazil became a republic in 1889. Military regimes prevailed until the accession of President Getúlio Vargas in 1930. A military coup overthrew the leftist civilian government of João Goulart in 1964. Often accused of torture and other human rights violations, the military continued to rule through a succession of generals who served as president. The first presidential election with civilian candidates in 20 years was held in Jan. 1985. Civilian rule was restored in the late 1980s. From 1995 onwards, the current president, Cardoso, has tried to reform the corrupt political system.

Brazil nut, South American tree (genus *Bertholletia*) of the Amazon and Negro rivers. The tree grows to 160 ft (50 m), bearing very hard 6 in (15 cm) fruit containing 10 to 20 nuts. The nuts are used as food and for lubricating oil. The trees are also used for hardwood lumber.

Brazilwood, heavy wood of various trees (genus *Caesalpinia*). Extracts from this wood produce bright crimson and deep purple colors. Once an important source of dye, it is still used for making violins and in cabinetwork.

Brazzaville (pop. 596,200), river port and capital of the Republic of the Congo, situated below the Stanley Pool on the right bank of the Congo River. Kinshasa lies on the other side of the pool. Brazzaville was formerly the capital of the French Equatorial Africa. It was the headquarters of the Free French in Africa during World War II and gained independence in 1960. Brazzaville has always been primarily a center of government and education, although since 1945 industries such as brewing, matchmaking, and sugar refining have become established. Contributing to this industrial development is the hydroelectric plant at the nearby Djoué Falls. The Center for Administrative and Advanced Technical Studies is located in Brazzaville.
See also: Congo.

Bread, one of humanity's earliest and most important foods, made of baked dough—a mixture of flour and water. In developed western societies, wheat flour is most commonly used and the dough is leavened (i.e., increased in volume by introducing small bubbles of carbon dioxide throughout) using yeast.

Breadfruit (*Artocarpus altilis*), tree of the mulberry family, whose fruit is the staple diet in the South Pacific. Breadfruit trees are now seen in much of tropical America. The fruit is melonlike, 8 in (20 cm) across, and is protected by a thick rind that can be woven into cloth. The pulp, which tastes like potato meal, is eaten cooked, and may be ground to make a flour.

Breakbone fever *See:* Dengue.

Breakwater, timber, masonry, or stone barrier constructed to give protection from heavy seas. Breakwaters built at right angles to the shore are called *jetties*; those built parallel with the shore (providing additional protection for a harbor), with a wharf on the sheltered side, are called *moles*.

Bream, any of a variety of European freshwater fishes of the carp family, growing up to 17 lb (8 kg). The freshwater sunfishes of the United States and the marine porgies and wrasses are also known as bream.

Breast, front of the chest; especially in female mammals, the modified cutaneous, glandular structure it bears—the mamma or mammary gland. In humans, each breast consists of 15 to 20 branching ducts surrounded by connective tissue that acts as a supporting framework. The larger partitions between the lobes form strands that extend from the skin to the underlying deep fascia. At puberty in the female, fat accumulates in the connective tissue of the breast and the overlying skin. The skin of the areola, the disk-shaped area surrounding the nipple, contains modified sweat glands and sebaceous glands. The breasts usually secrete a small quantity of fluid, or colostrum, from early pregnancy onwards, and for 2-3 days after childbirth. Milk begins about 3 days after childbirth, increasing to an average rate of about 28 fl oz (850 ml) per day. The principal constituents of breast milk are water, lactose,

fat, and protein. The ejection of milk is stimulated by sucking and by the release of the pituitary hormone oxytocin.
See also: Mammary glands.

Breast cancer, malignant growth in the breast or mammary gland. Breast cancer— carcinoma of the breast—is the most common malignancy among women and has the highest fatality rate of all cancers affecting them. The annual mortality rate since 1950 has remained at about 25 in every 100,000 women. Breast cancer in men is rare and tends not to be recognized until late, thus the results of treatment are poor. In women, breast carcinoma is rarely seen before the age of 30, and the incidence rises rapidly after menopause.
See also: Cancer.

Breasted, James Henry (1865-1935), U.S. archaeologist and historian, who advanced archaeological research in Egypt and western Asia. He specialized in Egyptology, and in 1919 organized the Oriental Institute at the University of Chicago, subsequently sponsoring expeditions at Megiddo and Persepolis.
See also: Archeology.

Brecht, Bertolt (Eugen Berthold Friedrich Brecht; 1898-1956), German Marxist playwright and poet, who revolutionized modern theater with his production techniques and concept of epic theater. He left Nazi Germany in 1933, returning to East Berlin in 1948 to found the Berliner Ensemble. His plays include *The Threepenny Opera* (1928), *The Life of Galileo* (1938), *Mother Courage* (1939), and *The Caucasian Chalk Circle* (1949).

Breckinridge, John Cabell (1821-75), congressman and vice-president of the United States, and major-general and secretary of war of the Confederate States of America. Breckinridge served as vice-president under James Buchanan 1857-61. During the 4-way race for president in 1860, Breckinridge was the candidate of the Southern Democrats on a pro-slavery, pro-Union platform, polling 18% of the popular vote. When Kentucky voted to remain in the Union, Breckinridge left his Senate seat, becoming brigadier-general and later, secretary of war for the Confederacy. When the South surrendered, he fled to Britain, but returned to the United States in 1868.
See also: Civil War, U.S.

Breckinridge, Sophonisba (1866-1948), U.S. pioneer teacher of social work. She wrote *The Delinquent Child and the Home* (1912) and *The Family and the State* (1934). She believed the government should play a key role in helping the needy.

Breedlove, Craig (1937-), U.S. racing-car driver. He set many records in *Spirit of America,* a car he designed and built himself. In 1963 he was the first U.S. driver since 1928 to hold the world land speed mark, achieving an average velocity of 407.45 mph (655.73 kph). Breedlove broke the 600 mph (966 kph) mark in the jetpowered *Spirit of America-Sonic I*, reaching 600.6 mph (966.6 kph) in 1965.

Breed's Hill *See:* Bunker Hill, Battle of.

Bremen (pop. 552,300), city in northwest Germany, situated on the Weser River, 38 mi (61 km) from Bremerhaven on the estuary. Founded by Charlemagne in A.D. 787, Bremen became a major medieval trading center, controlling its own small state within the Holy Roman Empire (from which it broke free in 1646), and acting as a leading force in the Hanseatic League of city-states. From 1806 to 1815 Bremen was in French hands. After the Congress of Vienna, it became one of the independent German states, and in 1871 merged with Bismarck's Germany. Commercial fishing, truck farming, and cattle raising are the main occupations in the rural areas surrounding the city. In the city itself, which retains much of its medieval character, the main occupations are shipbuilding and import and export shipping.
See also: Germany.

Brendan, Saint (c.A.D. 484-c.578), Irish monk, founder of Clonfert and other monasteries. Tales of his travels are recorded in the 8th-century *Voyages of St. Brendan*, and he is sometimes honored as having reached America 900 years before Columbus.

Brennan, William Joseph, Jr. (1906-   ), U.S. Supreme Court associate justice 1956-90, appointed by Eisenhower. He became leader of the court's liberal wing, and was a champion of civil rights, free speech, and labor relations.

Brenner Pass, important pass across the Alps, in the Tyrol, linking Innsbruck in Austria with Bolzano in Italy. The first good road along this ancient route was completed in 1772, and the railroad was built from 1864 to 1867.
See also: Alps.

Breslau *See:* Wroclaw.

Bresson, Robert (1907-), French film director, noted for the austere, penetrating quality of his work. His films include *Diary of a Country Priest* (1950), *The Trial of Joan of Arc* (1962), and *Lancelot of the Lake* (1976). In 1994, he received a "Felix" (European film prize) for his works.

Brest (pop. 153,100), seaport and naval station in Finistère department, northwest France. It is built on two hills overlooking an island harbor linked with the Atlantic Ocean by a natural 6-mi (9.7-km) channel. Brest is a commercial port, but important primarily as a naval base. During World War II the base was used by German submarines and was largely destroyed by Allied bombing.
See also: France.

Brethren, Children of the, Baptist sect organized in Germany in 1708. Following persecution, the church was reorganized in 1719 in Germantown, Pa., eventually spreading its doctrine of pacifism and simple living to the Pacific coast. Headquarters in Elgin, Ill., the church sponsors mission work around the world and operates six colleges and a seminary.
See also: Baptists.

Breton, André (1896-1966), French poet and critic, a founder of surrealism. Associated at first with Dada, he broke with it and in 1924 issued the first of three surrealist manifestos, becoming the new movement's chief spokesperson. Among his works is the poetic novel, *Nadja* (1928).
See also: Surrealism.

Bretton Woods Conference, international gathering at Bretton Woods, N.H., in July 1944, at which 44 members of the United Nations planned to stabilize the international economy and national currencies after World War II. They also established the International Monetary Fund and the World Bank.
See also: United Nations; World Bank.

Breuer, Marcel (Lajos) (1902-81), Hungarian-born U.S. architect. A student and teacher at the Bauhaus 1920-28, in 1937 he moved to Harvard and continued working with Walter Gropius. A pioneer of the international style, he collaborated in the design of the UNESCO headquarters, Paris (1953-58).
See also: Bauhaus.

Brewing, process of making beer from cereal grains, usually barley. Brewing is a major industry in the United States, with a total annual production of about 125 million barrels. In the first step of brewing, malting, cleaned barley is soaked in water 2-3 days, allowed to germinate, and dried in a kiln. The malt is stored for several weeks while the malt flavor develops and various enzymes are produced. In the next stage, mashing, the ground malt is mixed with water, maintained at a warm temperature, and stirred constantly. During this process the enzymes break down the insoluble starch into soluble carbohydrates. The liquor containing these substances is filtered out (the remaining solid mash is used as animal feed) and boiled to stop enzyme activity and sterilize the brew. Hops are added at this stage to impart their characteristic flavor. Yeast is then added for about 8 days of fermentation.
See also: Beer; Fermentation.

Brewster, William (1567-1644), leader of the Plymouth Colony in New England. He sailed with the Pilgrims on the *Mayflower* in 1620. Brewster played a major part in regulating the civil and religious affairs of the Plymouth Colony.
See also: Pilgrims; Plymouth Colony.

Brezhnev, Leonid Ilyich (1906-82), USSR political leader, who became first secretary of the Communist Party and effective head of the Soviet government in 1964. He first became a member of the party central committee in 1952, and was chairman of the Presidium of the Supreme Soviet 1960-64. Brezhnev, Aleksei Kosygin, and Nikolai Podgorny took control when Nikita Khrushchev was ousted in 1964. Brezhnev assumed the additional office of chief of state in 1977. He pursued a policy of détente with the West while overseeing a massive Soviet military buildup.
See also: Union of Soviet Socialist Republics.

Brian Boru (941-1014), king of Ireland from 1002. His reign marked the end of Norse domination, but unified rule ended when he was murdered after his victory against the Danes at Clontarf.
See also: Ireland.

Briand, Aristide (1862-1932), French politician, lawyer, and socialist leader who was 11 times premier of France. As foreign minister (1925-32), he was the author of the Kellogg-Briand Pact (1928). He was awarded the Nobel Peace Prize in 1926.
See also: Kellogg-Briand Peace Pact.

Briar *See:* Brier.

Briard, sheepdog first bred in France in the twelfth century. Used for herding and police work, the briard is strongly built and usually black, grey, or tawny in color. It stands 22 to 27 in (56 to 69 cm) and weighs about 70 to 80 lb (32 to 36 kg).

Brice, Fanny (Fannie Borach; 1891-1951), U.S. popular singer and performer of musical comedy. Acclaimed for her radio series in which she portrayed "Baby Snooks," she was also known for her satirical sketches and her long association with the *Ziegfeld Follies*.

Brick, building material made of clay, sometimes reinforced with straw, shaped into rectangles and hardened by heat. Sun-dried bricks were used as a building material at least 6,000 years ago in Mesopotamia. The discovery of the technique of firing clay in kilns enabled hard durable bricks to be made. Examples of fired bricks have been found in excavations at the city of Ur that are at least 5,000 years old. The Greeks used bricks, and the Romans made an art of brick masonry in their large-scale constructions. After the fall of Rome, bricks were not used again on a large scale until the 12th and 13th centuries.
Although bricks are important in the construction industry, concrete, plastics, and light alloys have taken over some of their functions. Modern bricks include: *common brick*, used for ordinary building purposes; *face brick,* used to resist erosion or for decoration; *firebrick* (refractory brick), which can withstand the high temperatures found in furnaces and kilns; *paving brick*, larger, harder, and more water-resistant than the common brick; and *insulating brick*, a porous type that insulates against extremes of temperature.

Bridge, card game developed from whist. Contract bridge, the form now universally adopted, was perfected by Harold S. Vanderbilt in 1925-26. It is played by 2 pairs of partners, who make bids according to how many tricks (rounds of cards played) they calculate they can win. Demanding great skill, bridge has become immensely popular as a social and competitive game, with international championships controlled by the World Bridge Federation.

Bridge, structure that spans an obstacle and permits traffic across it. The *beam* (or girder) *bridge* consists of a rigid beam resting at either end on piers. A development of this is the *truss bridge*, with a metal framework designed for greatest strength at those points where the load has greatest moment around the piers. Where piers are impracticable, a *cantilever bridge* may be built on beams (cantilevers) extending from each side. An *arch bridge* consists of one or more arches. A *suspension bridge* comprises two towers that carry one or more flexible cables that are firmly anchored at each end; the roadway is suspended by means of vertical cables. *Movable bridges* include the *swing bridge*, pivoted on a central pier; the *bascule* (a descendant of the medieval drawbridge), whose cantilevers are pivoted inshore so that they may be swung upward; the *vertical-lift bridge*, a pair of towers between which runs a beam that may be winched vertically upward; and the *retractable bridge*, whose cantilevers may be run inshore on wheels. Temporary bridges include the pontoon or floating bridge, in which floating structures support a continuous roadway.

Bridge of Sighs, landmark bridge in Venice, Italy. Spanning the canal between the Doges' Palace and the state prison, its name derives from the "sighs" of the unhappy prisoners who had to cross it. Renowned for its beauty, it was designed by Italian architect Antonio Contino and completed c.1600.

Bridgeport (pop. 141,686), city in southwestern Connecticut, about 65 mi (105 km) from New York City. Products include electrical and metal goods, sewing machines, munitions, airplanes, textiles, and clothing. It is the home of the Barnum Institute of Science and History and the University of Bridgeport, founded in 1947.
See also: Connecticut.

Bridger, James (1804-81), U.S. trader, explorer, and army scout. He traded in the unexplored American West and Southwest. He discovered Great Salt Lake (1824), and founded Fort Bridger, Wy.
See also: Western frontier life.

Bridges, Harry (Alfred Bryant Renton Bridges; 1901-90), U.S. labor leader, Australian- born. He helped form the International Longshoremen's and Warehousemen's Union (ILWU) in 1937, and as its president (until 1977) fought to improve dockworking conditions. Until 1955 there were many government attempts to deport him as a communist.

Bridgetown (pop. 7,500), capital and only port of Barbados. It is a crowded and attractive tourist center, with public buildings made of coral. It was founded in 1628, and then named Indian Bridge, from a crude structure over the creek. Its modernized port now handles sugar, molasses, and rum.
See also: Barbados.

Bridgman, Laura Dewey (1829-89), first blind and deaf child to be successfully educated in the United States. She was taught the names of objects by raised letters pasted onto the objects themselves and eventually learned finger-spelling, thus paving the way for the education of other deaf-blind youths such as Helen Keller.

Brier, shrubby plant (*Erica arborea*) of the heath family, known for its fragrant, white, globe-shaped flowers. Its thick roots are used in making pipes.

Bright, Richard (1789-1858), English physician who first identified the kidney disorder known as Bright's Disease, now called nephritis.
See also: Nephritis.

Brighton (pop. 143,000), popular English seaside resort on the south coast, 51 mi (82 km) south of London. The town first gained popularity when an 18th-century doctor claimed its seawater had curative power. In 1783 the Prince of Wales (later George IV) visited the town. The onion-domed Royal Pavilion was built to his orders. Originally in classical style, it was rebuilt in 1815 by John Nash, in the exotic style of Indian Mogul architecture.
See also: England.

Brisbane (pop. 1,301,700), city and seaport in eastern Australia, capital of the state of Queensland. The city is built on both banks of the navigable Brisbane River, about 15 mi (24 km) from the outlet to the Pacific Ocean. The area was a penal settlement in 1824, then in 1838 became a city. Queensland became a separate colony in 1859.
See also: Australia.

Bristlecone pine, evergreen tree (*Pinus aristata*) native to the Rocky Mountains of the United States. Some bristlecone pines are thought to be more than 4,000 years old, possibly the oldest living things on earth. The long life of the needles helps the tree survive years of harsh weather, when few new needles can grow.

Bristol (pop. 396,600), large city and port in southwestern England, situated at the confluence of the Avon and Frome rivers, 6 mi (9.7 km) from the mouth of the Avon. First a Saxon settlement called Brycgstowe ("the place of the bridge"), by Norman times it had become a wool center and the chief port for trade with Ireland. The textile trade flourished and in 1540 Bristol became a city. In the 17th and 18th centuries, when new trade routes had been established, Bristol shipowners engaged in "the triangular trade of the Atlantic," dealing in sugar, slaves, and tobacco. Another source of prosperity in the 18th century was the development of the city as a fashionable spa, making use of the hot mineral springs. There are some fine historic buildings and a famous suspension bridge (1864) that spans the precipitous Avon gorge.
See also: England.

Bristol Channel, inlet of the Atlantic Ocean between Wales and southwestern England. Extending 80 mi (130km) from the sea to the River Severn, it separates the heavily industrialized southwestern Wales from largely agricultural southwestern England.

Britain, modern form of the ancient name for the island now comprising England, Scotland, and Wales. The Romans referred to the 1st century B.C. Celtic inhabitants as Pritani, hence their own name for the island, Britannia.

Britain, Battle of,, air battle of World War II from Aug. 8 to Oct. 31, 1940, between the British Royal Air Force (RAF) and the German Luftwaffe. The Germans intended to weaken British defenses and morale before invading the country. The Luftwaffe forces were much larger than those of the RAF, but the latter proved technically and tactically superior. The Germans bombed shipping and ports, then airfields and Midland industries, and finally, London. Daylight raids proving too costly, the Germans turned to night attacks. At the end the RAF had lost some 900 planes, the Germans

over 2,300, causing Hitler to postpone his projected invasion indefinitely, thus tacitly admitted failure.
See also: Churchill, Sir Winston Leonard Spencer; World War II.

British Broadcasting Corporation (BBC), publicly financed company that runs all radio and 2 of the 3 television networks in Britain. The BBC first went on the air in 1922. Regular television programs, which began in 1936, were interrupted by World War II, but resumed in 1946. The BBC provides a wide range of news programs, documentaries, plays, comedies, concerts, and school programs, and is known for the excellence of its panel programs and educational broadcasts. The BBC has a considerable overseas audience.

British Cameroons, former UN trust territory on the west coast of Africa in what is now Nigeria and Cameroon. After World War I the former German colony of Camcroons was divided between France and Britain. After World War II both became UN trust territories. In 1960, French Cameroons became independent, and in 1961 the southern part of British Cameroons joined it to form the Republic of Cameroon. The northern part was incorporated into Nigeria.

British Columbia, westernmost of Canada's provinces, bordered by Alberta on the east, Montana, Idaho, and Washington on the south, the Pacific Ocean and Alaska on the west, and the Yukon and Northwest Territories on the north. Alberta is dominated by two mountain chains, the Coast Mountains in the west and the Canadian Rocky Mountains in the east. The 700-mi (1,127-km) coastline is broken by fjords. Vancouver Island and the Queen Charlotte Islands are the most important of the offshore chains. About 75% of the population lives in the relatively mild southwest corner of the province. Greater Vancouver alone accounts for about one-half of the total population. The provincial capital is Victoria. Forestry is the mainstay of British Columbia's economy and accounts for the province's major industries. Mining is second, including zinc, lead, silver, gold, and iron ore.
See also: Canada.

British Commonwealth of Nations *See:* Commonwealth of Nations.

British Empire *See:* Great Britain.

British Guiana *See:* Guyana.

British Honduras *See:* Belize.

British Indian Ocean Territory, British dependency in the Indian Ocean, about 1,180 mi (1,900 km) northeast of Mauritius. Consisting of the Chagos Archipelago Island group, it covers a land area of about 30 sq mi (78 sq km) and has a population of about 2,500 people. The United States maintains a naval base on the main island, Diego Garcia.

British Isles, island group bounded by the English Channel, the Strait of Dover, the North Sea, and the Atlantic Ocean. The British Isles consist of the island of Great Britain (England, Scotland, and Wales), Ireland, and about 5,500 small islands and inlets.

British Library, national library of Great Britain, one of the largest research libraries in the world. Located in London, it was originally a part of the British Museum. Its collection of rare books and manuscripts includes *Beowulf* and the Magna Carta. The library is also a depository for copyrights.

British Museum, national museum of antiquities and ethnography in London. Founded in 1753, when the British government acquired the art collection and library of Sir Hans Sloane, it opened to the public in 1759. Its present neoclassical premises were built 1823-47 and its natural history section was separated 1881-83. The museum has one of the world's foremost collections, including the Elgin Marbles.

British North America Act, act passed by the British Parliament in 1867 to create the Dominion of Canada, uniting Canada (Quebec and Ontario), New Brunswick, and Nova Scotia under a federal government. The act served as Canada's constitution until 1982; under it, amendments had to be submitted to the British Parliament for formal approval. The Constitution Act, 1982, superseded the earlier law (now also known as the Constitution Act, 1867), thus "patriating" the constitution.
See also: Confederation of Canada.

British thermal unit (BTU), quantity of heat required to raise the temperature of one pound of water 1°F at, or near, its point of maximum density (39.1°F). The BTU is equivalent to 0.252 kilogram-calorie.
See also: Calorie.

British West Indies, collective name for islands in the Caribbean Sea that are or have been dependencies of Great Britain, including Anguilla, the Bahamas, Barbados, Bermuda, Grenada, Jamaica, Trinidad and Tobago, and the British Virgin Islands. Although the British West Indies is not a political entity, the islands have formed such organizations as the West Indies Federation (1958-62) and Caricom, or the Caribbean Community, an alliance based on foreign policy and economic cooperation (1973).

Brittany, breed of hunting dog with a short, thick coat, white with orange or red-brown markings. Brittanies average 35-40 lbs (16-18 kg) and stand 18-20 in (45-50 cm) at the shoulder. A breed with a long history in France and Spain, the Brittany has the build of a spaniel but points at its quarry.

Brittany (French: *Bretagne*), historic penninsular region of northwestern France. The Romans conquered the area in 56 B.C. and named it Armonica. It was settled about 500 A.D. by Celtic Britons fleeing the Anglo-Saxon invasion. After struggles for independence from the Franks and from Normandy, Anjou, England, and France in turn, it became a French province in 1532. The Bretons retain their own cultural traditions and language.
See also: France.

Britten, Benjamin (1913-76), British composer. His works include the operas *Peter Grimes* (1945), *Billy Budd* (1951), *The Turn of the Screw* (1954), and *Death in Venice* (1973), as well as such instrumental and choral

works as the *Variations on a Theme by Frank Bridge* (1937) and *War Requiem* (1962).
See also: Opera.

Brittle star, marine invertebrate (class Ophiuroidea), 5-armed relative of starfish found in seas all over the world. The button-shaped body grows up to 2 in (5 cm), and the flexible arms, which break off readily but are regrown, grow to 2 ft (60 cm). Brittle stars feed by trapping minute particles in mucus on the arms and passing them to the mouth on the underside of the disk, or by holding animals or carrion in an arm and pushing them into the mouth. Eggs are fertilized after being released into the sea or retained in the female, where larval development takes place, the young being released as small adults.

Brno (formerly Brünn; pop. 388,300), city in the eastern part of the Czech Republic, chief city of Moravia. It was founded in the 9th century, flourishing as a free city within the kingdom of Bohemia in the 13th-14th centuries. In the 18th-19th centuries its Spielberg castle was used as a Hapsburg prison. Situated on the Svratka and Svitava rivers, Brno is a manufacturing center for cars, machinery, textiles, and other products, and is the seat of the Czech supreme court.
See also: Czech Republic.

Broad bean, Windsor bean, or horse bean (*Vicia faba*), annual plant producing seed pods up to 1 ft (30 cm) long, containing large edible beans. An important food in early civilizations of North Africa and southwest Asia, it is one of the most widely cultivated beans in Europe and Latin America, and is also grown for fodder.

Broadcasting *See:* Journalism; Radio; Television.

Broccoli, form of cabbage, a branching cauliflower (*Brassica oleracea botytis*), grown for the immature flowers. Originating in Italy, it is grown in Europe and America, where green-sprouting broccoli is the most popular variety.

Broglie, Louis Victor, Prince de (1892-1987), French physicist, awarded the 1929 Nobel Prize in physics for his suggestion that subatomic particles would display wave-like properties under appropriate conditions. The prediction was borne out experimentally, and de Broglie's theories led to the branch of quantum mechanics called wave mechanics.
See also: Physics; Quantum theory.

Bromegrass, any of about 60 kinds of grass of genus *Bromus*, found mostly in the Northern Hemisphere and including both weed grasses and grasses valuable as pasturage and soil binders. Plants have flat thin leaves 12-40 in (30-100 cm) tall, often with drooping flower clusters. Rescue grass (*B. unioloides*) and smooth brome (*B. inermis*) are the most economically important varieties. Some weed varieties, such as ripgut grass (*B. rigidus*) and foxtail brome (*B. rubens*), have spines on the flower clusters that can cause serious internal and external injury to grazing animals.

Bromeliad, large family of tropical plants, mostly native to the Americas, including the pineapple and epiphytes (air plants) such as Spanish moss. Most bromeliads have spike-shaped leaves that form a tight cluster, with flowers in the cluster or on spikes; the cup-shaped cluster holds water, allowing the plants to survive droughts.

Bromide, salt of hydrobromic acid, especially potassium bromide, that acts as a depressant of brain function and the heart and is used in medicine as a sedative and a hypnotic.

Bromine, chemical element, symbol Br; for physical constants see Periodic Table. Bromine was discovered by Antoine J. Balard in 1826. It belongs to the halogen group of elements and is obtained from natural brines and sea water by displacement with chlorine. Bromine, a heavy reddish-brown liquid, is the only nonmetallic element that is liquid at room temperature. It produces irritating red fumes at room temperature and produces painful sores on skin contact. Bromine is less active than chlorine. The major use of bromine is in the production of ethylene dibromide, a lead scavenger used in making gasoline antiknock compounds. It is also used in making fumigants, flameproofing agents, water purification compounds, dyes, medicinals, sanitizers, and photographic chemicals.

Bronchitis, inflammation of the bronchi, the main branches of the windpipe, caused by viruses or bacteria or by the inhalation of smoke. Coughing, fever, and chest pains are common symptoms.

Brontë sisters, 3 English novelists and poets, daughters of an Anglican clergyman. The isolated life of the Yorkshire moors, their mother's early death, and the dissipations of their brother, Branwell, informed much of their work. **Charlotte Brontë** (1816-55) published the partly autobiographical novel *Jane Eyre* (1847) under the name Currer Bell and met with immediate success. Together with *Shirley* (1849) and *Villette* (1853), it represents an important advance in the treatment of women in English fiction. **Emily Brontë** (1818-48), using the name Ellis Bell, published a single novel, *Wuthering Heights* (1847), a masterpiece of visionary power. **Anne Brontë** (1820-49) published two novels, *Agnes Grey* (1847) and *The Tenant of Wildfell Hall* (1848), under the name Acton Bell.

Brontosaurus, large, plant-eating, four-legged dinosaur whose fossilized skeletons have been found in the western United States. With its long neck and tail, small head, and huge body (about 68 ft/28 m long, weighing 35 tons), the brontosaurus was probably the largest land animal in the earth's history.
See also: Dinosaur.

Bronx, The, one of the 5 boroughs of New York City, the only one situated on the mainland, separated from Manhattan Island by the Harlem River. Jonas Bronck purchased the area from the Native Americans in 1639.
See also: New York City.

Bronze, corrosion-resistant alloy of copper and tin, used for machine parts, marine hardware, and casting statues. Aluminum, iron, lead, zinc, and phosphorus are often added to bronze to harden it.
See also: Alloy.

Bronze Age, phase of history in which metal was first used to make tools and weapons. Copper and bronze were used interchangeably in the first stage, called the Copper Age. Bronze casting began in the Middle East about 3500 B.C. and in the Americas, about 1100 A.D.

Brooke, Rupert (1887-1915), English poet whose patriotic war sonnets were widely popular during World War I, author of *Poems* (1911) and *1914 and Other Poems* (1915).

Brook Farm (1841-47), Utopian community, founded at West Roxbury, Massachusetts, by Unitarian minister George Ripley. The aim was to create an egalitarian community of workers and thinkers; many leading intellectuals were attracted, including the author Nathaniel Hawthorne, who was a member, and Horace Greeley, Margaret Fuller, and Ralph Waldo Emerson, who visited.

Brookhaven National Laboratory, center for nuclear research in Upton, Long Island, N.Y. Founded in 1947 under the aegis of the U.S. Atomic Energy Commission, it has facilities for medical and agricultural research.

Brookings Institution, public service corporation founded in 1927 in Washington, D.C., for research and information on government and economic issues.

Brooklyn, one of the 5 boroughs of New York City, situated at the southwest extremity of Long Island. First settled in 1636 by Dutch farmers, Brooklyn was chartered as a city in 1834 and gradually absorbed the surrounding communities until it became a borough of New York (1896). Though its large area is primarily residential, it also has a considerable business and industrial area and the port handles a great share of New York's oceangoing traffic. Brooklyn's facilities for higher education include Pratt Institute, Polytechnic University, Brooklyn College, and parts of Long Island University (LIU). The Brooklyn Museum, located on the edge of Prospect Park, has a fine collection of Egyptian and primitive art and a notable group of 18th-century and 19th-century American paintings. The Institute of Arts and Sciences, the Brooklyn Philharmonic Orchestra, and the Brooklyn Academy of Music have international reputations.
See also: New York City.

Brooklyn Bridge, world's first steel-wire suspension bridge. It spans 1,595 ft (486 m) over the East River and joins the boroughs of Brooklyn and Manhattan. Built 1869-83 by J. A. Roebling and his son, W. A. Roebling, it was the largest suspension bridge in the world at the time of its completion.

Brooks, Gwendolyn Elizabeth (1917-   ), U.S. poet. She was the first African American to win the Pulitzer Prize (1949), for her semiautobiographical *Annie Allen* (1949). Her books of poems include *Bronzeville Boys* *and Girls* (1956), *Selected Poems* (1963), *In the Mecca* (1968), and *To Disembark* (1981).

Brooks, Van Wyck (1886-1963), U.S. critic. In *America's Coming of Age* (1915), he saw the 19th-century United States as torn between the idealistic and the materialistic. He wrote critical biographies of Mark Twain, Henry James, and Emerson. His series *Makers and Finders: A History of the Writer in America, 1800-1915*, included the Pulitzer Prize-winning *The Flowering of New England* (1936).

Broom, any of various European and Asian leguminous shrubs with yellow flowers that "explode" when bees land on them. The seeds develop in pods that twist open suddenly, throwing the seeds out with an audible crackle.

Broom, Robert (1866-1951), Scottish anatomist and paleontologist, discoverer of fossils of the humanlike *Australopithecus*. From 1903 he lived in South Africa, where he taught at Victoria College and studied the fossils, important for their bearing on human evolution. His writings include *Mammal-Like Reptiles of South Africa* (1932) and *The South African Fossil Apemen* (1946).
See also: Paleontology.

Broun, Heywood Campbell (1888-1939), U.S. journalist. His column, "It Seems to Me," published in the *New York Tribune* (1912-21), *New York World* (1921-28), and *New York Telegram* (1928-39), was widely read for its liberal political and social views; he also wrote for the *Post* and *The New Republic*. His views, as in his defense of Sacco and Vanzetti, brought him into frequent conflict with his publishers. He ran for Congress as a Socialist (1930), and established the American Newspaper Guild (1933), serving as president until his death.
See also: Journalism.

Browder, Earl Russell (1891-1973), U.S. Communist party secretary-general 1930-44 and president of the Communist Political Association 1944-45. He was also the Communist presidential candidate in 1936 and 1940, but was expelled from the party in 1946 for advocating greater cooperation between the Soviet Union and the West.**Brown, Charles Brockden** (1771-1810), one of the first U.S. professional novelists. Influenced by William Godwin, his *Alcuin: A Dialogue* (1798) and novel *Edgar Huntly* (1799) plead for social reform. *Wieland* (1799) is an outstanding Gothic novel.
See also: Communism.

Brown, Jim (1936-), U.S. football player. A running back for the Cleveland Browns (1957-65), he was one of the greatest players in National Football League (NFL) history. Brown's achievements include winning a record 8 league rushing titles and placing second among all-time leading rushers (12,312 yards). Brown was inducted into the football Hall of Fame in 1971.

Brown, John (1800-59), U.S. abolitionist. After supporters of slavery burned down the town of Lawrence, Kansas, Brown retaliated by murdering five proslavery men at Pottawatamie Creek. In October 1859 Brown seized the government arsenal at Harper's Ferry, Virginia, attempting to ignite a massive slave insurrection. Troops under Robert E. Lee stormed the arsenal and captured Brown. He was tried for treason and hanged on Dec. 2, 1859. *See also:* Abolitionism.

Brown, Robert (1773-1858), Scottish physician and botanist. Brown discovered the natural continuous random movement of microscopic particles now known as Brownian motion (1827), and identified the nucleus as a constituent of nearly all living plant cells (1831). Brown studied and collected specimens of flora in Australia and Tasmania. He identified the two plant groupings of gymnosperms (conifers) and angiosperms (flowering plants), and otherwise elaborated the system of plant classification. He was also a pioneer in the microscopic examination of plant fossils. *See also:* Botany.

Brown, Sir Arthur Whitten *See:* Alcock and Brown.

Brownian motion *See:* Brown, Robert; Einstein, Albert.

Brownie, in British folklore, small creature that lives with a household and helps with chores while a family sleeps. It looks like an ugly, shaggy man and usually dresses in a brown cloak. The brownie, who accepts no pay, may also cause mischief. The name is also used for the youngest group (6-8 years) of the Girl Scouts.

Brownies *See:* Girl Scouts and Girl Guides.

Browning, Elizabeth Barrett (1806-61), English lyric poet best known for *Sonnets from the Portuguese* (1850), inspired by her husband, Robert Browning, who had "rescued" her from illness and family tyranny in 1846. Other works include *Casa Guidi Windows* (1851) and *Aurora Leigh* (1857), a novel in verse.

Browning, Robert (1812-89), English poet. He perfected the dramatic monologue in "Andrea del Sarto" and "My Last Duchess." His masterpiece is *The Ring and the Book* (4 vols., 1868-69), a 17th-century Roman murder story told from different viewpoints. His psychological insight and colloquial language profoundly influenced 20th-century poets.

Brown lung, or byssinosis, lung disease caused by inhaling of cotton dust. Symptoms include difficulty in breathing, a tight feeling in the chest, and coughing. Because cotton dust can permanently harm workers' health, the governments of many countries have set limits on their exposure to it.

Brown recluse, poisonous spider (*Loxosceles reclusa*) of the southern United States, member of the family of brown spiders (Loxoscelidae). It is about 3/8 in (1 cm) long, with a dark violin-shaped patch on its back and 6 eyes in 2 rows. The spider's poisonous bite, used to paralyze insects it eats, leaves a deep and long-lasting sore in humans, and may produce severe reactions, even death.

Brownsville (pop. 260,120), city in southern Texas near the mouth of the Rio Grande River. Named after Major Jacob Brown, who died defending the

settlement from Mexican troops in 1846, Brownsville was incorporated in 1850. Brownsville is a busy port on the Gulf of Mexico and a major industrial center producing chemicals, clothing, and petroleum products. The largest city in the Rio Grande Valley, Brownsville has a tropical climate. Its population is predominantly Latin American in origin although there has been an influx of Anglo Americans since World War II.
See also: Texas.

Brown-tail moth (*Nygmia phaeorrhoea*), member of the family of tussock moths (Liparidae, which also includes the gypsy moth), native to the northeastern United States, whose caterpillar is a serious pest to fruit and shade trees. The hairs of the caterpillars and female moths can be irritating to human skin. The moth is white with a brown abdomen, and a wingspan of about 1.5 in (3.8 cm). The female lays about 300 eggs, which hatch into hairy brown caterpillars with orange, white, or other markings. All summer the caterpillars eat leaves, spinning silk tents to winter over and emerging in spring to continue eating. Grown caterpillars spin cocoons and pupate, maturing by July.

Brown thrasher (*Toxostoma rufum*), bird of the mockingbird family (Mimidae), of the eastern United States and Canada. It is about 11.5 in (29 cm) long, with red-brown head and back, white-and-brown striped breast, long tail, and yellow eyes. The thrasher lives in brush and shrubs and eats insects. Its musical song, like the mockingbird's, resembles that of a variety of other birds.

Brown University, private coeducational school in Providence, R.I., established 1764. Its programs include undergraduate arts and sciences, a graduate program, and a medical school, and it awards bachelor's, master's, and doctoral degrees.

Brown v. Board of Education of Topeka, historic 1954 case in which the U.S. Supreme Court, influenced greatly by Chief Justice Warren's determination to provide a clear signal, unanimously held that racial segregation in public schools is unconstitutional. The Court thereby reversed the 1896 "separate but equal" case of *Plessy* v. *Ferguson*. The decision helped to stimulate the civil rights movement.
See also: Segregation.

Brubeck, Dave (1920-   ), U.S. pianist and composer in the classical and jazz idioms. He studied composition with Darius Milhaud and Arnold Schoenberg. His jazz quartet, founded in 1951 and active through the 1960s, featured alto saxophonist Paul Desmond. During the 1970s and 1980s Brubeck often performed with his three sons. His compositions, known for complex cross-rhythms and baroque counterpoint, include "Blue Rondo a la Turk" and "Take Five."

Bruce, Blanche Kelso (1841-98), public official, the first African American to serve a full term as a U.S. senator (1875-81). Born a slave in Virginia, he was educated on the plantation, then ran away in 1861 after the beginning of the Civil War. After founding schools for blacks in Kansas and Missouri and attending Oberlin College 1866-68, he became a wealthy planter in Mississippi. As a Republican senator from Mississippi, he was an advocate of civil rights for racial minorities, but also opposed discrimination against former rebels. With the end of Reconstruction, he was not reelected, but served as registrar of the U.S. Treasury under presidents James A. Garfield (1881-85) and William McKinley (1897-98).

Bruce, Robert the (1274-1329), claimant to the Scottish throne, which Edward I of England awarded to John de Baliol instead. In 1314 his forces defeated the English in the battle of Bannockburn, briefly interrupting English rule over Scotland.

Bruce, Sir David (1855-1931), British physician and bacteriologist, specialist in tropical diseases. Born in Melbourne, Australia, he studied in Edinburgh and Berlin. In Malta he discovered the bacillus causing brucellosis (1886) and its transmission in goat's milk; in Africa he discovered the organism causing sleeping sickness and its transmission by the tsetse fly (1903-10). An expert on trench fever and tetanus, he also studied the connection between human and animal diseases.
See also: Bacteriology.

Brucellosis, undulant fever, or Malta fever, infectious diseases of vertebrate animals, caused by any of a genus (*Brucella*) of bacteria. Symptoms are chills, fever, profuse sweating, slow pulse and, finally, enlargement of the spleen. Cattle, sheep, goats, and swine can pass the disease on to humans through contaminated meat, milk, and cheese, or by direct contact.

Bruch, Max (1838-1920), German composer and conductor. His best-known works are his Violin Concerto No. 1 in G minor (1868), *Scottish Fantasy* for violin and orchestra (1880), and *Kol Nidrei* for cello and orchestra (1881), based on a traditional Hebrew liturgical melody and written for the Jewish community of Liverpool, England (although Bruch himself was Protestant). He taught at the Berlin Academy of Arts 1891-1910.

Bruckner, (Josef) Anton (1824-96), Austrian composer, noted for his 9 symphonies and his choral music—Masses in D Minor (1864), E Minor (1866), and F Minor (1867-71). Richard Wagner greatly influenced Bruckner.

Bruegel, family of Flemish painters. **Pieter Bruegel the Elder** (c.1525-69) was a great painter of landscapes and allegories: *Peasant Wedding, Fall of Icarus*. Influenced by Bosch (*The Fall of the Rebel Angels*), his works are profoundly marked by his views of the human condition. **Pieter Bruegel the Younger** (1564-1637), also called Hell Bruegel, worked in his father's manner, often with an emphasis on the grotesque. **Jan Bruegel** (1568-1625), also called Velvet Bruegel, the second son, painted landscapes and still lifes with great subtlety and delicacy. He often collaborated with Rubens.

Brugge, or Bruges (pop. 116,700), well-preserved medieval city in north-western Belgium. Once a center for wool trade, in the 15th century it was home to a school of painting led by the van Eycks and Hans Memling. Its commercial interest revived in the 19th century when the Zeebrugge Canal

Brunei

Capital:	Bandar Seri Begawan
Area:	2,226 sq mi
	(5,765 sq km)
Population:	315,000
Language:	Malay
Government:	Absolute monarchy
	(sultanate)
Independent:	1984
Head of gov.:	Sultan
Per capita:	U.S. $14,938
Mon. unit:	1 Brunei dollar = 100
	cents

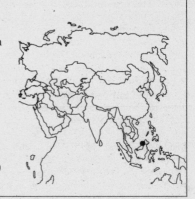

to the North Sea was opened. It manufactures lace and textiles.
See also: Belgium.

Bruhn, Erik (1928-86), Danish ballet dancer. He debuted with the Royal Danish Ballet in 1947 and became a soloist in 1949. For his roles in *Giselle*, *Swan Lake*, and *La Sylphide*, Bruhn is considered one of the greatest classical dancers of his time.
See also: Ballet.

Brulé, Étienne (1592?-1633), French-born Canadian explorer. He came to Quebec around 1608, and was sent by Samuel de Champlain to live with the Algonquins (1610) and the Hurons (1611), studying their language and becoming an interpreter. On another mission for Champlain, he was the first European to reach Lake Ontario (1615), and also explored the valley of the Susquehanna River. When Quebec was seized by the English (1629) he fled to the Hurons; according to some accounts, he was later killed by the Hurons.

Brummell, Beau (George Bryan Brummell; 1778-1840), English dandy, friend of the Prince of Wales (later George IV), and an arbiter of fashion in Regency society. The "Beau" window is named after him.

Brunei, sultanate on the north coast of the island of Borneo, on the South China Sea. It has a humid tropical climate that supports dense forests. Malay is the chief language, Islam the official religion. Rubber and timber were superseded as main products after petroleum was found in 1929. Petroleum and natural gas are now extracted both on and off shore. A local sultanate, established in the 15th century, controlled all of Borneo during the 16th century. It became a British protectorate in 1888, and a 1959 constitution gave it domestic autonomy. Brunei received full independence in 1984. At the end of the 1990s, the country suffered severely from the forest fires in Borneo.
See also: Borneo.

Brunel, Sir Marc Isambard (1769-1849), French-born British engineer and inventor who built the world's first underwater tunnel (Thames Tunnel,

1825). His son, **Isambard Kingdom Brunel** (1806-59), a civil engineer, designed the Clifton suspension bridge at Bristol, England, and built iron-hulled steamships, including the giant *Great Eastern* (1858).

Brunelleschi, Filippo (1377-1446), first great Italian Renaissance architect. One of the first practitioners of linear perspective, he was influenced by classical Roman and 11th-century Tuscan Romanesque architecture. His masterpiece is the dome of the Florence cathedral (1420-36).
See also: Renaissance.

Brunhild, Brünnehilde, or Brynhild, heroine of German and Scandinavian mythology dating back to A.D. 400. In the oldest Scandinavian version, Sigurd rescues her from a deep sleep imposed by Odin. In the medieval epic, she loves and is deserted by Sigurd, whose death she contrives, destroying herself on his funeral pyre. As Brünnhilde, the Valkyrie, she is the subject of German composer Richard Wagner's opera *Ring of the Nibelungs*.
See also: Nibelungenlied.

Bruno, Giordano (1548-1600), Italian philosopher. A Dominican who was expelled from the order for heresy, he held that the universe was infinite and that there is no absolute truth. He also defended the Copernican hypothesis. His major works were *On the Infinite Universe and Worlds* and *The Infinite* (both 1584). Brought to trial by the Inquisition, he refused to recant and was burned at the stake. His ideas later influenced Leibniz and Spinoza, making him an important philosophical influence on early modern science.
See also: Philosophy.

Brunswick (German: *Braunschweig*), descendants of the Wolf family. Great Britain's present line of monarchs are descendants of Brunswick dukes of Hanover, Germany. The duchy of Brunswick-Luneburg was established by Frederick II in 1235 and given to Otto, grandson of the Wolf family's founder, Henry the Lion. In 1714, Elector George Louis of Hanover suc-ceeded to the throne of Britain as George I. A reduced duchy of Brunswick existed as a separate state and after 1735 was associated with Prussia under the House of Brunswick-Beven. Brunswick remained a constituent state of Germany from 1871 to 1946.

Brussels (pop. c. 134,800), Belgian capital city, headquarters of the Euro-pean Common Market and NATO. First commercially important in the 12th century, it was granted a ducal charter in 1312. From the 16th to the 19th centuries it was subject successively to Spain, Austria, and France. It manu-factures textiles, lace, and furniture and is a transport center.
See also: Belgium.

Brussels griffon, breed of toy dog developed in 19th-century Belgium. The Brussels griffon may be reddish brown, black, or a combination of the two. It comes in two varieties, one rough and wiry and the other, called Brabançon, having a smooth coat. Standing about 10-12 in (25-30 cm) and weighing 8-10 lb (3.6-4.5 kg), it is noted for its intelligent and affectionate nature.

Brussels sprouts, variety of cabbage first grown on the outskirts of Brussels. The edible buds on the stem are best eaten after being touched by frost.

Brutus, Marcus Junius (85?-42 B.C.), Roman statesman who led the assassination plot against Julius Caesar. He committed suicide after being defeated by Mark Antony and Octavian at Philippi.
See also: Philippi; Caesar, (Gaius) Julius; Antony, Marc.

Bryan, William Jennings (1860-1925), U.S. political leader, orator, and lawyer. After serving in Congress in 1891-95, he ran unsuccessfully as Democratic candidate for president in 1896, 1900, and 1908. He was secretary of state under Woodrow Wilson in 1913-15. His famous "Cross of Gold" speech at the 1896 Democratic convention defended free silver. A Christian fundamentalist, he assisted in the prosecution at the Scopes Trial in 1925, when John Scopes was convicted for teaching evolution in public schools in Dayton, Tenn. Bryan was also a supporter of the income tax and of women's suffrage.
See also: Scopes trial; Darrow, Clarence Seward.

Bryant, Paul 'Bear' (1913-83), U.S. football coach. The all time winningest coach in Division I-A football, Bryant compiled a record of 323 wins, 85 losses, and 17 ties while coaching at Maryland (1945), Kentucky (1946-53), Texas A & M (1954-57), and Alabama (1958-82). Bryant won or shared six national championships at Alabama (1961, 64, 65, 73, 78, 79).

Bryant, William Cullen (1794-1878), U.S. poet and journalist. Editor of the New York *Evening Post* (1826) and later part owner (1829-78), he campaigned against slavery and for free speech. He wrote the pastoral odes "Thanatopsis" (1817) and translated the *Iliad* (1870) and the *Odyssey* (1872).

Bryce, James, 1st Viscount (1838-1922), British politician and historian. A professor of law at Oxford, he wrote *History of the Holy Roman Empire* (1864) and *The American Commonwealth* (1888). He was British ambassador to the U.S. 1907-13.

Bryce Canyon National Park, area of 5,835 acres in southwest Utah, created as a park in 1924. Its extraordinary formations in limestone and sandstone are the result of erosion.
Brynhild See: Brunhild.

Bryophyte, most primitive division of land plants, including liverworts and mosses. The life-cycle of bryophytes has two stages: the gametophyte, a sexual stage, and its offspring, the sporophyte, an asexual spore-bearing stage.

Bryozoan, freshwater and marine moss animals living in colonies encrusting seaweeds, stones, or the hulls of ships and sometimes forming lacy fans. Each colony is made up of minute, tentacled polyps.

Brzezinski, Zbigniew (1928-   ), Polish-born U.S. political scientist and national security adviser (1977-81), who advocated more vigorous anticommunist policies.

BTU *See:* British thermal unit.

Bubble chamber, device invented by Donald Glaser (1952) to observe the paths of subatomic particles. The particles are shot through pressurized liquefied gas; they create strings of tiny bubbles, leaving "tracks" of their path.
See also: Wilson cloud chamber.

Buber, Martin (1878-1965), Jewish philosopher, born in Austria. Editor of a major German-Jewish journal, *Der Jude*, 1916-24, he was a leading educator and scholar of Hasidism. He was forced to leave Germany in 1938 and moved to Jerusalem. His central philosophical concept, the direct relationship between God and the individual, is expressed in *I and Thou* (1923).
See also: Hasidism.

Bubonic plague, disease transmitted to humans by fleas from infected rats. One form of the plague called Black Death swept through Europe and parts of Asia in the 1300s, killing three-quarters of the population in 20 years. Symptoms include fever, chills, and enlarged, painful lymph nodes (buboes), particularly in the groin. In its black form, hemorrhages turn black. The antibiotics tetracycline and streptomycin as well as rat control and sanitation have greatly reduced the mortality rate.
See also: Epidemic.

Buchan, John, 1st Baron Tweedsmuir (1875-1940), Scottish author and politician. He wrote a four-volume history of World War I (1920-21), biographies (of Julius Caesar, 1932), and classic adventure stories (*The Thirty-Nine Steps*, 1915). From 1935 he was governor-general of Canada.

Buchanan, James (1791-1868), 15th president of the United States. Buchanan held office during the years of mounting crisis that led up to the Civil War. The bitter divisions between North and South over the issue of slavery intensified during Buchanan's administration. When he left office in Mar. 1861, 7 slave states had already seceded from the Union and the nation was on the verge of war.
Early life. Buchanan was born in a pioneer settlement near Mercersburg, Pa. He was graduated in 1809 from Dickinson College, studied law, and then served in the War of 1812. He became a state legislator (1814-16) and later a U.S. representative from Pennsylvania (1821-31). Initially a Federalist, Buchanan switched to the Democratic party after the Federalist party dissolved in the 1820s. After serving as U.S. minister to Russia (1832-33),

James Buchanan	
15th U.S. President	
Born:	Near Mercersburg, Pa., Apr. 23, 1791
Term:	Mar. 1857-Mar. 1861
Vice President:	John Cabell Breckinridge
Political Party:	Initially Federalist, later Democratic
Spouse:	None
Children:	None
Died:	Lancaster, Pa., June 1, 1868

Buchanan became a U.S. senator (1834-45). In 1845 President James K. Polk appointed him secretary of state, a position he held until 1849.

Buchanan's diplomatic career resumed in 1853, when President Franklin Pierce named him minister to Great Britain. In 1854 Buchanan, along with the U.S. ministers to France and Spain, formulated the Ostend Manifesto, which stated that the United States should try to purchase the island of Cuba from Spain but also suggested that the United States might, under certain circumstances, be justified in using force to "wrest" the island away from Spain.

President. In 1856 the Democratic party nominated Buchanan for president. He won the election, defeating two opponents from the Republican and Native American, or "Know-Nothing," parties. Although he opposed slavery on moral grounds, Buchanan felt that it was an issue for each state or territory to decide. One such territory was "Bleeding Kansas," which had been the scene of virtual civil war between proslavery groups and abolitionists.

Buchanan endorsed the principle of popular sovereignty, which would allow the people of Kansas to vote whether to enter the Union as a slave or a free state. He submitted to Congress the proslavery state constitution drawn up at Lecompton, Kans., in Sept. 1857. However, this constitution was not approved by antislavery forces in Kansas, and the U.S. House of Representatives rejected it. Buchanan's action on the Kansas issue and his endorsement of the Supreme Court's Dred Scott decision angered the North, and the 1858 elections returned majorities hostile to the president in both houses of Congress. The financial panic of 1857 further weakened confidence in Buchanan's administration.

In 1860 the nation elected Abraham Lincoln, a Republican, as president. In the months preceding his inauguration, 7 Southern states seceded from the Union, establishing the Confederate States of America.

Although war was imminent, Buchanan tried to maintain peace. A U.S. steamer attempting to bring supplies to U.S. troops at Fort Sumter, S.C., was fired upon by a Southern battery, but since no blood was shed, Buchanan chose not to regard this as an act of war. The nation he handed over to Lincoln was still precariously at peace. In his last annual message to Congress, On Dec. 4, 1860, Buchanan asserted that no state could secede from the Union. He professed that he knew of no legal authority to prevent it, but he said, "Secession is neither more nor less than revolution," and he supported the Union during the Civil War.

Bucharest (pop. c. 2,064,500), capital of Romania, on the Dîmbovita River. A medieval fortress, it became the residence of the princes of Walachia in 1459 and the capital when the new Romania was formed in 1861. It produces pharmaceutical and electrical goods, machinery, and automobiles. Bucharest was the site of violence during the 1989 overthrow of the communist government of Nicolae Ceausescu.
See also: Romania.

Buchenwald, Nazi concentration camp set up near Weimar, Germany in 1937 to hold political and "non-Aryan" prisoners. More than 100,000 (mostly Jews) died there through starvation, extermination, and medical experimentation.
See also: Holocaust.

Buchman, Frank Nathan Daniel (1878-1961), evangelist and founder of the Moral Re-Armament movement (1938), commonly known as the MRA, an anticommunist grouping that grew rapidly and spread to over 50 countries.

Büchner, Georg (1813-37), German dramatist, forerunner of expressionism. His *Danton's Death* (1835) and *Woyzeck* (1837) use colloquial language and sometimes sordid settings to trace the powerlessness of isolated individuals against historical forces of society. Woyzeck, for example, is a soldier pressured into murdering his unfaithful mistress. *Lenz*, an unfinished work, is about a dramatist on the verge of madness.

Buchwald, Art (1925-   ), U.S. political columnist. Known primarily for his satires, Buchwald began his column with the *International Herald Tribune* in 1949. Later syndicated, it appeared in more than 500 newspapers. Buchwald won a Pulitzer Prize in 1982. He remains an active columnist.

Buck, Frank (1884-1950), U.S. wild-animal authority and collector. In childhood he collected and maintained small birds and other animals. In 1911 he sailed to South America, where he bought birds to sell at considerable profit. He traveled to Africa, South America, Asia, and Australia, acquiring a financial fortune and a wide reputation while capturing for zoos and circuses everything from tiny birds to elephants. Buck came to public attention in 1930 with publication of his first book, *Bring 'Em Back Alive*, which was subsequently made into a successful motion picture in which he starred. He had exhibits at the Century of Progress Exposition in Chicago in 1933 and the New York World's Fair in 1939 and was associated with the Ringling Brothers-Barnum and Bailey circus in 1937-38.

Buck, Pearl Sydenstricker (1892-1973), U.S. author. Most of her novels are set in China, where she lived until 1934. She won the Pulitzer Prize in 1932 for *The Good Earth* (1931), and the 1938 Nobel Prize in literature.

Buckeye *See:* Horse chestnut.

Buckingham, George Villiers, 1st Duke of (1592-1628), English nobleman whose influence over James I and Charles I inflamed antimonarchical feeling. He promoted costly and unsuccessful military ventures, notably the expedition to relieve the Huguenots of La Rochelle. Charles, however, shielded him from impeachment. He was eventually assassinated.

Buckingham Palace, London residence of the British royal family since 1837, built in 1703 and bought by George III from the Duke of Buckingham in 1761. Queen Victoria was the first monarch to use it as an official residence.
See also: London.

Buckley, William F(rank), Jr. (1925-   ), U.S. author, editor, and lecturer. He founded the weekly *National Review* (1955) to voice his often controversial conservative views. He ran unsuccessfully for mayor of New York City as a Conservative in 1965, and served as a UN delegate in 1973.

Buckner, Simon Bolivar (1823-1914), U.S. politician and Confederate general. Taken prisoner by General Grant, Buckner was released in a prisoner exchange and was commander of the District of Louisiana when the war ended. He then edited the *Louisville Courier* and served 1 term as governor of Kentucky (1887-91).
See also: Civil War, U.S.

Bucktails, political group active in New York (1816-30). They sought to keep New York City in control of state politics and opposed reforms desired by rural districts. Bucktails were so called because members wore hats with a buck's tail emblem.
See also: Tammany, Society of.

Buckthorn, common name for thorny shrub (*Rhamnus cathartica*) of the family Rhamnaceae. It has oval leaves and small, green flowers that grow in clusters. Its fruit resembles small black berries. Buckthorns are sometimes grown to form hedges and may reach a height of 12 ft (3.7 m). The bark is used to produce a yellow dye. Buckthorns are found in Europe and the United States.

Buckwheat, any of a genus (*Fagopyrum*) of common weeds, including dock and sorrel and a few tropical trees. The name applies particularly to species *F. esculentum* and *F. tartaricum*, cultivated for seeds used as cereal grain and cattle fodder.

Budapest (pop. c. 1,992,300), capital of Hungary, on the Danube River. Two settlements, Buda on the right bank and Pest on the left, date from Roman times but were destroyed by Mongol invaders in 1241. Buda became Hungary's capital in 1361. Both cities declined under the Turks but revived under the Hapsburgs and were united in 1873. Textiles are the main industry. The city was virtually destroyed in World War II. It was the center of the Hungarian uprising in 1956.
See also: Hungary.

Budd, Lanny *See:* Sinclair, Upton.

Buddha, Gautama (c.563-c.483 B.C.), founder of Buddhism. He was born Siddhartha Gautama, son of the raja of Kapilavastu, India, near Nepal. At the age of 29, confronting human misery for the first time, he set out to find the path to peace and serenity. For 6 years he studied under Brahman teachers, living as a hermit. Enlightenment came to him while seated under a *bodhi* or pipal tree. Thereafter he preached and gathered disciples as Buddha ("The Enlightened One").
See also: Buddhism.

Buddhism, religion and philosophy originating in India in the 6th century B.C., based on interpretations of the teaching of Siddhartha Gautama, called the Buddha, or "Enlightened One." His first disciples became the Sangha, or original Buddhist monastic order, men (and later women) who gave up home and family, shaved their heads, dressed only in rags, and devoted their lives to practicing and spreading his philosophy of Enlightenment.

In the 5th century B.C. a council in Rajagaha resulted in the Pali Canon, a body of scriptures from the oral tradition of the Buddha's teaching, together with his rules for monastic life, a collection of his sermons, and a metaphysical analysis of his concepts. From a second council, held in Vesali in the 4th century B.C., there emerged 2 separate schools of thought, the Hinayana ("Small Vehicle," surviving as Theravada, "Doctrine of the Elders"), which elected to adhere to strict monastic rules, and the Mahayana ("Large Vehicle"), which adopted a more flexible approach. As a result of a third council, in the 3rd century B.C., called by the Indian emperor Asoka, an ardent convert to Buddhism, missionaries were sent throughout India, as well as to Syria, North Africa, Greece, and Ceylon (now Sri Lanka). From Ceylon, in the 4th century A.D., Buddhism reached Burma, and in the 7th century it reached Tibet, where it combined with existing beliefs to become Lamaism. It made a deep mark on Chinese thought in the 4th and 5th centuries A.D. In 630 an Indian Buddhist living in China, Bodhidarma, introduced his method of meditation and direct or "spontaneous" enlightenment, which led to the dominant School of Ch'an (Zen, in Japanese). Buddhism spread to Korea in the 4th century A.D., and from there in the 6th century it entered Japan. Eventually Buddhism declined in China, but more from its ever-tolerant absorption of other philosophies, which often blurred its intrinsic character, than from the failure of its teaching. By the 7th century, Buddhism had begun to recede from India itself and, by the year 1000, except in Nepal, Buddhist sects had been almost entirely absorbed back into the Brahman religion.

Today the world of Buddhism has 2 main divisions, Theravada, the Southern School, covering Sri Lanka, Burma, Thailand, and Cambodia, and Mahayana, the Northern School, covering Nepal, Korea, China, and Japan. In the 2 schools can be counted 300-500 million followers, and there are many millions more who practice the teaching alone, for Buddhism has no service, ritual, or church in the Western sense. It is a lone process of self-awareness and self-development aimed at the ultimate enlightenment known as nirvana, a state beyond intellect, words, and form. This attainment, Buddhism holds, is the sole means by which one can be liberated from the "wheel of life," the continual cycle of birth, death, and suffering. Human beings are bound to this cycle by the cause-effect of karma, in which present circumstances and experience are the result of past thoughts and actions, and present thoughts and actions are creating those of the future. Through Buddhist teaching and the use of meditation, one can begin to purify one's thoughts and thus improve one's destiny. Buddhist teaching uses the Pali Canon as its scriptural authority, Buddha's Four Noble Truths as its main premise, and the Noble Eightfold Path as its manual.

The Four Noble Truths are (1) suffering is omnipresent; (2) its cause is wrongly directed desire; (3) remove the wrong desire and the cause for suffering is removed; (4) the Noble Eightfold Path leads to the end of suffering. The Noble Eightfold Path consists of (1) right understanding, (2) right thought, (3) right speech, (4) right action, (5) right means of livelihood, (6) right effort, (7) right concentration, (8) right meditation.

Budge, Donald (1915-   ), U.S. tennis player. His team won the Davis Cup in 1937, and in 1938 he was the first player to win 4 top world championships (U.S., British, Australian, and French), now referred to as the Grand Slam.

Budget, document designed to estimate income and expenditures over a certain period of time, usually 1 year. The most important budget in the United States is the federal budget, prepared annually by the executive branch of government, and transmitted to the Congress, usually in January. Most aspects of the budget must be approved by Congress.

Budgie *See:* Parakeet.

Buenos Aires (pop. 2,908,000), capital of Argentina. On the Rio de la Plata, it is a port for Argentine agricultural products, meat, hides, wool, and cereals. It has several universities and an opera house (Teatro Colón), and is the world's leading Spanish-language publishing center. Industries include food processing, textiles, automobiles, and chemical manufacturing. Founded in 1536, it became the capital of Rio de la Plata viceroyalty in 1776. An impressive economic growth after 1850 attracted many immigrants.
See also: Argentina.

Buffalo, any of several humpbacked fishes (genus *Ictiobus*) of the sucker family. Related to the carp, buffalo are large freshwater fishes that inhabit the bottom of lakes and rivers and feed by sucking up tiny plant organisms. Some grow to 3 ft (91 cm) long and weigh 73 lbs (33 kg). Buffalo are fished for food.

Buffalo, any of several species of wild ox, members of the bovid family. The domesticated Indian water buffalo or carabao is used as a draft animal and for milk. It weighs about a ton, is 5 ft (1.5 m) high, and has large curved horns. Other types of Asiatic buffalo are the Philippine tamarau and the small anoa of Celebes. Cape buffaloes are dangerous big-game animals living in herds. The American bison is also incorrectly called a buffalo.

Buffalo (pop. 323,400), second largest city in the state of New York, situated at the eastern end of Lake Erie near Niagara Falls, in western New York. Buffalo was incorporated in 1832. Buffalo is at a natural junction point for lake, rail, and road transportation and is a hub of rail transport. The completion of the Erie Canal in 1825 was a turning point in the city's development. Buffalo is one of the United States' major centers of grain distribution and a leading flour-milling center and steel producer. Among the important institutions located in Buffalo are the Albright-Knox Gallery and one of the campuses of the State University of New York.
See also: New York.

Buffalo Bill (William Frederick Cody; 1846-1917), U.S. scout and showman. He claimed to have killed 4,280 buffalo to feed the builders of the Kansas Pacific Railway. He rode with the pony express in 1860, and during the Civil War was a scout in Tennessee and Missouri for the Union army. From 1872 he toured the United States and Europe with his Wild West Show.

Buffalo grass, low-growing grass (*Buchloë dactyloides*) that was once abundant on the central plains of North America and a main food of the bison and pronghorn.

Buffon, Georges Louis Leclerc, Comte de (1707-88), French naturalist who was the first modern taxonomist of the animal kingdom. He led the team that produced the 44-volume *Histoire Naturelle* (1749-1804).

Bug, name commonly given to all insects but properly applied to the order Hemiptera. These insects have pointed beaks with which they suck juice from plants or blood from animals, including humans.

Buganda *See:* Uganda.

Bugbane, any of several tall plants (genus *Cimicifuga*) of the buttercup family. They have broad leaves that divide into thin leaflets. Their small white flowers grow in branched clusters. Bugbanes are perennials that grow in mild climates. It was once thought that their unpleasant smell repelled bugs.

Bugging *See:* Wiretapping.

Bugle, wind instrument of the brass family, made of either copper or brass, with a conical bore and a cupshaped mouthpiece. The sound it produces is clear and penetrating. The bugle can produce only 7-8 different pitches; only 5 are needed in the military calls for which it is used. An instrument of great antiquity, it is mentioned in the Old Testament description of the siege of Jericho.

Buick, David Dunbar (1855-1929), Scottish-born U.S. plumber turned automobile maker. His Detroit manufacturing company produced the first Buick automobile in 1903. Money problems forced Buick to sell his interest in the company in 1906.

Building *See:* Architecture.

Bulb, short, underground storage stem composed of many fleshy scale leaves that are swollen with stored food and an outer layer of protective scale leaves. Bulbs are a means of overwintering; in the spring, flowers and foliage are rapidly produced when growing conditions are suitable. Examples of plants producing bulbs are the daffodil, tulip, snowdrop, and onion.

Bulbul, any of various species of tropical songbirds of the family Pycnonotidae, native to Africa and southern Asia. About 7 to 10 in (18 to 25 cm) long, bulbuls have plain, fluffy feathers and a slim, notched beak designed for eating fruits and insects. They tend to travel in noisy flocks and can cause damage to orchards and crops.

Bulfinch, Charles (1763-1844), U.S. architect. He designed the Massachusetts statehouse, Boston (1800); University Hall, Harvard University (1815); and the east portico of the Capitol, Washington, D.C. (1818). He emphasized the neoclassical style in U.S. civic architecture.

Bulganin, Nikolai Alexandrovich (1895-1975), Soviet leader. With the support of Nikita Khrushchev, he succeeded Georgy Malenkov as premier

Bulgaria

Capital:	Sofia
Area:	42,855 sq mi
	(110,994 sq km)
Population:	8,240,000
Language:	Bulgarian
Government:	Republic
Independent:	1908
Head of gov.:	Prime minister
Per capita:	U.S. $1,330
Mon. unit:	1 Lev = 100 stotinki

in 1955. He was expelled from the central committee when Khrushchev became premier in 1958.

Bulgaria, country in eastern Europe, in the Balkan mountains; bordered on the east by the Black Sea, on the west by Yugoslavia and Macedonia, on the south by Greece and Turkey, and on the north by Rumania, the Danube River forming the border.

Land and climate. The climate is continental in the north, with cold winters and hot summers, temperate continental in the center, and mediterranean south of the Rhodope Mountains and along the Black Sea coast. The country's capital is Sofia.

People. Nearly 90% of Bulgarians are descendants of the Bulgars, a migratory people of Mongol origin. About a tenth of the population is ethnically Turkish. Bulgarian is a southern-Slavic language similar to Russian.

Economy. Though agriculture still employs the majority of the work force, it accounts for only 14% of the national income. Modern industries produce trucks, ships, transistors, chemicals, cement, porcelain, and glass. Lead, zinc, iron ore, copper, and manganese are mined. There are also deposits of oil and natural gas.

History. In the 17th century, the Eastern Bulgars conquered and merged with the Slavic population and adopted their language and customs. Between the 7th and 14th centuries, Bulgarian empires were major participants in Balkan political life, but in 1396 the country was occupied by the Ottoman Empire, which ruled Bulgaria for nearly 500 years. The Congress of Berlin (1878) restricted Turkish hegemony and in 1908 Bulgaria proclaimed its independence under Ferdinand I of Saxe-Coburg-Gotha. Bulgaria supported Germany in World War I and World War II. In 1944 the USSR occupied the country; in 1946 the monarchy was abolished and a republic proclaimed, under the control of the Communist party. In the upheavals of 1989, the Bulgarian Communist party changed its name to the Socialists and won control of the parliament in the first free elections. After the electoral victory in 1997, the opposition was unable to revive the economy.

Bulge, Battle of the, last major western counteroffensive by the Germans in World War II. They planned to capture Liège and Antwerp, thus dividing

the Allied armies. The German assault in the Ardennes began on Dec. 16, 1944, and create a huge "bulge" in the Allied lines. Although suffering about 77,000 casualties, the Allies stopped the German advance by Jan. 16, 1945.
See also: World War II.

Bulimia, eating disorder characterized by insatiable appetite; eating binges are generally followed by self-induced vomiting. It is related to anorexia nervosa. Often observed in psychotics, it also commonly affects adolescent girls.
See also: Anorexia nervosa.

Bull, John *See:* John Bull.

Bulldog, medium-sized, low-slung dog originally bred in England for bull-baiting and related sports (outlawed in 1835). It has a massive head with an undershot jaw, broad shoulders, and strong legs. It weighs 40 to 50 lb (18 to 23 kg).

Bullfighting, Spanish national sport and spectacle, also popular in Latin America. Probably developed by the Moors, it was taken over by aristocratic professionals in the 18th century. The modern bullfight stresses the grace, skill, and daring of the *matador*. After a procession, the bull is released. Two mounted *picadors* jab the bull's neck with lances to lower its head for the matador's capework. Then three *banderilleros* thrust decorated wooden goads into the bull's back. The matador, after using his cape to make daring and graceful passes at the bull, kills it with a swordthrust between the shoulders. In Portugal, the matador is on horseback and does not kill the bull.

Bullfinch, any of several species of small songbirds native to Europe and Asia, named for their short, stout bill. The common bullfinch (*Pyrrhula pyrrhula*) is a popular cage bird that can be taught to sing tunes. The bullfinch's diet is mostly berries and seeds.

Bullfrog, large North American frog (*Rana catesbeiana*) named for its booming call, which is made by passing air up and down the windpipe, the swollen airsacs acting as resonators. Bullfrogs grow up to 8 in (20 cm) long and live near water, where they feed on many kinds of animals, including small snakes and alligators. They hibernate under logs or in holes, emerging in spring to lay up to 25,000 eggs.
See also: Frog.

Bullhead, North American freshwater catfish (genus *Ictalurus*) with broad head and tapering tail. Bullheads grow up to 1 ft (30 cm) long and weigh 2 lb (1 kg). Bullhead is also a name for a marine fish of the southern United States, and for the miller's thumb, a European freshwater fish.
See also: Catfish.

Bullmastiff, breed of dog obtained by crossing the bulldog and the mastiff. Standing about 24 to 27 in (61 to 69 cm) and weighing 100 to 130 lb (45 to 59 kg), this agile, powerful dog is used as a watchdog and bodyguard.

Bull Moose Party *See:* Progressive Party.

Bull Run, Battles of, 2 clashes in the American Civil War around Manassas Junction near Bull Run Creek, 25 mi (40 km) southwest of Washington, D.C. In the First Battle of Bull Run, July 1861, Union general Irvin McDowell was sent against Confederates led by P.G.T. Beauregard, but was repulsed by them. Gen. "Stonewall" Jackson was so nicknamed for his tenacity in this battle. In the Second Battle of Bull Run, Aug. 1862, Jackson attacked Union general John Pope and forced his retreat.
See also: Civil War, U.S.

Bull terrier, muscular dog that combines the strength of the bulldog and the speed and intelligence of the white English terrier, the 2 breeds from which it was first developed in 1835. The bull terrier has an oval head, pointed ears, a straight tail, a smooth white or brindled coat, and weighs 30-36 lb (13.5-16 kg).

Bulrush, any of a genus (*Scirpus*) of sedges growing in water or marshes, up to 6 ft (2 m) high, with narrow leaves and spiky flowers. Bulrushes grow from rhizomes, which help to anchor debris accumulating in the water, hastening the natural drying out of swamps. Bulrushes are used by Peruvian Indians to make boats.

Bulwer, Sir Henry *See:* Clayton-Bulwer Treaty.

Bulwer-Lytton, Edward George Earle Lytton, 1st Baron Lytton (1803-73), English author and politician. His best-known works include the historical novels *The Last Days of Pompeii* (1834) and *Rienzi* (1835), and the utopian *The Coming Race* (1871).

Bumblebee, insect belonging to the family Apidae, subfamily Bombinae, having a hairy coat, typically black with orange or yellow stripes, and a sting. Bumble bees range in length from 0.6 to 1 in (1.5 to 2.5 cm). They are social insects, living in colonies consisting of a queen, workers (females), and drones (males). In spring the queen comes out of hibernation and finds a nesting place. She begins laying eggs that develop into worker bees. All summer the workers gather pollen and care for the hive. At the end of summer unfertilized eggs, produced by either the queen or the workers, develop into drones; the colony also rears new queens. Once mature, these queens leave the nest, mate, and find a place to hibernate, while the old colony dies out.

Bunchberry, common name for a low-growing woody perennial (*Cornus canadensis*) related to dogwood. Its clusters of yellowish flowers, surrounded by white bracts, develop into red berries. Bunchberry is found in North America, Greenland, and Asia.

Bunche, Ralph Johnson (1904-71), U.S. diplomat. He entered the UN in 1946, and was undersecretary for political affairs 1958-71. Having supervised the 1959 Arab-Israeli armistice, he became the first African American to win the Nobel Peace Prize (1950).

Bunin, Ivan Alekseyevich (1870-1953), Russian novelist, short-story writer, and poet. He is best known for such short stories as *The Gentleman* *from San Francisco* (1916). He emigrated to France in 1919, and won the Nobel Prize in literature in 1933.

Bunker Hill, Battle of, one of the first engagements in the American Revolutionary War (June 17, 1775), involving some 2,300 British troops under generals Thomas Gage and Sir William Howe, and some 1,500 inexperienced American volunteers under Colonel William Prescott, Major-General Israel Putman, and General J. Warren. The British had planned to occupy Bunker Hill (near Charlestown, Mass.) as a good site for the defense of Boston. However, the rebels dug themselves into neighboring Breed's Hill under cover of night. Colonial troops opened fire on the arriving British troops, causing heavy casualties. Although the British eventually took Breed's Hill, the Americans, who had lost only about 450 men and proved their skills against seasoned troops, gained greatly in morale.
See also: Revolutionary War in America.

Bunsen, Robert Wilhelm Eberhard (1811-99), German chemist who conducted important work on organo-arsenic compounds and, with G.R. Kirchhoff, pioneered chemical spectroscopy, discovering the elements cesium (1860) and rubidium (1861). He also helped to popularize the gas burner known by his name.

Bunsen burner, gas burner consisting of a metal tube with a gas inlet and adjustable openings for air near the lower end. The air and the gas mix before ignition, producing an extremely hot and smokeless flame. Developed by the German chemist Robert Wilhelm Bunsen (1811-99), the Bunsen burner is used in scientific laboratories.
See also: Bunsen, Robert Wilhelm Eberhard.

Bunting, finchlike bird (especially, genus *Passerina*), with a conical seed-cracking bill. Buntings feed on seeds and live near the ground in woods or grasslands. They range from hot, humid forests of the tropics to polar regions. The snow bunting nests in northern Greenland, farther north than any other land bird.

Buñuel, Luis (1900-83), Spanish-Mexican director of films marked by fierce realism, social criticism, and wry humor. Surrealist fantasy is evident in his work ever since his first film, *Un Chien andalou* (made with Salvador Dali in 1929).

Bunyan, John (1628-88), English author. A tinker by trade, he became a Baptist preacher in 1657. While imprisoned for unlicensed preaching (1660-72; 1675) he wrote his most famous work, *The Pilgrim's Progress* (1678), an allegory in simple prose describing Christian's journey to the Celestial City.

Buonarroti, Michelangelo *See:* Michelangelo.

Burbank (pop. 93,643), city in southern California, 12 mi (19 km) north of Los Angeles in the San Fernando Valley. Incorporated as a town in 1911 and as a city in 1927, Burbank is famous today for its motion picture and television studios.
See also: California.

Burbank, Luther (1849-1926), U.S. horticulturalist who developed more than 800 varieties of plants, including the Burbank potato. *See also:* Horticulture.

Burchfield, Charles Ephraim (1893-1967), U.S. watercolorist known for his midwestern landscapes and small-town scenes. A leader of the realistic movement in American painting, he often depicted architectural relics of the late 1800s and was sensitive to lighting and atmospheric effects.

Burdock, any of a genus (Arctium) of plants with hairy stems, heart-shaped leaves, and burrs. A North American biennial, also called beggar's-button, burr-bur, cockle button, and stickbutton, it grows to heights of 4 to 9 ft (1 to 3 m).

Burger, Warren Earl (1907-   ), chief justice of the United States Supreme Court 1969-86. Appointed by President Richard M. Nixon, Justice Burger moved the court in a conservative direction. Before his Supreme Court appointment, he served as judge on the United States Court of Appeals (1955-69) and as an Assistant United States Attorney General (1953-5). Throughout his career, he tended to limit the number of appeals and trials for each court case, to give state courts more authority, and to loosen rules of admission for introducing confessions of the defendants as evidence in trials. *See also:* Supreme Court of the United States.

Burgess, Anthony (1917-93), English writer, best known for *A Clockwork Orange* (1962), a bitter satire about a violent gang leader in a corrupt, violent society of the near future. His other works include *Inside Mr. Enderby* (1961), *Earthly Powers* (1980), *The Kingdom of the Wicked* (1985), and the critical study *Re Joyce* (1965).

Burghley, Lord (1520-98), English statesman. He was chief advisor to Queen Elizabeth I (1558-98) and her spokesman in Parliament. A supporter of the Anglican Church, he repressed Catholic revolts and advocated the execution of Elizabeth's Catholic sister, Mary Queen of Scots.

Burgoyne, John (1722-92), British general in the American Revolutionary War. He fought in the Seven Years War (1756-63), and became a playwright, socialite, and member of Parliament. Posted to America, he attempted to put into effect his plan to split off the New England colonies, but was forced to surrender by Gen. Horatio Gates at Saratoga (1777). *See also:* Revolutionary War in America.

Burgundy (French: *Bourgogne*), historic region of eastern France, occupying what are now the departments of Côte-d'Or, Saône-et-Loire, Nièvre, and Yonne. It was named for the Burgundians, a Germanic tribe. A rich agricultural region, Burgundy is famous for its wines. *See also:* France.

Burke, Edmund (1729-97), Irish-born British statesman, political philosopher, and orator. He entered parliament in 1765, and advocated more just policies toward the American colonies, opposing the Stamp Act and (in 1775)

Burkina Faso

Capital:	Ouagadougou
Area:	105,869 sq mi
	(274,200 sq km)
Population:	11,266,000
Language:	French
Government:	Presidential republic
Independent:	1960
Head of gov.:	President
Per capita:	U.S. $230
Mon. unit:	1 CFA franc = 100
	centimes

arguing for conciliation. Concerned for justice in India, he promoted the im-peachment of Warren Hastings (1786-87). His famous *Reflections on the Revolution in France* (1790) presented his rational case against violent change.

Burke, Martha Jane *See:* Calamity Jane.

Burkina Faso, land-locked country in West Africa known as Upper Volta until 1984. It is bounded on the west and north by Mali, on the east by Niger and Benin, and on the south by Togo, Ghana, and the Ivory Coast. Burkina Faso is a broad expanse too dry to support much vegetation. Water is scarce. Temperatures range from 68ÉF to 95ÉF (20ÉC-35ÉC). The largest ethnic group in Burkina Faso is the Mossi tribe, but well over half a million nomadic Fulanis and others live in the north. Traditional African religions predominate, but there are also about a million Muslims and a quarter of a million Roman Catholics. The capital is Ouagadougou. French is the official language. Burkina Faso is one of the poorest countries of Africa, and the majority of its work force is engaged in subsistence farming. The country exports cotton, animals, meat, oil seeds, and karité nuts. There are deposits of manganese, limestone, and bauxite, but they have not been fully exploited.

What is now Burkina Faso was once the heart of the great Mossi kingdoms, which dated back to the 1100s and lasted some 500 years. The French made the area a protectorate in 1896 and a colony in 1919. Upper Volta became inde-pendent in 1960. The country had a series of civilian and military regimes. Although a new constitution was introduced in 1978, the military continued to dominate the country's politics until 1991 when a multi party system was introduced. At the end of the 1990s, the IMF acquitted part of the foreign debt.

Burleigh, Lord *See:* Burghley, Lord.

Burlington (pop. 131,439), city in northwest Vermont; seat of Chittenden County. The largest city in Vermont, situated on Lake Champlain, it was chartered in 1773 and named for the Burlington family, who were pioneer landowners. A summer and winter resort, Burlington is also the state's manufacturing center.
See also: Vermont.

Burma *See:* Myanmar.

Burnet, Sir Frank Macfarlane (1899-1985), Australian physician and virologist. He shared the 1970 Nobel Prize in physiology or medicine with P.B. Medawar for the suggestion that the ability of organisms to form antibodies in response to foreign tissues was acquired and not inborn.

Burnett, Frances (Eliza) Hodgson (1849-1924), English-born U.S. author. She is particularly famous for her children's stories, *Little Lord Fauntleroy* (1885-86) and *The Secret Garden* (1910).

Burney, Fanny (Frances Burney; 1752-1840), English novelist and diarist. Her first novel, *Evelina* (1778), won her the respect of Samuel Johnson. She was a member of Queen Charlotte's household 1786-91. Her *Early Diary: 1768-78* and *Diary and Letters: 1778-1840* provide interesting background to the period.

Burnham, Daniel Hudson (1846-1912), U.S. architect, a pioneer of city planning. He built some of America's early skyscrapers, including the Masonic Temple Building, Chicago (1892), and the Flatiron Building, New York City (1902). He also designed the plan for the Columbian Exposition in Chicago (1893). Much of his improvement plan for Chicago (1907-9) was subsequently put into effect.

Burns, Arthur Frank (1904-87), Austrian-born U.S. economist. An expert on the business cycle, he served as presidential adviser on economics 1953-56 and on labor management 1961-66. Among his many books, the most influential was *Measuring Business Cycles* (1946), written with Wesley Clair Mitchell.

Burns, Robert (1759-96), Scottish poet. The son of a poor farmer, he himself farmed for a living and later worked as a customs official. In 1786 he published *Poems, Chiefly in the Scottish Dialect* (enlarged 1787). His poetry, in Scots-English idiom, deals with rural life. He also wrote satirical poems such as "The Twa Dogs" and "The Jolly Beggars." Influenced by Scottish folk tradition, he was a master at writing songs to traditional airs ("Auld Lang Syne"). At first taken up by fashionable society, he died neglected and in debt. Other poems are "Tam O'Shanter," "To a Mouse," and "The Cotter's Saturday Night."

Burnside, Ambrose Everett (1824-81), Union general in the U.S. Civil War. Succeeding George McClellan as general of the Army of the Potomac, he resigned after the Union defeat at Fredericksburg in 1862. He was later governor of Rhode Island (1866-69) and U.S. senator (1875-81). *See also:* Civil War, U.S.

Burr, Aaron (1756-1836), U.S. lawyer and politician, vice president under Thomas Jefferson 1801-5, also known for having killed Alexander Hamilton in a duel (1804). Burr was admitted to the New York bar in 1782 and was attorney general (1789-91) and U.S. senator (1781-97). After his term as vice president he was involved in efforts to expand settlements in the West. He was accused of treason for allegedly trying to establish a private empire.

Though acquitted of the charge, in 1812, hĕ retired from public life and returned to practice law in New York.

Burroughs, Edgar Rice (1875-1950), U.S. writer of adventure novels. He is most famous for *Tarzan of the Apes* (1914), whose characters have passed into comic strips, films, and television.

Burroughs, John (1837-1921), U.S. naturalist and author, known for his philosophical nature essays. His *Notes on Walt Whitman* (1867) was the first biographical study of the poet, who was his friend.

Burroughs, William (1855-98), U.S. inventor, best known for his practical and commercially successful adding machine (1898). His firm, the American Arithmometer Company (1886), was later renamed Burroughs Adding Machine Company.

Bursitis, inflammation of a bursa (fibrous sac containing synovial fluid that reduces friction where tendons move over bones), commonly caused by excessive wear and tear or by rheumatoid arthritis, gout, or bacteria. It causes pain and stiffness, and may require cortisone injections and, if infected, surgical drainage.

Burton, Sir Richard Francis (1821-90), English explorer, writer, and linguist. His interest in Muslim culture led him to secretly visit shrines in the holy city of Mecca (1853). In the 1880s, he translated the *Arabian Nights* into English. He was the first European to see Lake Tanganyika in central Africa (1858), and he also explored Santos, Brazil (1865). The motion picture *Mountains of the Moon* is based on his adventures.

Burundi, one of Africa's smallest states, bordered on the east by Tanzania, on the west by Zaïre, on the north by Rwanda, and on the southwest by Lake Tanganyika. The capital, situated alongside the lake, is Bujumbura. The climate is tropical, with a rainy season from Oct. to April and a dry season in June, July, and Aug.

Burundi

Capital:	Bujumbura
Area:	10,747 sq mi
	(27,834 sq km)
Population:	5,537,000
Language:	French, Rundi
Government:	Presidential republic
Independent:	1962
Head of gov.:	Prime minister
Per capita:	U.S. $160
Mon. unit:	1 Burundi franc =
	100 centimes

The Hutu and Tutsi are the country's main ethnic groups. There is a small minority of Twa, a pygmy people. The official language is French; the chief African language is Kurundi; Swahili is also widely spoken. About 30% of the people adhere to traditional beliefs, the rest being Christian, principally Roman Catholic. The economy is mainly agricultural. Principal exports are arabica coffee and cotton.

The earliest inhabitants seem to have been the Twa, who were succeeded by the Hutu, who came from the Congo Basin. The Hutu were later subjugated by the Tutsi, who may have originated in northeast Africa. In 1899 Germany claimed Burundi as part of German East Africa. After World War I, Belgium was granted control of the area. In 1962, following a referendum, Burundi became an independent monarchy. The monarchy was overthrown and replaced by a republic in 1966. Since independence Burundi has been the scene of recurrent fighting between the Tutsi minority (who dominated the government for a long time) and the Hutu majority (*e.g.* in 1972, 1987 and 1993). In 1996 the army seized power.

Burying beetle, insect of the carrion beetle family (Silphidae). Averaging 1/2 in (12 mm) in length, the burying beetle digs around and beneath dead insects or animals, effectively burying them. Eggs are laid there, and the hatched larvae feed off the carrion until they reach maturity.

Bush, George Herbert Walker (1924-), 41st president of the United States. Bush's 2 terms as vice president to a popular president and his promise of "No new taxes" helped sweep him into the White House. Almost from the beginning of his time in office, Bush faced a series of crises both foreign and domestic, yet maintained a high level of popularity until well into his third year as president.

Early life. Bush was born in Milton, Mass., in 1924. Soon afterward, his family moved to Connecticut. Bush's father was a successful businessman and, later, a U.S. senator. Young Bush attended private schools, graduating from Phillips Academy in 1942. He then enlisted in the Navy. A fighter pilot, he flew hazardous missions in the Pacific during World War II, earning the Distinguished Flying Cross and three air medals. Returning home from the war in 1945, he entered Yale, from which he graduated in 1948. Also in 1945, he married Barbara Pierce. The Bushes had 6 children, 1 of whom died of leukemia.

Entering politics. After college, Bush moved to Texas and entered the oil business, at which he was very successful. He became interested in politics and was active in the Republican Party. In 1964, he ran for a U.S. Senate seat in Texas, but lost. Two years later, he won election to the U.S. House of Representatives and was reelected in 1968. In 1970, he again ran for Senate and lost. He then served as U.S. ambassador to the United Nations (1971-73), U.S. envoy to China (1974-75), and director of the Central Intelligence Agency (1976-77). In 1980, Bush ran for the Republicans' presidential nomination. Ronald Reagan, who won the nomination, chose Bush as his running mate. The Reagan-Bush team defeated the Democratic incumbents, President Jimmy Carter and Vice President Walter Mondale.

Vice presidency. Bush served two terms as vice president to Reagan, working closely with him. Bush filled in briefly for the president in 1981, when Reagan was wounded in an assassination attempt, and again in 1985, when Reagan had minor surgery. In 1988, Bush ran for the presidency, promising

---

George Herbert Walker Bush

41st U.S. President
Born: Milton, Mass.; June 12, 1924
Term: Jan. 1989-Jan. 1993
Vice President: Dan Quayle
Political Party: Republican
Spouse: Barbara Pierce Bush
Children: 6

"no new taxes," a war on drugs, to protect the environment, and to be "the education president." He and his running mate, Dan Quayle, defeated Democrats Michael S. Dukakis and Lloyd Bentsen by a landslide.

Presidency. Bush faced serious problems: a huge and growing federal budget deficit, foreign-trade deficits, and a financial crisis in which hundreds of failing savings-and-loan institutions required federal aid. Cleanup after the environmentally disastrous wreck of an oil tanker off the Alaska coast also required federal aid.

Overseas, the loosening of communist control in the Soviet Union and Eastern Europe eased long-held tensions between East and West. In 1989, Bush presented an arms-control plan to reduce U.S. military presence in Europe. He sent U.S. troops to Panama in 1989 to arrest strongman Manuel Noriega on drug-trafficking charges. In response to the Iraqi invasion of Kuwait in August of 1990, Bush initiated operation Desert Shield, which sent thousands of U.S. and allied troops to Saudi Arabia to deter further Iraqi aggression. After 6 months of economic sanctions and diplomacy failed to persuade Iraq to leave Kuwait, Bush and the allies initiated operation Desert Storm in January of 1991. After weeks of relentless air attacks and a ground assault, the Iraqis were forced out of Kuwait in March of 1991. In the aftermath of the war, Bush has set out to bring peace to the Middle East and to create his "New World Order." On the home front, Bush had problems between the executive and legislative branches in reaching a federal budget that would reduce the deficit without compromising a campaign promise for no new taxes.

See also: Persian Gulf War.

Bush, Vannevar (1890-1974), U.S. electrical engineer, director of the Office of Scientific Research and Development in World War II. In the 1930s he developed the differential analyzer—in effect the first analog computer. *See also:* Analog computer.

Bushmaster, large tropical American pit viper (*Lachesis muta*), which may grow up to 12 ft (4 m) long and feeds mainly on small mammals. It is light brown and has dark patterns on its back. Its long fangs and large venom glands make it dangerous to humans.

Business cycle, periodic fluctuation in the economy of an industrialized nation, between prosperity and recession or depression, with marked variations in growth rate and employment levels. Recession may be caused by overproduction, declining demand, changes in money supply, and general

loss of confidence. Government interventions to moderate the cycle have become common in recent years.
See also: Economics.

Business law *See:* Law.

Bustard, any of Otididae family of large-bodied, strong-legged birds of the Old World and Australia, usually with drab plumage but sometimes with ornamental plumes on the head and neck. They feed on seeds, leaves, and small animals and prefer to run rather than fly. The great bustard is the size of a turkey. Bustards are scarce in many places, as they have been killed for food.

Butane and propane, odorless, colorless, flammable gases. These hydrocarbons (compounds of hydrogen and carbon) are found in natural gas and crude petroleum, and can be produced by cracking, a chemical process by which gasoline is derived from heavy oil. In their liquid form (referred to as LPG, or liquified petroleum gas), they are used as fuels for industry and for isolated homes.

Butler, Benjamin Franklin (1818-93), U.S. politician and Union general in the Civil War. His autocratic rule as military governor of New Orleans (1862) earned him the appellation "Beast," and he was recalled by President Abraham Lincoln. As U.S. representative (1867-75, 1877-79), he supported Reconstruction and voted for the impeachment of President Andrew Johnson. As Populist party candidate, he was elected governor of Massachusetts in 1882 and ran unsuccessfully for president in 1884.

Butler, Nicholas Murray (1862-1947), U.S. educator. President of Columbia College (1902-45), he expanded it into Columbia University. He was president of the Carnegie Endowment for International Peace (1925-45) and, in 1931, shared the Nobel Peace Prize with Jane Addams. He also served as president of the American Academy of Arts and Letters (1928-41).

Butler, Samuel (1835-1902), English novelist. He considered Darwinism too mechanistic and satirized it in *Erewhon* (1872), his version of utopia. His major work is *The Way of All Flesh* (1903), an autobiographical novel satirizing Victorian morality.

Butler, Samuel (1612-80), English poet, author of *Hudibras* (1663-78), a mock-heroic, anti-Puritan satire. He attacked the hypocrisy and pedantry of the Puritans of the Commonwealth.

Butte (pop. 33,336), city in southwestern Montana; seat of Silver Bow County, situated on Silver Bow Creek on a plateau in the Rocky Mountains. The fourth largest city in the state, Butte was founded in 1864. It was first a gold mining camp and then a silver center, and copper was discovered there in 1880. Butte is an important mining center for zinc, silver, gold, copper, arsenic, and lead.

Butter, dairy product made by churning milk or cream, containing fat, protein, and water. Made in some countries from the milk of goats, sheep, or yaks, it is most often made from cow's milk. Continuous mechanized production has been general since the 1940s. After skimming, the cream is ripened with a bacterial culture, pasteurized, cooled to 40°F (4°C), and then churned, causing the butterfat to separate from the liquid residue, buttermilk. The butter is then washed, worked, colored, and salted.

Buttercup, any of 300 species of flower (genus *Ranunculus*), native to temperate North America; especially the familiar gold flower of meadows and pastures. Buttercups have five-petaled flowers and deeply notched leaves that give them the alternative name of crow foot. The common buttercup has an acrid taste and can be poisonous to cattle.

Butterfish, any of several fish of the family Stromateidae. They have mucous-coated slippery skins and live in temperate seas around the world. The most common U.S. butterfish, found along the Atlantic Coast, is also known as the dollarfish (*Poronotus triacanthus*).

Butterfly, flying insect of the order Lepidoptera (which also includes moths), characterized by wide, brightly colored wings. The butterfly undergoes metamorphosis (change in form) several times during its life. The egg grows into a larva called a caterpillar, which feeds on vegetation. During the next stage, the pupa, it does not feed, but is protected by a shell or cocoon while develping into the adult butterfly. Most species of butterflies are members of one of the main family groups: (1) skippers, (2) blues, coppers, and hairstreaks, (3) brush-foots, (4) sulphurs and whites, (5) metalmarks, (6) satyrs and wood nymphs, (7) swallowtail, (8) milkweed butterflies, and (9) snout butterflies. Although butterflies are found worldwide in a variety of climates, the greatest number of species are native to the tropical rainforests. Migratory butterflies such as the monarch may travel thousands of miles to reach warm winter habitats.

Butternut, or white walnut, tree (*Juglans cinerea*) of the walnut family. This deciduous tree with pale gray bark and ridged leaves grows in the eastern and southern United States. Its light brown wood produces fine furniture. *See also:* Walnut.

Butterwort, insect-eating plant (genus *Pinguicula*) that grows in damp places in Eurasia and the Americas. The yellow or violet flower grows on a 2 in (5 cm) stalk surrounded by a rosette of light green fleshy leaves that lie flat against the ground. At the slightest pressure, such as the weight of an insect, glands on the upper surfaces of the leaves secrete a sticky fluid and the insect becomes trapped. The fluid also contains a digestive juice that breaks down the insect's body and allows nitrogenous products to be absorbed.
See also: Carnivorous plant.

Buttress *See:* Architecture.

Buxtehude, Dietrich (1637? -1707), German composer and organist, possibly born in Denmark. His cantatas, organ toccatas, and chorale preludes influenced J.S. Bach.

Byelorussia

Capital:	Minsk
Area:	80,153 sq mi
	(207,600 sq km)
Population:	10,339,000
Language:	White Russian, Russian
Government:	Presidential republic
Independent:	1991
Head of gov.:	President
Per capita:	U.S. $2,070
Mon. unit:	1 Rouble = 100 kopecks

Buzzard, any of a group of medium-sized hawks of the family Accipitridae, identifiable by their soaring flight, widespread wings, and broad tail. They prey on small mammals by swooping from the air or from a perch. In North America they are called hawks, "buzzard" being applied to vultures.

Byelorussia, or Belarus, republic, also known as White Russia. Independent country in eastern Europe, bordered by Russia, Ukraine, Poland, Latvia and Lithuania.

Land and climated. Though mainly a plain, Byelorussia has hilly regions and extensive marshes, particularly in the southwest. The climate is mild. There are extensive waterways, in which the Dnieper, Pripet, Berezina, and Western Dvina rivers are linked by canals. About a quarter of the country is forestland.

People. White Russians constitute 78% of the population; the largest minorities are Russians (13%), Poles (4%), and Ukranians (3%). 60% of the population belongs to the Russian Orthodox Church. The official language is White Russian, which is usually written in Cyrillic script.

Economy. Natural resources include peat, rock salt, phosphorite, limestone, and iron ore. The people are dependent on both agriculture and industry. Products include agricultural machinery, trucks, timber, wood products, and textiles. Minsk, the capital, produces heavy vehicles and tractors. Other cities and industrial centers include Vitebsk, Gomel, and Mogilev.

History. Byelorussia was originally inhabited by Slavic tribes, became part of Lithuania in the 14th century, and was made part of Poland in the 16th century. When Poland was partitioned in the late 18th century, Byelorussia became part of the Russian Empire. By the Treaty of Riga in 1921, the western part of Byelorussia was ceded to Poland. When the USSR (Soviet Union) was formed in 1922, Byelorussia became one of the 4 original constituent republics. The region was the scene of bitter fighting during World War II. The collapse of communism in the USSR resulted in the republic's independence in 1991.

See also: Union of Soviet Socialist Republics.

Byrd, Richard Evelyn (1888-1957), U.S. aviator and pioneer of exploration and research in Antarctica. He led the air unit with D. B. MacMillan's 1925

Arctic expedition and, with Floyd Bennett, overflew the North Pole (1926).
In 1929 he flew over the South Pole. Beginning as a Navy flier, he rose to
the rank of Rear Admiral in 1930. He made 5 important expeditions to
Antarctica (1928-1956), established the Antarctic base camp Little America,
and spent the entire winter of 1933-34 alone at an advance camp. He was in
charge of the U.S. Antarctic program from 1955.
See also: Antarctica.

Byrd, Robert Carlyle (1917-   ), U.S. legislator. He belonged to the Ku
Klux Klan for a year and a half during the 1940s. He ran successfully for the
West Virginiaa. State Senate in 1950. After service in the U.S. House of
Representative (1953-59), he entered the Senate, 1959. He served as majority
whip for the Democrats (1971- 77) and then as majority leader (1977-80;
1987-88) and minority leader (1981- 87).

Byrd, William (1652-1704) and **William II** (1674-1744), colonial Virginian
father and son. The father attained wealth and influence after developing
farmlands at Westover, now Richmond, Virginia. The son, like his father, joined
the House of Burgesses (1692) and became a member of the Council of State
(1709). William II amassed an impressive library and produced diaries and
journals that give a detailed picture of aristocratic life in colonial Virginia.

Byrd, William (1543-1623), English composer. His choral music includes
the Great Service for the Anglican Church, Roman Catholic mass settings,
and *Cantiones Sacrae* (1589; 1591). He also wrote keyboard music and
madrigals. He was closely associated with Thomas Tallis, and in 1575 they
were granted a joint monopoly for the printing and sale of music.

Byrne, Jane (1934-   ), U.S. politician, mayor of Chicago (1979-83). In her
first bid for elected office she defeated the remnants of the Democratic
machine of her former patron Mayor Richard Daley, becoming the first
female mayor in Chicago's history.

Byrnes, James Francis (1879-1972), U.S. statesman. Democratic repre-
sentative (1911-25) and senator (1931-41) from South Carolina, he served
on the U.S. Supreme Court (1941-42), and was director of World War II
mobilization (1943-45). As secretary of state (1945-47), he worked to lessen
tensions with the USSR. As governor of South Carolina (1951-55), he
opposed racial integration.

Byron, George Gordon Byron, 6th Baron (1788-1824), English poet, a
leading figure of European Romanticism. Lameness and an unhappy child-
hood bred morbidity, a scorn for authority, and hatred for oppression. A
disastrous marriage and the strictures of English society drove him into exile
in Italy (1816). He later joined the Greek revolt against the Turks and
died of fever at Missolonghi, Greece. English Bards and Scotch Review-
ers (1809), a savage riposte to his critics, brought overnight fame, and
the first two cantos of Childe Harold's Pilgrimage (1812) established his
European reputation. The "Byronic" hero of the poetic drama, Manfred
(1817) became a great Romantic theme. Major works include the incom-
plete satiric epic Don Juan (1819-24) and The Vision of Judgement

(1812), satirizing the poet laureate Robert Southey and King George III.
See also: Romanticism.

Byssinosis *See:* Brown lung.

Byzantine art and architecture, aesthetic style that arose in the city of
Byzantium (Constantinople) after it became the capital of the Roman Empire
(330 A.D.), under Constantine the Great. The term also may be applied to art
and architecture heavily influenced by Byzantine forms, which spread to
Italy, Greece, Russia, and much of the Middle East. The greatest monument
of the early phase is the cathedral of Hagia Sophia (Santa Sophia), built
532-537 in Constantinople. Mosaics, the principal form of decoration in
Byzantine churches, were highly developed during this period.
The minor arts, including ivory carving, silverwork, illuminated manus-
cripts, and textiles, became very sophisticated. Stylized naturalistic motifs
and lavish decorative color were used.
The period after 1204 saw a second great flowering of Byzantine art, known
as the Second Golden Age. In church building the favored type, initiated by
Basil I, was a plan based on a circle inscribed in a square, a three-aisled plan
with five domes, the largest one in the middle. The most famous example of
this type is Saint Mark's Venice (11th-13th century). Manuscript illumina-
tion also flourished, the most famous example being the Paris Psalter.
Constantinople was sacked by the Crusaders in 1204, and during the next 2
centuries Byzantine art underwent profound changes. Fresco became the
most important form of decoration; by the late 14th century mosaics had
virtually disappeared. Work in the minor arts was generally of a lower
quality. During this late period it was in the outlying areas of the former
empire—Russia, Sicily, and the Balkans—that Byzantine art flourished. In
1453 Constantinople was conquered by the Turks, marking the end of the
Byzantine state. The style of art and architecture, however, continued to
flourish in Russia, Greece, and Bulgaria for several centuries.
See also: Byzantine Empire.

Byzantine Empire, historical term for the successor state to the Roman
Empire in the East. Its capital was Constantinople (now Istanbul), founded
by Constantine I in 330 at the site of the ancient Greek Byzantium. The
heartlands of the empire were Asia Minor and the Balkans, but at its height
it ruled southern Spain, Italy, Sicily, northern Africa, Egypt, Syria, Palestine,
the Crimean coast, Cyprus, and the Aegean islands. Its religion was Eastern
Orthodox Christianity. Byzantine missionaries carried Christianity to Rus-
sia, and Byzantine theologians were among the chief Church Fathers.
The Roman Empire was divided after the death of Theodosius I in 395. By
about 500 the Western Empire had fallen, Germanic invaders occupying
Italy, Spain, and northern Africa. In the East, however, Roman institutions
continued. However, after about 600, Roman institutions were replaced by
typically Byzantine (Greek) ones. From the late seventh century onward, the
Byzantine Empire was in frequent conflict both with the West and with the
rising Muslim civilization in the East. Much of the empire's territory was
lost, first to the Arabs, later to the Turks. The empire finally collapsed in
1453, when the Ottoman Turks captured Constantinople.

Byzantium *See:* Byzantine Empire; Istanbul.

C

C, third letter of the alphabet, derived from the letter *gimel* of the ancient Semitic alphabet and a rounded form of the Greek *gamma*. The Romans used *C* as an abbreviation for *Gaius*, and *Cn* for *Gnaeus* but also gave the letter a *k*-sound, which survives in modern English (*case*, *concrete*, etc.) *C* also has the "soft" sound of *s*, as in *face* and *city*. When *C* is combined with the letter *H*, 2 further sounds may be represented (*church*, *loch*); the combination can also have the *K* sound (*ache*, *anchor*, *chronicle*). *C* can also be a superfluous letter, as in *thick*. In musical notation, *C* is a note of the scale. In chemistry, it is the symbol of the element *carbon*, in roman numbers, *C* = 100.

Cabal, secret group or organization engaged in intrigues; also applied to the intrigues themselves. The term was already used in the 17th century for a secret council of the king. The conduct of English king Charles II's ministers *C*lifford, *A*rlington, *B*uckingham, *A*shley, and *L*auderdale (whose initials spelled "cabal") gave the word a sinister sense.

Cabala, or Kabbalah (Hebrew, "tradition"), body of esoteric Jewish mystical doctrines dealing with the manifestations of and revelation of God. The Cabala attaches mystical significance to every detail in the Torah, the first 5 books of the Bible. Its chief books are the *Sefer Yezirah* (Book of Creation; 3rd-6th centuries) and the *Sefer HaZohar* (Book of Splendor; 13th century). The Cabala arose in France and Spain in the Middle Ages and was later a major influence on Hasidism.
See also: Hasidism.

Cabbage, (*Brassica olearacea*), biennial vegetable from which other brassicas, such as kale, cauliflower, and broccoli, have been developed. The cabbage originated many centuries ago from the European wild cabbage. It has a characteristic tight "head" of leaves. Cabbages can be boiled or pickled, or fermented in salt to give sauerkraut; also used as animal feed.

Cabbage palm, name used for various palm trees with edible leaf buds, especially, the palmetto (*Sabal palmetto*), a common fan palm ranging from North Carolina through Central America. It can grow up to 80 ft (24 m) and thrives in swampy country such as Florida everglades. The terminal buds and fruit are edible, the trunks can be used for fences and posts.
See also: Palm; Palmetto.

Cabell, (James) Branch, (1879-1958), U.S. novelist, who combined an ironic, often antiromantic style with a strong element of fantasy in plots and settings. His best-known novel is *Jurgen* (1919).

Caber, trunk of a young tree, tossed in the Scottish sport of tossing the caber.

Cabeza de Vaca, Alvar Núñez (1490?-1557?), Spanish explorer. Shipwrecked off the coast of Texas and imprisoned by the Native Americans in 1528, he escaped and made his way to Mexico City (1530-36). His account of southwestern United States, including descriptions of "Seven Cities of Cíbola," supposedly laden with riches, stirred Spanish interest in the area. He was made governor of Paraguay (1542- 44), but after a rebellion against him, he was recalled to Spain.

Cabinda (pop. 163,000), city and district in Angola. This coastal district, separated from the rest of Angola by the Congo River and Zaire, produces large quantities of oil. The city is an important seaport. When Angola fought for independence from Portugal (1961- 75), Cabinda fought unsuccessfully for its independence from Angola.
See also: Angola.

Cabinet, top-level advisory council to the head of state, usually composed of the heads of the major executive departments. Though not mentioned in the Constitution, the U.S. cabinet has been a consultative body to the executive since George Washington. Normally the cabinet meets weekly with the president, though procedure varies. Members of the cabinet are individually appointed by and responsible to the president. They are not members of either house of Congress and may not address them, though they are often called to testify before committees.

Cable, electric, insulated conductor used to carry electric power or electric signals. A cable consists of a core conducting metal, usually of several wires twisted or stranded together, surrounded by insulating material. The conducting metal is usually copper, aluminum, or steel. The insulation is most often made of plastic or rubber. Multicore cables contain many cores, each insulated from the others, all contained inside a tube of plastic, rubber, copper, aluminum, or lead, which also serve to keep out moisture and heat. Telephone cables contain several thousand cores. Such cables run along the sea bed between the continents; however, satellite communications are replacing such long cables.
Electric power is distributed by power cables. Inside the home they carry electricity at low power (usually 110 volts). Electricity at high power is carried between cities by overhead cables slung from pylons. The cables do not need insulation around the cores as they are kept far enough apart for the air to act as an insulator and prevent sparking between them, but special glass or ceramic insulators are used to attach them to the pylons. Super-voltage power cables carrying currents at up to about 500,000 volts are usually buried underground and filled with oil or gas, such as nitrogen, to remove heat and increase insulation.
Radio, television, telephone, and other electronic equipment uses low-power signals with high frequencies, requiring a coaxial cable, which has a central core of wire surrounded by insulation, then a sheath of wire braid, and finally an insulating outer covering.

Cable, George Washington (1844-1925), U.S. author noted for his depiction of New Orleans and Creole life in works like *Old Creole Days* (1879) and *The Grandissimes* (1880).

Cable car, vehicle to carry passengers up steep gradients. The cable cars in San Francisco travel on rails like street cars, but they are pulled along by means of a continuous underground cable, to which the engineer can hook the car by pulling on a lever. Alpine cable cars are suspended from cables and usually operate on a funicular system, in which one car goes up a slope while another goes down, balancing each other, which demands much less power to operate.

Cable television, or CATV (community antenna television), broadcasting by means of coaxial cables rather than airwaves, used originally in areas where mountains or tall buildings made television reception poor or impossible, but now expanding throughout the United States because of the multiplicity of channels and programs it makes available.
See also: Television.

Cabot, John (Giovanni Caboto; c.1450-c.1499), Italian navigator and explorer, probably the first European to reach the North American mainland. In 1497, after receiving permission from Henry VII to sail for England, Cabot sailed in search of a western route to Asia and reached the coasts of Nova Scotia and Newfoundland, where he planted the English and Venetian flags. On a second voyage (1498) Cabot may have reached America again, or may have been lost at sea.

Cabot, Sebastian (1476-1557), explorer and navigator, son of John Cabot. Appointed pilot-major of Spain in 1518, he led an expedition to the Rio de la Plata region of South America in 1526. Its failure led to his banishment from Spain. Though eventually reinstated, he went to England in 1548, and later became governor of the Merchant Adventurers Company.

Cabral, Pedro Alvares (1467-1520), Portuguese navigator. Commanding a fleet that was meant to sail from Lisbon to India, in 1500, Cabral went too far southwest and sighted Monte Pascoal on the east coast of Brazil. After exploring the coast and claiming Brazil for Portugal, Cabral sailed on to India, where he founded a small factory at the port of Calicut. Very little is known of his life after his return to Portugal in 1501.

Cabrillo, Juan Rodríguez (João Rodrigues Cabrilho; d. c.1543), Portuguese explorer in the service of Spain, best known for his discovery of California. In 1542 he explored the coastline from lower California northwards to San Diego Bay.

Cabrini, Saint Frances Xavier (1850-1917), Italian-American nun, first U.S. citizen to be canonized (1946). She founded the Missionary Sisters of the Sacred Heart in 1880, and established 67 houses of the order throughout the world. In 1889 she immigrated to New York from Italy. Her feast day is Dec. 22.

Cacao (*Theobroma cacao*), tropical tree that produces cacao or cocoa beans. The raw material for chocolate is prepared by roasting, grinding, and pressing the dried seeds (or beans) from the woody cacao fruits. Pressing squeezes out cocoa butter and leaves a solid mass that is reground to make cocoa powder. The cacao tree has been cultivated since the time of the Aztecs, who used it for beverages and currency. Christopher Columbus introduced cocoa beans into Europe in 1502.
See also: Chocolate.

Cactus, name for over 1,500 kinds of succulent prickly plant of the Cactaceae family nearly all native to America. Cacti are well adapted for desert life. They have no leaves, allowing them to conserve water. Photosynthesis takes place in the swollen stem, which may be 98% water and can swell to store the water collected by the long roots during rare desert showers. The spines that cover the stem may have 2 functions, protecting the cacti from being eaten and, where the spines form a dense mat, helping to retain moisture. The cacti produce flowers that may last for only a few hours, in some cases opening only at night. The flowers are pollinated by bees, moths, humming-birds, and bats. Some cacti are edible. Cacti are grown for ornamental purposes and to form hedges. The peyote cactus is the natural source of the hallucinogenic drug mescaline.

Cadence, in musical harmony, successive chores that usually bring a passage of music to a close. One of the most common cadences consists of the chords traditionally sung to the word "Amen" at the end of a hymn or psalm.

Cadillac, Antoine de la Mothe (1658-1730), French colonial governor and founder of Detroit (1701). Governor of Mackinac in 1694, he felt the site of Detroit would be a better strategic position. He was appointed governor of Louisiana (1713) but recalled in 1716.
See also: Detroit.

Cádiz (pop. 154,100), ancient city and port in southwest Spain, on the Atlantic coast northwest of Gibraltar. Founded by the Phoenicians in 1130 B.C. as Gadir, the city came under the rule of Carthage c.550 B.C. and became prosperous under Roman rule after 205 B.C. After the discovery of America it became important as the headquarters of the Spanish fleets. It is now a commercial port noted for sherry exports.
See also: Spain.

Cadmium, chemical element, symbol Cd; for physical constants see Periodic Table. Cadmium was discovered by Friedrich Stromeyer in 1817. It is a soft, bluish-white metal, used in low melting alloys and solders. Compounds of cadmium are used in television tubes. Cadmium sulfide is used as a yellow pigment. Cadmium and its compounds are toxic and should be handled with care.

Cadmus, in Greek mythology, son of Agenor and founder of Thebes. With the help of the goddess Athena, he killed a dragon and sowed its teeth. Where the teeth were sown, soldiers sprang up and helped Cadmus build the city of Thebes.
See also: Mythology; Thebes.

Caecilian, wormlike amphibian that lives in underground burrows. Caecilians are found in America, from Mexico southward, as well as Africa and Asia. The largest species grows to 4 ft (1.4 m).

Caedmon (7th century), illiterate herdsman, English poet who reputedly became a poet overnight after a stranger commanded him in a dream to "sing of the beginning of created things." Author of the Caedmon Hymn, he spent the rest of his life rendering Bible history into verse.

Caesar, (Gaius) Julius (c.100-44 B.C.), Roman general, politician, and writer. Although a member of the ancient patrician Julian clan, he supported the antisenatorial party. His early career through various public offices won him popularity, and in 60 B.C. he formed the First Triumvirate with Pompey, who supplied the army, and Marcus Licinius Crassus, who provided the money. With Caesar as consul they succeeded in controlling Roman politics. Caesar's successful Gallic Wars (58-51 B.C.) gained him great esteem and a loyal and well- trained army. After the death of Crassus, Pompey tried to force Caesar to lay down his command, but in 49 B.C. Caesar crossed the Rubicon River (the boundary between Caesar's Gaúl and Rome), and civil war began. Pompey was finally defeated at Pharsalus in 48 B.C., and by 45 B.C. Caesar had secured the defeat of all the Pompeian forces. In 44 B.C. he was made dictator for life, but on the Ides of March (March 15) he was murdered.
See also: Rome, Ancient.

Caffeine, slightly bitter alkaloid used as a stimulant and diuretic and found in coffee, tea, cocoa, and other plants; poisonous when taken in large doses.

Cage, John (1912-92), U.S. experimental composer and musical theoretician. He composed for "prepared piano," attaching objects to strings to alter tone and pitch and get percussive effects. Later work included prolonged silences, improvisation, aleatoric (chance) music, and electronic music.
See also: Aleatory music.

Cagney, James (1904-86), U.S. film actor who played cocky, aggressive tough guys in such classic gangster movies as *The Public Enemy* (1931) and *The Roaring Twenties* (1939). He won an Academy Award for his portrayal of George M. Cohan in *Yankee Doodle Dandy* (1942).

Cahokia Mounds, group of prehistoric mounds, mostly in the form of truncated pyramids, near East St. Louis, Ill. The largest of these, Monks Mound, is about 1,200 ft (360 m) by 650 ft (200 m) at base and 100 ft (30 m) high, and is the largest mound in the United States. More than 300 of the mounds have in recent years been bulldozed to make way for agricultural and municipal expansion, but the 18 largest remain.

Cahow (*Pterodroma cahow*), bird in the petrel family (Procellariidae). This seabird, often referred to as the Bermuda petrel, was believed extinct for hundreds of years until its rediscovery in 1906. Cahows, of which there are only 100 or so alive today, are approximately 15 in (38 cm) long with dark tops and white undersides. They nest only in the Bermuda Islands.

Cain, in the Old Testament, eldest son of Adam and Eve (Gen. 4:1), a tiller of the ground. Because the offering of his brother Abel was accepted by God, and his own rejected, he murdered Abel, and was doomed to be a wandering fugitive. But God gave him a protective sign and promised sevenfold vengeance if he were slain. He built a city and named it Enoch for his son (Gen. 4:17).
See also: Old Testament.

Cain, James Mallahan (1892-1977), U.S. writer of crime novels admired for their accuracy of dialogue and characterization. His best-known works are *The Postman Always Rings Twice* (1934), *Serenade* (1937), *Mildred Pierce* (1941), and *Double Indemnity* (1943), which have been made into films.

Cairn terrier, breed of dog that originated in Scotland. Its name comes from its ability to dig under cairns (piles of stone) in order to hunt animals. It weighs 13-14 lb (5.9-6.4 kg). Its wiry topcoat is of various colors, but never white.

Cairo, or Al-Qhirah (pop. 6,663,000), capital of Egypt. It lies at the head of the Nile delta and is the largest African city. It was founded in A.D. 969 by the Fatimid dynasty. The founding of al-Azhar University (970-78) made it the intellectual center of the Islamic world. An allied base during World War II and site of the Cairo Conference, it became capital of Egypt (1952), and remains a major Arab political, economic, and nationalist center. The 1977 Egyptian-Israeli talks were held in Cairo. The nearby pyramids, sphinx, and Memphis ruins make it a tourist center.
See also: Egypt.

Caisson, concrete or steel box, open at both ends, used in civil engineering when excavation or construction must be carried out underwater, particularly in sinking foundations for bridges. Caissons are sunk in the required position and built up to keep the top above water. As the soil is dredged from the bottom, the caisson sinks. It is eventually filled with concrete and acts as part of the foundation of the bridge. Sometimes a pressurized, watertight chamber is built at the bottom of the caisson for workers.

Caisson disease *See:* Bends.

Cajuns (from "Acadian"), descendants of expatriate French-Canadians, living in Louisiana. Cajuns were deported from Acadia (Nova Scotia) by the British in 1755. They have a distinctive patois: a combination of archaic French forms with English, Spanish, German, Native American, and African American idioms.
See also: Acadia.

Calabash (*Crescentia cujete*), tree of tropical America, the woody shell of whose gourdlike fruit is used as a waterproof container. The flowers of calabash trees grow close to the trunk and main limbs, not on the tips of the branches among the leaves. They are pollinated by nectar-drinking bats and develop into 12 in (30 cm) pulpy fruit.

Caladium, genus of tropical American plant in the Arum family (Aracaea). Its large, arrow-shaped leaves have vividly colored markings. Caladiums are grown commercially as houseplants.

Calais (pop. 76,500), French seaport on the Pas de Calais (Strait of Dover), 170 mi (274 km) from Paris and 21 mi (34 km) from Dover. Calais is an important port, and the center of heavy passenger traffic between England and continental Europe. The city has fishing industries and textile and paper manufacturing.
See also: France.

Calamity Jane (Martha Jane Canary Burk; 1852-1903), frontier-town pros-
titute and campfollower who roamed the West in male garb. Famous in
Deadwood, S.D., during the 1870s gold boom, she claimed she had been an
army scout, a pony express rider, Custer's aide, and Wild Bill Hickok's
mistress.

Calcination, process of heating used in chemistry and industry to convert
salts containing oxides and to remove volatile constituents from substances.
In making quicklime, for example, calcium carbonate is changed into cal-
cium oxide by calcination. Calcination is also used to covert bones into
phosphates for use in fertilizer.
See also: Chemistry.

Calcite, soft mineral, consisting of calcium carbonate ($CaCO_3$), found
mainly in limestone. Most stalagmites and stalactites are made of calcite.
Calcite is usually white, but impurities may give it other colors. Very pure
calcite, such as Iceland spar, is often transparent and causes double refraction,
so that objects seen through it appear double, making it useful in some optical
instruments. Other forms of calcite include marble and Oriental alabaster.
Calcite is used to make lime, cement, and fertilizers.
See also: Calcium carbonate; Lime.

Calcium, chemical element, symbol Ca; for physical constants see Periodic
Table. It was first isolated in 1808 by Sir Humphry Davy. A member of the
alkaline earth group, calcium is the fifth most abundant element in the earth's
crust, occurring in numerous compounds. It is an essential constituent of
plants and animals, neccessary for building bones and teeth.

Calcium carbide, crystalline compound (CaC_2) made from calcium and
carbon. Produced by heating lime and coke, it is used in the manufacture of
fertilizers and acetylene, a gas used to cut or weld metals.
See also: Acetylene.

Calcium carbonate, mineral ($CaCO_3$) abundant in nature. Limestone, mar-
ble, coral, calcite, and chalk have calcium carbonate as a main ingredient.
Calcium carbonate is used in toothpaste, tooth powder, and stomach medi-
cine. Stalactites and stalagmites that form in caves are made from water that
deposited this white, crystalline mineral.
See also: Calcite; Chalk.

Calculator, mechanical or electronic machine for performing numerical
calculations. Calculators have number keys (0 through 9) and additional keys
for computing mathematical equations or functions, which are then displayed
on a small screen. Calculators, first made available in the early 1960s, were
miniaturized and marketed for consumers during the 1970s.

Calculus, branch of mathematics dealing with calculating rates of change
(differential calculus) and determining functions from information about
their rate of change (integral calculus).
Differential calculus is used to calculate accelerations, velocities, slopes of
curves, and maximum and minimum values, based on experimental or
theoretical relationships expressed as continuous equations. If a relationship

can be expressed as $y = f(x)$, where the response y is a continuous function of x, then the average rate of change can be found by determining the change in

$$y(\Delta y = y_2 - y_1 = f(x_2) - f(x_1))$$

and dividing it by the change in

x ($\Delta x = x_2 - x_1$).

The average speed traveling in a car, 55 mph (88.5 kmph), or the average fuel efficiency during a trip, 30 mi/gal (12.8 km/l), are examples. If we take the limit of the expression $\Delta y / \Delta x$ as $\Delta x = x_2 - x_1$ gets smaller and smaller, we arrive at the instantaneous rate of change, which is the derivative of the function $y = f(x)$ expressed as $f'(x) = dy/dx$:

$$f'(x) = \frac{dy}{dx} = \lim_{x_1 \to x_2} \frac{y_2 - y_1}{x_2 - x_1} = \lim_{\Delta x \to 0} \frac{\Delta y}{\Delta x}$$

"the derivative of the function $y = f(x)$ with respect to x." The symbol dy and dx are referred to as the differential of y and the differential of x respectively. In the automobile example above, although the average speed was 55 mph (88.5 kmph) over the length of a trip, each moment the traveler glanced at the speedometer different instantaneous speeds (rates) were observed.

When the derivative of a function $f'(x)$ is known, the function itself can be determined. This process of finding the *antiderivative* is done with integral calculus. Just as differential calculus is concerned with changes and differences, integral calculus is concerned with summations. Rearranging the expression above, $dy = f'(x)dx$. Summing each side of this equation over a range gives the expression:

$$y = \int_a^b f'(x)\ dx$$

read "y is the integral of f prime of x with respect to x." The elongated s stands for "sum" and is the symbol for integration. The range of summation indicated is from $x = a$ to $x = b$ and takes place over tiny intervals of x, dx. Integration is used to find lengths of curves, areas bounded by curves, volumes enclosed by surfaces, and centers of gravity of attracting bodies.

Many 17th-century mathematicians, astronomers, and physicists contributed to the development of calculus, predominant developers were Isaac Newton and Gottfried Wilhelm Leibniz .

See also: Newton, Sir Isaac; Leibniz, Gottfried Wilhelm von.

Calcutta (pop. 3,305,000), capital of West Bengal state, the leading transportation, industrial, financial, and commercial center of eastern India, and the largest city in India, situated on the Houghly River, in the Ganges delta, 80 mi (130 km) north of the Bay of Bengal. Calcutta is accessible to oceangoing vessels and has road and rail links with the whole of northern India, and an international airport. Calcutta was founded as a permanent settlement by the British East India Company in 1690. In 1756 the British were driven out by the nawab of Bengal, at the time of the infamous Black Hole of Calcutta incident. Robert Clive recaptured the town in 1757, and the British became virtual rulers of Bengal. In 1834 Calcutta became the capital of the British India empire. By 1900 it was the center of a strong nationalist

movement, and the developing unrest continued. The capital of India was transferred to Delhi in 1912, but Calcutta's commercial importance continued to grow.With the partition of India in 1947, Calcutta lost most of its jute-producing hinterland to Pakistan, and was faced with an influx of thousands of Hindu refugees. The city has often been the scene of religious and political strife. In spite of the overcrowding and poverty, Calcutta has continued its development as a commercial city and a vitally important port. Among the principal exports are tea, jute, iron, manganese, and mica. Calcutta's factories produce iron and steel, textiles, shoes, rubber, leather, glass, and cement.
See also: India.

Caldecott, Randolph (1846-86), British painter and illustrator, particularly of children's books. Among his best-known illustrations are those for Washington Irving's *Old Christmas* (1876) and William Cowper's *The Diverting History of John Gilpin* (1782). In 1938 the Caldecott Medal was established as an annual award for the best U.S. children's picture book.

Calder, Alexander (1898-1976), U.S. abstract sculptor and creator of the mobile. His mobiles consist of flat metal shapes connected by rods, wire, or string, which are hung or balanced and moved by motors or by air currents.

Calderón de la Barca, Pedro (1600-81), Spanish playwright and poet. He and Lope de Vega were the leading dramatists of Spain's Golden Age. He wrote over 200 plays, distinguished by their heightened style and poetic symbolism, many on religious themes. Among his most famous works are *The Constant Prince* (1629), *Life Is a Dream* (1635), and *The Surgeon of His Honor* (1635).

Calderone, Mary Steichen (1904-   ) U.S. physician, health official, and leader in sex education. As a founder (1964) and executive director of Sex Information and Education Council of the United States and earlier as director of Planned Parenthood and a physician in a New York public school system, her aim was to encourage sex education and health counseling.
See also: Sex education.

Caldwell, Erskine Preston (1903-87), U.S. author noted for his portrayal of poor Southern whites in short stories and novels such as *Tobacco Road* (1932), *God's Little Acre* (1933), and *Trouble in July* (1940).

Caldwell, Sarah (1924-   ), U.S. conductor and opera producer. She was director of the Boston University Opera Workshop (1953-57) and founded the Opera Company in Boston (1957). As its artistic director she staged more than 50 productions noted for their originality. She was the first woman to conduct at the N.Y. Metropolitan Opera, 1976.
See also: Opera.

Caledonia, ancient Roman name for what is now Scotland. The area was invaded by Agricola, a Roman general, in A.D. 83. Roman artifacts have been found in present-day Scotland. Caledonia is still used as a poetic name for Scotland.
See also: Scotland.

Calendar, method of reckoning days and months of the year. The earliest calendars were based upon the phases of the moon. The first day of each month was the day of the new moon. When the moon had gone through its cycle of phases 12 times, a year was said to have passed. Unfortunately, the moon takes about 29 days to go through its phases, and consequently 12 lunar months (354 days, 8 hrs, 48 min) are 11 days short of a full year. Only by adding an extra month every 3 years or so could the calendar be kept roughly in line with the seasons. The Jewish and Muslim calendars are lunar calendars. The ancient Egyptians used a solar calendar with 12 months of 30 days each and added 5 feast days at the end of the year, making it one of the most accurate early calendars. But the length of the solar year is about 365 days, so that the Egyptian calendar got 1 day out of step with the seasons every 4 years. The Roman calendar, originally contained only 10 months and began with March. Later January and February were added to the end of the year, and the months received their odd numbers of days in an attempt to fit every day of the year into months of roughly equal length. In 46 B.C. Julius Caesar reformed the calendar, making January the first month and adding a leap year day to February in every fourth year to prevent the calendar from getting out of step. This system, the Julian calendar, continued to be used in Europe for over 1,500 years. Because a year is not exactly 365 days long, but slightly shorter (365 days, 5 hrs, 48 min, 46 sec), adding an extra day every 4 years proved too much. By the 16th century the calendar was 10 days out of step with the seasons. Pope Gregory VIII decided that Thursday, Oct. 4, 1582, would be followed by Friday, Oct. 15, thus wiping out the error. To prevent a recurrence, he ruled that a century year could be a leap year only if divisible by 400. The Gregorian, or New Style, calendar, though not perfect, is adequate for most practical purposes and is the calendar in widest use today.

Calendula, or pot marigold (*Calendula officinalis*), annual plant. Infusions of the leaves and yellow flowers are used medicinally for gastrointestinal problems, fever, abscesses, and vomiting.

Calgary (pop. 754,000), city in southern Alberta, Canada, at the junction of the Bow and Elbow rivers, at a height of 3,438 ft (1,048 m). Its name is Gaelic for "clear running water." Founded as a Northwest Mounted Police fort in 1875, it is a center of grain and livestock marketing, located in a good farming and ranch region. Related industries are milling and meatpacking. Nearby coal, oil, and gas have resulted in a rapid expansion of the city. The city is famous for the annual Calgary Stampede, a 10-day rodeo that attracts cowboys from all over North America.
See also: Alberta.

Calhoun, John Caldwell (1782-1850), U.S. congressman, secretary of war, senator, and vice-president known for his lifelong defense of southern interests. Born in South Carolina, he was elected in 1811 to the U.S. House of Representatives, where he ardently supported the War of 1812. In 1817 he was appointed secretary of war by President James Monroe, and in 1824 was elected vice-president under President John Quincy Adams. Calhoun wrote a defense of the states' rights philosophy, which declared that when a state found a federal law in violation of the Constitution, the state had the right to consider the law void. Calhoun served a second term as vice-president under Andrew Jackson but resigned in 1832. He was soon elected to the

Senate, where he became the South's leading spokesman. He argued passionately in favor of slavery and the secession of the Southern states.
See also: Secession.

California, state in the southwest corner of the United States; bordered by Oregon in the north, Nevada and Arizona in the east, Mexico in the south, and the Pacific Ocean in the west.
Land and climate. Redwood forests and the San Andreas fault, origin of periodic earth tremors and occasional earthquakes, are important features of the Coast Ranges along the Pacific. The Sierra Nevada range to the east is the location of several national parks, including Yosemite and Sequoia, and of Mt. Whitney. Between these 2 mountain chains in the central part of the state is the Great Valley, whose fertile acres are drained by the San Joaquin and Sacramento rivers. To the north, Lassen Peak, an active volcano, and Mt. Shasta are found in the Cascade Mountains. East of the Sierra Nevada is the Basin and Range Region, which is largely desert. It includes Death Valley, with the lowest point in North America. Generally speaking, the state experiences hot, dry summers and warm, relatively wet winters. Principal cities are Los Angeles, San Diego, San Francisco, and Sacramento.

Economy. California is first among the states in manufacturing and agriculture and ranks among the leading states in fishing and mining. Major manufactures include electronic, electrical, and transportation equipment and processed foods, and some of the world's finest wines. California ranks second among the states in the production of milk, cotton, and oranges. It leads the nation in the production of many fruits, including grapes, avocados,

---

California

Capital:	Sacramento.
Statehood:	Sept. 9, 1850 (31st state).
Familiar name:	Golden State
Area:	158,706 sq mi (411,049 sq km; ranks 3rd)
Population:	32,268,000 (1997; ranks 1st)
Elevation:	Highest—14,495 ft (4,418 m), Mt. Whitney.
	Lowest—282 ft (86 m) below sea level near
	Badwater in Death Valley
Motto:	Eureka ("I have found it")
State flower:	Golden poppy
State bird:	California valley quail
State tree:	California redwood
State song:	"I Love You, California"

and lemons. Tourism is also a large industry, and Disneyland is a primary attraction. California is the nation's film and television production center.
Government. The constitution of 1879 provides for a governor serving a 4-year term. The state legislature consists of 40 senators, elected for 4-year terms, and 80 members of the Assembly, elected for 2-year terms. California sends 2 senators and 52 representatives to the U.S. Congress.
History. The Spanish explorer Juan Rodriguez Cabrillo is usually credited with California's discovery in 1542. The first California mission was established by a Franciscan missionary in 1769. In 1822 California became a province of Mexico. After Mexico's defeat in the Mexican War (1846-48), the area was ceded to the United States. The 1849 gold rush increased the population from 15,000 to over 100,000. The Central Pacific Railroad, completed in 1869, linked California with the East. California became the nation's aircraft center during World War II (1939-45). The postwar population expansion boosted the state's economy, but also created problems that exist today, such as smog and scarcity of water resources.

California, University of, large U.S. state university system, founded 1868. It is housed on 9 campuses (Berkeley, Davis, Irvine, Los Angeles, San Francisco, Riverside, San Diego, Santa Barbara, Santa Cruz). It comprises a library with more than 10 million items, the Lawrence Radiation Laboratory, the Scripps Institute of Oceanography at La Jolla, and the Lick Observatory at Mt. Hamilton.
See also: California.

Californium, chemical element, symbol Cf; for physical constants see Periodic Table. Californium is a radioactive element that does not occur naturally. It was produced in 1950 by Glenn Seaborg and others, by bombarding curium-242 with helium ions in a cyclotron. Californium is metallic, a member of the actinide series. It is produced in nuclear reactors and is a source of neutrons.

Caligula (Gaius Caesar; A.D. 12-41), nickname (meaning "little boots") of cruel and despotic Roman emperor (37-41). He believed he was a god. His demands that his statue be erected in Jerusalem's temple almost precipitated a revolt in Palestine.
See also: Rome, Ancient.

Calla, plant of genus *Calla* or *Zantedeschia* of the arum family *(Araceae)*. Genus *Calla* includes water plants such as the arum lily of North America(*C. palustris*). Plants of genus *Zantedeschia* have showy white, yellow, or pink funnel-shaped leaves (spathes) that look like flowers. The white calla lily (*Z. aethiopica*), golden calla lily (*Z. elliottiana*), and red calla lily (*Z. rehmannii*) are found in South Africa.
See also: Arum.

Callaghan, (Leonard) James (1912-), prime minister of the United Kingdom 1976-79. He was elected Labour party leader on the resignation of Harold Wilson and became prime minister immediately. Labour lost the 1979 general election to Margaret Thatcher's Conservatives.
See also: United Kingdom.

Callaghan, Morley Edward (1903-90), Canadian novelist and short story writer influenced by the style of Ernest Hemingway. His books include the novel *They Shall Inherit the Earth* (1935) and a memoir, *That Summer in Paris* (1963).

Callao (pop. 515,200), Peruvian seaport located 8 mi (13 km) west of the capital city of Lima. As Peru's chief seaport, most of this nation's imports and exports pass through its harbor. The city, which is part of Peru's largest metropolitan area, has survived major earthquakes, tidal waves, and foreign attacks since its founding by Spaniards (1537).
See also: Peru.

Callas, Maria (Maria Kalogeropoulos; 1923-77), leading Greek-American operatic soprano. She was famous for her expressive phrasing and acting ability in a wide variety of roles.
See also: Opera.

Calligraphy, art of penmanship. Combining beauty with legibility, it developed in the Far East, where it was a recognized art form as early as 250 B.C. In early medieval Europe calligraphy was practiced in monastic communities, which developed the Carolingian and Insular scripts. A high point was reached with the Book of Kells and the Lindisfarne gospels. The Italian Renaissance manuscripts provided models for the first printed books and for roman and italic types. Edward Johnston (1872-1944) and his pupil Graily Hewitt (1864- 1952) began the modern revival of calligraphy in the early 1900s.

Calliope, keyboard instrument dating from 1855 and much used in circuses and amusement parks. The original version was operated by steam forced through whistles controlled by a keyboard, but later models have used compressed air.

Calms, Regions of, areas characterized by little or no wind. They include *horse latitudes, subpolar regions*, and the equatorial *doldrums. Horse latitudes* lie between 30 degrees north latitude and 30 degrees south. The calms of Cancer and of Capricorn both fall within the horse latitudes. Calms in the subpolar regions are caused by the sinking of the cold air over the North and South poles, which forms high-pressure centers. In the equatorial doldrums, air masses are forced upwards after being heated in the tropics, causing a belt of low pressure to form.
See also: Doldrums; Horse latitudes.

Calorie, amount of heat required to raise the temperature of one gram of water one centigrade degree (more precisely, from 14.5C to 15.5C). One kilocalorie is the amount of heat required to raise 1 kg of water through 1 centigrade degree and is therefore equal to 1,000 calories. The calorific value of foods is actually a measure of the number of kilocalories that can be obtained by the body, in the form of energy, when the foods are broken down.
See also: British thermal unit.

Calvary, or Golgotha, Jerusalem hill site of the crucifixion of Jesus. It is traditionally accepted to be the hill on which Constantine founded the church of the Holy Sepulcher in the 4th century.

Calvert, English family that founded and owned colonial Maryland. **George, 1st Baron Baltimore** (c.1580-1632), founded Ferryland, Newfoundland (1621). He petitioned for a grant in northern Virginia (present-day Maryland), granted to his son Cecil in 1632. **Cecil** (or Cecilius), **2nd Baron Baltimore** (c.1605-75), left Maryland's administration to his younger brother **Leonard Calvert** (1606-47). **Charles, 3rd Baron Baltimore** (1637-1715), son of Cecil, governor of Maryland from 1661, and governed the colony in person, 1679-84. In 1689 his Roman Catholic Maryland Administration was overthrown by a Protestant rebellion, and in 1691 the Crown withdrew his authority to govern.
See also: Maryland.

Calvin, John (1509-64), French theologian. After a "sudden conversion" in 1533, Calvin became a leader of the Protestant Reformation, eventually systematizing his ideas with those of other reformers. His *Institutes of the Christian Religion* (1536) is one of the most important religious works ever written. Calvin's theology, which rejected the authority of the pope, focused on the faith of the individual and study of the Bible. Calvin also believed in predestination, the idea that God preordains some souls for salvation and others for damnation. His church organization became the model for Presbyterianism and the Reformed Churches. Calvin was active in politics, in 1541 establishing in Geneva a government based on his theology. The academy that he founded in 1559 later became the University of Geneva.
See also: Calvinism; Reformation.

Calvin, Melvin (1911-), U.S. biochemist who won the 1961 Nobel Prize for chemistry, having led the team that unraveled the details of the chemistry of photosynthesis.
See also: Calvin, John; Chemistry.

Calvinism, Protestant doctrine formulated by John Calvin and stated chiefly in his *Institutes of the Christian Religion* (1536). Its basic tenets are that God is omnipotent; His will is supreme and governs all actions; each person's life is predestined, the salvation or damnation of each soul determined by God before creation; God's elect will be saved and given eternal life, and those He has damned can find no release (justification) from the consequences of their sins except by dedicating themselves to His service. The strict Calvinist maintains that God sees humankind as loathsome and corrupt, with feeble delusions of virtue and worth. Calvinism preaches that the Bible is the only source of God's laws and refers more often to the Old Testament than the New, emphasizing the judgment of sinners more than the love and compassion of God.

Calvino, Italo (1923-85), Italian writer notable for his use of fantasy. Calvino has written in several genres, including science fiction and historical allegory, but he received his greatest acclaim for *Italian Folktales* (1956) and the experimental *If on a Winter's Night a Traveler* (1979; trans. 1981).

Calypso, West Indies musical style notable for its lyrics, which are usually improvised and often humorous or ironic. The music is typically played on steel drums, which carry the tune as well as provide the beat.

Cambodia *See:* Kampuchea.

Cambrian, earliest period of the Paleozoic Era, dated roughly 570-500 million years ago, immediately preceding the Ordovician period. Cambrian rocks contain the oldest fossils that can be used for dating.
See also: Paleozoic.

Cambridge (pop. 98,700), English market town, 51 mi (32 km) from London, and home of the Cambridge University. The town grew up in the 9th century at a ford on the Cam River, near what had been a Roman camp. The first university college, Peterhouse, was founded in 1284. Since then the growth of city and university have been closely linked.
See also: England.

Cambridge (pop. 95,802), city in Massachusetts on the Charles River opposite Boston; seat of Middlesex County. Since the establishment of Harvard University in 1636, the city has been an important educational center. In 1639 the first printing press in the American colonies was established there. In 1879, Radcliffe College for Women was opened, followed by the Episcopal Theological Seminary (1867) and the Massachusetts Institute of Technology (relocated from Boston in 1916). Principal industries include printing and publishing, baking, and the manufacture of light machinery.
See also: Massachusetts.

Cambridge University, one of the world's leading universities, at Cambridge, England. Its history dates from 1209, and its first college, Peterhouse, was established in 1284. Today the coeducational university has about 9,000 students and 29 colleges and approved societies.

Camcorder *See:* Video camera.

Camden (pop. 87,492), city in New Jersey on the Delaware River opposite Philadelphia. Formally laid out as a town in 1773 and chartered as a city in 1828, it is an important manufacturing and shipbuilding city.
See also: New Jersey.

Camel, 2 species of haired, cud-chewing animals with humped backs, long necks, and hooves. The 1-humped Arabian camel or dromedary (*Camelus dromedarius*) of Africa and the Middle East is a widely kept domestic animal. The 2-humped Bactrian camel (*C. bactrianus*) is found from Asia Minor to Manchuria, and a few still live wild in the Gobi Desert. Domesticated in Babylonia about 1100 B.C., camels are invaluable in the desert. They can carry enormous loads and are able to withstand the loss of about one third of their body fluid without danger. Their humps are fatty tissue, not water storage vessels. Their use as bearers has been greatly reduced by the use of motor vehicles.

Camellia, any of a genus *(Camellia)* of evergreen trees and shrubs of Asia that have large fragrant red, pink, or white flowers. The most important of the many cultivated varieties is the tea plant *(Co sinensis)*.

Camelot, in Arthurian legend, court of King Arthur and the Knights of the Round Table. It has been identified variously with Caerleon (Wales), Camelford (Cornwall), and South Cadbury (Somerset).
See also: Arthur, King.

Camera, device for forming an optical image of a subject and recording it on a photographic film or plate or (in television cameras) on a photoelectric mosaic.
See also: Photography.

Cameron, Julia Margaret (1815-79), Indian-born British pioneer photographer, best known for her portraits of such Victorians as Alfred, Lord Tennyson and Ellen Terry. Believing that a photograph should capture the spirit of its subject, Cameron put less emphasis on technique, and the blurred quality of some of her photographs is a distinction of her style. A revised edition of her book *Victorian Photographers of Famous Men and Women* appeared in 1973.

Cameroon, republic in West Africa. Cameroon is bordered by the Gulf of Guinea (west and southwest), Nigeria (northwest), Chad (northeast), the Central African Republic (east), and the Congo, Gabon, and Equatorial Guinea (south).
Land and climate. The narrow coastal plain of swamps and dense jungle rises to a plateau of savanna and forest some 2,000 ft (610 m) above sea level. The country's highest peak is the volcanic Great Cameroon (13,354 ft/4,070 m). The interior plateau covers about two-thirds of the country. The coast is tropical, the north, near Lake Chad, is semiarid. The central region receives about 30-40 in (76-102 cm) of rainfall annually. The country's capital is Yaoundé.

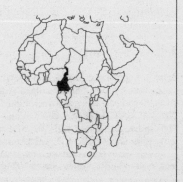

Cameroon

Capital:	Yaoundé
Area:	183,570 sq mi
	(475,442 sq km)
Population:	15,029,000
Language:	English, French
Government:	Presidential republic
Independent:	1960
Head of gov.:	Prime minister
Per capita:	U.S. $650
Mon. unit:	1 CFA franc = 100
	centimes

People. Cameroon's population consists of some 150 different tribes and ethnic groups. The official languages are English and French. Most of the people are Christian, but sizable minorities follow traditional African beliefs or the Islam.

Economy. The economy is based mainly on agriculture and forestry. Cameroon is mostly self-sufficient in food and exports coffee, cocoa, and timber as well as bananas, rubber, and aluminum. Aluminum smelting is Cameroon's largest industry.

History. The Sao people, who produced a distinctive kind of art and cast objects in bronze, settled near Lake Chad about 900 A.D.The Portuguese came in 1472 and established the slave trade. In 1884, Germany established a protectorate in the Cameroon area. British and French troops occupied the area in World War I and afterwards the League of Nations mandated the larger part (Cameroun) to France and the remainder (Southern and Northern Cameroons) to the British. In 1946 they became UN trust territories. In 1960, Cameroun became an independent republic after several years of guerrilla warfare. After plebiscites in 1961, the Northern Cameroons joined Nigeria, and the Southern Camerouns joined Cameroun to form the Federal Republic of Cameroon. In 1972, the federal system was replaced by a unified republic. In 1980, Ahmadou Ahidjo, president since independence, was reelected. President Paul Biya was elected unopposed in 1984 for his first full 5-year term and was reelected in 1988 and 1992. In the late 1990s the burden of debt increased as a result of the fact that prices plummeted at the world market.

Camomile, also spelled chamomile, any of a genus (*Anthemis*) of various strong-scented herbs with daisylike flowers. The bitter-tasting flowers and leaves have had uses in folk medicine ranging from malaria cure to mouthwash.

Camorra, Italian secret society started in the Kingdom of Naples (1830). Although it specialized in extortion, smuggling, robbery, and assassination, it was often used by the authorities, and it became very powerful. After Italian unification in 1861, attempts were made to suppress the society, but it survived until 1911.

Campanella, Roy (1921-   ), one of the most popular and successful catchers in baseball history. He signed with the Negro leagues in 1936, joining the Brooklyn Dodgers in 1948. Campanella's 10-year major league career was cut short by an automobile accident in 1958 that left him paralyzed. He won the National League's Most Valuable Player award 3 times (1951, 1953, and 1955) playing for the Dodgers.

Campanile, bell tower, usually adjacent to a church. The first campaniles appeared in Italy about the 7th century. As in the round campanile of Sant' Apollinare Nuovo in Ravenna, Italy, the earliest examples probably contained not bells, but semantra, planks of wood or metal that sounded when struck. In the following century, the square campanile became the standard. The campanile has been revived as an element of modern church architecture.

Campanula, plant genus of the family Campanulaceae containing some 700 species of mostly herbaceous (nonwoody) plants. Campanula is often called bellflower, and many of the species have showy, bell-like flowers.

Camp, Walter Chauncey (1859-1925), father of American football. As a player and coach at Yale and Stanford universities, he helped initiate, implement, and develop changes (such as the first down system and the line of scrimmage) that turned European rugby into the American game. Camp authored numerous books on athletics and physical fitness.

Campbell, Donald Malcolm (1921-67), English speedboat racer. The first man to break the 200 mph (320 kmph) barrier and survive, Campbell's run, on Ullswater Lake, Cumberland, England in 1955, established a watercraft speed record of 202.32 mph (325.602 kmph). Campbell died in an accident in 1967, while exceeding 300 mph (480 kmph) in his jet-propelled boat.

Campbell, Mrs. Patrick (1865-1940), English actress. Popular on stage for over 40 years, she created many classic roles, including Eliza Doolittle in George Bernard Shaw's *Pygmalion* (1914), a part written for her.

Campbell-Bannerman, Sir Henry (1836-1908), British prime minister 1905-08 and leader of the Liberal party from 1899. A member of the House of Commons from 1868 until his death, he championed progressive causes. *See also:* United Kingdom.

Camp David, woodland camp in the Catoctin Mountains in Maryland near Washington, D.C., that has been used by U.S. presidents since Franklin D. Roosevelt as a retreat, workplace, and environment to receive foreign dignitaries.
See also: Maryland.

Camp David Agreement, peace treaty formulated in 1979 at Camp David by Egyptian President Anwar Sadat and Israeli Prime Minister Menachem Begin with the assistance of U.S. President Jimmy Carter. It included a timetable for Israel's phased withdrawal from the Egyptian Sinai by 1982, mutual diplomatic recognition, and a framework for attempting to solve the Palestinian question.

Campeche, state in southeastern Mexico, on the Yucatán Peninsula. Although forest products yield a significant portion of the state's income, commercial fishing is also important. About a third of the inhabitants of Campeche are descended from the Mayas.
See also: Mexico.

Camp Fire, organization for children in the United States. Originally founded for girls in 1910 by Luther and Charlotte Gulick, Camp Fire began admitting boys in 1975. The organization has programs for kindergartners through high-school students. It stresses self reliance through safety courses, camping, and service activities.
See also: Gulick, Luther Halsey.

Camphor, white, crystalline compound ($C_{10}H_{16}O$) distilled from the wood of a species of laurel tree (*Cinnamonum camphora*). It has a strong odor that repels insects and is used medicinally—internally as a pain-killer and anti-spasmodic, and externally in linaments.

Campin, Robert (1375?-1444), Flemish painter best known for his religious works. His art reflects the influence of manuscript illumination, though with a keener sense of plasticity in rendering the forms. One of his major works is the triptych of the Annunciation (c.1428) known as the *Mérode Altarpiece*. Depicting in realistic detail the daily life of the rising bourgeoisie, Campin became a founder of the Netherlandish School, influencing Jan Van Eyck and Rogier Van Der Weyden, among others.

Campion, plant of genera *Lychnis* or *Silene* grown for showy flowers. Many have escaped from gardens and grow wild. Descriptive names include ragged robin, Maltese cross, and mullein pink.

Camus, Albert (1913-60), French writer and philosopher. He communicated a vision of humanity in an absurd universe and felt that the only possibility for freedom and dignity lay in the awareness of this absurdity. His works include the essay "The Myth of Sisyphus" (1942), which elucidated the philosophical basis of his novel *The Stranger* (1942); the novels *The Plague* (1947) and *The Fall* (1956); the essay "The Rebel" (1951); and the play *Caligula* (1945). He won the Nobel Prize in literature in 1957. *See also:* Philosophy.

Canaan, early name for Palestine. The region was inhabited from the 2nd millennium B.C. by Semitic peoples, mainly Amorites, whose script provides the earliest known alphabet. During the 13th century B.C. Canaan was occupied by the Israelites. In the next century its coasts were taken by the Philistines but later, King David (1000-961 B.C.) extended Israelite rule over all Canaan. *See also:* Palestine.

Canaanites, people who settled Canaan, the biblical name for Palestine, c.3000 B.C. The chief inhabitants of this land until the Israelites defeated them c.1200 B.C., the Canaanites spoke a Semitic language whose writing system influenced the development of the ancient Hebrew alphabet. *See also:* Canaan; Semites.

Canada, independent nation in North America, encompassing a land mass of 3,851,809 sq mi (9,976,185 sq km), making it the largest country in the Western Hemisphere and the second largest country in the world after Russia. Canada is an autonomous federation with 10 provinces and 2 federally administered territories. It is formally a constitutional monarchy under the British Crown and a member of the Commonwealth of Nations. French and English are the official languages. The federal capital is Ottawa.
Land and climate. Canada is divided into 7 regions. (1) The Appalachian region (New Brunswick, Nova Scotia, Prince Edward Island, and Newfoundland and the Gaspé peninsula) is a geological extension of the Appalachian mountain chain that runs along the eastern United States. The region is a source of varied farm products, timber, coal, and iron ore, and with numerous

Canada

Capital:	Ottawa
Area:	3,849,675 sq mi
	(9,970,610 sq km)
Population:	30,675,000
Language:	English, French
Government:	Parliamentary
	democracy in the
	British Commonwealth
Independent:	1931
Head of gov.:	Prime minister
Per capita:	U.S. $19,380
Mon. unit:	1 Canadian dollar =
	100 cents

natural harbors, a major commercial fishing center. (2) The St. Lawrence lowlands, adjacent to the desolate Canadian Shield in the north and bordering on the Great Lakes and the St. Lawrence River in the south, is one of its most productive agricultural belts, containing about half of the total population. The Hudson Bay lowlands, embracing the southwest shore of Hudson Bay and James Bay, are situated in an Arctic zone, the region's swampy subsoil, consisting mostly of clay and sand, frozen the year round. Most of the region's inhabitants are fur trappers and fishers. (3) The Canadian Shield, almost 50% of the country, is a horseshoe-shaped region encircling Hudson Bay and including large portions of the provinces of Quebec, Ontario, Manitoba, and Saskatchewan, the northeastern corner of Alberta, the Labrador portion of Newfoundland, and much of the Northwest territories. The area is characterized by rocky hills and ridges, numerous lakes, and muskeg (a type of bog). Though unsuitable for agriculture, the region is rich in natural resources; forests, mineral deposits, and water power. (4) The Interior Plains reach from the Rocky Mountains to the Canadian Shield and include southern Manitoba and Saskatchewan, almost all of Alberta, and part of British Columbia and the Northwest Territories. The northern half of the Interior Plains is heavily forested, and there is some muskeg and tundra. The southern half includes fertile prairies and also contains rich deposits of natural gas, oil, and coal. (5) The Cordilleran region, between the Pacific Ocean and the Interior Plains of western Canada, is a 500-mi- (800- km-) wide strip of mountainous terrain that includes most of British Columbia, the Yukon territory, and part of western Alberta. Second to the Canadian Shield in wealth of mineral deposits, the region has extensive forests, water resources for hydroelectric plants, fertile soils particularly suited to fruit production, and important commercial fishing areas along the Pacific coast.

(6) With very limited animal life and vegetation, the Inuitian region in the Arctic Archipelago includes the 800-mi-(1,300-km-) long and 300-mi-(480-km) wide mountainous region extending from northernmost Ellesmere Island south and west to Melville Island. The Arctic lowlands and plateaus include most of Banks Island, southern Ellesmere Island, and eastern Baffin Island. (7) Though rugged and virtually uninhabitable, the Arctic Archipelago possesses rich deposits of coal, salt, gypsum, oil, and natural gas. About 70% of Canadian soil is useless for agriculture, but most of the nonarable

soils support vast expanses of forests, and some are suitable for cattle raising. Covering about 40% of the country from coast to coast, the northern forests form Canada's largest belt of natural vegetation. The tundra extending across northern Canada can support only moss, lichens, and grass and flowers during the summer, when the surface layer is frost-free. Ever-frozen subsoil, or permafrost, prevents greater vegetation.

The government has created several game reserves; the land set aside for national parks totals about 29,500 sq mi (76,405 sq km). The largest of the national parks are Jasper, Wood Buffalo, Prince Albert, and Riding Mountain. Each province has also established its own provincial parks.

People. Canada's population is predominantly of British or French stock, though it includes many of German, Italian, Ukrainian, Dutch, and other origins. Native Americans number about 370,000 and Inuit (Eskimos) about 26,000. Population is concentrated in the southern part of the country, the most populous provinces being Ontario, Quebec, and British Columbia. About 76% of Canadians are urban.

Government. Canada has a parliamentary system of government, with executive power vested in a prime minister and cabinet. The federal legislature comprises a Senate of 112 appointed members and a House of Commons whose 295 members are elected for a 5-year term. Each of the 10 provinces has its own premier and elected legislature. The Yukon and Northwest Territories are governed by federally appointed commissioners and elected councils, and each sends 1 representative to the federal parliament.

Economy. Agriculture is responsible for 3% of Canada's employment and provides around 10% of Canada's total exports. One of the world's chief wheat producers, Canada grows other grains, oilseeds, fruit (especially apples), vegetables, and tobacco. Beef and dairy cattle, hogs, sheep, and poultry are reared. Forestry and fisheries are major industries, and Canada remains a leading source of furs, both farmed and trapped. Mineral resources include petroleum and natural gas, molybdenum, platinum, copper, nickel, iron ore, zinc, lead, silver, gold, asbestos, elemental sulfur, and coal. Most manufacturing plants are located in Ontario and Quebec. Manufacturing accounts for about 25% of all employment. Products include nonferrous metals, machinery, chemicals, plastics, electrical equipment, and textiles.

History. Visited by 11th-century Vikings, Canada was later penetrated by explorers such as John Cabot, Jacques Cartier, and Samuel de Champlain. The French founded Quebec in 1608 and made Canada the royal colony of New France (1663). Anglo-French rivalry culminated in the cession of New France to Britain (Treaty of Paris, 1763). French rights were guaranteed by the Quebec Act (1774). Only 1 serious revolt against British rule took place (1837-38), consisting of separate uprisings led by W.L. Mackenzie in Upper (English-speaking) Canada and Louis Papineau in Lower (French-speaking) Canada. The British North America Act (1867) established Canada as a dominion, the 4 founding provinces being Quebec, Ontario, Nova Scotia, and New Brunswick. The others entered later: Manitoba (1870), British Columbia (1871), Prince Edward Island (1873), Saskatchewan (1905), Alberta (1905), and Newfoundland (1949). The Northwest Territories, formerly administered by the Hudson's Bay Company, became a federal territory in 1870, and the Yukon was made a separate territory in 1898. Separatist tensions, particularly in French-speaking Quebec, developed during the

1960s and have continued. Efforts begun in 1978 to amend the British North America Act in order to "patriate" the Canadian constitution resulted in the Constitution Act (1982). At the end of the 1990s Canada, the United States, and Mexico formed a free trade association, NAFTA.

Canada goose (*Branta canadensis*), large migratory bird common to North America, Greenland, and parts of Asia. It has a long black head and neck and distinctive white cheek bars, and flies in group formations.

Canada thistle (*Cirsium arvense*), weed native to Europe and Asia and now widespread in the northern United States and southern Canada. The weed is difficult to control because new thistle can grow from bits of the old roots.

Canadian literature, body of literary works reflecting the English and French heritage of Canada, often focusing on national identity and duality. Since 1945 French-language Quebecois fiction has evolved into an intense and experimental body of writing, while English-Canadian literature has tended to be marked by well-crafted novels of life in the various regions of the country. Robertson Davies, many of whose widely praised novels are set in Ontario towns, and Margaret Atwood, a poet and novelist whose work often has a strong feminist component, are two of the leading figures of contemporary Canadian literature.

Canadian Mounted Police *See:* Royal Canadian Mounted Police.

Canadian Shield, or Laurentian Plateau, geologic designation of that area of North America (including the eastern half of Canada and small portions of the United States) that has remained more or less stable since Precambrian times.

Canal, artificial waterway used for transportation, drainage, and irrigation. In 521 B.C. a precursor of the Suez Canal joined the Nile to the Red Sea. In China, the Ling Ch'u canal was completed during the 3rd century B.C. and the Grand Canal, joining the Paiho, Yellow, and Yangtze rivers, had sections in use by the 7th century A.D. The Romans built many canals to supply their cities with water and canalized a number of European rivers to create an empire-wide transportation system. In the 15th century the lock, a device for raising boats from one land level to another, was invented. Although one of the great engineering projects of the 19th century, the Suez Canal to the Red Sea, was built entirely without locks, the other great international waterway, the Panama Canal, would not have been possible without them. In North America the canal system included the Erie Canal (1825), linking the Hudson River to Lake Erie and providing an opening to the Middle West. The Welland Canal (1828), between Lake Erie and Lake Ontario, was the next step in an inland waterway transportation network, completed by the opening of the St. Lawrence Seaway (1959). The longest canalized system is the Volga-Baltic Canal (1965), which runs 1,850 mi (2,977 km), from Astrakhan up the Volga, via Kuybyshev, Gorkiy and Lake Ladoga, to St. Petersburg, Russia.

Canal Zone *See:* Panama Canal Zone.

Canary, name of several small song birds, particularly a finch native to the Canary Islands (*Serinus canarius*). The wild canary is usually gray or green in color, but tame birds have been bred to produce the characteristic "canary yellow." Canaries have been bred in Europe since the 16th century and are valued for their song.

Canary, Martha Jane *See:* Calamity Jane.

Canary Islands, group of islands in the Atlantic Ocean off the northwest coast of Africa that make up 2 Spanish provinces. The main islands are Tenerife, Palma, Gomera, Hierro, Grand Canary, Fuerteventura, and Lanzarote; their land area is nearly 3,000 sq mi (7,770 sq km).

Canberra (pop. 310,100), capital city of the Commonwealth of Australia and the country's largest inland city. The Australian parliament first met there in 1927. The economy rests mainly on the public service and governmental departments.
See also: Australia.

Cancer, group of diseases in which some body cells change their nature, start to divide uncontrollably, and may revert to an undifferentiated type. They form a malignant tumor that enlarges and may spread to adjacent tissues or through blood and lymph systems to other parts of the body. The American Cancer Society has listed 7 warning signals: (1) change in bowel or bladder habits, (2) a sore that does not heal, (3) unusual bleeding or discharge, (4) thickening or lump in a breast or elsewhere, (5) indigestion or difficulty in swallowing, (6) obvious change in a wart or mole, and (7) nagging cough or hoarseness. Every diagnosis of cancer made by a doctor is subject to confirmation by a biopsy, in which a small piece of tissue is cut into very thin slices, stained with special dyes, and examined under a microscope. Routine periodic physical examinations are important, since the most successfully treated cancers are those that have not progressed to the stage of producing symptoms. The doctor feels, or palpates, parts of the body for unusual lumps or thickenings. A cervical smear is taken from adult women. The rectum and large intestine can be examined by means of a lighted tube, called a proctosigmoidoscope. Periodic self-examination of the skin, mouth, and genital organs is also important. Women should examine their breasts once a month after their menstrual cycles, and men should examine their testicles.
Successful treatment of cancer requires complete removal or destruction of the tumor by surgery, radiation, or drugs (chemotherapy). Some tumors cannot be destroyed by safe amounts of radiation, and some cannot be entirely removed surgically without destroying a vital organ, so surgery, radiation, and drugs may be combined.
Cancer is tenacious, sometimes subsiding but reappearing years after the patient has presumably been cured. For some cancers, even 5 years is not a long enough period; an indefinite length of time with frequent examinations is recommended. Physicians are increasingly reluctant to speak of "5-year cures," preferring more the realistic expression of "5-year survival without clinical evidence of disease."
Causes of cancer.
Chemical compounds.

Chemists have manufactured several hundred pure chemicals that produce cancer in animals. In humans, however, research has not found a relationship between chemical structure and cancer-producing activity. Some chemical carcinogens produce cancers at the site of contact, others at distant sites. Some are incomplete or weak in their action and need the action of other chemicals in order to induce tumors. The simultaneous injection of a chemical carcinogen and a closely related inactive compound (anticarcinogen) can prevent or retard the action of the carcinogen. This line of investigation may eventually uncover chemicals to prevent the development of cancer in individuals who are unavoidably exposed to certain cancer-producing hazards.

Environmental hazards.

Molds and bacteria growing naturally on food products may represent a source of environmental carcinogens. The human cancers due to industrial exposure include the following: (1) bladder cancer in aniline dye workers who handle betanaphtylamine, (2) bone cancer due to swallowing radium, (3) lung cancer caused by inhalation of chromium compounds, radioactive ores, asbestos, arsenic, and iron, (4) cancer of nasal sinuses and the lung in nickel mine workers, and (5) skin cancer from the handling of some products of coal, oil shale, lignite, and petroleum. Excessive or continuous exposure to inhaled impurities brings about changes in the bronchial linings and the lungs that may eventually result in disability and illness. If the impurities contain cancer-producing substances, prolonged exposure can lead to cancer. During the past 40 years, cancer of the lung in the United States has shown the greatest increase of any cancer type. At least 80% of the total increase can be attributed to cigarette smoking. An additional important factor is air pollution caused by industrial wastes, car exhausts, and household sources.

Radiation.

The cancer-producing effects of the ultraviolet rays of sunlight appear to be limited to the skin. Related to the cancer-causing effects of sunlight are those of ionizing radiation from radium and X-rays. Ionizing radiation can cause several forms of cancer in humans and animals. Radiologists and others exposed to increased doses of radiation are more likely to develop leukemia than are people who are not exposed. Radium salts, which are deposited in bone, give rise to cancers of the bone.

Cancer-causing viruses.

Cancer-causing viruses penetrate the cells of victims and become part of the structure of the chromosomes. The presence of the virus in the genetic mechanism of the cell may make the cell behave immediately as a cancer, or the virus can remain dormant until activated by another stimulus. Scientists have identified several dozen types of cancer that are caused by viruses, in many species of animals, including cats, monkeys, chickens, and rodents. It is inevitable that some human cancers will be found to be caused by viruses and that such discoveries may lead to the development of protective vaccines.

Hormones.

Large doses of the female hormone estrogen given over long periods will lead to the development of leukemia and tumors of the testes, uterus, and pituitary in some strains of mice. The increasing use of hormones as treatment for various human conditions does not seem to have led to an increase in the incidence of any specific type of cancer in women or men. However, some girls born of mothers who took large doses of a synthetic estrogen, diethylstilbestrol (DES), during their pregnancy have developed cancer of the vagina. Widespread use of "the pill" (the collective term for a variety of oral

contraceptives containing progestogen, often estrogen, and sometimes other hormones) has increased the number of younger women receiving additional hormones. Carefully controlled, long-term observations of "pill" users are necessary to assess increased risks for cancer of the breast, uterus, or ovary. Established tumors in both humans and laboratory animals have shown varying degrees of hormone dependency. For example, removal of the ovaries in some women with advanced breast cancer or removal of the testes in men with prostate cancer often leads to temporary regression of the tumors.
Nutrition.
There is no diet known to prevent cancer in humans. There is some evidence, that vitamin deficiency in humans plays a role in the occurrence of cancers of the mouth and the esophagus. However, such a deficiency is probably only 1 of a number of factors. The consumption of dietary fiber has been associated with reduced risk of colon cancer.
Heredity.
The limited data available suggest increased familial risk of developing cancer of the same site for cancers of the breast (female), stomach, large intestine, endometrium (lining of the uterus), prostate, lung, and possibly ovary. However, it is not known to what extent the tumors that have been observed to run in some families are due to genetic characteristics or to environmental factors such as diet or occupation that may remain the same from one generation to the next. Brain tumors and sarcomas seem to occur more frequently than expected in brothers and sisters of children with these tumors. When an identical twin has childhood leukemia, the probability that the other twin will develop the disease within 1 or 2 years of the date of diagnosis of the first twin is about 1 in 5. In addition, retinoblastoma, a rare form of cancer of the eye, is known to be due to inherited mutation.

Cancer, Tropic of *See:* Tropic of Cancer.

Cancer Society of America, voluntary organization founded in 1913 to provide a program of services for cancer patients and their families. The Cancer Society also directs public education programs and supports research through grants to individuals and institutions.
See also: Cancer.

Candela, or new candle (symbol: cd), basic unit of measurement of luminous intensity, or candle power. It is defined as equal to one sixtieth of the light reflected by one sq cm of a blackbody (a theoretically perfect absorber and emitter of radiation) at the freezing temperature of platinum (1,769° C) and at standard atmospheric pressure.

Candlepower *See:* Candela.

Candy, any of a great variety of sweet confections. Candy can provide quick energy because the body digests sugar, usually its main ingredient, more rapidly than any other food. Chocolate candies are the best selling among all the different types.

Candytuft, any of several species of a genus (*Iberis*) of low-growing, Old World plants of the mustard family. Often cultivated as a rock garden or border plant, candytuft has variously colored blossoms.

Canetti, Elias (1905-94), Bulgarian-born author of prose and plays in the German language. Major works include the novel *Auto da Fé* (1935) and the political study *Crowds and Power* (1960). He received the 1981 Nobel Prize for literature.

Canine *See:* Teeth.

Canis Major, constellation of stars visible in the Southern Hemisphere. It contains the brightest star in the sky, Sirius, (the Dog Star). Canis Major is visible on winter evenings.
See also: Constellation; Sirius.

Canis Minor, constellation appearing north of Canis Major in the Southern Hemisphere. Procyon in Canis Minor is one of the brightest stars in the sky.
See also: Constellation.

Cankerworm, or measuring worm, any of various larvae of insects, especially moths. Cankerworms feed on foliage and can seriously damage fruit and shade trees.

Canna, any of a genus (*Canna*) of tropical plants of the family Cannaceae. Widely cultivated in the United States, canna is bred in hybrid varieties.

Cannabis, tops and leaves of the female plant of Indian hemp (*Cannabis sativa*), from which marijuana, a mood-altering substance, is obtained.
See also: Marijuana.

Cannae, ancient town in southern Italy, site of Hannibal's decisive defeat of the Romans (216 B.C.). The encircling technique he perfected, regarded as a masterpiece of tactics, won him the battle and 10,000 prisoners.
See also: Hannibal; Italy; Punic Wars.

Cannes (pop. 72,300), French resort and seaport on the Mediterranean coast. Its superb climate makes it a center for tourism and festivals, notably the annual International Film Festival.
See also: France.

Cannibalism, consumption by humans of human flesh, common throughout the world at various times in the past and still occasionally practiced, though now generally taboo. Among primitive peoples, the motive appears to have been the belief that eating an enemy or a respected elder transferred that person's strength to the eater.

Canning, process of preserving foods in sealed metal containers, developed by the French chef Nicolas Appert in 1809 and first patented in the United States by Ezra Daggett in 1815. The fragile glass jars originally used were replaced by tin-coated iron cans after 1810. Today a production line process is used.

Cannizzaro, Stanislao (1826-1910), Italian chemist, teacher, and activist in Garibaldi's movement for Italian unification. Cannizzaro found that benzaldehyde treated with a concentrated alcoholic hydroxide produced

equal amounts of benzyl alcohol and the salt of benzoic acid. This became known as the Cannizzaro reaction. In 1858 he differentiated between atomic and molecular weights, a discovery that won him the Copley medal from the Royal Society of London.
See also: Chemistry.

Cannon, large firearm with a barrel, breech, and firing mechanism. First used in warfare around the middle of the 14th century, early cannons were cast of bronze and wrought iron. The term gradually came to refer to any gun that was fired from a carriage or fixed mount and had a bore greater than 1 inch in diameter.

Cannon-ball tree, South American tree (*Couroupita guianensis*) noted for its spherical woody fruit, which resembles a rusty cannon ball. Related to the Brazil-nut tree, the cannon-ball tree sheds its leaves more than once a year.
See also: Brazil nut.

Cano, Juan Sebastián del (1476-1526), Basque sailor who succeeded Ferdinand Magellan as commander of the expedition that completed the first circumnavigation of the globe (1522).
See also: Magellan, Ferdinand.

Canoe, long, narrow, lightweight boat used primarily for fishing and recreational activities on lakes and rivers. Originally canoes were made by hollowing out logs and were used for combat as well as transport. Now they are made from canvas, thin wood, and aluminum. In contrast to kayaks, canoes have an uncovered top.

Canon, form or procedure of contrapuntal musical composition in which one voice or instrument starts to sing or play a theme and other voices or instruments follow at a specified interval of time, all singing or playing the same theme according to the same rule (canon). The composer might specify that later voices enter at different pitches, or even execute the theme upside down or backwards (*cancrizans*, crabwise). In the best-known form of canon, the round, the theme is sung (played) identically by all voices, which enter at regular intervals. This very old musical form originated in the church music of the Middle Ages.

Canonization, process by which a Christian church declares a deceased person to be a saint. In the Roman Catholic Church the process involves a long and careful investigation of the individual's life for sanctity, heroic virtue, and orthodoxy.
See also: Saint.

Canopus, second brightest star in the sky. It lies in the constellation of Carina, the Keel, visible in the Southern Hemisphere. Canopus is used as a guide star for navigating spacecraft.

Canova, Antonio (1757-1822), Italian sculptor, a leading exponent of neoclassicism. His works include *Cupid and Psyche* (1787-92), several statues of his patron Napoleon, and a famous statue of Pauline Bonaparte Borghese as the reclining *Venus Victrix* (1808).

Cantaloupe *See:* Muskmelon.

Cantata (from: Italian *cantare*, "to sing"), musical composition for solo voice or choir, usually with an instrumental accompaniment. One of the earliest composers of cantatas was Giacomo Carissimi, who wrote such works both for entertainment and for the church. Another important composer in this field was Alessandro Scarlatti, some of whose cantatas were almost as elaborate as opera. J.S. Bach wrote hundreds of cantatas as part of his normal duties as a church choirmaster.
See also: Bach, Johann Sebastian.

Canterbury (pop. 34,400), city and county borough of Kent, on the Stour River 55 mi (89 km) southeast of London. It has been England's ecclesiastical capital since A.D. 597. The archbishop of Canterbury is primate of all England.
See also: England.

Canterbury bell, any of several biennial flowering plants with bell-shaped flowers, in particular the *Campanula medium*. Found wild in woods and stony places, the canterbury bell does not flower until the second (and final) summer of its life. The plant may grow to 3 ft (91 cm) and has hairy, oval leaves.

Canterbury Tales, best-known work of English poet Geoffrey Chaucer, written between 1387 and his death in 1400. In 17,000 lines (mostly heroic couplets) it describes a party of 30 pilgrims going to the shrine of St. Thomas à Becket, and their plan to tell 4 tales each on the journey. Only 24 tales were written, 4 of them unfinished, but the work presents a vivid cross section of medieval society and the tales cover most medieval literary genres.
See also: Chaucer, Geoffrey.

Canticle, piece of religious music, similar in character to a psalm, but using a passage from the Bible other than the psalms themselves. Some canticles actually date from biblical times and are therefore very ancient. More recently the word has come to be used for shorter choral works with any kind of religious or semi-religious basis.

Canticles *See:* Song of Solomon.

Canton (pop. 394,106), city in northeastern Ohio, about 60 mi (97 km) southeast of Cleveland; seat of Stark County. An important industrial center, Canton manufactures rubber goods, steel, bearings, electrical appliances, paints, motors, and bricks. Settled in 1805, Canton was the home of President William McKinley, who is commemorated there by the National McKinley Memorial.
See also: Ohio.

Canton, China *See:* Guangzhou.

Canute (995?-1035), king of England, Norway, and Denmark. The younger son of Sweyn of Denmark, Canute invaded England with his father in 1013. He withdrew in 1014, when Sweyn died, but invaded again in 1015 and became king in 1016 on the death of Edmund II. In 1019 he succeeded his brother as king of Denmark, and in 1028 he conquered Norway, ousting Olaf II. Canute is noted in English history for having brought peace and codifying English law. Anglo-Saxon rule was reestablished in England in 1042, when Edward the Confessor became king.

Canvasback (*Aythya valisneria*), diving duck found in coastal and inland waters of North America. About 2 ft (0.6 m) long and 3 lb (1.4 kg) in weight, it feeds on aquatic plants, shrimps, and small fish.

Canyonlands National Park, in eastern Utah, established in 1964. It covers an area of 337,258 acres (136,488 hectares) and contains red rock canyons, stone needles, arches, rapids, and rock carvings.

Canzoniere *See:* Petrarch.

Capacitance, ability of a system to store an electric charge, measured by the charge that must be communicated to a body to raise its potential 1 unit. Electrostatic unit capacitance is that which requires 1 electrostatic unit of charge to raise the potential 1 electrostatic unit. The farad $= 9 \times 10^{11}$ electrostatic units. A capacitance of 1 farad requires 1 coulomb of electricity to raise its potential 1 volt. A conductor charged with a quantity Q to a potential V has a capacitance $C = Q/V$. The capacitance of a spherical conductor of radius r is $C = Kr$. The capacitance of 2 concentric spheres of radii r and r' is $C = K[rr'/(r-r')]$. The capacitance of a parallel plate condenser, the area of whose plates is A and the distance between them d, is $C = KA/4\pi d$. Capacitances are given in electrostatic units if the dimensions of condensers are substituted in cm. K is the dielectric constant of the medium.

Capacitor, or condenser, electrical component used to store electric charge and to provide reactance in alternating current circuits. In essence, a capacitor consists of 2 conducting plates separated by a thin layer of insulator. When the plates are connected to the terminals of a battery, a current flows until the capacitor is "charged," with 1 plate positive and the other negative. The ability of a capacitor to hold charge, its capacitance C, is the ratio of the quantity of electricity on its plates, Q, to the potential difference between the plates, V. The electric energy stored in a capacitor is given by CV^2. The capacitance of a capacitor depends on the area of its plates, their separation, and the dielectric constant of the insulator. Small fixed capacitors are commonly made with metal-foil plates and paraffin-paper insulation; to save space, the plates and paper are rolled up into a tight cylinder. Some small capacitors have a mica dielectric. Variable capacitors used in radio tuners consist of intermeshing metal vanes separated by an air gap. In electrolytic capacitors, the dielectric is an oxide film formed on the plates by the action of a solid electrolyte.

Cape Breton Island, island in northeast Nova Scotia, 110 mi (177 km) long, up to 75 mi (121 km) wide, separated from the Canadian mainland by the Strait of Canso (since 1955 joined by a causeway).
See also: Nova Scotia.

Cape Canaveral, promontory on the eastern coast of Florida, site of the John F. Kennedy Space Center called Cape Kennedy 1963-73. It became famous with the launching of the first U.S. satellite, *Explorer 1*, in 1958, and the first manned lunar exploration in 1969. The cape was established as a national seashore in 1975.
See also: Florida; National Aeronautics and Space Adminstration.

Cape Cod, peninsula in Barnstable County, southeast Massachusetts, surrounded by the Atlantic Ocean and Cape Cod Bay. It is 65 mi (105 km) long and up to 20 mi (32 km) in width. Site of the first Pilgrim landing in 1620, shipping, whaling, fishing, and salt production were early industries. Today the cape is famous for its cranberries and its summer resorts.
See also: Massachusetts.

Cape Cod Canal, sea-level channel cutting through the Cape Cod (Massachusetts) peninsula. The canal was a private commercial project built between 1909 and 1914. In 1928 it was purchased by the U.S. government and since has operated as one of the most heavily used toll-free waterways in the world. The canal, which is 17.5 miles (28 km) long, shortens the shipping route between New York and Boston by more than 75 mi (121 km).
See also: Cape Cod.

Cape Hatteras, promontory lying 30 mi (48 km) off the North Carolina coast and long known as "the graveyard of the Atlantic" because of its rocky shoals.
See also: North Carolina.

Cape Horn, southernmost tip of South America, known for its cold, stormy climate. Part of Chile, the cape's bare headland lies well south of the Strait of Magellan on Horn Island.
See also: Chile.

Capek, Karel (1890-1938), Czech writer whose works, known for their humor and antiauthoritarian stand, include the plays *R.U.R. (Rossum's Universal Robots*, 1920) and *The Insect Play* (1921) and the novel *The War with the Newts* (1936).

Cape Kennedy *See:* Cape Canaveral.

Capella, brightest star of the constellation Auriga, the charioteer. It is a yellow star, about 10 times the diameter of our sun. In midnorthern latitudes Capella appears overhead in winter.
See also: Constellation.

Cape May, oldest beach resort in the United States, on Cape May Peninsula, N.J.
See also: New Jersey.

Cape of Good Hope, rocky promontory near the southern tip of Africa, 30 mi (48 km) south of Cape Town, chief navigational hazard in rounding Africa. It was discovered by Bartholomeu Dias in 1488, who named it Cape

of Storms. Vasco da Gama first sailed around it in 1497 into the Indian Ocean.
See also: South Africa.

Cape Province, former province of South Africa, 278,465 sq mi (721,224
sq km) in area. The capital and chief city is Cape Town. A Dutch colony
from 1652, the cape became British in 1806. Many Dutch settlers (Boers)
migrated north and west to found independent states. Self-governing after
1872, Cape Colony joined the Union of South Africa in 1910. In the early
1990s the province was subdivided into three new provinces.
See also: South Africa.

Caper (genus *Capparis*), prickly Mediterranean shrub cultivated for its tender
aromatic buds, which are pickled for use in sauces such as tartare sauce.

Capet, Hugh *See:* Hugh Capet.

Capetians, ruling house of France (987-1328) that laid the basis for the
French state by consolidating and extending its power. Hugh Capet, founder
of the dynasty, was elected king in 987. Though his rule and territory were
limited, his successors gradually increased their land and control. Under the
Capetian dynasty many basic administration characteristics of the French
monarchy were established, including the parliaments (courts) and the
States-General (national assembly).
See also: Louis ; Philip ; Hugh Capet.

Cape Town (pop. 911,500), legislative capital of South Africa and capital
of WestCape Province. Founded by the Dutch East India Company in 1652,
it has a pleasant climate, excellent beaches, attractive scenery, and the
country's largest harbor. Exports are gold, diamonds, fruits, wines, skins,
wool, mohair, and corn.
See also: South Africa.

Cape Verde (Republic of), independent nation in Africa, lying in the Atlan-
tic Ocean some 400 mi (644 km) west of Senegal. The area is about 1,550

Cape Verde

Capital:	Praia
Area:	1,557 sq mi
	(4,033 sq km)
Population:	400,000
Language:	Portuguese
Government:	Republic
Independent:	1975
Head of gov.:	Prime minister
Per capita:	U.S. $960
Mon. unit:	1 Escudo = 100
	centavos

sq mi (4,015 sq km). Cape Verde consists of 10 islands and 5 islets, forming a horseshoe. The islands are volcanic—only about 10% of the land is cultivable. The climate is tropical, with a rainy season, although recently there has been cyclical drought. Over half of the population is of Portuguese and African extraction. Living standards and the rate of literacy are low. Despite a paucity of fertile land, the country is primarily agricultural. However, most food must be imported. The fishing industry provides the major source of exports. Canned fish, salt, bananas, and frozen fish are the primary exports, most going to Portugal. The Portuguese discovered the island in the 15th century. Cape Verde became a supply station for ships and a transit point during the Atlantic slave trade. Blacks from Guinea were taken to the islands to work on Portuguese plantations. Portugal ruled the islands until 1975, when they became independent. Since the 1991 elections, the Movimento para Democrazia (MpD) is in power.

Cape York, point of land on the northwest coast of Greenland. Well north of the Arctic Circle and extending into Baffin Bay, it was used as a base by Admiral Robert E. Peary in his North Pole explorations.
See also: Greenland.

Cap-Haitien (pop. 70,500), seaport on the north coast of Haiti and the country's second largest city. Under French rule it was the capital of the colony ("the Paris of the Antilles"). Today it has less than 10% of the population of Port-au-Prince, the capital.
See also: Haiti, Republic of.

Capillarity, or capillary action, rise or fall of a liquid within a narrow tube (less than 0.02 m/0.5 mm in diameter) when one end is placed beneath the surface of a liquid, caused by its surface tension, which is due to the forces of attraction between the molecules of the liquid. Where, in the case of adhesion, these forces are weaker than the attraction of the molecules for the walls of the tube (as with water surrounded by a glass tube), a concave meniscus is formed (that is, the water level is higher wherever the water touches the tube). Surface tension pulls the rest of the surface upwards, and the level rises until the weight of the column balances the surface tension. In the case of cohesion, with a liquid like mercury, where the molecules of the liquid are more strongly attracted to each other than to the walls of the vessel, the reverse takes place and the level falls. Plants obtain food and water from the soil by capillary action, and it also helps the flow of sap up the stem. Blotting paper, towels, and sponges soak up moisture by capillarity.

Capillary, minute blood vessel that connects the arteries and veins. In general, the capillaries comprise fine tubes, approximately 0.004 in (0.1 mm) in diameter, the same order of size as the red blood corpuscles. The capillary walls are one cell thick and arranged in a network throughout every tissue of the body. Here, the primary functions of the circulation—the exchange of gases, nutrients, metabolites, and heat—take place.
See also: Circulatory system.

Capital, in economics, those goods that are used in production, such as plant and equipment (fixed capital) and raw materials, components, and semifin-ished goods (circulating capital), as opposed to goods intended for immediate consumption. To classical economists, 3 main factors of production were capital, labor, and land. Modern economists add management skill and human capital (education and training). The decision to invest in capital is determined by the cost and availability of labor and natural resources and the cost of capital (e.g., interest on the money used to buy equipment). Modern industrial countries are highly capitalized, but among the less developed countries the lack of capital is often acute.

Capitalism, economic system in which goods and services are provided by the efforts of private individuals and groups (firms) who own and control the means of production, compete with one another, and aim to make a profit. The concept has several overlapping senses, but the idea of private ownership of the means of production and their employment in the search of profit are common to all of them. Capitalism is usually regarded as having developed through a number of stages, beginning with *commercial capitalism*, under which large merchants came to dominate trade. This was succeeded by *industrial capitalism*, dominated by the owners of factories and mines, and then by *finance capitalism*, in which control passed into the hands of bankers and financiers, who exerted indirect control over industries they did not manage in person. Reference is sometimes made to a fourth form—*state capitalism*—defined by Lenin as a system under which the State owns and uses the means of production in the interests of the class that controls the State. A fifth term, *welfare capitalism*, is used to describe capitalist economies in which there is an increased element of state intervention, either by welfare programs or by taking responsibility for maintaining full employment.
Socialists criticize the system on the grounds that in practice it produces luxuries for the rich rather than necessities for all. Capitalism is defended by the argument that an economic system based on private ownership and investment, if left to operate with a minimum of state interference, will be the most efficient method of raising production, distributing scarce resources rationally, and balancing supply with demand.

Capital punishment (from Latin *caput*, "head"), originally, death by decapitation; now, execution in general. Historically, there has been a wide variety of death penalties, but in the United States electrocution is the most common, followed by lethal gas and hanging. It has long been debated whether capital punishment deters serious crime or is only a form of revenge. Its use has been declining recently as belief in rehabilitation has grown. In most civilized countries, capital punishment has been discontinued. But those who believe that capital punishment is necessary as a deterrent see their argument supported by recent statistics showing that violent crime has been increasing. In the U.S. it is the state government that determines the use of capital punishment.

Capitol, U.S., building in Washington, D.C. that houses the Congress of the United States. The U.S. Senate occupies the north wing of the Capitol, and the U.S. House of Representatives the south.
The Capitol is a brilliant white structure in the classical style. It occupies about 3 1/2 acres of high ground known as Capitol Hill (a term also used for Congress) in the center of Washington. The most striking feature of the building is its great white-painted iron dome, 288 ft (88 m) high and 135 1/2

ft (41 m) in diameter, with a statue representing freedom on the top. William Thornton designed the Capitol in 1792 and construction began in 1793 when President George Washington laid the cornerstone. Disagreements and war repeatedly delayed completion until 1906, when the wings were finished. In the late 1950s, the central portico of the east façade was extended, adding 2 more acres of floor space.

Capitol Hill *See:* Washington, D.C.

Capone, Al (1899-1947), U.S. gangster. He became head of a lucrative Chicago crime syndicate in the 1920s, and was involved in many gang murders, including the St. Valentine's Day Massacre. Because of the difficulty in securing evidence against him, he was eventually convicted only of income-tax evasion (1931).

Capote, Truman (1924-1984), U.S. writer. His best-known works are *Breakfast at Tiffany's* (1958) and *In Cold Blood* (1965). His earlier works include *Other Voices, Other Rooms* (1948) and *The Grass Harp* (1951). He was also coauthor of the motion picture *Beat the Devil*, cowrote the screenplay for *The Innocents*, and adapted some of his stories for television.

Capp, Al (1909-79), U.S. cartoonist, creator of the comic strip "Li'l Abner." The *New York Mirror* first published this famous comic about the residents of "Dogpatch U.S.A." in 1934. The characters entertained readers and allowed Capp to develop social commentary on the current events and celebrities of his time.

Capra, Frank (1897-91), U.S. film director and 3-time Academy Award winner. With a gift for gentle satire and comic improvisation, he directed *Mr. Deeds Goes to Town* (1936), *Lost Horizon* (1937), *You Can't Take It with You* (1938) and *It's a Wonderful Life* (1946).

Capri (pop. 7,500), Italian island resort in the Bay of Naples, site of the Villa Iovis of Roman Emperor Tiberius. Capri produces olive oil and wine, but its main industry is tourism. Anacapri, at the island's western end, is approachable from the sea by hundreds of steps, called the "Phoenician Stairs." *See also:* Italy.

Capricorn, Tropic of *See:* Tropic of Capricorn.

Capsicum, genus of the nightshade family, cultivated in warm climates for its fruit (pepper); also, pod of the cayenne pepper plant, which, when dried and prepared, is used in medicine as an irritant and a stimulant.

Captain Kidd *See:* Kidd, William.

Capuchin (*Cebus capucinus*), small tree-dwelling monkey with a long, prehensile tail. Native to South America, capuchins are popular as pets in North America and Europe because of their great intelligence. They are the traditional organ-grinder's monkey. Capuchins live in troops and feed on fruit, shoots, and small animals.

Capuchins, Roman Catholic order of friars and an independent branch of the Franciscans. Founded (1525) by Matteo di Basico, a Franciscan who sought a return to the simplicity of St. Francis's life, the order is distinguished by the pointed hood, or *capuccino*.
See also: Franciscans.

Capybara (*Hydrochoerus capybara*), world's largest rodent. It looks like a large guinea pig, weighing up to 120 lb (54 kg) and standing 21 in (53 cm) at the shoulder. The fur is coarse and grey-brown. Capybaras are found in wet areas of northern South America where they live a largely aquatic life, swimming with only their high-set nose, eyes, and ears showing.

Car *See:* Automobile; Railroad.

Caracal, or desert lynx (*Felis caracal*), medium-sized cat of Africa and southern Asia that is distinguished by a fawn coat, long legs, and long black ear tufts. It lives in grassland, bush, or rocky country and feeds on small animals.

Caracara, any of a variety of long-legged South American hawks with long narrow wings, related to the falcon. The patch of bare skin at the base of the bill, a characteristic shared with vultures, is an adaptation for carrion-eating, but caracaras also hunt for live prey and will eat fruit. They rob other birds of their food, and the red-throated caracara raids wasps' nests. The Guadeloupe caracara was exterminated before 1911.

Caracas (pop. 3,435,800), Venezuelan capital, near the Caribbean Sea at an altitude of 3,020 ft (920 m). Founded in 1567 by Diego de Losada, it was the birthplace of Simón Bolívar (1783). Independence from Spain was achieved in 1821, as part of the Republic of Gran Colombia. In 1829 Caracas became the capital of independent Venezuela. After World War II and the discovery of oil in Maracaibo, Caracas greatly expanded. Industries include textiles, cement, steel products, paper, leatherwork, and furniture.
See also: Venezuela.

Caramanlis, Constantine (1907-98), Greek premier (1955-63, 1974-80) and president (1980-85, 1990-95). Following a dispute with then King Paul, he resigned as premier and went into exile in Paris (1963). He returned 11 years later when the military junta ruling Greece fell because of the Cyprus crisis. He helped restore constitutional government and his party, New Democracy, won a big victory in 1975. The republican form of government he advocated was also approved, and in 1980 he was elected president.
See also: Greece.

Carat, measure of the weight of gems and pearls or of the purity of precious metals. The name comes from the dried seeds of the carob tree, which were used to weigh gold in Africa and diamonds in India. The value of the carat varied from 190 mg to almost 210 mg until 1913, when a standard carat of 200 mg was adopted. As a measure of purity, 1 carat represents 1 part in 24 of the precious metal. Thus 22-carat gold contains 22 parts of gold and 2 of other metal.

Caravaggio, Michelangelo Merisi da (1573-1610), Italian Baroque painter who achieved startling and dramatic effects with a technique of shadow and light called *chiaroscuro*. Among his finest works are the *Death of the Virgin*, the *Fortune Teller*, and *Supper at Emmaus*. *See also:* Baroque.

Caraway (*Carum carvi*), biennial or perennial plant of the carrot family, the seed of which is used for flavoring medicinal purposes. The hollow, furrowed, angular, branched stem grows in the second year from a white, carrot-shaped root. The leaves are deeply incised, the small white or yellow flowers form a flat, round cluster, and the fruit is dark brown, oblong, flattened, and 2-seeded.

Caraway, Hattie Ophelia Wyatt (1878-1950), first woman elected to the U.S. Senate. Although Caraway was appointed by the governor of Arkansas to take her husband's place in the Senate when he died in 1931, she won a special election in 1932. She served 14 years in the Senate and was the first woman to head a Senate committee and to preside over a Senate session.

Carbide, any chemical compound of carbon and a metal. Calcium carbide is one of the important ones, a source of acetylene, while carbides of silicon, tungsten, and other elements are known for being hard, strong, and resistant to high temperatures. *See also:* Calcium carbide.

Carbine, short, lightweight rifle most useful to soldiers fighting from tanks and other cramped spaces. It fires ammunition heavier than a pistol's but lighter than the larger assault rifles.

Carbohydrate, any of a group of chemical compounds—including sugars, starches, and cellulose—containing carbon, hydrogen, and oxygen only, with the ratio of hydrogen to oxygen atoms usually 2:1. Carbohydrates provide the chief source of energy in most diets; about 50% of the total calories in the diet of a prosperous industrial community come from carbohydrates. In a poor agricultural community, living largely on cereals, the proportion is higher and may be as much as 85%. The chief dietary carbohydrate is starch, which is present in all cereal grains, roots, and tubers.

Carbolic acid, or phenol (C_6H_5OH), first chemical to be used as an antiseptic. Though poisonous and corrosive to the skin, in dilute form it is lethal to microorganisms, without many undesirable side effects on the patient. *See also:* Antiseptic.

Carbon, chemical element, symbol C; for physical constants see Periodic Table. Carbon is nonmetallic and was discovered in ancient times. It occurs in 3 allotropic forms: amorphous (as in coal or charcoal), graphite, and diamond. All living things contain carbon, which forms more compounds than any other element. Organic chemistry, the study of carbon compounds, is therefore a major field in biology and medicine.

Carbon 14 *See:* Radiocarbon.

125 *Carboniferous*

Carbonate, salt of carbonic acid that contains the carbonate ion $CO_3=$. They are produced by reacting a base, such as metal oxide or hydroxide, with carbonic acid, which is formed by dissolving carbon dioxide in water. Calcium carbonate is very abundant in nature, occurring as limestone, chalk, and marble. The mineral dolomite is a mixture of calcium and magnesium carbonates. Commercially, the most important carbonate is sodium carbonate, also called soda ash and washing soda. Carbonates are decomposed by acids, carbon dioxide being given off. Heating carbonates also drives off carbon dioxide, leaving the metal oxide.

Carbon bisulfide *See:* Carbon disulfide.

Carbon black *See:* Carbon.

Carbon dating *See:* Radiocarbon.

Carbon dioxide (CO_2), colorless, odorless, incombustible gas, consisting of 1 carbon atom and 2 oxygen atoms. Carbon dioxide is formed during respiration (as a waste product of the body), combustion, and organic decomposition. The air we breathe is 0.03% carbon dioxide. It is used by plants during photosynthesis.
See also: Photosynthesis.

Carbon disulfide (CS_2), clear, inflammable liquid chemical compound, composed of 1 carbon atom and 2 sulfur atoms, used in the manufacture of viscose rayon and cellophane, as a solvent for fats, rubber, resins, waxes, and sulfur, and in matches, fumigants, and pesticides. It is a typical toxic industrial chemical. The principal route of exposure in humans is by inhalation; skin contact is much less significant, and other routes are of negligible importance. Carbon disulfide is distributed in an organism through the bloodstream. Readily soluble in fats and lipids and binding to amino acids and proteins, it disappears rapidly from the bloodstream and has a high affinity for all tissues and organs. Hyperactive poisoning caused by massive short-term exposure to high concentrations of carbon disulfide is characterized by sudden coma and eventual death. Cases of poisoning due to relatively short exposures to concentrations of 3,000-5,000 mg per cubic meter are predominantly associated with psychiatric and neurological symptoms: (1) extreme irritability, (2) uncontrolled anger, (3) rapid mood changes, (4) hallucinations, (5) paranoia and suicidal tendencies, and (6) manic delirium. Other symptoms include: (1) memory defects, (2) severe insomnia, (3) nightmares, (4) fatigue, (5) loss of appetite, and (6) gastrointestinal problems. Exposure over many years may produce chronic damage to the brain at first associated with psychological and behavioral changes, later with neurological changes, both in the brain and peripheral nerves. Changes in the blood vessels due to exposure are similar to those of atherosclerosis and mainly affect the arteries supplying the brain and heart muscle. Incidence of coronary heart disease is disproportionately high in exposed workers.
See also: Sulfide.

Carboniferous, collective term used mainly in Europe for the combined Mississippian and Pennsylvanian periods of the geological time scale, 345-280 million years ago.

Carbon monoxide (CO), colorless, odorless, very poisonous gas that burns with a pale blue flame and is a component of coal gas, exhaust fumes, and most smoke (including cigarette smoke). Inhalation of carbon monoxide causes dizziness, headache, and convulsions, and can lead to brain damage, paralysis, and death.

Carbon tetrachloride (CCI_4), colorless liquid with a distinctive smell, used mainly as a solvent. It dissolves fats and oils, and can be used as a dry-cleaning fluid. Widely used in industry to dissolve resins, rubber, and many other organic chemicals, it must be handled carefully. It is not inflammable, but forms highly poisonous substances when heated in a flame. Breathing the fumes over a long period can itself cause kidney and liver damage, so carbon tetrachloride should be used only in well-ventilated places. Carbon tetrachloride is manufactured by passing chlorine gas over red-hot coke.

Carborundum, commercial name for silicon carbide (SiC), widely used abrasive and one of the hardest substances known. Carborundum has a very high melting point (about 4,892F/2,700C) and is used in the manufacture of heat-resistant materials. It conducts electricity and is used in electronic equipment. Carborundum is found in a variety of colors, ranging from blue-black to green, all with a lustrous sheen. A very pure colorless form also exists. Carborundum is widely found over the earth's surface and has also been found in meteorites that have landed on earth. It was first synthesized in 1891 by the American chemist Edward Acheson, who heated coke and clay in a furnace at very high temperatures.

Carbuncle, infection under the full thickness of the skin caused by the pus-forming germ *Staphylococcus*. It produces a large infected area from which the pus escapes by making numerous openings for itself through the skin, producing a sieve-like appearance.

Carburetor, device that mixes air and gasoline in the correct proportion for efficient combustion (about 15:1 by weight) in internal combustion engines (as in automobiles). In its simplest form a carburetor is a tube that is constructed at one point into a narrow throat or venturi. As air flows through the venturi, it speeds up and its pressure decreases. Gasoline from a reservoir (the float chamber) is piped to the venturi and sucked into the airstream. The fuel mixture then passes through a "butterfly" throttle valve into the engine cylinders. The throttle valve controls the rate at which the fuel mixture enters the engine and therefore the engine speed. A butterfly choke valve is fitted in the air intake to the carburetor to cut off the air supply when the engine is started from cold.
See also: Gasoline engine.

Carcassonne (pop. 41,200), city in southern France, southeast of Toulouse. Carcassonne is divided by the Aude River into the old town (Cité) and the newer Ville Basse. The old town is a medieval walled city whose architecture has made Carcassonne a tourist attraction.
See also: France.

Carcinogen *See:* Cancer.

Carcinoma, malignant tumor or new growth (neoplasm) derived from epithelial and glandular tissues, a form of cancer.
See also: Cancer.

Cardamom (*Elettaria cardamomum*), perennial plant the seed of which is used as a spice and for medicinal purposes. The simple erect stem of the plant grows to a height of 6-10 ft (1.8-3 m) from a thumbthick, creeping rootstock. The leaves are lanceolate (spear-shaped) and dark green. The small, yellowish flowers grow in loose groups on prostrate flower stems. The fruit is a 3-celled capsule holding up to 18 seeds. These are useful in controlling flatulence, but they are usually used to increase the efficacy of other remedies.

Cárdenas, Lázaro (1895-1970), Mexican soldier and politician. He joined the Mexican revolutionary forces in 1913, rising to the rank of general. President from 1934 to 1940, he initiated many radical reforms, including the expropriation of land and nationalization of foreign-owned oil companies.
See also: Mexico.

Card games, games played with rectangular cards marked with number (rank) and symbol (suit). Playing cards probably developed from small stones, scratched with various symbols, used in early cultures for religious ceremonies and magical purposes. These pebbles were eventually used for competitive games, often involving gambling. Cards were used in China in the 10th century A.D. By about the 13th century they had been introduced in Europe by travelers and gypsies from the East. Early cards varied greatly in design. The 14th century Italian tarocchi or tarot deck had 78 cards that included 22 picture cards bearing mainly religious illustrations, and 4 suits each of 14 plain cards. Today, many different decks exist, but the most popular contains 52 cards divided into 4 suits. First used in 14th-century Europe, this 52-deck was introduced to Britain, modified, and eventually popularized by the invention of games requiring such a deck. As games became more sophisticated, it became desirable to have written rules. The English writer Edmond Hoyle (1672-1769) produced a rule book giving details of many games.

Cardiac *See:* Heart.

Cardiff (pop. 295,600), city and seaport near the mouth of the Taff River in southern Wales. The town was established in the 11th century around a Norman castle. Development was gradual until the discovery of coal in the valleys to the north made Cardiff a natural outlet for the export of coal, iron, and steel. Shipping of coal, coke, and steel is still the major industry; there are massive iron and steel works, and copper and tin are also produced. Flour milling and manufacture of chemicals and paper are valuable secondary industries. The city is the administrative center for Wales, and has important educational and cultural institutions including the National Museum of Wales.
See also: Wales.

Cardigan Welsh corgi, breed of dog first raised in Wales. The name derives from the Welsh words for "dwarf dog". The Cardigan Welsh corgi stands about 12 in (30 cm) high. Used for centuries to herd sheep, the corgi makes an affectionate and spirited pet.

Cardinal, or redbird (*Cardinalis cardinalis*), familiar songbird of the finch family, found in North America. It is about 9 in (23 cm) long, with a pointed crest and red beak. The male is scarlet with a black bib and face; the female is a dull brown.
See also: Roman Catholic Church.

Cardinal, hierarchically high-ranking official of the Roman Catholic Church, whose principal duties include the election of the pope, counseling the papacy, and administrating Church government. Cardinals are chosen by the pope and have the title of Eminence. Their insignia consists of scarlet cassock, sash, biretta (skullcap) and hat, and ring. There are three orders: cardinal bishops of the sees near Rome; cardinal priests (cardinal archbishops) with responsibilities outside the district of Rome; and cardinal deacons, who have been titular bishops since 1962. Cardinal bishops and cardinal deacons are members of the Curia, the central administrative body of the Church. They head the tribunals, or the courts of the Church. Together, the cardinals form the Sacred College, which elects the pope. The cardinalate originated in early 6th-century Rome.

Cardinal flower, tall plant (*Lobelia cardinalis*) native to North and Central America. Cardinal flowers thrive in wet soil. Their leafy stems grow up to 5 ft (1.5 m) and bear spikes of bright red flowers.

Cardiology, science of the heart, including the study of its diseases and functions.
See also: Heart.

Cardiopulmonary resuscitation (CPR), restoration of hearbeat and breathing by external cardiac massage and mouth-to-mouth breathing.
See also: First aid.

Cardozo, Benjamin Nathan (1870-1938), U.S. jurist and Supreme Court justice (1932-38) after an impressive career at the bar and in the New York courts. His many significant decisions reflect his view that the courts should not merely interpret the law but help create it, particularly in adapting it to changing social conditions.
See also: Supreme Court of the United States.

Cards *See:* Card games.

Carducci, Glosuè (1835-1907), Italian scholar and patriotic poet. His *Hymn to Satan* (1863) is an anticlerical political satire; the *Barbarian Odes* (1877-89) are perhaps his best work. He won the 1906 Nobel Prize for literature.

CARE (Cooperative for American Relief to Everywhere, Inc.), charity founded in 1945, initially for aid to Europe but now operating worldwide. MEDICO (Medical International Cooperation Organization), a medical relief agency, became part of CARE in 1962.

Caribbean Sea, warm oceanic basin off Central America, partly enclosed by islands. The waters of the Caribbean flow into the Gulf of Mexico and thence into the Atlantic Ocean through the narrow strait of Florida. They create the warm current known as the Gulf Stream, which reaches Europe. The lands bordering the Caribbean have a warm and humid climate, with almost continuously high temperatures. The Caribbean was the route taken by the Spanish treasure ships, and became known as the "Spanish Main." It was an area overrun with buccaneers and fiercely disputed by France, England, Spain, and later the United States. At the end of the 19th century U.S. control over the Caribbean area was officially recognized. The building of the Panama Canal increased the importance of this "Mediterranean of the West."

Caribou (*Rangifer tarandus*), the only member of the deer family (Cervidae) in which both sexes bear antlers. They were at one time essential food animals for Native Americans of Canada. They live wild in Canada and Siberia, while the semi-domesticated reindeer, a subspecies, live in Greenland and Scandinavia. They can travel over boggy or snow-covered ground and live on lichen, dry grass, and twigs.

Caribs, Native American tribe encountered by the Spanish conquerors of America in the 16th century. They inhabited the islands of the Lesser Antilles in the Caribbean (which was named after them) and parts of the South American mainland, notably the Guianas. The Caribs grew a variety of crops and hunted with clubs, spears, bows, and blowguns. They were strongly independent and formed no political bonds between their own groups. Their raids on other tribes—including the more peaceful Arawaks—whom they dispossessed of their land, were made in large dugout canoes, and their conquests were celebrated by killing and eating the male captives. After Spanish settlement of the Antilles in 1527, most Caribs were exterminated except for some on the island of Aruba.

Caricature, sketch exaggerating or distorting characteristics of its subject for satirical purposes. It became an established form by the 18th century, in the hands of Francisco de Goya in Spain and William Hogarth in England, followed by Thomas Rowlandson, the Cruikshanks, and John Tenniel, and the savagely witty Honoré Daumier in France. Today, artists such as David Levine and Albert Hirschfeld continue the tradition in the United States.

Carillon, musical instrument, usually permanently set in a bell-tower, consisting of a series of bells on which melodies and simple harmonies are played from a keyboard and pedal console much like that of an organ. Some carillons are played automatically by a pegged rotating drum that operates the bell clappers or hammers. Modern instruments are electrically operated, and some do not have cast bells, but are completely electronic. Carillons originated in the Low Countries, and the old cities of Belgium and Holland have many notable examples, the oldest being the 24-bell carillon (1554) at the Rijksmuseum, Amsterdam.

Carleton, Sir Guy, 1st Baron Dorchester (1724-1808), English soldier and governor. He was responsible for the Quebec Act of 1774, which guaranteed the French the right to speak French and to practice Roman

Catholicism. During the American Revolution, he led the defense of Quebec (1775) against Benedict Arnold and later captured Crown Point, N.Y. (1776). In 1782-83 he was commander-in-chief of the British army in North America; he was governor of Quebec (1786-91, 1793-96) and governor-general of Canada (1793).
See also: Quebec Act.

Carl Gustaf (1946-), king of Sweden (Charles XV Gustavus) from 1973. Carl Gustaf's father died when his son was less than a year old, and Carl Gustaf therefore succeeded his grandfather, Gustavus VI (Gustaf Adolf).
See also: Sweden.

Carlos, Juan *See:* Juan Carlos I.

Carlota, Empress *See:* Maximilian.

Carlsbad Caverns National Park, national park in southeastern New Mexico. Its major site is a series of limestone caves about 60 million years old, among the largest caverns in the world. The caverns have spectacular stalagmite formations. The Big Room is a single chamber 1,800 ft (550 m) long, 1,100 ft (335 m) wide, and   225 ft (78 m) at its highest point. Several million bats still inhabit the caverns, which were designated a national park in 1930.

Carlyle, Thomas (1795-1881), Scottish essayist and historian. His writings greatly influenced literature and political and religious thought in mid-19th-century Britain. Carlyle was much influenced by Johann Wolfgang von Goethe, whose *Wilhelm Meister* he translated (1824). In 1826 he married Jane Welsh, who greatly helped his literary career. At her farm near Dumfries he wrote *Sartor Resartus* (The Tailor Retailored, 1833-34). Moving to London (1834), he wrote his famous *French Revolution* (1837), which won him immediate recognition. Carlyle believed that progress was due to "heroes" in history. He scorned the idea of democratic equality, exaggerated the importance of individual great men (*On Heroes, Hero-Worship and the Heroic in History*, 1841), and failed to realize the dangers inherent in hero-worship. His capacity for throwing new light on familiar subjects was shown by *Cromwell's Letters and Speeches* (1845), which many regard as his historical masterpiece, and *Frederick the Great* (1858-65), his largest work.

Carman, (William) Bliss (1861-1929), Canadian poet and essayist. His work includes *Low Tide on Grand Pré* (1893) and *Songs from Vagabondia* (1894, 1896, 1901), volumes of love and nature poems.
See also: Transcendentalism.

Carmel-by-the-Sea, or Carmel (pop. 4,239), town in California situated on Carmel Bay south of Monterey. Long an art and literature center that has attempted to maintain its quiet charm free from modern encroachments, Carmel is especially well known as the home of such artists as Henry Miller, James D. Nash, and Joan Baez.
See also: California.

Carmelites, friars of Our Lady of Mount Carmel, a religious order of the Roman Catholic Church. It is named for Mount Carmel, in Israel, where it originated about 1150. The Carmelites' strict rule was based on silence and solitude, but it was slightly relaxed by the English prior, Saint Simon Stock. The order's typical clothing consists of a brown habit and scapular, with a white mantle and black hood.
See also: Roman Catholic Church.

Carmichael, Hoagy (Hoagland Howard Carmichael; 1899-1981), U.S. songwriter. His 1929 ballad "Star Dust" became a popular classic. Other compositions include "Georgia on My Mind" (1930), "Lazybones" (1933), and "The Nearness of You" (1940). He appeared as a pianist in several films including *To Have and Have Not* (1944), and his song "In the Cool, Cool, Cool of the Evening" won an Academy Award in 1951.

Carmichael, Stokely (1941-), U.S. Black Power leader. Prominent in the civil rights movement in the 1960s, he then advocated violent revolution and spent some time in exile in Algeria. He later argued for the use of political and economic power to attain African American demands.

Carnap, Rudolf (1891-1970), German-U.S. logician and philosopher of science, a leading figure in the Vienna Circle and founder of logical positivism, who later turned to studying problems of linguistic philosophy and the role of probability in inductive reasoning.
See also: Positivism.

Carnarvon, George Edward Stanhope Molyneux Herbert, 5th Earl of (1866-1923), English Egyptologist. His excavations with Howard Carter in the Valley of Kings area revealed tombs of the 12th and 18th dynasties and, in Nov. 1922, the tomb of Tutankhamen.
See also: Tutankhamen.

Carnation, flower popular for buttonholes and in horticulture, subspecies of pink (*Dianthus caryophyllus*). Each carnation has a cluster of flowers, which are pink in the wild state. They have been cultivated since the time of ancient Greece, and their cultivation has become such a popular pastime that the American Carnation Society was established in 1891.

Carneades (213?-129? B.C.), Greek philosopher who rejected the notion of an absolute standard of truth. He founded and led the New Academy at Athens, and although he left no writings, his teachings were preserved by the philosopher Cleitomachus.
See also: Philosophy.

Carnegie, Andrew (1835-1919), U.S. steel magnate and philanthropist. A Scottish emigrant, Carnegie rose from bobbin-boy in a cotton factory to railroad manager and then steel producer at a time of great demand. He believed that the duty of the rich is to distribute their surplus wealth, and in 1900 he began to set up a vast number of charitable foundations and educational institutions.

Carnegie, Dale (1888-1955), U.S. author and lecturer whose *How to Win Friends and Influence People* (1936) became the best-selling nonfiction work of modern times, second only to the Bible. He offered courses in effective speaking and human relations in more than 750 U.S. cities and 15 foreign countries.

Carnegie Foundations, philanthropic organizations established by Andrew Carnegie to advance education, research, and world peace. The Carnegie Institution of Washington, D.C., supports research in physical and biological sciences. The Carnegie Foundation for the Advancement of Teaching works to improve higher education, and the Carnegie Corporation of New York endows projects in preschool education and education for the disadvantaged. The Carnegie Endowment for International Peace promotes peace through studies of international law and diplomacy. These and other organizations set a pattern for other major institutions, such as the Ford and Rockefeller foundations.
See also: Carnegie, Andrew.

Carnelian, or cornelian, one of the chalcedony group of crystalline quartz forms. Carnelian is typically red, but is sometimes yellow or brown, the latter kind being the most precious and known as sard. Used in jewelry, the stones are often artificially colored by heating and dyeing with iron compounds.
See also: Chalcedony.

Carnival, term for any festive season with processions and masquerades, and particularly for the period preceding Lent. Historically, carnival can be traced back at least to the Dionysian festivals of Athens in the 6th century B.C., when a float dedicated to the god was escorted through the city, and to the Saturnalia of ancient Rome. The word *carnival* may have been derived from the Latin *carnem levare* (to put meat aside), a reference to Lenten abstinence. The Christian Church, unable to suppress the traditional pagan festivals, had to adapt and recognize them. Italy, Rome, Venice, and Florence have long been famed for their carnivals. Rio de Janeiro in Brazil, Nice in France, and Cologne in Germany are still noted carnival centers. The festivities traditionally reach their climax on the last night, Mardi Gras (Shrove Tuesday).

Carnivore, order of flesh-eating mammals with daggerlike canine teeth, cutting cheek teeth, and sharp claws. Bears, dogs, cats, hyenas, foxes, and racoons are land carnivores; seals, sea lions, and walruses are fin-footed aquatic carnivores.

Carnivorous plant, or insectivorous plant, term used for plants that have mechanisms for trapping and digesting insects. Over 500 known species of these plants are divided into 6 unrelated families. The diverse group ranges in size from microscopic fungi to the large Pitcher Fungi.

Carnot, Lazare Nicolas Marguerite(1753-1823), French soldier and politician, "Organizer of Victory" for the Revolutionary armies. He later served as minister of war under Napoleon I, resigning in 1800.

Carnot, Nicolas Léonard Sadi (1796-1832), French physicist. Seeking to improve the efficiency of the steam engine, he devised the Carnot cycle (1824), on the basis of which Lord Kelvin and R. J. E. Clausius formulated the second law of thermodynamics. The Carnot cycle demonstrates that the efficiency of a heat engine working at maximum thermal efficiency does not depend on its mode of operation, but only on the temperatures at which it accepts and discards heat energy.
See also: Physics.

Carnotite, yellow mineral found in sandstone and limestone deposits in the Colorado Plateau. Carnotite is a valuable source of radium, uranium, and vanadium.

Caro, Joseph ben Ephraim (1488-1575), Jewish Talmudist and philosopher whose codification of Jewish law, the *Shulhan Arukh* (1565), became the standard authority. Caro's family were Spanish Jews who settled in Constantinople; in later life he became a leader of the Jewish community in Palestine.
See also: Philosophy; Talmud.

Carob, evergreen tree (*Ceratonia siliqua*) native to the Mediterranean but also cultivated elsewhere. The carob, a member of the pea family, has pods that contain a sticky pulp that tastes similar to chocolate. Roasted and ground, it can be used as a chocolate substitute. Untreated carob pods are used as feed for cattle and horses.

Carol, name of 2 kings of Romania. **Carol I** (1839-1914), Romania's first king, brought economic development but no solution to political problems. **Carol II** (1893-1953) became king in 1930. He established a royal dictatorship to counter the growing Fascist movement, but after losing territory to the Axis powers in World War II, he abdicated in 1940 and went into exile.
See also: Romania.

Carol, cheerful song sung at Christmas, but once also performed (as a dance song) at other festive seasons. Some carols have pagan origins, and some of the older carols such as "The Holly and the Ivy" (c.1710) have a folklore element. Certain 19th-century Christmas hymns now rank as carols. Among the oldest is the "Boar's Head Carol," in the collection printed by Wynkyn de Worde (1521). The German *Weihnachtslieder* (Christmas Eve Songs) and French *Noëls* have also provided carols.

Caroline Islands, volcanic islands in the Pacific Ocean, administered as a trust territory by the United States. The 900 islands are inhabited mainly by Malays, with some Japanese, Chinese, and Americans. The Spanish claimed the islands in 1696 and in 1899 sold them to Germany. After World War I they became a Japanese mandate and were invaded by U.S. troops in World War II.

Carolingian, Frankish dynasty founded in the 7th century by Pepin of Landen, whose successors ruled as mayors under the Merovingians until A.D. 751, when Pepin III made himself king. His son Charlemagne, crowned emperor in 800, reigned in the golden age of the Carolingians.

His son Louis (814-840) and the Treaty of Verdun (843) partitioned the empire.
See also: Charlemagne; Pepin the Short.

Carolingian art, style created in France and western Germany in the late 8th and 9th centuries. The style, named for Charlemagne, who was crowned emperor of the restored Holy Roman Empire in 800, was an attempt to revive the arts of antiquity. Instead of the abstract geometric patterns and mythical animals used by artists of this region in the preceding centuries, Carolingian artists reintroduced the human figure in natural settings. Carolingian church architecture adopted the basilican plan of the early Christian era, adding towers, chapels, and crypts. Abbots built monasteries in which the church and living and working quarters were joined by covered walks. Artists also worked in metal, manuscript illumination, and ivory carving, combining the ornamental motifs of Anglo-Saxon and Irish art with figures from antiquity. Among the era's most important works still in existence are Charlemagne's chapel in Aachen, West Germany, built in 805, and the Utrecht Psalter, a religious manuscript written in France about 830.
See also: Charlemagne.

Carp (*Cyprinus carpio*), freshwater, bottom-feeding fish native to Asia but now found in Europe and America. It grows up to 3 1/3 ft (1 m) and 60 lb (27 kg) in weight and has a long dorsal fin and 4 barbels (whiskers) around the mouth.

Carpaccio, Vittore (c.1460-1526), Venetian Renaissance narrative painter, influenced by Gentile Bellini. A major work is the cycle of 9 paintings of the *Legend of St. Ursula* (1490-95), typical in its atmospheric use of color and meticulous detail to create fantasy settings.
See also: Renaissance.

Carpal tunnel syndrome, sensation of pins-and-needles or numbness in the thumb and first two fingers, plus pain in the wrist, in the palm, or in the forearm. The carpal tunnel is the part of the wrist that encloses all the wrist tendons and the median nerve, one of the main nerves supplying the hand. This syndrome results from the compression of the median nerve when the fibrous tunnel becomes swollen. This may occur during pregnancy when the tissues are more likely to swell. The syndrome is relatively common, and is seen more often in women. A mild condition that usually responds rapidly to treatment, it can become chronic, and then surgery to remove swollen or damaged tissue may have to be considered. The condition is common among typists and keyboarders.

Carpathian Mountains, European mountain range, about 900 mi (1,448 km) long, an extension of the Alps running from Czechoslovakia through Poland, the USSR, and Rumania. Gerlachovka (8,737 ft/2,663 m) is the highest point.
See also: Alps.

Carpenter, M. Scott (1925-), second U.S. astronaut to circle the earth in a spacecraft. Carpenter served in the Navy in both World War II (1930-45) and the Korean War (1950-53), becoming a test pilot in 1954 and completing

Naval Air Intelligence School in 1958. In 1959, he was selected as one of 7 men for the National Aeronautics and Space Administration's (NASA) Project Mercury. He made a 3- orbit flight in the Aurora 7 on May 24, 1962. In 1965, he became an aquanaut and directed the Navy's Sealab II experiment, living and working 205 ft (62 m) under the Pacific Ocean, to improve submarine rescue efforts. He returned to NASA in 1966 as branch chief for advanced programs. A year later he resigned from NASA to continue deep-sea research for the Navy, helping to develop Sealab III. In 1969, he retired from the Navy.
See also: Astronaut.

Carpentry, craft of laying floors, building stairways, and erecting ceiling joists and roof rafters of wood using traditional tools such as the hammer, chisel, pincers, plane, square, plumb line, and tape measure. Modern building techniques have created new applications for carpentry, most notably, the development of wooden molds for casting concrete.
See also: Woodworking.

Carpetbagger, Northerner who moved into the South during the Reconstruction after the Civil War. Although many such Northerners legitimately ran businesses and were elected to office on the Republican ticket (with the help of newly enfranchised African Americans), the term is generally used to apply to those corrupt opportunists who sought to make their fortunes and seize political power out of postwar chaos,earning a reputation for graft and wasteful spending.
See also: Reconstruction.

Carpet beetle (*Anthrenus scrophulariae*), destructive household insect whose larvae feed on carpets, rugs, furniture, fur, and clothing. The tiny (under 0.2 in/5 mm long), wormlike larvae, which do more damage than the adult, are the only beetle larvae covered with hair. Adult carpet beetles, which are brownish-black or marked with red or yellowish-white spots, are discovered in infested houses during spring, and are usually found on windowsills attempting to get out to feed on pollen.

Carracci, family of Bolognese painters. **Lodovico Carracci** (1555-1619), a painter of the Mannerist school, founded an academy of art in Bologna. **Agostino Carracci** (1557-1602) is famous primarily for his prints and *Communion of St. Jerome* (c.1590). **Annibale Carracci** (1560-1609) is considered the greatest painter of the family. Much influenced by Correggio, his work, particularly the vast decorations for the Farnese palace (1597-1604), introduced a strong classical element into a basically Mannerist style.

Carrageen *See:* Irish moss.

Carranza, Venustiano (1859-1920), Mexican political leader. He overthrew General Huerta in the Mexican revolution and became president (1914). The new constitution he supported established basic reforms in land ownership and national control of natural resources. Carranza fled an uprising led by General Obrégon, but was assassinated.
See also: Mexico.

Carrel, Alexis (1873-1944), U.S. surgeon and biologist who received the 1912 Nobel Prize in physiology and medicine for his work in suturing blood vessels, in transfusion, and in organ transplantation. During World War I he developed a treatment for wounds (the Carrel-Dakin method) that reduced the necessity for amputations.
See also: Biology.

Carrier pigeon, breed of show pigeon derived from the rock pigeon. Although this breed is not used for message carrying, the name is also used for the message- carrying homing pigeon.
See also: Pigeon.

Carroll, Charles (1737-1832), U.S. revolutionary leader, member of the Continental Congress, signer of the Declaration of Independence. A Federalist party member, Carroll was elected to Maryland's first state senate (1777), where he served until his retirement in 1801.

Carroll, Daniel (1730-96), U.S. revolutionary politician, signer of the Articles of Confederation and the U.S. Constitution. In 1789 he was elected to the first U.S. House of Representatives.

Carroll, John (1735-1815), first U.S. Roman Catholic bishop, elected by U.S. priests in 1789 and consecrated Bishop of Baltimore in 1790. A friend of Benjamin Franklin and supporter of the American revolution, Bishop Carroll founded Georgetown University and fought against anti-Catholic prejudice in the early United States. He became an archbishop in 1808.

Carroll, Lewis (Charles Lutwidge Dodgson; 1832-98), English mathematician best known for his children's books, *Alice in Wonderland* (1865) and *Alice Through the Looking Glass* (1872), built on mathematical illogic and paradox.

Carrot (*Daucus carota*), biennial vegetable of the parsley family with a swollen, edible root, grown extensively in America and Europe. Its carotene is changed by the body to vitamin A, an essential chemical in the process of vision.

Carson, Kit (Christopher Carson; 1809-68), American frontiersman. Carson worked as a trapper, hunter, and guide throughout the Southwest and accompanied John C. Fremont on his Western expeditions (1842-46). In 1854 he became an Indian agent in New Mexico. He was a Union general in the Civil War.
See also: Pioneer life in America.

Carson, Rachel Louise (1907-64), U.S. marine biologist and science writer whose *Silent Spring* (1962) first alerted the U.S. public to the dangers of environmental pollution.
See also: Marine biology.

Carson City (pop. 40,443), state capital of Nevada, south of Reno. Established as a trading post on the trail from Utah to California, Carson City became important with the discovery of the Comstock Lode in 1859, and as the location of a United States mint from 1870 to 1893.
See also: Nevada.

Cartagena (pop. 168,800), city and seaport on the Mediterranean coast in southeastern Spain. The Carthaginians, attracted by the gold and silver ores there, founded the city about 225 B.C. During the Civil War of 1936-39, Cartagena was a naval base for General Franco.
See also: Spain.

Cartel, formal organization of producers in a particular industry, designed to set prices, control levels of production, and divide markets. Cartels normally attempt to gain sufficient control over supply, demand, and price to produce higher profits for their members. Cartels are illegal in the United States, though U.S. firms are permitted to join international associations. The best known international cartel of the 1970s and 1980s was the Organization of Petroleum Exporting Countries (OPEC).

Carter, Don (1926-   ), U.S. bowler. Voted the best bowler in history in a 1970 poll of bowling writers, he achieved the sport's first grand slam by winning the 4 major competitions of his day—the World Invitational All-Star, Professional Bowlers Association (PBA) National, and American Bowling Conference (ABC) Masters. He continued to win bowling championships throughout the 1950s and early 1960s. He was named to the ABC Hall of Fame in 1970 and to the PBA Hall of Fame in 1975. He was a founder and first president of the PBA.

Carter, Elliott Cook (1908-), U.S. composer, Pulitzer Prize winner (1960, 1973). Marked by unusual instrumentation and structure, his work is complex and highly contrapuntal, sometimes employing *metric modulation*, a technique he developed for creating subtle shifts in tempo. Among his best-known works are a ballet *The Minotaur* (1947), the *Double Concerto* (1961), and *Concerto for Piano and Orchestra* (1965).

Carter, Howard (1873-1939), English Egyptologist, famous for excavations in the Valley of the Kings at Luxor, Egypt, with Lord Carnarvon that discovered the tomb of Tutankhamen in 1922.
See also: Tutankhamen.

Carter, Jimmy (James Earl Carter, Jr.; 1924-), 39th president of the United States.
Early life. Carter grew up on a Georgia farm and graduated from the U.S. Naval Academy in 1946. In the navy he studied nuclear physics and worked on the atomic submarine program. In 1953 he returned to Georgia, built the family's farm into a prosperous peanut business, and entered politics as a Democrat.
Politics. As governor of Georgia (1971-75) he encouraged electoral and social reforms. Carter rose from relative obscurity to win the Democratic nomination in 1976 after a 2-year campaign in which he cast himself as a political outsider. He defeated Republican incumbent Gerald R. Ford.
President. Carter's relations with Congress were strained. His revision of the Social Security system was passed, but his comprehensive energy program was not. The economic growth rate fell in the last years of his administration, and both inflation and interest rates were high. His anti-inflation program, emphasizing cooperation among government, business, and labour had little success. In 1977 Carter won congressional approval of a treaty to cede control of the Panama Canal to Panama at the end of 1999. In 1979 the United

---

James Earl (Jimmy) Carter, Jr.

39th U.S. President
Born: Plains, Ga.; Oct. 1, 1924
Term: Jan. 1977-Jan. 1981
Vice President: Walter F. Mondale
Political Party: Democratic
Spouse: Rosalynn Smith Carter
Children: 4

States established full diplomatic relations with China. But Carter's most significant foreign policy achievement was his brokering of a peace treaty between Egypt and Israel, signed in 1979. In Nov. 1979, Muslim militants in Iran seized the U.S. embassy in Tehran, taking some 60 Americans hostage. Carter's failure to win their release was an important factor in his defeat by Ronald Reagan in the 1980 election.

Retirement. After leaving office, Carter returned home to Plains, Ga. He wrote several books, established an institute at Georgia's Emory University for discussion of international political and social issues, and took part in various international fact-finding and diplomatic missions.

Carteret, Sir George (c.1610-80), English politician, admiral, and lieutenant-governor of East Jersey from 1643. A staunch Royalist, he was rewarded after the Restoration with proprietorships in New Jersey and Carolina.

Cartesian philosophy *See:* Descartes, René.

Carthage, ancient North African city established in 814 B.C. by the Phoenicians, traders of the Mediterranean. Carthage colonized new lands and became the prominent center of the Phoenician world.
See also: Hannibal; Punic Wars.

Carthusians, contemplative and austere Roman Catholic monastic order founded in France in 1084 by St. Bruno. Each monk spends most of his life in solitude in his private cell and garden. Lay brothers prepare the Chartreuse liqueur for which the order is known.
See also: Roman Catholic Church.

Cartier, Jacques (1491-1557), French explorer who discovered the St. Lawrence River while in search of a Northwest Passage in Canada. Between 1534 and 1542 he made 3 voyages, discovering the Magdalene Islands and Prince Edward Island.
See also: Saint Lawrence River.

Cartier, Sir George Étienne (1814-73), Canadian statesman and leading French-Canadian advocate of confederation. Elected to the Canadian parliament in 1848, he was joint prime minister (1857-62) with Sir John Macdonald, under whom he later served as minister of defense in the first dominion government.
See also: Canada.

Cartier-Bresson, Henri (1908-), international French documentary photographer who rose to fame with his coverage of the Spanish Civil War. He has published many photographic books, including *The Decisive Moment* (1952), *China in Transition* (1956), and *Henri Cartier-Bresson, Photographer* (1979), and has also made films.

Cartilage, tough, flexible connective tissue found in all vertebrates, consisting of cartilage cells in a matrix of collagen fibers and a firm protein gel. The skeleton of the vertebrate embryo is formed wholly of cartilage; in most species much of this is replaced by bone during growth. There are 3 main types of cartilage: (1) hyaline, which is translucent and glossy and found in the joints, nose, trachea, and bronchi; (2) elastic, which is found in the external ear, Eustachian tube, and larynx; and (3) fibrocartilage, which attaches tendons to bone and forms the disks between the vertebrae.
See also: Bone.

Cartoon, originally, preparatory sketch in the fine arts; since the mid-19th century, humorous or satirical drawing. Today the term also includes the comic strip, the political cartoon, and cartoon animation. Prominent U.S. cartoonists include Charles Addams, Al Capp, Charles Schulz, Garry Trudeau, and Herblock.

Cartwright, Edmund (1743-1823), English inventor of a mechanical loom (1785) that was the ancestor of the modern power loom. He also invented a woolcombing machine (1789).

Cartwright, Peter (1785-1872), U.S. Methodist preacher, frontier circuit rider (the "Kentucky Boy") and Illinois politician. The life of circuit riders is vividly described in his *Autobiography* (1856).

Caruso, Enrico (1873-1921), Italian operatic tenor famous for his voice and his artistry. Caruso sang over 50 roles in Europe, the United States, and Latin America, excelling in works by Puccini and Verdi. His recordings brought him worldwide fame.
See also: Opera.

Carver, George Washington (1860-1943), U.S. chemist, botanist, and educator, born of slave parents in Missouri. As director of agricultural research at Tuskegee Institute, Alabama (1896-1943), he fostered soil improvement by crop rotation, and developed hundreds of industrial uses for peanuts and sweet potatoes.
See also: Botany.

Carver, John (1576-1621), first governor of Plymouth Colony (1620-21). As leader of the Pilgrims, he was largely responsible (1617-20) for getting a charter and financial aid, and for chartering the *Mayflower*.
See also: Plymouth Colony.

Cary, Joyce (1888-1957), English novelist most famous for 2 trilogies: the first on art—*Herself Surprised* (1941), *To Be a Pilgrim* (1942), and *The Horse's Mouth* (1944), and the second on politics—*Prisoner of Grace* (1952), *Except the Lord* (1953), and *Not Honour More* (1955).

Cary, Mary Ann Shadd (1823-1893), U.S. teacher and journalist, first North American black woman to establish and edit a weekly newspaper. Born to free parents, she taught in and established schools for blacks in Delaware, Pennsylvania, and New York (1839-51). After the U.S. Congress passed the Fugitive Slave Act of 1850, allowing for the return of slaves who had escaped into another state, she began actively working to help slaves who had escaped to Canada. In 1851 she moved to Windsor, Ont., where she helped found the *Provincial Freeman*, a weekly newspaper for blacks in Canada. She moved to Washington, D.C. (1869), where she taught school and received a law degree from Howard University. She was active in the suffrage movement.

Casaba (*Cucumis melo*), type of muskmelon, also called winter melon because it ripens in fall and is available in winter. The casaba is round or oval, with a pointed stem, and weighs 2-9 lbs (1-4 kg). Its hard outer skin, which ripens from green to yellow, is smooth but wrinkled. Rich in vitamin C and potassium, its flesh is sweet and juicy and ranges in color from green to white. The casaba, which originated in Iran and the Transcaucasia, is named for the town in southwest Turkey (Kasaba) from which it was introduced in the United States in 1871. It is now grown in California and the Southwest. It is a member of the gourd family and grows on vines.

Casablanca (pop. 3,210,000), largest city in Morocco and the country's leading port. Casablanca handles most of Morocco's foreign trade, exporting grain and phosphates. In 1907 the French occupied the port, and remained in control until 1956.
See also: Morocco.

Casals, Pablo (1876-1973), virtuoso Spanish cellist and conductor, brilliant interpreter of the music of J.S. Bach. In 1919 he founded an orchestra in Barcelona to bring music to the working classes. An outspoken antifascist, he left Spain after the Spanish Civil War to settle in Prades, France, and then (1956) in Puerto Rico, organizing music festivals in both places.

Casanova (De Seingalt), Giovanni Giacomo (1725-98), Venetian author and adventurer whose name became a synonym for seducer. His memoirs, both sensual and sensitive, show him as a freethinking libertine; they also give an excellent picture of his times.

Cascade Range, mountain range extending 700 mi (1,127 km) from northern California to British Columbia. Its highest peak is Mt. Rainier (14,410 ft/4,392 m). There are 4 dormant volcanos and the recently active (1980) Mt. Saint Helens.

Cascade Tunnel, longest railroad tunnel in North America, cutting across 7.79 mi (12.5 km) of the Cascade range in the central part of Washington. The tunnel was completed in 1929 at a cost of 25 million dollars.
See also: Cascade Range.

Cascara sagrada, small buckthorn tree of the Western United States whose bark is used in making a laxative. It is also known as coffeeberry, as its berries were used by the pioneers to make a substitute coffee.

Casehardening, treatment of mild steel to give it an extremely hard surface. The steel is heated for several hours in carbon-containing material, such as powdered charcoal. During this process carbon is slowly absorbed to a shallow depth, converting this part to high-carbon steel. On quenching with cold water this "case" becomes hard. An even harder case is produced by "nitriding," in which the steel is heated in gaseous ammonia, from which the surface absorbs nitrogen. Casehardening is commonly used on gears, roller bearings, and crankshafts to produce a wear-resistant surface.
See also: Steel.

Casein, important protein that accounts for 80% of the protein content of milk. It occurs as calcium caseinate. It coagulates to form curds when acted upon by certain acids and by the enzyme rennet. The curds are used to make cheese. Casein also has many industrial uses, especially as paper coatings, adhesives, paints, plastics, and synthetic fibers.

Case method, system of teaching law by the study of actual cases. Introduced in 1870 by Christopher C. Langdell, a Harvard Law School professor, by the early 1900s the case method was adopted by most law schools.
See also: Law.

Cashew (*Anacardium occidentale*), tropical American tree of the sumac family cultivated in Africa and India. It grows up to 40 ft (12 m) high and bears a kidney-shaped nut in a hard covering underneath a fleshy edible "pear," which can be made into "cajee" wine. The nuts are roasted, and the oil surrounding each nut can be used in cooking.

Cashmere, very fine natural fiber, the soft underhair of the Kashmir goat, bred in India, Iran, China, and Mongolia. Cashmere is finer than the best wools, although the name may be applied to some soft wool fabrics.

Caslon, William (1692-1766), English typefounder, inventor of Caslon type, for many years the standard typeface in the 18th century. Although superseded by the "newstyle" faces of John Baskerville and others, versions of it are much in use today.

Casper (pop. 61,226), second largest city in Wyoming, on the North Platte River, at an altitude of 5,140 ft (1,566 m). First a cavalry post, the city became a trading center for sheep and cattle ranchers. Over 400 oil companies are now represented in Casper; coal and uranium ore are mined as well.

Caspian Sea, world's largest inland sea (143,000 sq mi/370,370 sq km), in the southwestern part of the former USSR and Iran. Tideless, it is 92 ft (28 m) below sea level and fed mainly by the Volga River. Astrakhan and Baku are the main ports. The northern part of the sea produces caviar.

Cass, Lewis (1782-1866), U.S. soldier and political leader. He rose to the rank of brigadier general in the War of 1812, was governor of Michigan Territory (1813-31), and became secretary of war under Andrew Jackson. He ran as the Democratic presidential candidate in 1848 but lost to Zachary Taylor, due largely to the defection of the Barnburners (radical New York

State Democrats) to the Free Soil Party. Twice serving in the Senate (1845-48, 1849-57), he also served as secretary of state (1857-60).

Cassandra, in Greek mythology, prophetess of doom whose warnings were never heeded. The daughter of Trojan King Priam, she was taken prisoner by Agamemnon after the Trojan War and later murdered with him by his wife, Clytemnestra.
See also: Mythology; Troy.

Cassatt, Mary (1845-1926), U.S.-born impressionist painter who lived mainly in Paris. Strongly influenced by her friend Edgar Degas, she painted domestic scenes, especially mother-and-child studies: "The Cup of Tea" (1879), "The Bath" (1891), "The Boating Party" (1893).
See also: Impressionism.

Cassava, or manioc (genus *Manihot*), potato-like tuber plant, staple in its native Central and South America and in West Africa and southeastern Asia. After being peeled to remove most of the poisonous prussic acid, the tubers are soaked. Lumps of cooked tuber form tapioca, which can be ground to make a flour.

Cassette *See:* Tape recorder; Videotape recorder.

Cassia, genus of tropical plants. Sennas, best known as medicinal plants, are a common species.

Cassino (pop. 26,300), Italian town about 75 miles southeast of Rome, site of Monte Cassino, a Benedictine monastery founded in A.D. 529. During World War II, Cassino was strategically important to the German defense of Rome, and the town and abbey were nearly destroyed in heavy fighting. Both have since been rebuilt.
See also: Italy.

Cassiopeia, w-shaped constellation of the northern hemisphere, which appears between the North Star and the Big Dipper, directly north of the constellation Andromeda. An exploding star (supernova) was observed in Cassiopeia in 1572 by the Danish astronomer Tycho Brahe.
See also: Constellation.

Cassirer, Ernst (1874-1945), German-born philosopher. His work, based on the ideas of Immanuel Kant, examines the ways in which a person's symbols and concepts structure his or her world. He fled Nazi Germany in 1933 and taught at Oxford, in Sweden, and, from 1941, in the United States.
See also: Philosophy.

Cassiterite, or tinstone, principal ore of tin. The brown-to-black-colored mineral is found in veins, along with granite and quartz, and in riverbeds as pebbles. It is mined commercially in Malaysia, China, Bolivia, Indonesia, Thailand, the Congo, and Nigeria.
See also: Tin.

Cassius Longinus, Gaius (d. 42 B.C.), Roman general, conspirator to assassinate Julius Caesar in 44 B.C. He fled to Syria and joined Brutus to fight Octavian and Mark Antony at Philippi. Despairing of victory, he committed suicide.
See also: Rome, Ancient.

Cassowary, large, flightless bird of northern Australia and New Guinea. The largest species is nearly 5 ft (1.5 m) tall. The plumage is coarse. The head and neck are naked and brightly colored with wattles and a bony helmet. The legs are strong, and cassowaries can run at 30 mph (48 km per hour), but they are shy and hide in thick cover. Cassowaries have large, sharp claws on their 3 toes that can be formidable weapons. The eggs are incubated by the male, who also cares for the chicks. They feed on insects and fruit.

Castagno, Andrea del (1423-57), Florentine painter of church frescoes, portraits, and murals. Best known for his *Last   Supper* (1445-50) and *Crucifixion* (1499-50), he stressed perspective and a stark, dramatic illumination. He is notable for the vigor and strength of his figure rendering.

Castanets, small percussion instrument consisting of 2 shell-shaped halves, usually made of wood or ivory. They are held in the palm of the hand and tapped by the fingers to produce a clicking sound. Castanets have been used for hundreds of years in Spanish flamenco dancing. More recently some composers have included a part for castanets in their music, especially to suggest a Spanish flavor.

Caste system, division of society into closed groups, primarily by birth, but usually also involving religion and occupation. The most caste-bound society today is that of Hindu India; its caste system, dating from 3000 B.C., was not discouraged until recently.

Castiglione, Comte Baldassare (1478-1529), Italian courtier, diplomat, and author. His *Il Cortegiano* (The Courier) (1528), a portrait of the ideal courtier and his relationship with the prince he serves, greatly influenced Renaissance mores and inspired writers like Edmund Spenser, Sir Philip Sidney, and Miguel Cervantes.
See also: Renaissance.

Castile and Aragón, 2 kingdoms of Spain, united in 1479 by Isabella of Castile and her husband, Ferdinand V. Aragón is in the northeast of Spain, bordering France; Castile, in central and northern Spain, surrounds the city of Madrid. The union of Castile and Aragón formed the core of the modern Spanish state and served as Ferdinand and Isabella's base in their struggle, eventually successful, to drive the Moors from southern Spain (Andalusia).
See also: Spain.

Castilla, Ramón (1797?-1867), president of Peru, 1845-51 and 1855-62. He joined the Peruvian independence movement in 1821 and fought the Spaniards alongside José de San Martín and Simón Bolívar. When he assumed the presidency, he ended a period of anarchy and is credited with bringing peace, stability, and economic improvements. Slavery and the taxation of Indians were abolished under his administration.
See also: Peru.

Casting, production of a desired form by pouring the raw material (alloys, fiberglass, plastics, steel) in liquid form into a suitably shaped mold. In *die casting*, molten metal is forced under pressure into a die; in *centrifugal casting*, used primarily for pipes, molten material is poured into a rapidly rotating mold; in *continuous casting*, material is poured into water-cooled, open-ended molds; in *sand casting* fine sand is packed tightly around each half of a permanent pattern, which is removed, after which the 2 halves of the mold are placed together.

Castle, Vernon (1887-1918), and **Irene** (1893-1969), couple who revolutionized ballroom dancing. They introduced the one-step and the Castle walk and popularized the hesitation waltz and tango during a meteoric career that began in 1912 and ended with Vernon's death in an air crash.

Castle, fortified dwelling, built to dominate and guard a region. The term derives from the Roman *castellum* (fort or frontier stronghold). In Western Europe, most of the extant castles were built between 1000 and 1500, often on an artificial mound, with a palisaded courtyard. Later, the stockade was replaced by masonry keeps, or dungeons; defensive outer walls; and frequently a moat and drawbridge. With the decline of feudalism, the castle evolved into the Renaissance château, with its emphasis on splendor rather than on fortification.

Castlereagh, Robert Stewart, 2d Viscount (1769-1822), Irish born British statesman, creator of the Quadruple Alliance that defeated Napoleon. As secretary for Ireland, he suppressed the 1798 rebellion and forced the Act of Union through the Irish Parliament (1800). He was war minister (1805-6, 1807-9), and as foreign secretary (1812-22), played a major role in the organization of Europe at the Congress of Vienna (1814). Much maligned in his time, he committed suicide.
See also: Vienna, Congress of.

Castor and Pollux, in Greek mythology, twin heroes, called the Dioscuri. Castor the horseman was the son of Leda and Tyndareus; Pollux the boxer was the son of Leda and Zeus.
See also: Mythology.

Castor oil, thick oil obtained from the castor bean, used as a purgative and a lubricant.

Castries (pop. 52,900), capital and largest city of the Caribbean island nation of St. Lucia. Bordered by a deep-water harbor on the island's northwest coast, Castries is the chief port, exporting bananas, sugarcane, molasses, cacao, and other tropical products. Colonized by France in 1651, St. Lucia was fought over by the French and British until 1814, when Great Britain took control. Britain ruled St. Lucia until 1979, when it became an independent nation.
See also: Saint Lucia.

Castro, Fidel (1926-) Cuban premier (1959-) and revolutionary. He led an abortive revolution in 1953 against dictator Fulgencio Batista, and was imprisoned and exiled. In 1956 he invaded Cuba with 81 men and overthrew the regime, establishing himself as premier in 1959. He nationalized industry

and collectivized agriculture, becoming increasingly dependent on the USSR for financial support. The U.S. has attempted to isolate Cuba both economically and politically but has not achieved success.
See also: Cuba.

Castro, Raul Hector (1916-), governor of Arizona (1975-77). Born in Mexico, Castro moved to Arizona in 1926 and became a U.S. citizen in 1939. He earned a law degree from the University of Arizona in 1949. He was U.S. ambassador to El Salvador 1964-1968, and to Bolivia 1968-1969. In 1977 he was named U.S. ambassador to Argentina.

Cat, hunting carnivore of the family Felidae, varying in size from the small domestic cat and the small wild cats (lynx and ocelot) to the great cats (lion, tiger, leopard, and cheetah). Cats have short snouts, large eyes, sensitive whiskers, and sharp claws and teeth.
See also: Lion; Tiger.

CAT (computerized axial tomography) scan, painless, quick diagnostic procedure in which hundreds of X-ray pictures are taken as a camera revolves around a body part. A computer integrates the pictures to reveal structures within the body. The CAT scan has created a new era in the history of diagnostic medicine. It is especially effective in the diagnosis of neurologic disorders and cancers.

Catacombs, underground cemeteries of the early Christians, who did not follow the Greek and Roman practice of cremation. The best known and most extensive are outside Rome, built from the 1st to the 5th century A.D.

Catalepsy, condition of loss of voluntary motion in which the arms and legs remain in any position they are placed in. Causes may be organic or psychological. Catalepsy is often associated with severe cases of schizophrenia.
See also: Schizophrenia.

Catalonia, region in northeastern Spain, comprising the provinces of Lérida, Gerona, Barcelona, and Tarragona. It was occupied by the Romans and Goths, who called it Gothalonia. It maintained its own customs and language after its union with Aragon in 1137. There is also a rich body of Catalan literature. It is now the chief industrial area of Spain, and is dependent on the interior for grain and protected markets. It experienced a brief period of independence during the 1930s. In 1980 the Spanish government handed over certain limited functions to a Catalan regional government with its own parliament and premier.
See also: Spain.

Catalpa, genus of ornamental shade tree of the bignonia family, growing naturally in eastern Asia, the West Indies, and the southern United States. Its tubular white or yellow flowers have purple or brown markings.

Catalysis, change in the rate of a chemical reaction by an additive (a catalyst speeds up reactions; an inhibitor slows down reactions) that is itself unchanged at the end of the reaction. Catalysts are widely used in industry. All living organisms are dependent on the complex catalysts called enzymes, which regulate biochemical reactions.

Catamaran, boat with 2 narrow, identical hulls connected by a flat bridge deck. They are driven by sail or power and are extremely fast and stable. Trimarans are similar, but have 3 hulls, the center 1 being longer than the outer 2.

Catamount, folk name for the puma and the lynx. The word is a shortened form of *catamountain*, a form of *cat of the mountain*.

Cataplexy, condition of abrupt and temporary loss of voluntary muscle control brought on by some extreme emotional stimulus, especially fear, anger, or mirth. An attack may last from a few seconds to several minutes, and symptoms may range in severity from a mild weakening to paralysis of most of the muscles of the body.

Catapult, ancient military weapon used for hurling missiles. Some catapults were large crossbows, with a lethal range of over 400 yd (366 m), while others (*ballistas*) used giant levers to hurl boulders. In the Middle Ages catapults were an important part of siege artillery, but they were made obsolete by the cannon. A modern steam-powered version of the catapult launches jets from aircraft carriers.

Cataract, opacity of the lens of the eye, causing a progressive loss of vision. Aging is the most common cause, but cataracts may be hereditary or due to disease, such as diabetes. Cataracts are treated by lens extraction, followed by wearing corrective lenses or having a plastic lens implant.
See also: Blindness.

Catarrh, mild inflammation of a mucous membrane, associated with a copious secretion of mucus. Medically speaking, this refers to any mucous membrane in the body, but popularly it refers to nasal or bronchial catarrh.
See also: Sinus; Cold, common.

Catbird (*Dumetella carolinensis*), songbird of the thrush family, named for the mewing notes in its imitative song. Catbirds, which are gray with a black cap, live in the United States and in Canada, migrating in winter to Central America or to the West Indies.

Catechism, manual of religious instruction arranged in question-and- answer form. First appearing in the 8th and 9th centuries, catechisms were widely used during the Middle Ages. The Anglican catechism is included in the Book of Common Prayer, and the Baltimore Catechism (1885) is used by Roman Catholics.
See also: Book of Common Prayer.

Catechu, strong, astringent substance prepared from the wood of various tropical Asiatic plants and used in medicine with prepared chalk to treat diarrhea.

Caterpillar, larva of a moth or a butterfly, with 13 segments, 3 pairs of true legs, and up to 5 pairs of soft false legs.
See also: Butterfly.

Catfish, freshwater, bottom-feeding fish (suborder Nematognathi) with barbels, or whiskers, around the mouth, tough scaleless skin, and sharp spines. Catfish are an important food source.

Catharsis, in psychoanalysis, bringing into the open of a previously repressed memory or emotion, in the hope of releasing and eliminating stress.

Cathay, name by which China was known in medieval Europe. The word derives from the Khitai, a seminomadic people of southern Manchuria whose rule extended to northern China in the 10th century A.D.
See also: China.

Cathedral, principal church of a diocese, in which the bishop has his *cathedra*, his official seat or throne. A cathedral need not be particularly large or imposing, though its importance as a major center led to the magnificent structures of the Gothic and Renaissance periods. By its prominent position and size, a cathedral often dominated a city and served as the focus of its life. In Europe, most of the older cathedral cities were already important centers in Roman and early Christian times.
See also: Architecture.

Cather, Willa Sibert (1876-1947), U.S. novelist noted for her psychologically astute portrayals of the people of Nebraska and the Southwest. Her works include *O Pioneers!* (1913), *My Antonia* (1918), and *Death Comes for the Archbishop* (1927). She was also a brilliant writer of short stories, the most famous being "Paul's Case."

Catherine, name of 2 Russian empresses. **Catherine I** (1684-1727), wife of Peter I, succeeded him to the throne on his death in 1725. **Catherine II, the Great** (1729-96) married the future Peter III in 1745. After his deposition and murder in 1762, she became empress. Her liberalism was quenched by Pugachev's peasant uprising (1773 - 74) and the French Revolution. She greatly extended Russian territory, annexing the Crimea (1783) and partitioning Poland (1772-95).

Catherine de' Medici (1519-89), daughter of Lorenzo de' Medici, Duke of Urbino; wife of King Henry II of France; and mother of 3 kings of France. After the death of her eldest son, King Francis II (r.1559-60), she acted as regent of France (until 1563) and was adviser to her son, King Charles IX, (r.1560-74) until his death. She helped Charles IX plan the St. Bartholomew's Day Massacre against the Protestants in 1572. Her third son, Henry III, ruled from 1574 to 1589.
See also: Saint Bartholomew's Day, Massacre of.

Catherine of Aragon (1485-1536), first wife of Henry VIII of England. The daughter of Ferdinand and Isabella of Spain, she married Prince Arthur (1501) and, after his death, his brother, Henry VIII (1509). Henry's annul-

ment of the marriage (1533) without papal consent led to the English Reformation. She was the mother of Mary I of England.
See also: Henry (England).

Catherine of Braganza (1638-1705), Portuguese wife of King Charles II of England. The marriage (1662) was intended to promote the Anglo-Portuguese alliance, but she produced no heir. After Charles's death, she returned to Portugal (1692), serving as regent (1704-5).

Catherine of Siena, Saint (1347-80), Italian religious and mystic known for her visions, charity, and diplomatic skill. Her influence over Pope Gregory XI (1331-78) led him to leave Avignon in 1377 and return the papacy to Rome, thus ending the "Babylonian captivity" of the papacy. Her feast day is Apr. 30.

Catherine the Great *See:* Catherine.

Cathode ray, stream of electrons that flows from a cathode (negative electrode) to an anode (positive electrode) in a vacuum tube when a potential of 4,000-10,000 volts is applied across them. Cathode rays were first detected when a glowing light was seen to emanate from a cathode; this is a secondary effect the rays produce only when traces of certain gases are present.
See also: Electrolysis; Electronics; Vacuum tube.

Catholic Church, Roman *See:* Roman Catholic Church.

Catholic Emancipation Act, British law enacted on Apr. 13, 1829, removing most of the civil disabilities imposed on British Roman Catholics from the time of Henry VIII. A controversial measure, it was introduced by Sir Robert Peel after considerable pressure from Irish campaigners headed by Daniel O'Connell.

Catiline (c.108-62 B.C.), Roman aristocrat who tried to seize power in 63 B.C. He was trapped and killed in battle at Pistoria. Cicero attacked him in a series of 4 celebrated orations.

Catkin, reproductive organ of many common trees. Each catkin bears a cluster of primitive flowers that lack petals and sepals. Instead, the stamens and pistils are protected by small leaves called bracts. 1 Catkin bears either male or female flowers. Plants bearing catkins include beech, birch, walnut, and willow families.

Catlin, George (1796-1872), U.S. artist, noted for his paintings of U.S. Native American life based on his trips to the American West. His books include *Notes on the Manners, Customs, and Conditions of the North American Indians* (1841). A large portion of his work is in the Catlin Gallery of the National Gallery of Art in Washington, D.C.

Catnip, or catmint (*Nepeta cataria*), Eurasian mint naturalized in North America. It is grown for its aromatic leaves, which are stimulating to cats.

Cato, name of 2 Roman statesman. **Marcos Porcius Cato the Elder** (234-149 B.C.), was an orator and prose writer. He became consul in 195 B.C. and censor in 184 B.C. His only surviving work is a treatise on agriculture. **Marcus Porcius Cato the Younger**, (95-46 B.C.), great-grandson of Cato the Elder, was a model stoic and defender of Roman republicanism. He supported Pompey against Gaius Julius Caesar in the Civil War, but after the final defeat of the republican army at Thapsus (46 B.C.), he killed himself at Utica.
See also: Rome, Ancient.

Cat's eye, any of several gemstones that, when cut to form a convex surface, resemble the eye of a cat. Common cat's eye is chalcedony, a form of quartz. The most kind is a variety of chrysoberyl.

Catskill Mountains, group of mountains west of the Hudson River in the southeastern region of New York, part of the Appalachian system. Geologically unique, with flat- topped plateaus divided by narrow valleys, they are a popular recreational area.
See also: Appalachian Mountains.

Catt, Carrie Lane Chapman (1859-1947), U.S. feminist, suffragist, and founder of the League of Women Voters. She was also an active advocate of international disarmament.
See also: Woman suffrage.

Cattail, wild plant (genus *Typha*) that grows in marshes and other wetland areas. Also called clubrushes and, on the Pacific Coast, tule-reeds, cattails have long, slender leaves and a single tall stem. The female flowers form long brown spikes. The roots, which contain starch, are edible. The soft down produced by cattails is sometimes used for furniture upholstery.

Cattle, large ruminant mammal of the family Bovidae, most of which have been domesticated, including bison, buffalo, yak, zebu, and European cattle. By 2500 B.C. the Egyptians had several breed of cattle, which may have been used as draft animals and for leather . Their dung served as fuel and manure. Today, beef cattle (like Aberdeen Angus or Hereford) are square and heavily built commonly kept on poor grazing land, whereas dairy breeds (like Holstein or Guernsey) have good grazing. Recent breeds are mixed beef and dairy animals. A dairy cow can give as much as 14,000 lb (6,350 kg) of milk in 1 year.

Cattle tick, brown parasitic insect (*Boophilus annulatus*) that lives on cattle. It carries an infectious cattle disease known as Texas fever, which in the mid-1800s threatened cattle throughout the U.S. Southwest. Control measures have all but eliminated cattle ticks in the United States, but they are still common in Mexico.

Catton, Bruce (1899-1978), U.S. journalist and Civil War historian. He is best known for his trilogy on the Army of the Potomac: *Mr. Lincoln's Army* (1951), *Glory Road* (1952), and *A Stillness at Appomattox* (1953). He won the Pulitzer Prize in 1954.
See also: Civil War, U.S.

Catullus, Gaius Valerius (c.84-54 B.C.), Roman lyric poet influenced by Hellenistic Greek poetry. He wrote passionate lyrics, epigrams, elegies, idylls, and vicious satires, of which only 116 survive. He influenced the later Roman poets Horace and Martial.

Caucasia, oil-rich region that straddles the Caucasus Mountains in the southwest of the Russian Federation. After the Russian Revolution the southern part, called Transcaucasia, was organized as the republics of Georgia, Armenia, and Azerbaijan. In 1922, they became the Transcaucasian Soviet Federated Socialist Republic, but in 1936 they were again reorganized as 3 distinct republics of the Soviet Union and gained independence in 1991. *See also:* Union of Soviet Socialist Republics.

Caucasus, mountain range in the Russian Federation between the Caspian and Black seas, 700 mi (1,127 km) long and up to 120 mi (193 km) wide, including the highest mountain in Europe, Mt. Elbrus (18,481 ft/ 5,633 m). Its northern parts belong to Europe, but its southern regions, bordering on Turkey and Iran, are part of Asia. *See also:* Union of Soviet Socialist Republics.

Caucus, closed party meetings to decide on policy or select candidates for public office. The term, possibly derived from the Algonquian *Kaw-Kaw-was* (to talk), originated as the name of a political club in 18th-century Boston. From 1800 until 1824 presidential candidates were nominated by the 2-party caucuses in Congress. Although the national convention system replaced the Congressional nominating caucus, party caucuses are important forums for deciding legislative policy, and they fill party posts such as floor leader and whip. A special form of caucus is the meeting of local party members to nominate candidates for office or elect delegates to party conventions. In the late 19th century political "bosses" and their followers came to dominate these meetings, and primary elections were introduced in order to avoid such abuses in the nominating system.

Cauliflower, *(Brassica oleracea)*, variety of cabbage similar to broccoli, in which the edible portion consists of a large mass of unopened flowers.

Caustic, general name for chemicals that burn or corrode other materials such as metal, plastics, and organic substances. Caustic soda, also known as lye, is used in household drain cleaners and in making soap, paper, and textiles. Caustic potash is used in the manufacture of soaps that dissolve easily in water. *See also:* Lye.

Cavalry, military force that fights on horseback. It played a key role in warfare from about the 6th century B.C. to the end of the 19th century, when the development of rapid-fire rifles began to reduce its effectiveness.

Cavazos, Lauro Fred (1927-), named secretary of education in 1988, first Mexican American to hold a cabinet post. He was president of Texas Tech University from 1980 to 1988, when he was named secretary of education by President Ronald Reagan; he remained in the post under President George Bush.

Cave, natural hollow or cavern found in rock. The most spectacularl caves are found in limestone rocks beneath the earth's surface. These caves were formed thousands of years ago by water erosion.
See also: Speleology.

Cavefish, common name of several varieties of small, blind, cave-dwelling fish of the family Amblyopsidae. Also known as blindfish, they navigate with the help of rows of small projections on their skin.

Cavell, Edith Louise (1865-1915), British nurse who became a World War I heroine. She was responsible for updating nurses' training in Belgium and eventually was executed by the Germans for helping some 200 Allied soldiers escape.

Cavendish, Henry (1731-1810), English chemist and physicist who showed hydrogen to be a distinct gas, water to be a compound—not an elementary substance, and the composition of the atmosphere to be constant. He also used a torsion balance to measure the density of the earth (1798).
See also: Chemistry; Hydrogen.

Cavour, Count Camillo Benso of (1810-61), Italian statesman largely responsible for the unification of Italy. Cavour, under Victor Emmanuel II, became premier of Piedmont in 1852 and sought to unite the country by making piecemeal additions to Piedmont. A subtle diplomat, he secured the central Italian states. The unification, except for Venice and the province of Rome, was completed in 1861, only a few months before Cavour's death.
See also: Italy.

Cavy, any of a number of related South American rodents (family Caviidae), of which the guinea pig is the best known. Cavies typically have short hair and legs and thick bodies. They are social animals, vegetarians, and generally nocturnal.

Caxton, William (c.1422-91), English printer, trained in Cologne. He produced *The Recuyell of the Historyes of Troye* (Bruges, c.1475), the first book printed in English, and *Dictes and Sayenges of the Phylosophers* (1477), the first dated book printed in English.

Cayenne (pop. 41,100), capital of French Guiana, situated on an island in the Cayenne River. It was founded by the French in 1643 and from the late 17th century until 1946 was a notorious French penal colony. Gold, hides, rum, cocoa, and cayenne pepper pass through the port.
See also: French Guiana.

Cayley, Sir George (1773-1857), British inventor who pioneered the science of aerodynamics. He built the first man-carrying glider (1853) and formulated the design principles later used in airplane construction.
See also: Aerodynamics.

Cayman, crocodilian of South America, notably of the Amazon basin. The dwarf cayman is up to 4 ft (1 m) long but the black cayman may grow to 15

ft (4-1/2 m). Similar to alligators, caymans can be distinguished by bony plates on the underside.
See also: Crocodile; Alligator.

Cayman Islands, British dependency in the Caribbean Sea, about 200 mi (320 km) northwest of Jamaica, consisting of 3 islands: Grand Cayman, Little Cayman, and Cayman Brac. Georgetown, on Grand Cayman, is the capital and largest city. Tourism is the main industry, but low taxes and banking secrecy laws have attracted a variety of companies.

Cayuga, Native American tribe, member of the Iroquois League. They inhabited the area of Cayuga Lake, N.Y., until the American Revolution. Favoring the British, many then moved to Canada, while others dispersed.

CB radio *See:* Citizens band radio.

CD *See:* Compact disc (CD).

Ceausescu, Nicolae (1918-89), president of Romania from 1967 until 1989, when he was overthrown and executed. First elected member of the Romanian Communist Party Central Committee in 1948, he became head of the committee in 1965. As president, he instigated a policy of independence within the Soviet bloc.
See also: Romania.

Cebu, densely populated Philippine island with a narrow coastal plain and interior mountains. The city of Cebu is the main port and commercial center for the surrounding islands. It was the first permanent Spanish settlement in the Philippines (1565).
See also: Philippines.

Cecilia, Saint, early martyr of the Christian church, in 2nd or 3rd century Rome. According to legend, she converted St. Valerian and his brother Tiburtius. The Roman prefect Almachius ordered her burned to death for distributing goods to the poor. Tradition says that she was beheaded when her body would not burn. Though her authenticity is doubted, she continues to be popular and is represented on the church calendar (Nov. 22). She is considered the patron saint of music.
See also: Christianity.

Cedar (genus *Cedrus*), evergreen, cone-bearing tree with fragrant wood. The timber trade calls several unrelated trees "cedar" but the true cedars are species found in the mountains of North Africa and Asia. They are distinguished by being the only evergreen conifers with needles in tufts along the branches.

Cedar Rapids (pop. 168,767), city in east central Iowa, seat of Linn County. Cedar Rapids is situated on the Cedar River in an agricultural area. It produces radio and electronic equipment, corn products, cereal, and meat products.
See also: Iowa.

Celandine (*Chelidonium majus*), low-growing biennial of the poppy family with yellow flowers that are open for most of the spring and summer.

Celery, biennial vegetable (*Apium graveolens*) related to parsley and carrots, eaten either raw or cooked. The seeds are used for seasoning. Celery grows best in cool weather and consists of long stalks topped with feathery leaves. It was first cultivated in France in the early 1600s.

Celery cabbage *See:* Chinese cabbage.

Celesta, keyboard musical instrument that looks like a miniature upright piano. The hammers strike metal bars, producing a delicate, bell-like sound. Introduced during the late 19th century as an improvement on the glockenspiel, the celesta is often used in orchestral compositions.

Celibacy, voluntary abstinence from marriage and sexual intercourse. Celibacy of Roman Catholic church clergy was instituted by Pope Siricius (386), but abandoned by Protestants during the Reformation. In the Eastern Church, married men can be ordained as priests, though bishops must be celibates or widowers.

Céline, Louis-Ferdinand (Louis-Ferdinand Destouches, 1849-1961), French novelist. His first novels, *Journey to the End of Night* (1932) and *Death on the Installment Plan* (1936), made his vivid, hallucinatory style notable.

Cell, in biology, smallest unit that possesses all the essential properties of a living organism: metabolism, reproduction, differentiation, regeneration, and excitability (response to stimulus). A living cell can also be described as having a flow of matter: Chemicals come into the cell; they are broken down or transformed into other chemicals that then leave the cell. There is also a flow of energy: Energy comes into a living system either as chemical energy or as radiant energy from the sun. However, a third element is crucial: information. A living system is a directed and responsive system in which there is control and regulation of chemical reactions. The cell contains a specific information system: the nucleic acids and the proteins, DNA (deoxyribonucleic acid) and RNA (ribonucleic acid). These molecules contain and transmit the genetic information of the cell. All cells have an outer membrane, or cell boundary, cytoplasm (the contents of the cell excluding the nucleus), a cell nucleus, more or less spherical, containing specific molecules, a nucleolus, and organelles (cytoplasmic structures) to which the diverse functions are attributed.
See also: Biology.

Cellini, Benvenuto (1500-71), Italian metalsmith, sculptor, and writer. Of his work in precious metals little survives except the gold and enamel saltcellar made for Francis I of France in 1543. His most famous sculpture is *Perseus with the Head of Medusa* (1545-54). His celebrated *Autobiography* (1558-62) is colorful and vigorous, though somewhat exaggerated.

Cello, or violoncello, second largest instrument of the violin family, with 4 strings and a range starting 2 octaves below middle C. Dating from the 16th century, it is the deepest-toned instrument in the string quartet.
See also: Violin.

Cellophane, transparent, nonpenetrable film of cellulose used in packaging, first developed by J. E. Brandenburger (1911). Wood pulp is soaked in sodium hydroxide, shredded, aged, and mixed with carbon sulfide to form a solution of viscose. After an acid bath, the cellulose is regenerated as a film, dried and waterproofed.
See also: Cellulose.

Celluloid, first commercial synthetic plastic, developed by J. W. Hyatt (1869), made by treating nitrocellulose with camphor and alcohol. It is tough, strong, and resistant to water and oils. Used in dental plates, combs, billiard balls, lacquers, and spectacle frames, celluloid is highly inflammable and has been largely replaced by newer plastics.
See also: Plastic.

Cellulose, main constituent of the cell walls of plants. Cellulose is a complex carbohydrate with a structure similar to that of starch. Processed cellulose is used in the manufacture of many goods, among them, paper, explosives, fibers, plastics, and adhesives.

Celsius scale, system for measuring temperature in which the interval between the freezing point and boiling point of water is divided into 100 equal degrees. In the Celsius scale, also called the centigrade scale, water freezes at 0 degrees and boils at 100 degrees. Invented by the Swedish astronomer Anders Celsius in 1742, the Celsius scale is widely used in scientific work and is the common system of measuring temperature in most of the world.

Celts, prehistoric people speaking Indo-European dialects, whose numerous tribes occupied much of Europe between 2000 and 100 B.C. They grouped together in small settlements. Their social unit, based on kinship, was divided into a warrior nobility and a farming class. Their priests or druids were recruited from the nobility.

Cement, most important modern construction material, notably as a constituent of concrete. Cement generally is composed mostly of limestone, clays, gypsum, and crushed rock.

Cenozoic Era, third and current geologic era. Beginning about 65 million years ago, the Cenozoic is characterized by mammals and flowering plants.

Censorship, supervision or control exercised by authority over public communication, conduct, or morals. Early censorship in the Greek city-states curbed conduct considered insulting to the gods or dangerous to public order. In Rome the censor dictated public morality. Censorship of books was not widespread (although some books were publicly burned) until the invention of printing in the 15th century. The first *Index of Prohibited Books* was drawn up by the Roman Catholic Church in 1559 in an effort to stop the spread of

subversive literature. Similar tactics were employed by Protestants and secular authorities. In the United States, freedom of the press is protected from federal interference by the First Amendment to the Constitution.
See also: Bill of rights.

Census, enumeration of persons, property, and other items within a community, state, or country. A population census has been conducted in the United States every 10 years since 1790. In addition to population, the United States conducts a census on agricultural production every 5 years on the years ending in 4 and 9. Manufacturing, mining, and business censuses are also performed every 5 years on the years that end in 2 and 7.
See also: Population.

Centaur, in Greek mythology, a creature with the torso, arms, and head of a man and the body of a horse. Most centaurs were considered savages, but a few, such as Chiron, a son of Cronus, the titan, were wise teachers of humans.
See also: Mythology.

Centennial Exposition, International, world's fair held in Philadelphia from May to Nov. 1876, celebrating the 100th anniversary of the Declaration of Independence. Exhibits from the arts and sciences were displayed by 49 nations. The United States exhibited its new mass production techniques. The fair attracted almost 10 million visitors.

Centipede, long-bodied member of the class Chilopoda, phylum Arthropoda with 2 legs to each of their 15 to 100 segments. They are usually 1-2 in (2.5-5 cm) long, though in the tropics some reach 1 ft (30 cm). Normally insectivorous they paralyze their food by injecting poison through a pair of pincers located near the head. Centipedes live in moist places under stones or in soil.

Central African Republic, landlocked country in equatorial Africa, bordered by Chad, Sudan, Zaire, Congo and Cameroon.
Land and climate. The republic lies north of the equator and is a rolling plateau at about 2,500 ft (763 m). In the east the Fertit Hills rise to 4,200 ft (1,280 m), and in the northeast the Ouanda-Djale Hills reach 3,750 ft (1,143 m). A dense tropical rainforest covers the southern part of the country; the rest is grassland, becoming drier and treeless toward the northern border. Jungle wildlife is abundant. Rain is abundant in the south, but mainly confined to the season from June to October in both central and northern areas. The chief rivers are the Ubangi and the Shari.
People. The Central African Republic has a population density of 5 persons per sq mi (2 per sq km). Ethnic groups include the Zandé, the Banda, and the Mbaka. The small European group is mainly French. French is the official language, but Sango is the language most commonly spoken. Religion is mainly animism, but a growing number of Muslims live near the Chad border. Illiteracy is high, but school attendance is rising. There are technical schools, but no university.
Economy. The country's poor economy is based on farm crops for home consumption and cotton and diamonds for export. The tsetse fly prevents significant expansion of the cattle industry. There are plans to exploit the

Central African Republic

Capital:	Bangui
Area:	240,535 sq mi
	(622,984 sq km)
Population:	3,376,000
Language:	Sangho, French
Government:	Presidential republic
Independent:	1960
Head of gov.:	Prime minister
Per capita:	U.S. $340
Mon. unit:	1 CFA franc = 100
	centimes

deposits of iron, limestone, silver, and uranium. The one large industrial complex is the textile plant at Bouali, which uses hydroelectric power. The country's economy suffers from the lack of a seaport and the absence of railways. The capital, Bangui, is a river port, located on the Ubangi, a tributary of the Congo River.

History. The first French outposts were established in 1886. In 1894 the area was called the territory of Ubangi-Shari. In 1910 it was incorporated into French Equatorial Africa. After World War II demands for independence were led by M. Barthélemy Boganda, resulting in the inclusion of Ubangi-Shari in the French Community in 1958. Two years later, on August 13, the country became an independent nation as the Central African Republic. In 1959 David Dacko became the independent nation's first president. He was overthrown in 1966 by a military coup, led by Colonel Jean-Bedel Bokassa, who assumed the presidency and had the nation's sole political party appoint him president for life in 1972. In 1979 Dacko regained control with support from the French, and Bokassa went into exile. Dacko, elected to a 6-year term in 1981, was ousted in a military coup later that year. The country returned to a civilian government in 1993 when Ange-Felix Pattass was democratically elected as the new president. His policy is aimed at a socio-economic reconstruction of the country.

Central America, North America southeast of Mexico, land bridge to South America, separating the Pacific Ocean from the Caribbean Sea. Its north and south land boundaries, about 1,100 mi (1,770 km) apart, are the Isthmus of Tehuantepec in Mexico and the valley of the Atrato in Colombia. Within this area are the republics of Guatemala, Honduras, El Salvador, Nicaragua, Costa Rica, Belize, and Panama. Most of the people are of Spanish or Native American ancestry, living as farmers in the mountain valleys or working in the forests or mines. The dominant feature of the region is a string of mountain ranges characterized by great volcanic activity and earthquakes. They are part of the same mountain system as the islands of the Greater and Lesser Antilles. Most of the mountains are no more than 6,000 ft (1,829 m), though some volcanoes are higher than 10,000 ft (3,048 m), with Mt. Tajumulco in Guatemala rising to 13,845 ft (4,220 m). The volcanic deposits in the northwest have produced very fertile highlands. Relatively level tracts of land occur on the Yucatán Peninsula and along the coast. These limestone plains of the peninsula are the most extensive in Central America, and support dense tropical forests. The rolling coastal lowlands appear insignificant by comparison, broadening to a width of only 90 mi (145 km) along the Mosquito Coast (on the Caribbean) and never exceeding 30 mi (48 km) along the Pacific coast. A trough, the Nicaraguan Depression, divides the northern part of the isthmus from the narrower southern part and encloses lakes Nicaragua (3,000 sq mi/7,770 sq km) and Managua (386 sq mi/1,000 sq km), the largest in Central America. The climate is basically tropical, but is drier on the Pacific side. The considerable variations in temperature and rainfall are due mainly to differences in elevation. The 2 early civilizations of the region were the Mayan and the Toltec. The Maya reached their highest cultural state between A.D. 300 and 900. They were familiar with mathematics, astronomy, and agricultural techniques; they built cities of stone, erected fine monuments, and developed intricate handicrafts. The Toltec of central and southern Mexico spread their influence to the Yucatán Peninsula and into Guatemala. The Spanish conquerors arrived in the early 1500s to destroy what were already dying civilizations. Hernando Cortes completed the conquest of the whole area by 1525, and it remained a Spanish colony for nearly 300 years. Foreign rule ended in 1821, when a sympathetic Spanish governor was elected the first head of the independent United Provinces of Central America. The union was dissolved in 1838, and the 5 states (Costa Rica, El Salvador, Guatemala, Honduras, and Nicaragua) became independent. Subsequent attempts to reestablish the confederation have failed. A looser form of cooperation was begun with the creation of the Organization of Central American States in the 1950s. Costa Rica is politically the most stable country; the others have suffered from external conflicts, dictatorships, and revolutions.

Central Intelligence Agency (CIA), U.S. government agency established in 1947 by the National Security Act to coordinate, evaluate, and disseminate intelligence from other U.S. agencies and to advise the president and the National Security Council on security matters. The CIA has done much to further the interests of the United States and its allies, but such fiascos as the Bay of Pigs invasion of Cuba, as well as concern over possible misuse of its considerable independence in the wake of "Watergate," led to a major investigation and internal reorganization in 1975.
See also: Intelligence service.

Central Park *See:* New York City.

Central Powers *See:* World War I.

Centrifugal and Centripetal Forces, forces acting on a body as it moves along a curved path. If a stone is whirled in a circular path on a piece of string, it is acted on by a force pulling it toward the center of the circle (centripetal force). The stone also appears to be acted upon by an equal and opposite force pulling it outward (centrifugal force). An example of centripetal force is the force of gravity exerted on the moon by the earth to keep it in orbit. The value of the centripetal force (F) is given by the equation $F=mv^2/r$ where m equals the mass of the body, v is its velocity, and r is the radius of curvature of its path.
See also: Inertia; Newton, Sir Isaac.

Centrifuge, machine for separating mixtures of different densities by rotating them in a container at high speed. The centrifugal force experienced in a rotating frame causes the heavier elements to sink. Centrifuges are used in drying clothes, in separating milk from cream, in chemical analysis, and in atomic isotope separation.

Century of Progress Exposition, international exhibition celebrating Chicago's centenary, held on the shores of Lake Michigan, 1933-34. Primarily concerned with science and technology, it also stimulated design and architecture.

Century plant, any of several desert plants (genus *Agave*) native to warm climates in the Americas. The name arose from the misconception that the plant bloomed only once every 100 years. The century plant, also known as the American aloe, has thick fleshy leaves and produces a yellow flower spike. In Mexico, the sap of some agaves is used to make beverages, and the long tough fiber is formed into cord and rope.

Cephalopoda, class of predatory mollusks including the cuttlefish, octopus, and squid. They swim by forcing a jet of water through a narrow funnel near the mouth. Cephalopods have sucker-bearing arms and a horny beak. The shell, typical of most mollusks, is absent or reduced.

Cephalosporins, group of broad-spectrum antibiotics, most of which are derived from the penicillinlike cephalosporin C that was discovered in sewage in Sardinia. They act against the same bacteria as natural penicillin and can produce allergic reactions.
See also: Antibiotic.

Cepheid variables, yellow giant stars whose brightness varies regularly with a period of 1 to 50 days. The length of their cycle is directly proportional to their brightness, making them useful mileposts for computing large astronomical distances.

Ceram *See:* Indonesia.

Ceramics, materials produced by treating nonmetallic, inorganic substances (originally clay) at high temperatures. Modern ceramics include such diverse products as porcelain and china, furnace bricks, electric insulators, ferrite magnets, rocket nosecones, and abrasives. In general, ceramics are hard, are chemically inert under most conditions, and can withstand high temperatures in industrial applications. Primitive ceramics in the form of pottery date from the 5th millennium B.C.
See also: Pottery and porcelain.

Cerberus, in Greek mythology, huge multiheaded dog, with a mane and tail of snakes, that guarded the entrance to Hades.
See also: Hades.

Cereal, generic name for annual plants of the grass family, including wheat, rice, corn, barley, sorghum, millet, oats, and rye. Cereal is richer in carbohydrates than any other food, and also contains protein and vitamins. About

1,757 million acres of the world's arable land are sown with cereal crops each year.

Cerebellum *See:* Brain.

Cerebral hemorrhage, bleeding from a broken blood vessel in the brain, with damage to or destruction of surrounding tissues. The interruption of circulation also causes damage to tissue elsewhere in the brain. Cerebral hemorrhages are often fatal, and can leave victims suffering from various disabilities, including loss of speech and loss or impairment of muscle control.
See also: Stroke.

Cerebral palsy, diverse group of conditions caused by brain damage around the time of birth and resulting in a variable degree of nonprogressive physical and mental handicap. The condition is often accompanied by abnormalities of muscle control, loss of sensation, and some degree of deafness. Speech and intellectual development can also be impaired but may be entirely normal.

Cerebrospinal fluid, serum-like fluid produced in the lateral ventricles of the brain; it bathes the brain and spinal cord.
Lumbar puncture (spinal tap) between the third and fourth lumbar vertebrae is performed to obtain a specimen of cerebrospinal fluid for diagnostic study of brain and spinal cord disease.
See also: Human body.

Cerebrum *See:* Brain.

Ceres, in Roman mythology, goddess of grain, agriculture, and the harvest. A daughter of Saturn, she was the counterpart of the Greek Demeter. She was honored annually with a festival called Cerealia. The word "cereal" is derived from her name.
See also: Mythology.

Ceres, largest and first discovered (1801) of thousands of asteroids, or minor planets, that orbit the sun between Jupiter and Mars. It is named after the Roman goddess of grain.

Cerium, chemical element, symbol Ce; for physical constants see Periodic Table. A malleable metal, cerium is the most abundant of the rare-earth metals. Cerium was discovered in 1803 by Jons Berzelius and Wilhelm van Hisinger. It is found in various minerals monazite, being the most important source. Cerium and its compounds are used for decolorizing and polishing glass, in incandescent gas mantles, in carbon-arc lighting, and as catalysts.

Cermet, or ceramal, composite material made from mixed metals and ceramics. Cermets combine the hardness and strength of metals with a high resistance to corrosion, wear, and heat, qualities that make it invaluable in jet engines, cutting tools, brake linings, and nuclear reactors.

Cervantes Saavedra, Miguel de (1547-1616), Spanish novelist, poet, and playwright, a major figure of Spanish literature. In 1585 he wrote *La Galatea*, a pastoral novel in verse and prose. In 1605 he published the first part of *Don Quixote de la Mancha*, his masterpiece. A debunking of pseudo-chivalric romance and a rich tragi-comic novel, it was an immediate success. He also wrote about 30 plays, of which 16 survive, a volume of short stories, and the second part of *Don Quixote* (1615). His last work was the prose epic *Persilas and Sigismunda* (1617).
See also: Don Quixote.

Cesarean section, surgical incision through the abdominal wall and uterus, performed to deliver a baby. Usually done when a vaginal delivery is considered dangerous because the woman's pelvis is too narrow or the baby is in an abnormal position.
See also: Birth.

Cesium, chemical element, symbol Cs; for physical constants see Periodic Table. Cesium was discovered spectroscopically by Robert Bunsen and Gustav Kirchhoff in 1860. It is a metal belonging to the alkaline group. Elemental cesium is silvery-white, soft, and ductile; it is one of the three metallic elements that is liquid at room temperature. Cesium is used in ion propulsion systems and in atomic clocks, as well as in optical instruments and in glass and ceramic production.

CETA (Comprehensive Training and Employment Act of 1973), federally funded system for training unemployed people and providing them with jobs and job- related services. The Neighborhood Youth Corps, the Job Corps, and the Young Adult Conservation Corps are CETA programs. In 1981 severe cutbacks in Federal funding eliminated many programs.

Cetacean, any of the mammalian order (Cetacea) comprised of whales, porpoises, and dolphins. Cetaceans have fishlike bodies with virtually no hair and thick layers of blubber to keep them warm. They bear their young alive and live entirely in water.

Cetewayo, or Cetshwayo (1826-84), fourth and last Zulu king (1873-79). In 1879 he declared war on British and Boer settlers in the Transvaal, but was captured and deposed.
See also: Zulu.

Ceylon *See:* Sri Lanka.

Cézanne, Paul (1839-1906), French painter. His early work is impressionist in style, but he later abandoned that mode to develop an approach of his own, lyrical and vibrantly colorful, as in the *Grandes Baigneuses* (1905). Cézanne sought to suggest depth through the use of color and to give his paintings structural strength and formal integrity. He became a prime innovator of modern art, anticipating Cubism and other movements.

Chabrier, Alexis Emmanuel (1841-94), French composer best remembered for orchestral works such as *España* (1883) and various piano pieces. His work influenced Claude Debussy, Maurice Ravel, and Erik Satie.

Chad

Capital:	N'Djamena
Area:	495,755 sq mi
	(1,284,000 sq km)
Population:	7,359,000
Language:	French, Arabic
Government:	Presidential republic
Independent:	1960
Head of gov.:	Prime minister
Per capita:	U.S. $180
Mon. unit:	1 CFA franc = 100
	centimes

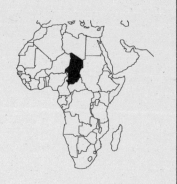

Chad (Republic of), landlocked state in north-central Africa bordered by 6 states, including Libya to the north and the Central African Republic to the south. N'Djamena is the capital.

Land and Climate. Its northern part extends into the Sahara desert, where the Tibesti highlands rise to 11,000 ft (3,353 m). The southern part consists largely of semiarid steppe with wooded grasslands (savannas) near Lake Chad, watered by the Shari and Logone rivers.

People. Northern and central Chad are inhabited chiefly by nomadic Arab-influenced tribes, who are predominantly Muslim; many speak Arabic as well as their tribal language. In the savanna regions the black population speaks tribal languages and includes chiefly animists, although small groups have adopted Islam. Fewer than 5,000 Europeans, mainly French, live in Chad. French is the official language.

Economy. Chad's economy is very poorly developed. The great majority of the population is engaged in subsistence farming. The chief export crop is cotton; some rice, peanuts, meat, hides, and smoked fish are also exported. A major obstacle to economic development is the lack of adequate roads, along with the absence of railroads. Chad depends on air and river transport, but the Shari River is navigable only 4 months of the year from Fort Lamy to Fort Archambault, and other rivers are even less reliable in the dry season.

History. Chad was penetrated by Arab traders and Berbers from the Sahara in the 7th century. The black kingdoms of Wadai and Baguirmi suffered from these incursions, but later became powerful sultanates. The Muslim empire of Kanem controlled most of the area around Lake Chad in the 16th century. The Chad area, lying in the heart of Africa, was not affected by the slave trade. Lake Chad was reached by British explorers in 1823. In 1850 the first German explorer mapped the area between Lake Chad and the Nile. By 1890 the French were arriving in considerable numbers, and by 1900 the French conquest of the whole area was completed. When French Equatorial Africa was formed in 1910, Chad was part of Ubangi-Shari-Chad and, 10 years later became the separate territory of Chad. In Aug. 1960 Chad became an independent republic within the French Community, with François Tombalbaye as the first president. Tombalbaye was killed in a coup in 1975. A new coalition government took power in 1979, but civil war soon broke out between rebels backed by Libya's Muammar Qadhaffi and government forces supported by France. The conflict has continued, in various forms. In the late 1990s the conflict focused on the exploitation of the oil fields.

Chadwick, Sir James (1891-1974), English physicist who was awarded the 1935 Nobel Prize in 1932 for his discovery of the neutron.
See also: Physics.

Chagall, Marc (1887-1985), Russian painter. His style is characterized by dreamlike, lyrical fantasy and bright but never harsh colors. His subjects are often derived from the traditions of folklore and Jewish life in Russia before World War I. Chagall also illustrated a number of books and created memorable works in stained glass. Two large murals (1966) are in the Metropolitan Opera House, New York City.

Chagres, river in eastern Panama that was dammed during construction of the Panama Canal, thus forming Gatun Lake.

Chaikovsky, Peter Ilich *See:* Tchaikovsky, Peter Ilich.

Chain, Sir Ernst Boris (1906-79), German-born English biochemist who helped develop penicillin for clinical use. He shared with Howard W. Florey and Alexander Fleming the 1945 Nobel Prize for physiology or medicine.
See also: Biochemistry; Penicillin.

Chain reaction *See:* Nuclear energy.

Chair, everyday piece of furniture that in early civilizations was reserved for persons in high authority. This historical significance is reflected in the term "chairman." A skilled craft became an art in the hands of English makers Thomas Chippendale (1718-79) and George Hepplewhite (d.1786); and U.S. cabinetmakers William Savery (1721-87) and Duncan Phyfe (c.1786-1854). Wood remains a favorite material, but steel and plastics are also now used. Modern chairs are designed on ergonomic principles; to conform to the structure of the body, thus providing support at anatomically correct points.

Chalcedony, mineral consisting of microcrystalline silica (silicon dioxide) with a glassy or waxy luster, sometimes translucent. Chalcedony occurs in a wide range of colors, some forms valued as gems and ornamental stones. Bloodstone (heliotrope), a dark green variety with red spots, was often used in the Middle Ages in sculptures showing martyrdom. Other chalcedonies are jasper, carnelian, agate, and onyx.

Chalcocite, sulfide mineral (Cu_2S) that is an important ore of copper. Shiny gray in color, chalcocite is formed at fairly low temperatures.
See also: Copper.

Chalcopyrite, most important copper ore. It contains iron and sulfur as well as copper, and has the formula $CuFeS_2$. Chalcopyrite has a yellowish coloration with a metallic luster, though it easily tarnishes to produce iridescent colors. It is found worldwide.
See also: Copper.

Chaldea, name for southern Babylonia after its occupation by the Chaldeans in the 10th century B.C. The Chaldeans were accomplished astronomers and astrologers, and ancient writers often used their name as a synonym for "magician." In 626 B.C. Nabopolassar founded the Chaldean Neo-Babylonian Empire, which held sway over the area until it was captured by the Persians in 539 B.C.

Chaliapin, Feodor Ivanovich (1873-1938), Russian operatic bass. Famous for his acting as well as for his voice, he settled in France after the Russian Revolution. His main successes were as Mussorgsky's *Boris Godunov* and Boito's *Mefistofele*.
See also: Opera.

Chalk, soft, white rock composed of calcium carbonate, $CaCO_3$, a type of fine-grained, porous limestone containing the shells of minute marine animals. Widely used in lime and cement manufacture and as a fertilizer, chalk is also used in cosmetics, plastics, crayons, and oil paints.
See also: Calcite; Calcium carbonate.

Challenger, one of the 4 space shuttles of the NASA space program. On Feb. 3, 1984, it began a spectacular flight (its fourth mission) during which 2 astronauts became the first human beings to fly freely in space. On Jan. 28, 1986, Challenger exploded shortly after lift-off with a crew of 7 aboard.

Chamberlain, family name of 3 prominent British statesmen, **Joseph Chamberlain** (1836-1914) entered Parliament in 1876 as a Liberal. He fought for integration of the Empire through preferential tariffs. His son, **Sir Joseph Austen Chamberlain** (1863-1937), entered Parliament as a Conservative in 1892, and held various government offices from 1902. As foreign secretary (1924-29), he helped secure the Locarno Pact, which encouraged stability and good will in Europe following World War I, and shared the 1925 Nobel Peace Prize. Austen's half-brother, **Arthur Neville Chamberlain** (1869-1940), was a Conservative member of Parliament from 1918. He became prime minister in 1937. In his efforts to avert war with Germany, he followed a policy of appeasement and signed the Munich Pact (1938), which surrendered part of Czechoslovakia to Hitler.

Chamberlain, Wilt (1936-   ), U.S. basketball player. The 7-ft 1-in (216-cm) center, is regarded as one of the most dominant players of all time. Chamberlain holds National Basketball Association (NBA) records for most points in a season (4,029), in a game (100), and most rebounds per season (2,149), and is second on the all-time regular season scoring list (31,419 points). He played for the Philadelphia (now Golden State) Warriors, Philadelphia 76ers, and Los Angeles Lakers of the NBA (1959-72). He was inducted into the Basketball Hall of Fame in 1978.

Chamber music, musical composition intended for a small ensemble. Originally the term meant domestic music, written by a house composer for a patron. It became established as a special genre during the 17th and 18th centuries. The instrumental combinations are varied, usually with not more than 15 instruments. Chamber music is characterized by an intimacy of communication between the performers. The principal form of composition is the string quartet (2 violins, viola, and cello), which was developed by Franz Joseph Haydn and Wolfgang Amadeus Mozart, and expanded to new dimensions by Ludwig van Beethoven.

Chamber of Commerce, association of businesspeople set up to improve business conditions and practices, and to protect business interests. The first in the United States was the New York Chamber of Commerce (1768); now most sizeable cities have one. Activities are coordinated through the U.S. Chamber of Commerce, founded in 1912.

Chambers, Whittaker (1901-61), U.S. journalist and main witness in perjury trial of State Department official Alger Hiss. Chambers joined the Communist Party in 1924, became a Soviet agent during the 1930s, and in August 1948, testified that Alger Hiss passed him U.S. military secrets. Chambers' autobiography, *Witness*, was published in 1952.

Chameleon, lizard of the family Chamaeleonidae, found in Africa and Madagascar, that is well adapted to living in trees. Its tail is prehensile, and its eyes can turn independently in all directions. It feeds on insects that it catches with its long, sticky tongue, and the color of its skin alters swiftly in response to changes of emotion or temperature. There are over 80 species, ranging in length from 2 in to 2 ft (5 cm to 0.6 m).

Chamois (*Rupicapra rupicapra*), goatlike mammal of the family Bovidae found in the mountain forests of Europe and Asia Minor. Famous for their agility, chamois are capable of leaps of over 20 ft (6 m). They have thick brown coats and stand about 3 ft at the shoulder. Their hides were used for making the original chamois leather.

Chamomile *See:* Camomile.

Champagne, historic province in northwestern France, famous for the effervescent sparkling white wines from vineyards between Reims and Epernay. The ruling counts of Champagne were especially powerful during the 12th and 13th centuries, and the region had a central role in French history.
See also: France.

Champlain, Samuel de (1567-1635), French explorer, first governor of French Canada. He explored the St. Lawrence Gulf and River (1603) as far as the Lachine Rapids. He explored much of what is now Nova Scotia, founded Quebec in 1608, discovered Lake Champlain in 1609, and was named commandant of New France in 1612. When Quebec surrendered to the English in 1629, Champlain was imprisoned in England; on his release in 1633 he returned to Canada as governor.
See also: Lake Champlain; Quebec.

Champollion, Jean François (1790-1832), French linguist and historian. Professor of history at Grenoble University (1809-16), he was the first to effectively decipher Egyptian hieroglyphics, a result of his research on the Rosetta stone.
See also: Rosetta stone.

Champs Élysées *See:* Paris (city).

Chancellorsville, Battle of, U.S. Civil War battle, May 1-5, 1863. Gen. Joseph Hooker's Union forces crossed the Rappahannock River to Chancellorsville, west of Fredericksburg, Va., in a bid to encircle Gen. Robert E. Lee's Confederate forces protecting Fredericksburg. The ploy failed; Lee's counteroffensive led to a Confederate victory in a battle that claimed 30,000 lives, including that of Gen. Stonewall Jackson.
See also: Civil War, U.S.

Chandler, Raymond Thornton (1888-1959), U.S. detective novelist whose works combine wit and pace with strong characterization, particularly of their hero, Philip Marlowe, a tough but honest private detective. Among Chandler's best- known works are *The Big Sleep* (1939) and *The Long Goodbye* (1953).

Chandler, Zachariah (1813-79), U.S. politician, a founder of the Republican Party. Elected to the Senate in 1857, he firmly opposed slavery and the Confederate cause. He was secretary of the interior, 1875-77.
See also: Republican Party.

Chandragupta, Maurya (4th century B.C.), Indian emperor c.321-297 B.C., founder of the Maurya dynasty. He rose to power after Alexander the Great's withdrawal from India, extending his realm into Afghanistan. His grandson was the emperor Asoka.
See also: Maurya Empire.

Changamire Empire *See:* Zimbabwe.

Channel bass *See:* Redfish.

Channel Islands, archipelago totaling 75 sq mi (194 sq km) in area, in the English Channel off northwestern France. Dependencies of the British crown since 1066, they are administered according to their own local constitutions. The main islands are Jersey, Guernsey, Sark, and Alderney.

Channel Islands National Park (est. 1980), 8 islands off South California, extending over 150 mi (241 k) in the Pacific Ocean. The islands include Santa Barbara, Anacapa, San Miguel, Santa Rosa, and Santa Cruz, known for sea mammals, including the California sea lion, and rich fossil beds.

Channing, William Ellery (*1*780-1842), U.S. theologian, writer, and philanthropist, leader of the Unitarian movement in New England. Active in antislavery, temperance, and pacifist causes, he believed that moral improvement was humanity's prime concern. He influenced Emerson, Holmes, and Bryant.
See also: Unitarianism.

Chansons de Geste, medieval French epic poems written from the 11th through the 13th centuries. Most deal with the legendary exploits of the Emperor Charlemagne and his knights. The best known is the *Chanson de Roland*, composed c.1098-1100.
See also: Charlemagne.

Chanukah *See:* Hanukkah.

Chaos, in Greek mythology, first being to be created, represented as a living creature made up of all the world's components. It was believed that all other beings emanated from Chaos.
See also: Mythology.

Chaparral, area of plant growth dominated by shrubs, evergreen oaks (including the mountain mahogany and scrub oak), and the chamiso scrub. North American chaparrals exist in southern California, some slopes of the Rocky Mountains, the Sierra Nevada, and Baja California, in Mexico.

Chapel, place of Christian worship, usually located in a chamber within a church. Chapels originated after the early Middle Ages because the increase of relics and altars devoted to certain saints required them. The Sistine Chapel in the Vatican is probably the best known.

Chaplin, Charlie (Sir Charles Spencer Chaplin; 1889-1977), English film actor and director, great comedian of the silent cinema. A vaudeville player, he rose to fame in Hollywood, 1913-19 in a series of short comedies, in which he established his Little Tramp character. After 1918 he produced his own feature-length films, including *The Gold Rush* (1925) and, with sound, *Modern Times* (1936) and *the Great Dictator* (1940).

Chapman, George, (1559?-1634), English poet and dramatist. His translations of Homer (1598- 1616), although imprecise and full of his own interjections, long remained standard, and they are still recognized as masterpieces. His plays include *Bussy d'Ambois* (1607).

Chapman, John *See:* Appleseed, Johnny.

Chapultepec, historic hill near Mexico City, site of an Aztec royal residence and religious center in the 14th century. American forces stormed the Spanish- built fort in the Mexican War of 1847. It is now a museum and state residence.
See also: Aztecs; Mexico.

Char, or brook trout, North American member of the trout family, (genus *Salvelinus*) prized for its flesh.

Charcoal, form of amorphous carbon produced when wood, peat, bones, cellulose, or other carbonaceous substances are heated with little or no air present. A highly porous residue of microcrystalline graphite remains. Charcoal as a fuel was used in blast furnaces until the advent of coke. A highly porous form, activated charcoal, is used for adsorption in refining processes and in gas masks.
See also: Carbon.

Charcot, Jean Martin (1825-93), French neurologist whose researches advanced knowledge of hysteria, multiple sclerosis, locomotor ataxia, asthma, and aging. Freud was one of his many pupils.
See also: Neurology.

Chard *See:* Swiss chard.

Chardin, Jean-Baptiste-Simeon (1699-1779), French painter. He is best known for his still-lifes and for his middle-period genre paintings, affectionate depictions of the everyday life of the bourgeoisie (*The Kiss, The Grace*). His work is characterized by a straightforward realism, with atmospheric use of light and color.

Chardonnet, Hilaire (1839-1924), French chemist, industrialist, and physiologist who did pioneering work on synthetic fiber, developing what later became known as rayon, first shown to the public at the Paris Exposition of 1889.
See also: Chemistry; Rayon.

Charlemagne (Charles the Great; 742?-814), King of the Franks, founder of the Holy Roman Empire. He waged war against the Saxons for 32 years, eventually compelling them to adopt Christianity. Crowned Emperor in Rome by Pope Leo III (800), Charlemagne ruled over a kingdom that included most of the lands that are now France, West Germany, Austria, Switzerland, the Netherlands, Belgium, and Luxembourg. It also included about half of Italy. The establishment of his reign sealed the break between the remnants of the Roman Empire and Byzantium, and thus the split between Roman Catholicism and the Greek Orthodox church. Charlemagne fostered a rich culture that inaugurated the Carolingian Renaissance.
See also: Holy Roman Empire.

Charles, name of 7 rulers of the Holy Roman Empire, starting with Charlemagne.

Charles, name of 10 kings of France. **Charles I** was Charlemagne. **Charles II** (the Bald; 823-77) reigned as king of the West Franks from 843 and as emperor of the West from 875. Numerous revolts and invasions troubled his reign, culturally the last flowering of the Carolingian renaissance. **Charles III** (the Simple; 879-929), grandson of Charles II, reigned (893-923). **Charles IV** (the Fair; 1294-1328) reigned from 1322. **Charles V** (the Wise; 1337-80) reigned as regent 1356-60 and as king from 1364. In poor health, he nevertheless put down a peasant uprising and various plots by his nobles. He declared war upon England in 1369 and before his death had regained most French territory occupied by the English. **Charles VI** (the Mad; 1368-1422) reigned from 1380. Corrupt advisers often ruled in his stead. England overran most of northern France, and Charles was forced to name Henry V of England his heir. **Charles VII** (1403-61) reigned from 1422. Early in his reign he was unwilling to challenge the English occupation of France, and he allowed Joan of Arc to be burned as a heretic. Later Charles introduced tax reforms, rebuilt his army, and regained all occupied territory except Calais. **Charles VIII** (1470-98) reigned from 1483. **Charles IX** (1550-74), who reigned 1560-98, was dominated by his mother, Catherine de Médici. **Charles X** (1757-1836) reigned 1824-30. He returned to France from exile after the restoration of the monarchy, becoming king on the death of his brother Louis XVIII. He was exiled again after the 1830 revolution.

Charles, Stuart kings of England, Scotland, and Ireland. **Charles I** (1600-49), a Catholic, came to the throne in 1625. His reign is most notable for his continual conflicts with the mainly Puritan Parliament. From 1629 to 1640 he ruled without a parliament, having dissolved it. Civil and religious liberties were eroded, leading to widespread emigration to America and finally, in the 1640s, to a civil war. In 1646-48 the king's supporters were defeated. Charles I was executed. His son, **Charles II** (1630-85) took refuge in France in 1646. In 1651 he returned to Scotland and was crowned king. He attempted to retake England, but was defeated by Oliver Cromwell and fled to France again. In 1660, 2 years after the death of Cromwell, Charles II took the throne again in the Stuart Restoration. Despite his dissolution of Parliament in 1681, that institution's power increased during his reign. Political parties were born, and colonization flourished.

Charles I (1887-1922), last emperor of Austria and King of Hungary (1916-18). When coming to the throne, during World War I, he made peace overtures to the Allies, which provoked opposition in Germany. He abdicated after Austria's defeat in the war, going into exile in Switzerland. Three years later he unsuccessfully tried to regain the throne of Hungary.

Charles, Philip Arthur George (1948-), Prince of Wales and Duke of Cornwall, heir apparent to the British throne. The first child of Queen Elizabeth II and Prince Philip, he was educated at Cheam, Gordonstoun, and Cambridge. In 1981 he married Lady Diana Spencer.

Charles, Ray (Ray Charles Robinson; 1930-), U.S. singer, composer, and pianist, credited with synthesizing aspects of gospel, blues and country, and jazz to create a new form of music known as soul. He lost his eyesight at age 6 to untreated glaucoma. Charles's first popular successes were "Baby Let Me Hold Your Hand" (1951) and "I've Got a Woman" (1955). His albums include *Ray Charles* (1957), *Modern Sounds in Country and Western Music* (1962), and *Wish You Were Here Tonight* (1983).

Charles Martel (A.D. 688-741), Frankish ruler who, as mayor of the palace (chief minister) from 714, ruled in place of the weak Merovingian kings. The son of Pepin II, he received his surname Martel (the Hammer) after his victory against Muslim invaders in 732. His policies assured Frankish preeminence in northern Europe, which culminated in his grandson Charlemagne's coronation as emperor (800).
See also: Merovingian.

Charles the Great *See:* Charlemagne.

Charleston (pop. 506,875), capital of South Carolina and major regional port. The oldest and largest city in the state, Charleston is a tourist center famous for its 18th-century buildings and monuments. It is also a producer of chemicals and steel. In 1861 it was the scene of the first military incident of the Civil War, the firing on Fort Sumter.
See also: South Carolina.

Charlotte (pop. 1,162,093), largest city in North Carolina, seat of Mecklenburg County. A flourishing commercial, industrial, and railroad center, it

produces textiles, manufactures chemicals and cottonseed oil, and is the central market for the region's agricultural products. Johnson C. Smith University, Queens College, and a campus of the University of North Carolina are located there.
See also: North Carolina.

Charlotte Amalie (pop. 11,800), capital of the U.S. Virgin Islands, located on St. Thomas. Founded by Danish colonists in 1673, it was purchased by the United States in 1917.
See also: Virgin Islands.

Charlottestown (pop. 15,800), capital of Prince Edward Island, Canada, on an estuary of the Hillsborough River. When the city was founded in 1720 by French colonists, it was known as Port de la Joie, but it was renamed in 1763 for the wife of King George III. Incorporated in 1875, it is now a fishing and shipbuilding center.
See also: Prince Edward Island.

Charlottesville (pop. 131,107), city in Virginia situated in the foothills of the Blue Ridge Mountains; seat of Albemarle County. Founded in 1762, it was named after the wife of King George III. Charlottesville is the site of the University of Virginia, founded in 1819 by Thomas Jefferson, whose home, Monticello (now a national monument), stands on a hill overlooking the city. The area's industries involve agricultural products, textiles, lumbering, and precision instruments.
See also: Virginia.

Charon, in Greek mythology, son of Erebus (the belt of darkness between Earth and Hades) and Nyx (night). His task was to ferry dead souls across the rivers Acheron and Styx to Hades, the underworld.
See also: Mythology.

Charter Oak, celebrated oak tree in which the Connecticut colonial charter was hidden in 1687 to prevent its surrender to the royal governor of New England. The tree was uprooted in a storm in 1856, at an estimated age of 1,000 years.

Chartism, radical and unsuccessful attempt by voteless British laborers to gain economic and social equality, 1838-48. It was one of the first working-class political movements in Britain. William Lovett of the London Workingmen's Association drafted the "People's Charter."

Chartres (pop. 37,100), historic city in northwestern France, capital of Eure-et-Loire department and commercial center of the Beauce region. It is famous for its Gothic Cathedral of Notre Dame, built in the 12th and 13th centuries.
See also: France.

Chartres Cathedral *See:* Chartres.

Charybdis *See:* Scylla and Charybdis.

Chase, Salmon Portland (1808-73), U.S. senator (1849-55, 1860-61), governor of Ohio (1855-59), secretary of the treasury (1861-64), and chief justice of the U.S. Supreme Court (1864-73). An abolitionist, he instituted a national banking system under the Lincoln administration and presided over the impeachment trial of President Andrew Jackson.
See also: Supreme Court of the United States.

Chase, Samuel (1741-1811), U.S. Supreme Court justice (1796-1811). A signer of the Declaration of Independence, he was also a member of the Maryland legislature and the Continental Congress. In 1804 an unsuccessful attempt to impeach him was made by President Jefferson, who believed Chase to be a partisan pro-Federalist.
See also: Supreme Court of the United States.

Chase, William Merritt (1849-1916), U.S. painter and art teacher known for his portraits and still lifes. Chase taught in New York City and on Long Island. Among his students were Sheeler, Hopper, and O'Keeffe.

Chat, any of several singing birds. The yellow-breasted chat (*Icteria virens*) is the largest wood warbler and is common in thickets over much of the United States.

Château, French term for castle, often applied to any stately mansion; originally a well-fortified medieval castle with a moat, used for defense rather than residence. The 16th century château contained outbuildings and were of a more residential nature. Elegant châteaus in the Loire valley in France are Chenonceaux and Chinon.
See also: Castle.

Chateaubriand, François René, Vicomte de (1768-1848), French writer and diplomat, a founder of the Romantic movement in 19th-century French literature. His works include the North American romance *Atala* (1801), *René* (1802), and *Mémoires d'outre-tombe* (1849-50).
See also: French language.

Chatham, Earl of *See:* Pitt.

Chattanooga (pop. 162,000), city in southern Tennessee, on the Tennessee River near the Georgia border. Chattanooga's strategic position as a railroad junction made it an important Northern stronghold in the Civil War. It later grew into a major transportation and industrial center for textiles and metals.
See also: Tennessee.

Chattanooga, Battle of *See:* Civil War, U.S.

Chatteron, Thomas (1752-70), English poet who at the age of 12 wrote poems in pseudomedieval English that he presented as the work of a 15th-century monk, Thomas Rowley. Despite the success of a burlesque opera, The Revenge (1770), he remained destitute and poisoned himself at age 17.

Chaucer, Geoffrey (c.1340-1400), English poet. His early writing, including an incomplete translation of *Le Roman de la Rose*, shows strong French

influence. In the 1370s, growing familiarity with Boccaccio and Dante influenced *The Parliament of Fowls* and *Troilus and Criseyde*, a powerful love poem. His masterpiece was *The Canterbury Tales*, a 17,000-line poem, in which pilgrims on their way to the shrine of St. Thomas à Becket pass the time by telling stories ranging from the serious to the comedic and ribald. Apart from creating vivid characters, the tales portray contemporary attitudes toward religion, love, and sex. The language of *The Canterbury Tales* is Middle English, sufficiently different from modern English to require translation to be understood. Changes in the language, particularly the emergence of Early Modern English less than a century after Chaucer's death, vastly reduced the popularity of his work, but since the 18th century, he has come to be regarded as one of the masters of world literature.
See also: Canterbury Tales.

Chauncy, Charles (1705-87), influential American Congregationalist minister, a critic of the Great Awakening religious revivalists. He supported the American Revolution in his sermons.

Chautauqua Movement, U.S. adult education movement that began at Lake Chautauqua, N.Y., in 1874, as a course for Sunday school teachers. The founders, John H. Vincent, a Methodist minister, and Lewis Miller, a businessperson, organized lectures, concerts, and recreation activities attended by thousands each year until c.1924.

Chavez, Carlos (1899-1978), Mexican composer who founded the Symphony Orchestra of Mexico (1928), which he conducted until 1949. His compositions include the ballet *El fuego nuevo* (1921), the ballet-symphony *H. P.* (1926-27), and *Invention*, for string trio (1965).

Chavez, Cesar Estrada (1927-), Chicano (Mexican-American) labor leader, founder of the United Farm Workers (UFW), an affiliate of the AFL-CIO. The early history of the UFW was marked by bitter strikes and violent clashes with both growers and the Teamsters. In the 1960s and 1970s, Chavez was instrumental in organizing national boycotts of table grapes and lettuce in solidarity with the struggle of the farm workers.

Chayote, climbing vine of the gourd family cultivated chiefly for its pear-shaped, round fruit, which is used in puddings, pies, and salads. The plant is also used as livestock feed.

Checkers, or draughts, game played by two people on a board of 64 alternating light and dark squares. Each player begins with 12 red or black checkers placed on the 12 dark squares nearest him or her. Taking turns, players advance their checkers diagonally in a forward direction. Once the last row of the board is reached, checkers are crowned, becoming kings, which may move forward or backward and can jump backwards over their opponents. The game became popular in Europe in the 16th century, but its origins go back to ancient times.

Checks and balances, term that describes the powers of the 3 branches of government: the legislature, which makes laws; the executive, which enforces them; and the judiciary, which interprets them. Each branch acts

independently and participates in the realms of the other 2, thus limiting potential abuse of power.
See also: Government.

Cheese, food made from the milk of cows, sheep, or goats, with a high content of protein, calcium, and vitamins. Hard cheeses include Cheddar and Parmesan, soft cheeses may be unripened (cottage cheese) or ripened (Brie, Camembert) to develop flavor.

Cheetah, tawny-coated, black-spotted cat (*Acinonyx jubatus*), native to Africa and southwest Asia, the fastest land animal, capable of running at speeds of up to 70 mi (113 k) per hr. The average adult weighs 100 lb (45 kg). Hunting has greatly reduced their numbers.

Cheever, John (1912-82), U.S. author. Noted for his irony and poetic style in portraying the lives of the upper middle classes in suburbia, he was awarded the Pulitzer Prize for fiction (1978) for *The Stories of John Cheever*. His novels are *The Wapshot Chronicle* (1957), *The Wapshot Scandal* (1964), *Bullet Park* (1969), *Falconer* (1979), and *Oh What a Paradise It Seems* (1982).

Cheka, Russian abbreviation of "Extraordinary Commission for Combatting Counter-Revolution, Speculation, Sabotage, and Misuse of Authority," the secret police set up by the Bolsheviks in 1917 to eliminate their opponents. Reorganized by Lenin in 1922 and renamed the GPU (State Political Directorate), it was the ancestor of the modern KGB.
See also: KGB.

Chekhov, Anton Pavlovich (1860-1904), Russian dramatist and short story writer. The Moscow Art Theatre produced his 4 major plays, depictions of Russian rural upper- and middle-class life: *The Seagull* (1898), *Uncle Vanya* (1899), *The Three Sisters* (1901), and *The Cherry Orchard* (1904). Chekhov's works emphasize mood and character development more than plot. He was also a physician, and ran a free clinic for peasants in Melikhovo, where he lived.

Chemical and biological warfare, military use of chemical poisons or disease-causing agents against enemy troops, civilians, animals, and plants. In World War I chlorine, mustard gas (causing skin blistering), and phosgene (causing fatal lung irritation), killed 100,000. Newer, deadly nerve gases are weapons of mass destruction. In the war in Vietnam U.S. forces used riot-control gases and chemical defoliants with carcinogenic effects. The Iraqi regime of Saddam Hussein used poison gas against the Kurdish population in Iraq and against Iranian troops during the Iran-Iraq War (1980-88).

Chemical bond *See:* Chemistry; Mineral.

Chemical element *See:* Element.

Chemical engineering *See:* Engineering.

Chemical reaction, process whereby 1 substance is changed chemically into another through the formation or destruction of bonds between atoms. Chemical equations, consisting of formulas and symbols representing elements and compounds, express the events of chemical reactions.
See also: Chemistry.

Chemical warfare *See:* Chemical and biological warfare.

Chemistry, science dealing with the composition of substances and the changes that occur when they react with one another. All chemical changes take place by the linking-up of atoms into molecules, a molecule being the smallest particle of a chemical compound that has that compound's characteristic properties. Chemical reactions may involve elements themselves, elements and compounds, or compounds and other compounds. Atoms themselves remain fundamentally unchanged in chemical reactions. It is the grouping of the atoms into molecules that is altered. Some chemical changes are relatively simple, while others, such as those that occur during the chemical processes of living matter, are highly complex, involving molecules that may consist of thousands of atoms. Organic chemistry deals with the chemistry of compounds of carbon (the chemical processes of life take place between substances in which carbon plays a major role). Inorganic chemistry is concerned with all the remaining elements. Apart from that broad division, there are other specialized fields. Physical chemistry deals with the physical properties and behavior of chemicals. Analytical chemistry develops laboratory methods of determining the chemical structure of materials. Chemotherapy is the treatment of diseases with chemical drugs; biochemistry is concerned with living processes; chemurgy deals with agricultural products; electrochemistry studies the electrical effects of chemical change.

Chemotherapy, use of nonantibiotic chemical substances to treat disease, most often cancer. The drug destroys rapidly spreading cancer cells without significantly affecting normal cells in the body.
See also: Cancer.

Chénier, André Marie de (1762-94), French poet. His work forms a bridge between classicism and romanticism: *Le Jeune Captive* (1795), *Elégies* and *Bucoliques* (1819). He was guillotined during the French Revolution for writing pamphlets against the Reign of Terror.

Chennault, Claire Lee (1890-1958), U.S. pilot. In 1937 he went to China to organize Chiang Kai-shek's air force in the war against Japan. In 1941 he organized in China the American Volunteer Group, the Flying Tigers. From 1942 to 1945 he served as commander of the U.S. air forces in China.
See also: Flying Tigers.

Cheops *See:* Khufu.

Cherbourg (pop. 28,400), seaport and naval station in France, on the English Channel. The harbor is a base for French fishing fleets and a port of call for oceangoing vessels.
See also: France.

Cherimoya (*Annona cherimola*), tropical tree native to Peru and Ecuador. It grows to about 25 ft (7.5 m), bearing oval, deciduous alternate leaves about 10 in (25 cm) long. Its round or conical edible fruit is pale green, 5 in (13 cm) long and weighing 1 lb (.45 kg), with an inner white pulp tasting of pineapple and banana. The cherimoya is cultivated in California and Florida.

Chernenko, Konstantin Ustinovich (1911-85), leader of the Communist Party of the Soviet Union (1984-85). He joined the Communist Party in 1931 and became a protege of Leonid Brezhnev, thus rising in the hierarchy of the party. In 1978, Chernenko was elected a full member of the Politburo, the policymaking body of the Communist Party. He became general secretary of the Communist Party in Feb. of 1984. As its leader, Chernenko renewed arms control talks with the United States. He was succeeded by Mikhail Gorbachev.
See also: Union of Soviet Socialist Republics.

Cherokees, once the largest Native American tribe in the southeast United States. The Iroquis-speaking Cherokees were decimated by smallpox and by conflicts with European settlers in the 18th century. They were deprived of their lands, and thousands of them died on a march west in 1838, an event known in Cherokee history as the "trail of tears." Today nearly 45,000 Cherokees live in Oklahoma. Several thousand remain in N. Carolina.

Cherry, any of several trees (genus *Prunus*) best known for their red, fleshy fruits with hard pits. Varieties of sweet and sour cherries are grown widely in the United States. Cherry blossom trees are also grown as ornaments and for their fine-grained timber.

Cherry laurel (family Rosaceae, genus *Prunus*), any of various evergreen shrubs native to southeastern Europe and the Orient. The cherry laurel is grown for ornamental use in the United States. Reaching to 18 ft (5.4 m), the shrub bears small, glossy, poisonous leaves, fragrant clusters of small white flowers, and dark purple, foul-tasting friut.

Cherubini, Maria Luigi (1760-1842), Italian composer who spent most of his life in France. He wrote operas: *Medea* (1797) and *Les Deux journées* (1800), which influenced Beethoven, and sacred works, such as the *Requiem in D minor* (1836).
See also: Opera.

Chesapeake and Ohio Canal, waterway along the Potomac River between Washington, D.C., and Cumberland, Md. Planned as a route to the Midwest, it went bankrupt because of competition from the railroads. The canal became a historical park in 1961.

Chesapeake Bay, large inlet of the Atlantic Ocean on the east coast of the United States, an important trade route for oceangoing vessels. About 200 mi (320 km) long and 30 mi (48 km) wide, the bay separates the Delmarva Peninsula from sections of Maryland and Virginia.
See also: Atlantic Ocean.

Chesapeake Bay retriever, medium-sized breed of water-loving hunting dogs of the sporting group. The dog stands 21-26 in (53-66 cm) at the shoulder and weighs 55-75 lbs (25-34 kg), and possesses yellowish eyes. Its short, thick, oily coat ranges from dark brown to light tan in color, resists cold, and easily sheds water. The breed was developed in the United States when two English-stock puppies were found shipwrecked off the Maryland coast (1807) and were bred with local retrievers.

Chesnutt, Charles Waddell (1858-1932), African-American educator, lawyer, and fiction author. *The Conjure Woman* (1899), a group of short stories, related incidents of slavery in a dialectic, folktale style and was his first and best-known book. Chesnutt was the recipient of the Spingarn Medal (1928) for his literary depictions of the struggles faced by blacks in America. He ceased writing in 1905 but continued to practice law until his death. Other works include *The Wife of His Youth and Other Stories of the Color Line* (1899), *The House Behind the Cedars* (1900), and *The Marrow of Tradition* (1901).

Chess, sophisticated board game for 2 players probably invented in India in ancient times. It was introduced into Persia in the 6th century A.D. and was brought to Europeans by the Arabs, probably at the time of the Crusades. By the 13th century, the game was widespread in Europe, and the rules of the modern version were definitively stabilized in the 16th century. The first modern world championship was held in 1851, and world champions have been recognized continuously since then. The game board has 64 squares in 8 rows of 8, and each player has 16 pieces. Each piece moves in specific ways, and the players alternate moves. The object of the game is to capture the opponent's king. If neither player is able to do this, the game is drawn. At the highest levels of international play, draws are common.

Chesterfield, Philip Dormer Stanhope, 4th Earl of (1694-1773), English politician and author chiefly remembered for his posthumously published *Letters to His Son* (1774), which offer vivid, amusing insights into the morality of the age.

Chesterton, G(ilbert) K(eith) (1874-1936), English author and critic, noted for his lyrical style and delight in paradox. He wrote poetry, stories (the Father Brown detective stories, 1911-35), novels (*The Napoleon of Notting Hill*, 1904), literary criticism (on Browning, 1903, and Dickens, 1906); and essays, collected in *Tremendous Trifles* (1909).

Chestnut, any of various deciduous trees (genus *Castanea*) of the beech family, with edible nuts. The American chestnut is rare, having been nearly wiped out by a fungus, "chestnut blight," introduced from Asia in 1904 and spread by woodpeckers. The related chinquapin of the southeastern states appears to be immune. Chestnuts are highly valued for their timber, nuts, and bark.

Chevalier, Maurice (1888-1972), French singer and film star. He gained international fame in the 1920s and 1930s as the embodiment of French charm and light-heartedness. His films include *The Love Parade* (1930), *Gigi* (1958), and *Can-Can* (1959).

Chevrolet, Louis (1879-1941), Swiss-born U.S. automobile racer and designer; in 1911 he designed and built (with William C. Durant) the first Chevrolet, a 6-cylinder car produced to compete with the Ford. He later designed the racers that won the 1920 and 1921 Indianapolis 500-mile race. *See also:* Automobile.

Chewing gum, confection made from chicle, other resins and waxes, sugar, and corn syrup. For centuries Native American tribes chewed chicle (gum from the juice of the sapodilla tree) or spruce resin. Early European settlers adopted the habit, and chewing gum has been made commercially in the United States since the 1860s.

Cheyenne (pop. 73,142), capital of Wyoming and center of its agriculture. Founded in 1867 by U.S. Army officers and Union Pacific Railroad engineers, the town became an outfitting station for prospectors going West and a haven for outlaws until vigilantes gained control. Its annual Frontier Days attract thousands of tourists. *See also:* Wyoming.

Cheyenne, North American tribe speaking an Algonquian language. By the mid 19th century the Cheyenne had become nomadic hunters on the Great Plains, and after 1860 their fierce battles against encroaching whites culminated in the defeat of General Custer in 1876 by an alliance of Sioux and northern Cheyenne forces. Eventually the Cheyenne were resettled in Oklahoma and Montana.

Chiang Ching-kuo (1910-88), leader of the Nationalist Chinese government on Taiwan (1975- 88). The son of Chiang Kaishek and his first wife, he was born in Zhejiang province. He attended Chinese schools before going to the Soviet Union to study in 1925, where he graduated from the military-political institute in Leningrad. In 1937 Chiang returned to China, where he advanced rapidly in the Nationalist government, becoming defense minister in 1965, prime minister in 1972, and president in 1978. Chiang was popular for his efforts in eliminating corruption in government. *See also:* Taiwan.

Chiang Kai-shek (1887-1975), Chinese Nationalist leader. After Sun Yat-sen's Revolution (1911), Chiang joined the Kuomintang, the governing party, organized the nationalist army, and rose rapidly to power. After Sun's death (1925), Chiang made an alliance with the Communists, but in 1927 he reversed course, initiating a 22-year-long civil war against them. Chiang became president of the Nationalist government in 1928, and he commanded Chinese and later (1942) Allied forces in the war against Japan. In 1949, with the victory of the Communists in the civil war, Chiang withdrew from the mainland to Taiwan, where he became president of Nationalist China (1950). *See also:* China.

Chibcha, inhabitants of the plateau of Bogota in central Colombia. Their highly developed society was based on farming and the worship of the Sun God. The Spaniards destroyed their culture in the 16th century. Over a million descendants survive in the area today.

Chicago (pop. 2,768,500), third-largest city in the United States, on Lake Michigan in Illinois, hub of the U.S. road, rail, and air systems. Industry is diverse, including the famous meatpacking plants, grain elevators, and chemical, metal, and printing industries. Chicago grew as a French trading post in the 1700s, but it was not until after the Black Hawk War (1832) that the city began to grow rapidly. Even the Great Fire of 1871, which destroyed 2,000 acres of property, could not end Chicago's vitality. Downtown Chicago has some of the world's tallest buildings. The North Side, along the lake, is residential. The West Side is a largely white mixture of various ethnic groups, while the South Side is home to most of the city's African-Americans, who constitute nearly 40% of the population.
See also: Illinois.

Chicago, University of, private, nondenominational, coeducational institution in Chicago, Ill, incorporated in 1890. It has about 7,500 students and over 1,000 faculty members. The Pritzker School of Medicine, the Enrico Fermi Institute for Nuclear Studies, and the department of education are among its best-known facilities.

Chicano, person of Mexican-American descent. Chicanos first came to the United States as seasonal field workers. Over 8 million Chicanos now live in mainly southern U.S. cities. A Chicano labor leader, Cesar Chavez, organized the United Farm Workers (1962) and achieved bargaining power for Chicano field workers after years of bitter struggle.

Chichén Itzá, archeological remains of a Maya city in Yucatan, Mexico. Founded c.514 by the Itzá, abandoned (692), reoccupied (c.928), and finally abandoned in 1194, the city connected two great periods of Maya civilization. Its astronomical observatory and temples show Toltec influence.
See also: Yucatán Peninsula.

Chickadee, any of various common small songbirds of the family Paridae (genus *Penthestes* or *Parus*), with dark caps and bibs and white faces. They are noted for their tameness and agility.

Chickamauga, Battle of, bloodiest single battle of the U.S. Civil War, fought in northern Georgia, Sept. 19-20, 1863. The Union forces lost about 16,000 troops, the Confederates some 18,000.
See also: Civil War, U.S.

Chickasaw, Native American tribe speaking a Muskogean language of the Hokan-Sioux grouping. The Chickasaw were moved from northern Mississippi to Oklahoma in 1834.

Chicken, domesticated bird raised for its meat and eggs, originating in northern Asia from the jungle fowl. The Leghorn, leading egg breed in the U.S., lays over 300 eggs a year. Chickens raised for meat are marketed as broilers and fryers when under three months old (weighing 2-4 lb/1-2 kg) and as roasters when 4-8 months old (weighing up to about 7 lb/3 kg).

Chickenpox, or varicella, contagious disease caused by a virus and affecting mainly children, usually in epidemics. Its characteristic blister-like, itching rash appears two to three weeks after infection.

Chickpea, or garbanzo bean (*Cicer arietinum*), bushy annual legume cultivated from antiquity in southern Europe, India, and the Middle East, and grown for its edible seeds. The chickpea plant grows to 1-2 ft (30-60 cm) and bears rectangular pods containing 1 or 2 3/8 in (9.5 mm), seeds, which may be white, light yellow, red, brown, or near-black. The chickpea is a good source of protein and carbohydrates.

Chicle, latex of the sapodilla tree, a tropical American evergreen, and the raw material of chewing gum. Obtained by cutting grooves in the bark, the latex is boiled to remove excess water, then molded into blocks.

Chicory, blue-flowered perennial herb (*Cichorium intybus*) of the Composite family, native to the Mediterranean and now grown in the United States. Its leaves are used in salads, and its roasted roots are sometimes added to coffee. Endive is a type of chicory used in salads.

Chigger, larva of the harvest mite, a small arachnid. Chiggers burrow beneath the skin of mammals and can produce troublesome ulcers.
See also: Mite.

Chihuahua, small terrierlike dog. It stands about 5 in (13 cm) high at the shoulder and weighs about 1-6 lbs (0.5-2.7 kg), and possesses a smooth or a long coat of any color or markings. The chihuahua has a friendly and loyal temperament. Native to Mexico, it is named for the Mexican state of Chihuahua, and is called the "royal dog of the Americas."

Chihuahua (pop. 530,500), capital of the Mexican state of the same name. Founded as a mining community in northern Mexico in 1707, the city is still a center of silver mining, and of ranching as well. Father Miguel Hidalgo y Costilla, a hero of the Mexican independence struggle, was executed in Chihuahua in 1811. The city was later headquarters for Pancho Villa during the Mexican revolution of 1910- 15.
See also: Chihuahua.

Chihuahua, geographically largest state 95,376 sq mi (247,086 sq km) in Mexico, bordering both Texas and New Mexico. With extensive forests, deep canyons, mineral deposits, and rich grasslands, Chihuahua is the leading cattle-raising and mining state in Mexico.
See also: Mexico.

Chilblain, reaction to cold with pain and itching that can lead to the formation of blisters and ulcers. The blue-red lesions are particularly common on fingers, toes, shins, nose, and ears.

Child abuse, physical, emotional, or sexual injury caused to a child under age 16 by an adult. It is often manifested in cuts, abrasions, bruises, and burns. Incidents of abuse are often detected by an inconsistency between an injury and the explanation of how it occurred. Emotional manifestations of abuse are less easily discovered. Small children who have been abused may be distrustful, passive, and overly concerned with pleasing adults. The emotional impact on children usually becomes obvious at school age, when difficulties in forming relationships with teachers and other children arise.

Child labor, employment of children in industrial or agricultural work, a practice common in the United States in the 19th century. The Fair Labor Standards Act of 1938 forbade the employment of children under 16 in heavy industry, transport, or commerce, and under 18 in occupations detrimental to health.

Children's home, or orphanage, place where foundlings and homeless children live. Children may live in one of these institutions because both parents are deceased or because one or both parents are unable to care for them properly.

Children's literature *See:* Literature for children.

Child welfare, any of various programs, services and, institutions designed to administer to the well-being of children. In the United States such agencies are paid for in part by federal and state taxes. They strive to ensure that children who are suffering from poverty, from the inability of parents to care properly for them, or from neglect or abuse, are provided with food, shelter, medical care, education, and other social services. Some services and organizations that deal with the welfare of children are Aid to Families with Dependent Children (AFDC), Head Start, Medicaid, Department of Health and Human Services, and the Children's Defense Fund.

Chile, country on the Pacific coast of South America, stretching 2,650 mi (1,643 km) from its northern borders with Peru and Bolivia to Cape Horn at the tip of the continent. Chile is narrow, sandwiched between the Pacific Ocean to the west and Argentina to the east; the average distance across the country is only 110 mi (68 km). The Andes Mountains run along the eastern length of the country, and Cerro Ojos del Salado, in the north, is the

Chile	
Capital:	Santiago
Area:	292,135 sq mi
	(756,626 sq km)
Population:	14,677,000
Language:	Spanish
Government:	Presidential republic
Independent:	1818
Head of gov.:	President
Per capita:	U.S. $4,160
Mon. unit:	1 Chilean peso =
	100 centavos

second-highest peak in the western hemisphere. Most Chileans live in the central part of the country, nearly a third of them in Santiago, the capital and chief industrial city. About 90% of Chileans are Roman Catholics. The national language is Spanish. Chile is a major mining and manufacturing nation (a leading exporter of copper). Colonized by Spain in the 16th century, the country won its independence in 1818. In the 20th century Chile was one of Latin America's most stable democracies. In 1970, the election of Salvador Allende, a Marxist, led to a period of political polarization and economic and civil conflict. It ended in 1973, with a bloody military coup that established the right-wing dictator Pinochet. Civilian rule was restored only in 1990. Pinochet stepped down as commander-in-chief of the army in 1998, when he became senator for life.

Chillicothe (pop. 21,923), industrial city and agricultural trade center in south central Ohio on the Scioto River and Paint Creek, seat of Ross County. Paper, shoes, and aluminum products are manufactured here. The city, founded in 1796 and incorporated in 1802, was capital of the Northwest Territory 1800-03 and of Ohio 1803-10 and 1812-16.
See also: Ohio.

Chimborazo, inactive volcanic mountain in the Cordillera Occidental of the Andes, located in central Ecuador about 120 mi (193 km) from the Pacific Coast. The peak is 20,561 ft (6,267 m) above sea level and Ecuador's highest mountain.

Chimera, in Greek mythology, fire-breathing female monster with a lion's head, goat's body, and serpent's tail. By extension, the word is applied to any imaginary being of incongruous parts, or to any unrealizable plan or scheme. In biology, the term is used for any individual or organ that is composed of tissue of varying genetic origin (e.g. from transplantation).
See also: Mythology.

Chimpanzee, black-haired ape (genus *Pan*) native to central and west Africa. Adult chimpanzees stand up to 5 ft (1.5 m) tall and may weigh 150 lb (68 k). They are the primates most closely related to humans genetically and are considered the most intelligent apes. They eat mainly fruit, leaves, nuts, and termites.

Chimu, ancient Indian culture of coastal northern Peru, developed c.1200. Its capital was the great city of Chan Chan. The Chimu built many cities and had efficient military and social systems, but were overcome by the Inca (c.1400- 60).

China, officially the People's Republic of China, world's most populous country and the third-largest in area. Located in the heart of Asia, China is bordered by the Russian Federation and Mongolia to the north; by North Korea and the Pacific Ocean (East China Sea and South China Sea) to the east; by Vietnam, Laos, Burma, Nepal, and India and Pakistan to the south; and by Afghanistan, Kazachstan, Kirghizstan and Tadjikistan to the west.
Land and climate. The country is made up of 3 large geographic regions. Western China is dominated by the high Tibetan Plateau, the mountain ranges that radiate from it, and a great belt of steppe and desert. North China

China

Capital:	Beijing
Area:	3,695,500 sq mi
	(9,571,300 sq km)
Population:	1,236,915,000
Language:	Chinese (Mandarin)
Government:	People's republic
Independent:	1949 (people's
	republic)
Head of gov.:	Premier
Per capita:	US $620
Mon. unit:	1 Renminbi (yuan)= 10
	jiao = 100 fen

contains lowland areas, dusty highlands, and part of the Gobi Desert. South China is a maze of hills and valleys. The chief rivers are the Yangtze in central China and the Huang He (Yellow) in the north. The capital is Beijing (formerly spelled Peking). The largest city is Shanghai, with a population of over 13 million. Other large cities are Tianjin (Tientsin), Harbin, Shenyang, Lüda (Lüta), Xi'an (Sian), Qingdao (Tsingtao), Taiyuan, Wuhan, Canton, Chongqing (Chungking), Chengdu (Chengtu), and Nanjing (Nanking).

People. The Han ethnic Chinese constitute nearly 95% of the population, but there are 56 officially recognized minority groups. The national language Putonghua, previously called Mandarin, is based on the spoken form of the Chinese language prevalent in the north, principally Beijing. Different spoken dialects persist in the south, including Cantonese, Wu, and Hakka. The written language, however, is the same everywhere. Traditional Chinese religions were Taoism, and Confucianism. There are substantial minorities of Catholics and Protestants.

History. China has one of the world's oldest civilizations, dating back some 3,500 years. Though ravaged by floods, famines, and wars, it remained politically intact through the centuries, often enjoying levels of civilization unparalleled in the world. The first historic dynasty that ruled the country, the Shang (or Yin) dynasty, arose about 1500 B.C. and lasted for some 500 years. It was under this dynasty that the Chinese writing system developed. The next dynasty, the Chou (c.1027-256 B.C.), saw the rise of classical Chinese philosophy, including such thinkers as Confucius and Lao-Tze. Under a later dynasty, the Han (202 B.C.-A.D. 220) Confucianism became the official state philosophy, but Buddhism also began to be introduced, and Taoism also grew in influence.

Other major dynasties include the T'ang (618-906), an age of great achievements in poetry and painting; the Sung (960-1279), during which gunpowder was first used for military purposes; and the Yüan (1260-1368), the Mongol dynasty founded by Kublai Khan, the grandson of Jenghiz Khan. It was during the Yüan dynasty that Marco Polo visited China, beginning a period of contact with the West.

The last Chinese monarchy was the Manchu (or Ch'ing) dynasty (1644-1912), founded by the Manchus, a non-Chinese people from Manchuria. It was in the later years of this dynasty that Chinese power gradually weakened, the country losing much of its territory to European, especially British, encroachments.

The monarchy was overthrown in 1912, and a republic was established under Sun Yat-sen. After his death in 1916, China was fragmented among various warlords. In 1927, Chiang Kai-shek (leader of the Nationalist Party) gained control of the government and launched a civil war against the Chinese Communist Party, led by Mao Zedong. The Communists and Nationalists briefly cooperated to resist the Japanese invasion during World War II, but in 1945 civil war broke out again, leading to the victory of the Communists in 1949. The Communist Party established the People's Republic of China. From 1966 to 1969 Mao Zedong, supported by paramilitary groups known as the Red Guard, led the Cultural Revolution, which was an effort to purge the society and government of counterrevolutionary and bourgeois tendencies. During this period many government officials were removed from office, violent demonstrations took place in many cities, and all universities were closed. The late 1980s and early 1990s saw the rise of popular unrest; millions of citizens demanding democratic reforms in the political system. In 1989 student demonstrations were crushed by force, by order of Deng Xiaoping. When he died (1997) a generation of leaders came to power who advocate economic reform. In the same year, Hong Kong was returned to China. In 1998 the ecomony suffered due to continuous floods.

China Sea, western part of the Pacific Ocean, bordering the east coast of China. Taiwan divides it into the East China Sea to the north, 485,300 sq mi (1,256,927 sq k), maximum depth 9,126 ft (351 m), and the South China Sea to the south, 895,400 sq mi (2,319,086 sq k), maximum depth 15,000 ft (4,572 m). Major seaports are Canton and Hong Kong.

Chinch bug (*Blissus leucopterus*), small insect found in the United States, Canada, Central America, and the West Indies. The adult, about one-fifth in (5 mm) long, is black with red legs and white wings. In spring adults lay eggs on roots and stems in grain fields.

Chinchilla, rodent (genus *Chinchilla*) noted for its soft gray fur. Wild chinchillas were once common in the Andes from Peru to Argentina, but extensive hunting has made them rare. Now reared on fur farms, 100 chinchillas provide the pelts for a single coat.

Chinese, major language of the Sino-Tibetan family, with more native speakers (over 800 million) than any other language in the world. Most Chinese speak Mandarin, a form based on the speech of the educated classes of northern China, particularly the city of Beijing (Peking). Since the early 1950s, this has been called the national language. Other dialects include Cantonese, Hakka, Wu, Fukienese, and Amoy-Swatow. In written form, all these dialects are the same, but the pronunciation may be mutually incomprehensible. Chinese is a tonal, monosyllabic language. The writing system uses an individual character for each syllable, every character representing a word or idea rather than a sound. The characters range from one stroke to as many as 32, but the average is about 11. The earliest witten records in Chinese date back to about 1400 B.C., making Chinese one of the world's oldest, continuously written languages.

Chinese cabbage, common generic name for *pak-choi*, *pe-tsiao*, and *wong bok*, cabbagelike vegetables of the mustard family with wide, thick leaves on a celerylike stalk used raw in salads and cooked in casseroles and Chinese-style dishes. It is an annual or biennial crop grown in many cool areas of eastern Asia and northern United States.

Chinese Exclusion Acts, legislation limiting immigration of Orientals to the United States. Anti-Chinese prejudice and competition for jobs led to riots preceding the first act (1882), banning Chinese immigration for 10 years. Congress continued these 10-year exclusions until the 1924 law excluded all Asians. In 1943 an immigration quota of 105 Chinese annually was established; the quota was abolished in 1965.

Chinese-Japanese Wars, 2 wars between China and Japan (1894-95 and 1937-45). The first war began after both countries sent troops to quell a rebellion in Korea and ended April 17, 1895 with the Treaty of Shimonoseki granting Korea independence, but giving Japan Taiwan and the Liadong Peninsula. Weakened, China became vulnerable to increased foreign imperialism. Japan seized territory from China (1931-35) resulting in an undeclared war (1937-41). After China declared war on Japan, German, and Italy, and Japan attacked the United States and Great Britain in 1941, the war became part of World War II. When Japan surrendered to the Allies in 1945 the second war ended.
See also: World War II.

Chinese literature, among the world's oldest and greatest, Chinese literary works can be traced back almost 3,000 years. Literature was not considered a separate art form and all cultured people were expected to write with style. As a result, literary topics include history, politics, philosophy, religion, and science.

Historically, government service was the most prestigious vocation in China and most government appointments were made on the basis of an examination which tested the ability to compose both poetry and prose.

Much of Chinese literature deals with moral lessons or the expression of political philosophy. Two early works were *The Book of Songs*, a collection of poems, and *The Book of Documents*, a prose work. Together with *Spring and Autumn Annals*, the *Book of Changes* and the *Book of Rites*, they form the Five Classics as the basis for Confucianism and the ideals of duty, moderation, proper conduct and public service.

Taoism, founded by the Laozi during the 300's B.C., was partly a reaction to Confucianism. In contrast to the Confucians, Taoists avoided social obligations and lived simple lives close to nature. *The Classics of the Way and the Virtue* and *The Zhuangzi* are the two literary masterpieces of Taoist thought.

The T'ang dynasty (A.D. 618-907) was the era of four great masters of poetry: Wang Wei, Li Bo, Du Fu and Bo Juyi. Wang Wei's four line poems describe nature. Li Bo wrote of his dreams, fantasies and his love of wine. Du Fu surpassed all others in his range of writing styles and subject matter. Some of his earliest works deal with his disappointment over failing a government service examination. Bo Juyi used satire to protest against numerous government policies.

Both drama and fiction evolved as important forms of Chinese literature in the 1200s. Two famous plays, *The Western Chamber*, by Wang Shifu, and

Injustice to Tou O, by Guan Hanqing, were written in this period. Tang Xianzu, one of the greatest Chinese playwrights, wrote *Peony Pavillion*, his most notable work, around 1600. Luo Guanzhong wrote in a style resembling the novels of Western writers. In *Romance of the Three Kingdoms*, he describes a power struggle among 3 rival states in the A.D. 100 and 200s. In *The Journey to the West*, also called *Monkey*, Wu Cheng'en uses allegory to relate the adventures of a Buddhist monk on a pilgrimage to India. *Dream of the Red Chamber*, written by Cao Xueqin in the 1700, describes the decline of an aristocratic family. It is perhaps the greatest Chinese novel.

By the 1800, the Chinese had been exposed to Western culture and this influence was evident in the works of Chinese authors in the 1900. With the coming to power of the Communists in 1949 under the leadership of Mao Zedong, literature changed and was directed towards peasants, soldiers and workers. Today, the poems and sayings of Mao Zedong are the most widely read writings in China.

Chinook, Native American tribe of the Pacific Northwest. The Chinook lived along the mouth of the Columbia River, trading, fishing, and gathering berries, nuts, and roots. Religion centered on a ritual welcoming the annual salmon run. Epidemics and contact with European American civilization destroyed Chinook culture in the 1800s. Modern Chinook live in Washington and Oregon making a living by ranching and fishing.

Chinook, warm, dry, westerly wind occurring in winter and spring on the Rocky Mountain eastern slopes. Pacific air condensing moisture on the mountains' western slopes result in air that increases in temperature 1°F for every 180 ft (1°C for every 99 m) as it descends the eastern slope. Chinooks, called snow eaters, rapidly melt and evaporate ground snow. The wind was named by settlers who thought it came from the direction of the Chinook Indian camp along the Columbia River. Similar winds blowing elsewhere are called *foehns*.

Chipmunk, any of various small, striped ground-living rodents (genera *Tamias* and *Eutamias*) of the squirrel family. There are 16 species in North America and 1 in Asia. They feed on fruits and nuts, which they carry in their cheek pouches. Though they do not hibernate, they sleep for long periods in winter.

Chippendale, Thomas (1718-79), English cabinetmaker whose elegant, individual style blended aspects of Gothic, Rococo, and Chinoiserie. Much 18th-century English furniture is given his name.

Chippewa, or Ojibwa, one of the largest Algonquian-speaking tribes of Native Americans, traditionally living in woodland areas around Lakes Superior and Huron, and to the west. They fought frequently with the Sioux. Longfellow's *The Song of Hiawatha* was based on Chippewa mythology. Today Chippewa live in both the United States and Canada.

Chirac, Jacques (1932-), French political leader, president of the republic since 1995. A Gaullist, he was in the cabinets of 4 premiers before serving as premier (1974-76). He resigned over differences with President Giscard d'Estaing, formed his own party, was elected mayor of Paris (1977-86).

Premier from 1986-88 under president Mitterand. In 1995 he succeeded Mitterand as president.

Chirico, Giorgio de (1888-1978), Greek-born Italian painter who founded "metaphysical painting" and influenced surrealism. His works depict desolate, harshly hued scenes and solitary figures that might be seen in a nightmare: *The Soothsayer's Recompense* (1913), *Melancholy and Mystery of a Street* (1914), and *The Poet and His Muse* (c.1925).

Chiron, in Greek mythology, wisest centaur, famous for his knowledge of healing. He taught many Greek heroes, including Achilles. Wounded by Hercules' arrow, he gave up his immortality to Prometheus and was placed in the heavens as the constellation Sagittarius.
See also: Mythology.

Chiropractic, medical therapy based on the theory that disease results from misalignment of the vertebrae, which causes nerve malfunction. Manipulation of the spinal column, massage, and dietary adjustments are the principal methods used.

Chisholm, Shirley (1924-), first black woman to serve in the U.S. Congress, Democratic Representative from 1969-83. She criticized the Vietnam War, and the seniority system in Congress, and advocated for the inner-city poor. From 1964-69 she served in the New York Assembly and campaigned for the 1972 Democratic presidential nomination.

Chisholm Trail, 19th-century route (c.1866-86) for cattle drives between Texas and Kansas, named after the scout and trader Jesse Chisholm. It was superseded by the spread of the railroads.

Chiton, any of an order (Polyplacophora) of primitive mollusks with shells of light overlapping plates and a muscular foot that clings to rocks. Found on shores worldwide, chitons feed on algae scraped from the rocks. They range in length from 1/2 in (1.2 cm) to 1 ft (28.8 cm).

Chivalry, knightly code of conduct in medieval Europe combining Christian and military ideals of bravery, piety, honor, loyalty, and sacrifice, virtues valued by the Crusaders. Chivalry flourished in the 12th to 14th century and declined in the 15th century although it continues to be the basis for gentlemanly behavior. Examples of chivalric literature are the Arthurian legends and the Chansons de Geste.
See also: Knights and knighthood.

Chive, perennial plant (*Allium schoenoprasum*) of the lily family, of the same genus as the onion. Found wild in Italy and Greece, its leaves are used in salads.

Chlamydia, infectious sexually transmitted disease, caused by various strains of bacteria. Symptoms may include inflamed eyes (conjunctivitis) and pelvic inflammation disease in women. Babies born to mothers with untreated chlamydia may develop pneumonia or the infection itself. One of the most widespread sexually transmitted diseases in the United States, chlamydia is treated with antibiotics.
See also: Venereal disease.

Chloride, chemical compound of chlorine with another element or radical. *See also:* Salt; Salt, chemical.

Chlorine, chemical element, symbol Cl; for physical constants see Periodic Table. Chlorine was discovered by Karl Scheele in 1774. It is a highly reactive, greenish-yellow poisonous gas that combines directly with nearly all elements. It is one of the top 5 industrial chemicals and is used throughout the world to make drinking water safe. It is also used in manufacturing products for sanitizing, bleaching, and disinfecting. Chlorine is a severe respiratory irritant; has been used as a weapon in war.

Chloroform, or trichloromethane, dense, colorless, volatile liquid ($CHCI_3$) produced by chlorination of ethanol or acetone. One of the first anesthetics to be used in surgery, it has since been replaced by less toxic anesthetics, such as ether. It is used in cough medicines and as an organic solvent.

Chlorophyll, green pigment of plants that gives them their color and traps and stores the energy of sunlight required for photosynthesis. The energy is used to convert water and carbon dioxide into sugars. *See also:* Photosynthesis.

Chocolate, confection made from cacao beans, used to make candy and beverages. Fermented beans are roasted and ground, then mixed with cacao butter, sugar, and milk solids. The process for making chocolate was perfected in Switzerland around 1876.

Choctaw, Native American tribe traditionally living in what is now southeast Mississippi, speaking a Muskogean language of the Hokan-Siouan family. Under the Removal Act of 1830, they were driven off their lands and transferred to what is now Oklahoma.

Cholera, acute infectious disease involving the small intestine, characterized by diarrhea, vomiting, muscular cramps, and severe loss of body fluid. The disease is caused by a toxin produced by the bacillus *Vibrio cholerae* and is spread by ingestion of water and of foods contaminated by the excrement of infected persons. Cholera can be fatal if untreated. Outbreaks still occur in regions of Africa and Asia where sanitation is poor.

Cholesterol, basic component of fats or lipids, a steroid found in nearly all tissues. Cholesterol is present in large quantity in the nervous system, where it is a compound of myelin, the greasy substance that acts as a sheath around nerve fibers. It is a precursor of bile salts and of adrenal and sex hormones. Large amounts are synthesized in the liver, intestines, and skin. Since abnormal depositing of cholesterol in the arteries is associated with aterio-arteriosclerosis, some doctors advise avoiding high-cholesterol foods and substituting unsaturated for saturated fats. Cholesterol is also a major constituent of gallstones. *See also:* Arteriosclerosis.

Chomsky, Noam (1928-), U.S. linguist that revolutionized the study of language structure with his theory of generative grammar, first outlined in

Syntactic Structures (1957). He was also an influential critic of U.S. foreign policy both during and after the Vietnam War.

Chongqing (pop. 2,980,000), Chungking, or Ch'ung-ch'ing, city in Sichuan province, southwest China, on the Jialing and Yangtze rivers. It is a densely populated political and industrial center, producing steel, medicine, and silk. It became part of China in 220 B.C., served as a treaty port (1891-1943), and was capital of the Nationalist government (1937-46) under Chiang Kai-shek. *See also:* China.

Chopin, Frédéric François (1810-49), Polish composer and pianist. In 1831 he moved from Poland to Paris. His chief works are for the piano and include piano concertos in E minor (1833) and F minor (1836), 24 preludes (1838-39), and many waltzes, mazurkas, and polonaises that were inspired by his Polish nationalism. In 1837 he began his friendship with the novelist George Sand. Their relationship ended unhappily in 1847. Chopin died 2 years later of tuberculosis.

Chorale, type of hymn tune developed in Germany during the Reformation. Chorales formed the basis of the new Protestant church music. J.S. Bach harmonized many of these chorale tunes for the Lutheran Church, and used them as a basis for many organ and choral compositions. *See also:* Reformation.

Choral music, unaccompanied choral music sung in monasteries during the early Christian era, known as plainsong. Choral music without accompaniment continued through the 16th century. The development of instrumental accompaniment in the 17th and 18th centuries culminated in J. S. Bach's orchestrated cantatas and passions and the oratorios of Handel. Beethoven's inclusion of a choir in the finale of his *Ninth Symphony* (1817-23) marks a turning point in the history of music. Notable among 20th-century choral works are Elgar's *Dream of Gerontius* (1900) and Stravinsky's *Symphony of Psalms* (1930).

Chordate, animal possessing a primitive backbone-like structure (notochord) at some stage in its development. Grouped in the phylum Chordata, chordates include all vertebrates and many small aquatic invertebrates such as the tunicates.

Chorea, disease of the central nervous system causing abnormal, involuntary movements of the limbs, body, and face. Sydenham's chorea (St. Vitus' dance) is a childhood illness associated with rheumatic fever; Huntington's chorea is a rare, fatal hereditary disease of adulthood associated with progressive dementia. *See also:* Nervous system.

Chorus, in ancient classical Greek drama, group of actors who commented upon the action. The origin of the chorus is probably the dithyramb, a hymn to the god Dionysus. By the 6th century B.C. the formal dramatic chorus was an integral part of the performance. Gradually the size and role of the chorus was reduced as the actor's role grew. It disappeared by the 2nd century B.C.

Chou En-lai (1898-1976), first prime minister of the People's Republic of China, 1949-76. A founder of the Chinese Communist Party, in 1926 he organized the Shanghai Strike for Chiang Kai-shek and escaped when Chiang betrayed the communists. Director of military affairs for Mao Tse-tung's guerrilla forces, he commanded the first stage of the Long March (1934-35). He won support for China in the Third World and was a major force in taking China into the United Nations (1971) and reestablishing contact with the West in the 1970s.
See also: China.

Chouteau, family of fur traders who helped to open up the Middle West. **(René) Auguste Chouteau** (1749-1829) co-founded with Pierre Laclède the trading past that became St. Louis (1764). Auguste's brother, **(Jean) Pierre Chouteau** (1758-1849), an Indian agent for tribes west of the Mississippi River, co-founded the St. Louis Missouri Fur Company (1809). His son, **Auguste Pierre Chouteau** (1786-1838), was an Indian treaty commissioner and made many expeditions into the West. Auguste Pierre's brother, **Pierre Chouteau** (1789-1865), headed the American Fur Company from 1834. By pioneering the use of steamboats he monopolized trade on the Missouri River.

Chow chow, breed of nonsporting dog believed to have come from China, with a thick, soft coat, and a unique blue-black tongue. The chow chow stands 18-20 in (46-51 cm) at the shoulder and weighs 50-60 lb (23-27 kg).

Chrétien de Troyes (1135-83), French poet who wrote romances rooted in Arthurian legend. His work, including *Erec et Enide, Cligès*, and *Perceval*, influenced French and English literature through the next 2 centuries.

Christ, Jesus *See:* Jesus Christ.

Christchurch (pop. 312,800), New Zealand's third largest city, located on South Island near the east coast. A tourist and commercial center, it produces clothing, electrical goods, and fertilizers, and is served by an international airport, railroads, and tunnels linking the city with Lyttelton, the chief port. An Anglican church group settled Christchurch in 1850 and established the University of Canterbury there in 1873.

Christian *See:* Christianity.

Christian IV (1577-1648), king of Denmark and Norway 1588-1648, longest reigning Danish monarch. He involved Denmark in wars with Sweden (1611-13, 1643-45), and helped Protestants fight Roman Catholics in Germany (1625-29) during the Thirty Years' War. These wars left Denmark bankrupt.

Christian IX (1818-1906), king of Denmark 1863-1906. During his reign, Denmark acquired the territory of Schleswig in 1863, but in 1864 Prussia and Austria invaded, gaining control of Schleswig and Holstein. Although against democracy, in 1901 he recognized a democratic parliament.

Christian X (1870-1947), king of Denmark (1912-47), king of Iceland (1912-44), symbol of Danish resistance to German occupation during World War II. In 1915, he granted a new constitution ending privileges of upper classes and admitting to women's rights. After the German invasion of Denmark in 1940 he continued to occupy the throne, but was under house arrest 1943-45 for refusing to cooperate with the Germans.

Christian, Charlie (1919-42), influential jazz guitarist who pioneered the use of electrically amplified instruments. While playing in the Benny Goodman orchestra (1939-41), Christian joined with Dizzy Gillespie and Thelonious Monk to create bebop, a modern style of jazz. Christian's career ended when he contracted tuberculosis in 1941.
See also: Jazz.

Christianity, religion founded on the life and teachings of Jesus, acknowledged by all Christians to be the Son of God. Christianity had its beginnings when a small band of Jews recognized Jesus of Nazareth, who died about A.D. 33, as the Messiah, or Christ. Immediately after the crucifixion of Jesus, Christianity counted only a few hundred members, among them the Apostles, who followed Christ's teachings and preached his Gospel, particularly as it concerned the life, sufferings, death, resurrection, and divine nature of Jesus. The Christian community had its center in Jerusalem but soon spread into Asia Minor, Syria, Macedonia, and Greece. While St. Peter was the leader of the Jewish Christian community, Saul of Tarsus (later known as Paul the Apostle) was preeminent in the task of converting the Gentiles and establishing churches in the Greco-Roman world. As the faith spread, an ecclesiastical structure evolved. Bishops replaced the Apostles as celebrants of the ritual of the Eucharist. They were assisted by presbyters, or elders, who were given the right to perform the sacred duties connected with the Eucharist, while the bishops retained the right of consecrating the presbyters and of confirming the faithful. Various regions were organized into dioceses and provinces. Within 3 centuries, despite persecutions, the Christian religion had become firmly established; in A.D. 324 the emperor Constantine established Christianity as the official religion. In order to settle doctrinal disputes and establish basic tenets, Constantine called the first ecumenical council at Nicaea in 325. The Nicene Creed, adopted at this council, stated the basic truths of the Christian Church; departures from this statement of faith were thereafter regarded as heresy. From earliest times the preeminence of the bishop of Rome was recognized by the entire Western Church. However, the Eastern Church, headed by the patriarch of Constantinople, had traditionally retained jurisdiction over organizational and doctrinal matters in its own sphere. The question of papal authority led to the Great Schism (1054), when the Eastern Church broke its ties with the West. The popes emerged as influential rulers in western Europe during the Middle Ages, contending with the Holy Roman emperors for temporal power as well as spiritual authority. Disputes arose concerning papal succession, and popes and antipopes, supported by rival kings and princes, fought for the right to rule with the authority of the Holy See.
The entire structure of the Church was shaken by this dissension, and abuses such as simony and the sale of indulgences also cried out for reform. In the 14th century reform was advocated by John Wycliffe in England and Jan Hus in Czechoslovakia. The Reformation of the 16th century was led by

Martin Luther, who denied the supreme authority of the pope and rejected all but 2 of the 7 sacraments, Baptism and the Eucharist. He affirmed the supreme authority of the Bible in all matters of faith. The Catholic Church responded to the Reformation with the Counter-Reformation, during which abuses were corrected, several new religious orders were formed, and a spirit of Christian mission was fostered among the faithful. It was a highly active era for proselytizing the faith and a period of great creativity in religious art. Since the 16th century there have existed 2 main currents of western Christianity: Protestantism and Roman Catholicism. In Switzerland the Reformation was led by Huldreich Zwingli in Zürich and John Calvin in Geneva. Calvinism, which teaches the predestination of the elect and was adopted by the French Huguenots, forms the basis of modern Presbyterianism and the Reformed churches. During the 18th century John Wesley, who turned from Calvinism to a more traditional Christian view, founded the Methodist church in England.

After the pope refused to annul his first marriage, King Henry VIII declared the Church of England to be free of papal jurisdiction. Under Edward VI and Elizabeth I, the Anglican church became truly Protestant; its tenets were set forth in the Thirty-nine Articles of 1576. The Puritans considered these doctrinal reforms inadequate, however, and sought a form of worship based strictly on the Scriptures. Puritan sects later gave rise to the Baptist and Congregational churches and to the Religious Society of Friends, or Quakers. The settlements founded throughout the American colonies by dissenting members of Protestant churches gave impetus to the development of independent American church bodies, such as the Protestant Episcopal Church, an offshoot of the Church of England. Some distinctly American churches sprang up, among these the Church of Jesus Christ of Latter-Day Saints (Mormons), founded in 1830, and the Church of Christ Scientist (Christian Science), founded in 1882. In all there are more than 200 branches of the Christian Church in the United States.

One of the most significant developments in the continued growth of the Christian church in the 20th century is the ecumenical movement. Although still in an early phase, with its progress often slowed by organizational and doctrinal difficulties, ecumenicism has caught the imagination of a majority of the clergy and the faithful, who envision a future in which the Christian Church will again be one universal body, as it was established by Christ. *See also:* Jesus Christ.

Christian Science, religion based on belief in the power of Christian faith to heal sickness. It was founded by Mary Baker Eddy, who organized the first Church of Christ, Scientist at Boston, Mass., in 1879.

Christie, Dame Agatha (1891-1976), British writer of popular detective novels and plays. Her works, which include *The Murder of Roger Ackroyd* (1926), *The Mousetrap* (1952), and *The Pale Horse* (1962) feature her 2 central characters, the egotistical Hercule Poirot and the elderly Miss Jane Marple.

Christmas (Christ's Mass), annual Christian festival observed on Dec. 25 to commemorate the birth of Jesus Christ. The exact date of Christ's birth is unknown. The origin of the Christmas story is based on the Gospels of Luke and Matthew in the New Testament. The first reference to the celebration of

Christmas occurred in a Roman calendar of A.D. 336. By the Middle Ages, Christmas had become the most significant religious holiday in Europe, with Saint Nicholas as a symbol of giving. In the 19th century Christmas trees and Christmas cards became customs of the holiday. In the United States, Santa Claus replaced Saint Nicholas as the great gift giver.
See also: Christianity; Jesus Christ; Santa Claus.

Christmas Island *See:* Kiritimati Atoll.

Christmas Tree *See:* Christmas.

Christ of the Andes, statue of Christ created by Mateo Alonzo, in Uspallata Pass on the Argentine-Chile border in the Andes Mountains. It was dedicated on March 13, 1904 to commemorate treaties for perpetual peace between Argentina and Chile.

Christophe, Henri (1767-1820), king of North Haiti. A freed black slave, he became president of Haiti in 1806, after plotting the assassination of Dessalines. After 1811 he ruled North Haiti, as King Henri I. Faced with a revolt, he shot himself.

Christopher, Saint (3rd century A.D.), Christian martyr and patron of travelers. According to legend, he carried the Christ child across a river. The Roman Catholic Church removed his feast day (July 25) from its liturgical calendar for lack of historical evidence as to his existence.

Christus, Petrus (fl. c.1442-73), Flemish painter, early Netherlandish school. His work, strongly influenced by Jan van Eyck, was important in the 15th-century development of realistic perspective: *Madonna with S. S. Francis and Jerome*, *Lamentation*, and *Nativity*.

Christy, Edwin P. (1815-62), U.S. actor who organized the successful Christy Minstrels troupe at Buffalo, N. Y., in 1842. He established the basic format of the minstrel show, popular in the 19th century.

Chrome *See:* Chromium.

Chromic acid, common name for chromium trioxide (H_2CrO_4), an industrial compound used in chromium plating and the manufacture of fire resistant chemicals. Poisonous and caustic, most chromic acid takes the form of bright red crystals.

Chromium, chemical element, symbol Cr; for physical constants see Periodic Table. Chromium was discovered by L.N. Vauquelin in 1797. It is a steel-gray, lustrous, hard metal. Elemental chromium is prepared by reduction of its oxide with aluminum. It is used in the production of stainless steel, in plating, and in the production of other metal alloys. Many compounds of chromium are used to color glass, as pigments, and as mordants in the textile industry.

Chromosome, threadlike body in the cell nucleus, composed of genes, which carry genetic information responsible for the inherited characteristic

of all organisms. Chromosomes consist of deoxyribonucleic acid (DNA), a sequence of nucleotides composed of 4 different bases, allowing over 500 million alternatives. The basic proteins are found in a complex with DNA in the cells of human organs and tissues; in general, these are called histones. The microscope shows that the chromosome is a coiled structure. This coiling should not be confused with the structure of the DNA molecule—a double helix— because there is a difference of several orders of magnitude in the scale. Mitosis is the normal process by which a cell divides, each new cell ending up with the same number of chromosomes as the original cell. Mitotic division occurs in somatic cells (i.e., not sex cells) during periods of growth, when the total number of cells is increasing, or during repair processes, when lost or damaged cells are being replaced. In the resting cell (interphase of mitosis) the chromosomes cannot be detected inside the nucleus as discrete structures. As a cell approaches mitosis, the chromosomes become visible as threads within the nucleus (prophase of mitosis). At the same time, cytoplasmic bodies, the centrioles, divide, and the 2 new centrioles move to opposite poles of the cell. The protein fibers that control the separation of the chromosomes radiate from these bodies. The chromosomes line up in the equatorial plane of the cell (metaphase of mitosis) and separate to form the chromosomes of the 2 new nuclei (anaphase of mitosis). A cleavage furrow begins to divide the cytoplasm of the cell, the chromosomes elongate, and a nuclear membrane re-forms around them. This stage (telophase of mitosis) results in the reconstruction of 2 nuclei that are genetically identical with the parent nucleus.
See also: Genetics; Heredity; Deoxyribonucleic Acid.

Chronicles, 2 Old Testament books summarizing Jewish history from Adam through the Babylonian Captivity.
See also: Old Testament.

Chronometer, extremely accurate clock, used especially in navigation. The chronometer invented by John Harrison (1759) allowed navigation to determine longitude accurately for the first time. The mechanical chronometer is spring- driven, like a watch, but its parts are larger and devices in the spring minimize effects of temperature changes and the ship's rolling movements.

Chrysalis, pupa of certain insects, especially butterflies and moths at the state between caterpillar or larva and fully developed imago (winged adult).

Chrysanthemum, genus of popular flowering annual or perennial herbaceous plants of the daisy family (Compositae). The national flower of Japan, chrysanthemums are usually white, yellow, pink, or red and are native to temperate and subtropical areas.

Chrysler, Walter Percy (1875-1940), U.S. industrialist who produced the first Chrysler car (1924) and established the Chrysler Corporation (1925), which became a major auto producer in the United States.

Chrysostom, Saint John (c.347-407 A.D.), Greek Father and Doctor of the Church. He was called Chrysostom ("golden mouthed") for his powers of oratory. He was patriarch of Constantinople (398-404) and became its patron saint.

Chub, any of several small, freshwater carp (family Cyprinidae) found in flowing waters, common to Europe and North America. The chub, 4-12 in (10-31 cm) long, has a large head and wide mouth and is usually a gray-brown or blue and silver color. Being a generally coarse and bony fish, it is not much valued as food, but is popularly used for bait and is caught for sport.

Chuckwalla (*Sauromalus obesus*), lizard of the North American desert. Stoutly built and 1 ft (30 cm) long, it ranges from Arizona and Utah to northern Mexico, feeding on the flowers and leaves of desert plants. During the summer it lives below ground, and when alarmed it retreats into crevices, wedging itself by blowing up its body.

Church, Frederick Edwin (1826-1900), U.S. landscape painter noted for his portrayal of light on large canvases. He was a student of Thomas Cole and the most famous member of the Hudson River School. Among his best known works are *Niagara* and *Heart of the Andes*.
See also: Hudson River School.

Church and state, phrase that refers to the relations between organized religion and organized government. This question, which for centuries has been a source of controversy, is whether the religious and political powers in a society should be kept clearly separate from one another. In the United States, due to various legislative acts, neither a state nor the federal government can openly or secretly participate in the affairs of a religious organization, and vice versa. This has led directly to the barring of prayer in U.S. public schools.

Churches of Christ, evangelical Protestant Christian body that teaches strict adherence to principles and practices set forth in the New Testament. Formerly one with the Church of the Disciples of Christ, believed to have been founded at Pentecost and refounded by Thomas Campbell (1763-1854), this conservative church is one of the largest denominations in the United States.
See also: Protestantism.

Churches of God, group of U.S. Pentecostal religious sects. Most of the churches of the group originated as Holiness, Pentecostal, or Adventist churches, which are evolved from Methodism. The Churches of God teach a doctrine of sanctification obtained by "second blessing" or forgiveness, and stress literal interpretation of the Bible.
See also: Adventists; Pentecostalism.

Churchill, Jennie Jerome *See:* Churchill, Sir Winston Leonard Spencer.

Churchill, John *See:* Marlborough, Duke of.

Churchill, Sir Winston Leonard Spencer (1874-1965), British statesman, soldier, and writer. The son of Lord Randolph Churchill and his U.S. wife, Jennie Jerome, he was educated at Harrow and Sandhurst. He fought in India (1897), the Sudan (1898), and South Africa. A Conservative member of Parliament (1900), he changed to the Liberal party in 1905 and became first lord of the admiralty by 1911, in which office he was held accountable for

the failure of the Dardanelles campaign during World War I. Churchill left government and saw active service in France until he was recalled by Lloyd George to serve in several cabinet positions (1917-22). In 1924 he regained a seat in Parliament and was chancellor of the exchequer in Stanley Baldwin's Conservative government (1924-29). Out of favor with his own party, he held no office for the next 10 years, during which time he voiced strong warnings regarding Hitler's activity in Germany. When World War II broke out (1939), Chamberlain appointed him first lord of the admiralty. Upon Hitler's invasion of the Low Countries, Churchill was made prime minister (1940) and minister of national defense. His persuasive oratory and unswerving confidence were instrumental assets in Allied resistance, as were his contributions to military strategy. He was coauthor, with President F.D. Roosevelt, of the Atlantic Charter, and played a key role in the diplomatic conferences that were to shape postwar Europe (e.g., Yalta Conference). In 1951 Churchill returned to power as prime minister for the second time, serving until his retirement from politics (1955). His extensive writings, for which he received the Nobel Prize (1953), include an autobiography, *My Early Life* (1930), *The Second World War* (6 vols., 1948-53), and *A History of the English-Speaking Peoples* (4 vols., 1956-58).
See also: World War II.

Churchill Downs *See:* Kentucky; Kentucky Derby; Louisville.

Churchill River, formerly Hamilton River, river rising in Ashuanipi Lake in southwestern Labrador and flowing about 600 mi (970 km) through Newfoundland in eastern Canada to Lake Melville on the Atlantic Ocean. A large hydroelectric power plant, with a capacity of more than 5 million kilowatts of electricity, was completed in 1974 on the river at Churchill Falls.

Church of Christ *See:* Churches of Christ.

Church of Christ, Scientist *See:* Christian Science.

Church of England, national church of England and parent church of the Anglican Communion. Its doctrine is basically Protestant and its hierarchy and ceremony are rooted in Catholic tradition. The church broke with Rome in 1534 when Henry VIII assumed the title of the head of the church. In the 16th and 17th centuries the church was troubled by Puritan agitation and later by nonconformity. But it remains the established state church and its 26 senior bishops (lords spiritual) sit in the House of Lords, led by the archbishop of Canterbury.
See also: Anglicans.

Church of God in Christ, large Pentecostal denomination. Founded in the United States in 1895 by Bishop Charles H. Mason as a Holiness church, the church now has over 3 million members. It bases its generally fundamentalist faith on personal experience, morality, and the experiences of the Apostles on Pentecost.

Church of Jesus Christ of Latter-Day Saints *See:* Mormons.

Church of the Nazarene, Protestant evangelical denomination. It was created in Texas in 1908 when 3 Holiness church groups merged.

Churriguera, José Benito (1665-1725), Spanish architect and sculptor who gave his name to the Spanish Baroque style featuring extravagant design, Churrigueresque (1650-1740). Churriguera designed grandiose theatrical altars and the entire urban complex of Nuevo Baztán in Madrid. He was also the architect for the cathedral of Salamanca. His style influenced the Spanish missions of colonial North America.

Chu Teh (1886-1976), Chinese Communist leader. He helped form the Chinese Red Army and joined Mao Tse-tung (1927). As commander in chief, he led the Long March (1934-35) and defeated the Nationalists (1949). He held various high posts in the Communist government including chairman of the National People's Congress in 1959.
See also: China.

CIA *See:* Central Intelligence Agency (CIA).

Ciardi, John (1916-86), U.S. poet, translator, and teacher. His poetry volumes include *Homeward to America* (1940) and *For Instance* (1979), and notable translations include Dante's *Inferno* (1954), *Purgatorio* (1960), and *Paradiso* (1970).

Cibber, Colley (1671-1757), English actor-manager and dramatist who introduced sentimental comedy to the theater. He wrote over 30 plays including *Love's Last Shift* (1696) and *Apology* (1740) which offers a vivid depiction of the contemporary theater. He was made poet laureate in 1730.

Cibola, Seven Cities of, golden cities reported in the North American Southwest in the 16th century. The legend attracted Spanish exploration, notably by Francisco Coronado and his 300 Spanish cavalry and 1,000 Native American allies (1540).

Cicada, large insect (order Homoptera) known for its monotonous whining song produced by the rapidly vibrating, drumlike membranes on the male's abdomen (the female is mute). The larvae develop in the soil, feeding on roots; the periodical cicada (genus *Magicicada*) spends 17 years underground and live for 1 week above it.

Cicero, Marcus Tullius (106-43 B.C.), Roman orator, statesman, and philosopher. As consul (63 B.C.) he crushed the Catiline conspiracy. His refusal to submit to the First Triumvirate resulted in banishment in 58 B.C., but he was recalled the next year by Pompey, with whom he sided in the civil war. Cicero's tacit approval of Caesar's murder and his defense of the Republic against Mark Antony in his first and second *Philippics* led to his execution after Octavian took Rome. A master of Latin prose, his great works include personal letters and orations (57 extant).
See also: Rome, Ancient.

Cid, El (Rodrigo Díaz de Bivar; 1040?-99), Spanish soldier and hero. His name comes from the Arabic *El Sayyid*, which means "the Lord." El Cid led the forces of Sancho II of Castile and Alfonso VI of Leon until banishment by Alfonso (c.1081). He then fought for the Arab kings of Saragossa, capturing Valencia (1094), where he remained as ruler until his death. His romanticized exploits appear in literature, notably *The Song of the Cid* (c.1140) and Corneille's *Le Cid* (1636).

Cilia, hairlike projections, often part of a fringe, that provide locomotion for 1-celled organisms, and move fluid within higher forms of life. Cilia protruding from the lining of the upper respiratory tract move to pass on dust, germs, and mucus.
See also: Protozoan.

Ciliate *See:* Protozoan.

Cimabue, Giovanni (Cenni di Pepo or Peppi; c.1240-c.1302), Italian painter. His work shows the transition from the formal Byzantine style of painting to the more lyrical Florentine school of the 14th century. His best known work, *Madonna and Child Enthroned with Angels and Prophets*, is now at the Uffizi Gallery in Florence, Italy.

Cimarosa, Domenico (1749-1801), prolific Italian composer famous for his comic operas, notably *Il Matrimonio Segreto* ("The Secret Marriage"; 1792). He was court composer to Catherine the Great of Russia, 1787-91.

Cimmerians, ancient nomads of the Crimea and Asia Minor. First mentioned in Homer's *Odyssey*, they lived from about 1200 B.C. to 700 B.C., in an area of the Caucasus Mountains, near the Black Sea in what is now the southern USSR. The Cimmerians were warriors who rode horses and used bows and arrows. According to the Greek historian Herodotus, they were driven into Asia Minor by the Scythians. About 700 B.C. the Cimmerians battled the Assyrians, and plundered and destroyed the Phrygian dynasty.

Cimon (c.507-c.449 B.C.), Athenian statesman and military leader in the Greco-Persian Wars. He became the leader of the aristocrats, those opposing the democrat Pericles and his reform-minded followers. He was exiled by Pericles, but returned to Athens in 451 B.C., and eventually effected a reconciliation between Sparta and Athens.
See also: Athens; Greece, Ancient.

Cinchona, or chinchona, genus of evergreen tree of South and Central America, cultivated for its bark, which yields quinine and other antimalarial alkaloids.

Cincinnati (pop. 364,300), city in southwest Ohio, on a height overlooking the Ohio River. First settled in 1788, the city grew rapidly after the War of 1812. Manufacturing industries today include chemicals, automobile parts and bodies, soap, machine tools, and engines. Publishing and printing industries also contribute to the economy. The city is a major river and rail transportation center and inland port. Cincinnati's cultural life offers museums (including the Taft Museum; Cincinnati was the birthplace of William Howard Taft and Robert A. Taft), its symphony orchestra, opera, and conservatory.
See also: Ohio.

Cincinnatus, Lucius Quinctius (c.519-c.439 B.C.), statesman and Roman patriotic hero. Cincinnatus was named dictator by the Senate in 458 B.C. When Rome was threatened by the Aequians, he left his farm, defeated the enemy, resigned, and returned to his farm all within 16 days of taking office. *See also:* Rome, Ancient.

Cinema *See:* Motion pictures.

Cinnabar, bright-red mercuric sulfide mineral (HgS), an important source of mercury and used in the pigment vermillion. Large deposits are found in Spain, Yugoslavia, Italy, China, and southern California. *See also:* Mercury (element).

Cinnamon (genus *Cinnamomum*), tree or shrub of the laurel family. The inner bark of the Ceylon cinnamon (*C. zeylanicum*) is used as a spice; in medicine, *C. camphora* serves as a digestion stimulant and to treat dyspepsia.

Cinquefoil, low-growing plant (genus *Potentilla*) of the rose family, named for its 5-fingered leaves. The bright yellow and white flowers are widespread over North America and the Pacific coast.

CIO *See:* Congress of Industrial Organizations.

Circadian rhythm *See:* Biological clock.

Circe, in Greek mythology, daughter of Helios (the Sun), enchantress who transformed Odysseus' men into swine; Odysseus himself escaped her spell. Later legends say she had 3 sons by Odysseus, including Telegonus, doomed to slay his father. *See also:* Mythology.

Circle, closed plane curve every point of which is at equal distance from a fixed point (center). A line segment between the center and the curve is called a *radius* (r); the word is also used for the length of that segment. A line segment whose 2 ends lie in the curve is a *chord*, and a chord passing through the center point is called the *diameter* (d). The distance around the edge is known as the *circumference* (C); $C = \pi d$. The area of a circle (A) is given by $A = \pi r^2$. The circle has been used to symbolize eternity, the universe, or heaven.

Circuit, electric *See:* Electric circuit.

Circuit breaker, electric device, like a fuse, that will automatically interrupt an electrical circuit (by separating the contacts) when the current exceeds a desired value. Circuit breakers may be reset by hand or automatically, whereas a fuse has to be replaced. *See also:* Electricity.

Circuit rider, itinerant preacher of the Methodist church who visited scattered communities to conduct services. John Wesley originated the practice in England in the 18th century, and Francis Asbury adapted

itin America. The term also refers to judges in the early days of the United States who were appointed to ride the circuit to hear cases.
See also: Methodists.

Circulation *See:* Circulatory system.

Circulatory system, system of organs that carries blood throughout the body. It consists chiefly of a pump (the heart) and a network of blood vessels (arteries, veins, and capillaries). The circulatory system provides the body with essential food and oxygen while eliminating carbon dioxide and other wastes. In addition, as blood circulates, white blood cells help protect the body from disease by engulfing harmful invaders, and body temperature is regulated by absorbing heat from the cells' production of energy.
Disease or injury may damage the circulatory system, possibly affecting blood flow. Arterioscleroisis, an accumulation of fatty deposits in the arteries, is one such condition. This disease may be associated with high blood pressure, which results from the heart's need to work harder, and may lead to complications such as heart attack, a stroke, or kidney failure.

Circumcision, removal of the foreskin covering the glans of the penis, as a religious requirement (among Jews and Muslims) or as a surgical measure for sanitary reasons. In ancient Egypt circumcision was regarded as an initiation into puberty. For Jews it symbolizes a male's induction into the covenant between God and Abraham, usually 8 days after birth. In some tribes of Africa and South America, and in Islam, female circumcision, involving removal of all or part of the clitoris, is practiced.

Circumference *See:* Circle.

Circumstantial evidence *See:* Evidence.

Circus, form of entertainment featuring trained animals and performances by acrobats, trapeze artists, horseback riders, and clowns, presented within a circular enclosure. Historically, "circus" (the Latin for "ring") referred to chariot races, gladiatorial fighting, and animal events in ancient Rome. U.S. circuses date from colonial times, but the modern circus became popular in the 19th century.

Cirrhosis, chronic disease of the liver marked by progressive destruction and regeneration of liver cells and increased connective tissue (scar) formation. Cirrhosis ultimately results in blockage of portal circulation, raised blood pressure in the portal vein, liver failure, and death. Causes include alcohol consumption (Laennec's cirrhosis, the most prevalent), hepatitis and other infections, and severe malnutrition in children of tropical countries (a condition known as kwashiorkor). Results include jaundice, gastrointestinal problems, and edema. Though irreparable, treatment includes vitamin intake, controlled diet, and diuretics.
See also: Liver.

Cirrus *See:* Cloud.

Cisneros, Henry Gabriel (1947-), first Hispanic mayor of a major U.S. city. Cisneros, a Democrat, was elected to 4 terms as mayor of San Antonio. Tex., (1981-89). Born in San Antonio, Cisneros earned degrees from Texas A&M, Harvard, an George Washington University. As mayor, he was credited with advancing economic development and lessening ethnic polarization. He is now employed in the private sector.

Cistercians, Roman Catholic monastic order. Monks and nuns of this order are often referred to as Trappists, after a 17th-century order of Cistercians in La Trappe, France. Their order is based on principles of prayer, manual work, and study. Its followers often lead secluded lives.
See also: Trappists.

Citadel, fortress protecting or dominating a town.

Cities of refuge, 6 cities of ancient Palestine. People accused of murders, committed by accident or in self-defense remained safe in these cities until they were tried. If found innocent, they continued to live in the cities of refuge. If found guilty, they were returned to the place of the crime for punishment.
See also: Palestine.

Citizens band radio (CB), radio with a short range. These radios operate on frequencies reserved for private use and transmit signals from 5 mi (8 km) in the city to 20 mi (32 km) in rural areas. Frequencies used for CB radios also operate remote controlled devices, such as garage doors and model airplanes.
See also: Radio.

Citizenship, legal relationship between an individual and the country of nationality, usually acquired by birth or naturalization. Though laws regarding citizenship by birth vary from country to country, such citizenship is generally based on place of birth or the nationality of one or both parents. Some countries grant citizenship by marriage, adoption, long residence, land purchase, entrance into public service, or annexation of territory. It is possible for an individual to be a citizen of more than 1 country or to possess no citizenship at all. Citizenship implies both rights (to a passport, to the protection of the government when appropriate, to constitutional rights) and duties (to pay taxes, to serve in the armed forces) between the citizen and the country.

Citizenship Day, day that honors citizens of voting age and naturalized foreign-born citizens of the United States, Sept. 17 (anniversary of the signing of the U.S. Constitution). Congress passed this act to replace the earlier May celebration called I Am an American Day.

Citrange, hybrid orange produced by crossing the sweet orange and the trifoliate orange. It is stronger and hardier than the sweet orange plant. Citrange is used for cooking and flavoring beverages.

Citric acid, tricarboxylic acid ($C_6H_8O_7$) derived from lemons and similar fruits or obtained by fermentation of carbohydrates; used as a flavoring and to condition water.

Citrin, one of a group of chemicals known as flavinoids. Also referred to as vitamin P and used in medicine, citrin helps control bleeding within capillary (tiny blood vessels) walls. Citrin is often formulated from a mixture of lemon peel and paprika.

Citron, *(Citrus medica)*, fruit tree in the citrus family (Rutaceae); also its fruit. The citron is a large yellowish fruit with a thick white rind and a small pulpy though acidic center. It was the first of the citrus fruits to be introduced into Europe from India and Asia. The rind is crystallized as candy, while the juice flavors syrups and beverages.

Citrus, genus of tropical trees of the rue family, providing such edible fruits as the orange, lemon, citron, grapefruit, lime, tangerine, and shaddock, all of which are rich in vitamin C, sugars, and citric acid.

City, large center of population, often distinguished from a town or village by the diversity of its economic and cultural activities; also, a center officially designated as a city for purposes of local government.

City government, government that manages affairs for cities and various other communities. Most cities are incorporated municipalities, that is, corporations defined and empowered by the state through charters. An elected council or commission forms the legislature. The executive branch may be headed by an elected mayor, an appointed city manager, or elected commissioners. Larger cities also have their own court system. The branches of government, its related agencies, and the individual city workers (civil servants) make up a bureaucracy governed by city laws, also known as municipal ordinances. These ordinances cover day-to-day needs of city residents. Property taxes and state or federal grants-in-aid generate most of the money on which cities run.
See also: City.

City planning, planning for the growth of a city or town, taking into consideration the economic, physical, social, and aesthetic needs of its populace and government. Examples of such planning range from the grid-iron organization of ancient Roman cities to the grandiose planning of the Renaissance, usually intended to glorify a ruler or to strengthen his military position; to the piecemeal development of the Industrial Revolution, chaotic due to the enormous population movement; to Pierre L'Enfant's design for Washington, D.C. (1791) and Frederick L. Olmsted's city park designs. In the United States civic reform movements, already active before the Civil War, instigated legislation to enforce slum clearance and to provide better educational and recreational facilities. Today's city planners, many dealing with housing projects and city-center renewal projects, take into account such factors as existing roads and traffic patterns; availability of sanitation service, police and fire protection, employment; zoning regulations; location of schools, hospitals, and recreational facilities.

City-state, independent political community (particularly in ancient Greece) made up of a city and its surrounding countryside, from which it draws food and labor. The Greek city-state, or *polis*, which emerged around 700 B.C., ranged in size from Athens (1,000 sq mi/2,590 sq km) to minute states less than one-hundredth of its size, and ranged in government from monarchies to democracies. The Greeks colonized much of the Mediterranean, spreading the city-state form of organization until Rome became the nucleus of an empire that turned all the city-states into subunits of its administration. City-states have flourished during 3 major periods of Western civilization: the ancient civilizations of the Middle East, the classical period of Greece, and in Europe from the 11th to the 16th centuries.

Ciudad Bolívar (pop. 249,600), commercial center and port of eastern Venezuela, located on the Orinoco River. It was originally founded by Spaniards and called Angostura (1764). Here Simon Bolívar, known as the liberator of South America, claimed independence for Colombia and Venezuela (1819). It was subsequently named after him (Spanish: *ciudad*, city). Exports such as latex, animal skins, and lumber are shipped through Ciudad Bolivar.
See also: Venezuela.

Civet, weasel-like carnivorous mammal of the family Viverridae, found in Africa and South Asia. The African civet, (*Civettictis civetta*), is reared for the musky-smelling oily substance, used as a base for perfumes, that is produced by glands under its tail.

Civics, study of the rights and duties of citizenship. Civics became part of the school curriculum in the United States in the 19th century, after the influx of immigration. Courses cover national and international events, community affairs, political and economic problems, elections, and government.

Civil Air Patrol (CAP), voluntary civilian auxiliary of the United States Air Force. CAP organizes and runs state or district groups (wings) with teenaged cadets as well as adult members. CAP operates an extensive radio network and an educational program, and participates in an international exchange program. Most search and rescue missions in the United States are directed by CAP. Originated in 1941 to organize civilian air participation for wartime tasks, this group is now a nonprofit private organization.

Civil code *See:* Code Napoléon.

Civil defense, nonmilitary measures taken to protect a nation's civilian population and its resources in case of enemy attack. Organized civil defense programs began shortly before World War II, when it was realized that powerful air forces greatly increased the wartime danger to civilians. In the United States, civil defense efforts, including warning systems, the construction and stocking of shelters, and survival planning, are directed and coordinated at the national level by the Office of Civil Defense.

Civil disobedience, form of political action involving intentional violation of the law in order to force concessions from a government or to draw attention to alleged injustices. Henry David Thoreau, in his 19th-century essay *On Civil Disobedience*, expounded on these methods, which were essential in Mohandas Gandhi's 20th-century struggle for India's independence and which have been employed by the suffragettes, the civil rights movement, and Vietnam War protesters. Martin Luther King, Jr. was an advocate of civil disobedience and used it successfully during his career. *See also:* Thoreau, Henry David; Gandhi, Mohandas Karamchand.

Civilian Conservation Corps (CCC), agency founded in 1933 by the U.S. Congress as part of the New Deal. The agency trained and hired unemployed men to develop and conserve natural resources through tree planting, firefighting, and dam construction. Congress abolished the corps in 1942.

Civilization (Latin *civis*, "citizen of a city"), stage of societal development in which complex economic, social, and governmental systems arise. Civilizations first arose as farming on permanent sites replaced the nomadic life of hunters and gatherers. In these new, permanent groups, inventions such as metal tools led to advances in the lives of people, and complex economic, social, and political structures evolved. The Tigris-Euphrates River valleys of the Middle East, the Nile River Valley of Egypt, the Indus River Valley in India, and the Huang He River Valley of China are sites of early civilizations.

Civil law, body of law based on Roman law, dealing with private rights claims between individuals, as opposed to criminal law (offenses against the state). After the fall of the Roman Empire, the customs of the ruling tribes developed into customary law throughout most of continental Europe, including England. Roman law was rediscovered in the 12th century, and European jurists began to codify the existing legal systems with Roman additions. The *Corpus Juris Civilis* of Justinian I (6th century) was of special importance for these evolving legal systems. The development of civil law was further enhanced by the Code Napoleon (1804), which gave France a unified national code. Other countries, mainly in continental Europe and Latin America, followed the French lead. Codes of civil law countries state general legal principles that courts must interpret in the light of particular cases. In common law countries such as Great Britain, Canada, and the United States (excluding Louisiana), the courts are bound by previous decisions (the rule of precedent). Trial by jury and the law of evidence are key features of legal practice in common law countries; they have no counterpart in civil law.

Civil liberties *See:* Civil rights.

Civil rights, rights and privileges enjoyed by citizens. A distinction is sometimes made between civil rights and civil liberties: Civil rights must be granted by the government (for example, the right to vote), while civil liberties are inalienable individual freedoms the government may be prohibited from restraining. In the United States "civil rights" also includes the rights of individuals, particularly members of minority groups, to nondiscriminatory treatment. The concept of civil rights arose in the Roman Empire, whose courts protected the rights of Roman citizens against arbitrary acts by the government. In the Middle Ages nobles issued charters to their followers to protect against other nobles and the king. The rise of absolute monarchs in France, Spain, and other European nations ended many of the civil rights of their subjects. In England, however, the nobles, and later the House of Commons and the common law courts, defended and extended the rights of the people against the crown. The Magna Carta of 1215, under which the king granted specific rights to his lords in return for their support, and the Bill of Rights in 1689 established a basis in common law for the inviolable liberties of individual citizens. Many U.S. and Canadian concepts of civil rights and individual liberty derive from the English example. The so-called natural law theorists of the 17th and 18th centuries, such as Jean-Jacques Rousseau and John Locke, taught that the natural law, reflecting divine law, confers certain rights upon the individual that cannot be legitimately taken away by governments. These ideas are enshrined in the famous words of the Declaration of Independence: "that all men are created equal, that they are endowed by their Creator with certain inalienable Rights..."

With some exceptions, civil rights in American colonial times were often restricted, particularly in matters of religion. The Declaration of Rights and Liberties, passed in 1774 by the Continental Congress, was an important part of the agitation against the British government preceding the American Revolution. The Northwest Ordinance of 1787, which provided for settlement and organization of new territories, established certain liberties for settlers in the new area, including the right of *habeas corpus*, trial by jury, and religious freedom. The basis for the civil rights of all Americans is the Constitution, whose first 10 amendments, known as the Bill of Rights, provide for fundamental liberties: freedom of speech, assembly, the press, and religion; protection against unreasonable searches and seizures; prohibition of double jeopardy and self-incrimination; and the right to a speedy and public trial. The 13th amendment (1865) abolished slavery, and the 14th (1868) established the standards of due process of law and equal protection of the laws of all citizens. The 15th amendment (1870) states that no male citizen could be denied the right to vote because of his race. The rights of women lagged behind those of former slaves: Women did not receive the right to vote in federal elections until 1920 (the 19th amendment).

The massive civil rights legislation of the Reconstruction era was followed by a prolonged legislative silence on racial discrimination. Moreover, the constitutional amendments and civil rights measures enacted by Congress after the Civil War were largely negated by 2 Supreme Court decisions—the first holding that only the states were prohibited from discriminating, while individuals were not (1883), the second establishing the criterion of "separate but equal" facilities as fulfilling legal requirements (1896). In 1954 the Supreme Court declared "separate but equal" facilities a violation of civil rights and ordered public schools to be integrated "with all deliberate speed." In 1957, after years of effort by civil rights activists, Congress set up the Civil Rights Commission to investigate discrimination, established a Civil Rights Division in the Department of Justice to investigate and prosecute violations of federal law, and empowered the attorney general to bring suit against any person or civic body that denied another's voting rights. The Civil Rights Act of 1960 outlawed infringements of voting rights and ordered all the armed forces desegregated. The 24th amendment (1964) outlawed poll taxes; literacy tests as a means of racial discrimination were brought under control in 1965 legislation. The Civil Rights Act of 1964 prohibited discrimination in public accommodations and by employers or labor unions. It also created the Equal Employment Opportunity Commission to ensure that persons were not barred from employment on the grounds of race, religion, or sex. Many women have since successfully sued for their rights under this act. The Civil Rights Act of 1968 outlawed discrimination in the sale or rental of housing and established the protection of the law for those exercising their civil rights or urging others to do so. In 1970 the 1965 Voting Rights Act was renewed and extended, lowering the voting age from 21 to 18. During this same period major strides were being made to ensure and extend individual civil liberties. The most far-reaching and controversial decisions were in the field of criminal procedure. The *Miranda* case (1966) resulted in a ruling that a citizen placed under arrest must be made aware of his or her constitutional rights and be free to exercise them; a confession obtained in violation of this rule is excluded from evidence in a court of law. The Court further established that a citizen placed under arrest must be made aware of his or her constitutional rights and be able to exercise them.

The international movement to secure civil rights for all people has been strengthened by the work of many agencies, including UNESCO, the International Labor Organization, the European Commission on Human Rights, the Inter-American Commission on Human Rights, the International Commission of Jurists, and the International League for the Rights of Man. The Universal Declaration of Human Rights, endorsed by the General Assembly of the United Nations (1948), includes a list of basic civil rights that should be available to all persons. In December 1965 the General Assembly approved the convention on the elimination of all forms of racial discrimination.

Civil Rights, Commission on, independent U.S. government agency whose role is to advance the cause of equal opportunity, established 1957. Public hearings are conducted to assure legal protection of citizens of all races, religions, gender, and national origins. Issues for which the commission seeks equality are voting rights and opportunities in education, housing, and employment. Through investigations initiated by charges of civil rights denials and independent studies, the commission makes recommendations to the President and Congress.

Civil Rights Act of 1866 *See:* Reconstruction.

Civil service, body of civilian (non-military) employees of a government, excluding elected officials. Civil service dates from ancient China, where officials were chosen through competitive exams. It was also found in ancient Rome, and in France after Napoleon I. In the United States the civil service suffered from the spoils system (gifts of government jobs as political rewards), firmly established from 1828 under President Andrew Jackson. Attempts to establish a merit system (appointment and promotion based on merit, to secure efficiency and freedom from political influence) failed until the Pendleton Act (1883), which set up the Civil Service Commission to administer federal employment. The Hatch Acts (1939, 1940) forbade federal employees to play any active part in politics beyond voting.

Civil War, U.S. (1861-65), conflict between 11 Southern states (Confederate States of America) and the U.S. federal government (Union). Because the 11 states had attempted to secede from the Union, in the North the conflict was officially called the War of the Rebellion. Since the war was a sectional struggle, North against South, it is sometimes also known as the War Between the States.

Origins. The economy of the South was based on the plantation system of agriculture, which absolutely depended on slave labor. Great staple crops— cotton, tobacco, sugar, and rice—were grown largely for export. The North had no need for slavery; its agriculture, which produced corn and wheat largely for subsistence and internal consumption, was based on small family farms; its industry and towns were expanding rapidly, and it welcomed European immigrants in large numbers to supply its growing labor needs. Political differences came to a head over the question of whether slavery would be permitted in the newly settled western territories, soon to become states. The Missouri Compromise (1820) was the first attempt to ease North-South tensions by admitting Missouri as a slave state and Maine as a free state and forbidding slavery in the Louisiana Territory north of latitude 30°30'. As a long-term solution it failed because expansion continued westward, raising the issue again and more acutely, and also because of the growth of abolitionism in the North.

The admission to the Union of the huge slave state of Texas (1845) and the resultant Mexican War renewed the fears of Southern political dominance and the possible extension of slave territory. The Compromise of 1850 seemed to solve the problem, but it was nullified by the Kansas-Nebraska Act of 1854, which gave the residents of those territories the right to vote on whether or not slavery would be permitted. This opened the way for opponents and supporters of slavery to begin a virtual civil war in "Bleeding Kansas." The Dred Scott Decision (1857) further inflamed the problem as the Supreme Court's decision had the effect of declaring the Missouri Compromise unconstitutional. The presidential election of 1860 raised the fears of the South as Abraham Lincoln, the candidate of the newly formed Republican party, was known to be opposed to the further extension of slavery. Lincoln declared: "My paramount object is to save the Union, and not either to save or destroy slavery," but South Carolina voted to secede from the Union (Dec. 20, 1860) and was followed by 6 more states by Feb. 1861. Representatives met at Montgomery, Ala., to draw up a constitution for these Confederate states and elected Jefferson Davis provisional president. When Lincoln announced he was sending supplies to the federal garrison of Fort Sumter, in Charleston harbor, Confederate guns opened fire on the fort (Apr. 12), which surrendered 2 days later. The outbreak of hostilities drove 4 more slave states (North Carolina, Virginia, Arkansas, and Tennessee) into the Confederacy.

First phase of the war—Union defeats. The capture of the Confederate capital seemed the natural objective, and the first rallying cry of the North was "On to Richmond." This simple aim of frontal attack led to the first major encounter, at Bull Run (July 21, 1861), and the Federals were routed. In the meantime the North blockaded the South, but chances of capturing a Southern blockade runner were rated at 1 in 10 and 800 vessels got through in the first year. The blockade, however, became increasingly effective. In Apr. the Union fleet under David Farragut took New Orleans, the first of many essential ports to fall to the North. Northern General George McClellan's Peninsular Campaign (1862) nearly reached Richmond but ended in defeat in the Battles of the Seven Days, and Southern General Robert E. Lee was again victorious at the second Battle of Bull Run. This opened the way for a Confederate invasion of Maryland that was thwarted by a Union victory at Antietam, and Lincoln seized the political initiative by issuing the preliminary Emancipation Proclamation (Sept. 1862) promising freedom to slaves held in the Confederacy. The year closed with a shattering defeat for the Union at Fredericksburg, Va.

Second phase—the Confederacy crushed. The first Union victories had come in the West in 1862, when General Ulysses S. Grant took forts Henry and Donelson, opening the Tennessee River. After the bloody battle of Shiloh, the Federals commanded nearly the entire length of the Mississippi. In 1863 Lee defeated the North at Chancellorsville, but General Stonewall Jackson, one of the ablest Confederate generals, was mortally wounded. Lee struck north into Pennsylvania, but Union forces won the decisive battle of the war after 3 days of costly fighting at Gettysburg (July 1863). On the following day Grant took Vicksburg, which finally gave the Union forces control of the Mississippi, cutting the Confederacy in two and opening the way for the invasion of Tennessee. Grant's attempt to capture Richmond in 1864 was halted in the Wilderness Campaign, but soon after he began the 9-month siege of Petersburg. Sherman meanwhile moved east from Chattanooga to take Atlanta in September 1864. His army marched through Georgia to the sea, leaving behind it a trail of devastation. The capture of Petersburg and Richmond on Apr. 2, 1865, led to Lee's surrender to Grant at Appomattox Court House a week later. Although Confederate forces in the South and West fought on for several weeks, the war was effectively over.

Civitan International, service organization of business and professional men and women, striving to promote good citizenship, locally, nationally, and internationally. Founded in 1920, Civitan consists of approximately 50,000 people in about 1,500 clubs. Projects include special olympics and other activities for the physically and mentally handicapped, scholarships, and awards for good citizenship and service.

Claiborne's Rebellion, outbreak of conflict in colonial United States caused by the refusal of William Claiborne, a Virginia fur trader, to accept the authority of Leonard Calvert, governor of Maryland. Kent Island in the Chesapeake Bay area, where Claiborne had established his fur trade, lay within the boundaries of Maryland, according to a charter issued to the Calvert family in 1632. Claiborne, however, had obtained a trading license in England in 1631. Claiborne drove Calvert's forces off the island, but Calvert restored his rule there in 1657.

Clair, René (René Chomette; 1898-1981), French film director, producer, and writer, especially of screen comedies. Born in Paris, he worked on both silent and sound films, including *Sous les Toits de Paris* (1929).

Clam, name given to many edible marine bivalve mollusks that live in sand or mud, including the jacknife clam, the quahog or cherrystone clam, and the pismo clam; also refers to some freshwater bivalves. The giant clams of Indian Ocean and Pacific Ocean coral reefs may reach a diameter of 4 ft (2.4 m) and weigh one-quarter ton (0.27 metric tons).

Clan, social group claiming descent from a common ancestor. Clans have existed all over the world, from primitive societies to the famous Highland clans of Scotland (said to have originated in the 11th century). Some clans have expressed their unity in the symbol of the totem (an object, animal, or plant revered as the ancestor of the group). Most, but not all clans, are exogamous, requiring marriage outside of the clan (marriage within being regarded as incest). Several clans may organize into a larger social structure known as phratry.

Clarendon, Edward Hyde, 1st earl of (1609-74), English statesman and historian. He originally opposed King Charles I, but supported him in 1642 when civil war started. Although Clarendon favored religious toleration, Parliament made him enforce the Clarendon Code, which strengthened the position of the Church of England. In 1667 Charles II made him a scapegoat for failures in the second Dutch War. He was forced into exile, from which he wrote the 10-volume *History of the Rebellion*, defending Royalist activities during the civil war.

Clarinet, single-reed woodwind instrument comprising a cylindrical tube (usually wooden) with a flared bell and tapered mouthpiece, played vertically. Tones are produced by opening and closing holes (some covered by keys) in the tube while blowing air through the mouthpiece. The clarinet, developed in Germany from the chalumeau by Johann Christoph Denner early in the 18th century, features in dance bands, military bands, woodwind groups, symphony orchestras, and as a solo instrument.

Clark, Abraham (1726-94), political leader during the American Revolutionary War, member of the 1776 Continental Congress, and a New Jersey signer of the Declaration of Independence. After the Revolution, he called for a bill of rights to be included in the projected U.S. Constitution and earned his nickname, the "Poor Man's Counselor," by defending poor farmers in land cases.

Clark, (Charles) Joseph (1939-   ), Canadian prime minister (1979-80). After election to the House of Commons in 1972, he was elected leader of the Progressive Conservative party in 1976, and prime minister in 1979, replacing Pierre Trudeau and marking the beginning of western Canada's political importance.
See also: Canada.

Clark, George Rogers (1752-1818), U.S. frontiersman and Revolutionary War general who led the campaign against the British in the Northwest Territory. With about 175 volunteers, he succeeded in capturing key British forts north of the Ohio River, principally Kaskaskia (1778) and Vincennes (1779). His brother was William Clark, the explorer.
See also: Revolutionary War in America.

Clark, Kenneth Bancroft (1914-   ), U.S. psychologist whose 1950 report on school segregation was cited in the Supreme Court's 1954 ruling against segregated public schools. A professor at City College of New York (1942-75), he was active in many civil rights and educational organizations and was the first black member of the New York State Board of Regents (1966). His books include *Prejudice and Your Child* (1955), *Dark Ghetto* (1965), and *The Pathos of Power* (1974).
See also: Psychology; Segregation.

Clark, Mark Wayne (1896-1984), U.S. general, commander of Allied ground forces in North Africa and Italy in World War II and commander of UN operations in the Korean War (1952-53). He led the invasion of Italy in 1943.
See also: World War II.

Clark, Ramsey (1927-   ), U.S. lawyer and politician. He served in the Department of Justice (1961-66) as assistant attorney general and deputy attorney general, becoming U.S. Attorney General in 1966, under President Lyndon B. Johnson. Clark was a strong proponent of civil rights and of the Vietnam War.

Clark, Tom Campbell (1899-1977), U.S. jurist and lawyer, Attorney General under President Harry S. Truman (1945), and associate justice of the U.S. Supreme Court, 1949-67. Generally a conservative supporter of the government's "antisubversion" actions after World War II, Clark was often at odds with the Warren Court. However, he joined the other justices in voting to outlaw school segregation in *Brown* v. *Board of Education*, 1954. He retired in 1967 when his son, Ramsey Clark, became attorney general.
See also: Supreme Court of the United States.

Clark, William (1770-1838), U.S. explorer, a leader of the Lewis and Clark Expedition, 1804-6, and brother of George Rogers Clark. He was superintendent of Indian affairs and governor of Missouri Territory, 1813-21.
See also: Lewis and Clark expedition.

Clarke, Arthur C(harles) (1917-   ), British science fiction and science writer. Clarke is best known as co-author of the screenplay for the film *2001: A Space Odyssey* (1968) and for his detailed design for communications satellites in 1945. His novels include *Childhood's End* (1953) and *The Fountains of Paradise* (1979). In 1996 Clarke was awarded a Sri Lankan prize for his "contributions to the development and realization of communications satellites".

Class, level of social stratification (e.g., upper, middle, and lower class). Classes lack the rigid boundaries characterizing caste, so that mobility between classes is possible.

Class action, lawsuit in which 1 or more persons represents a group (class) of persons having similar claims. U.S. citizens first used class action suits to recover money in bankruptcy cases. In the 1950s and 1960s civil rights groups used class action to fight school segregation, housing or voting restrictions, and job discrimination. Since then, class actions have expanded to cases involving price fixing, environmental issues, and other social problems.

Classical music, or art music, music composed by individuals and written for instruments, for voices, or for combinations of voices and instruments. Classical music is more complex than *popular music* (country, folk, rock, jazz). Christianity helped spread Western classical music, which began in ancient times. Instrumental music includes solo, chamber, and orchestral music. Perhaps the most popular chamber group is the string quartet, consisting of 2 violins, a viola, and cello. Opera combines a large orchestra with soloists and chorus, and tells a story. Nonwestern classical music includes the music of the highly developed cultures of India, China, and Japan.

Classicism, in painting, sculpture, architecture, literature, and music, the emulation of classical antiquity, emphasizing harmony, order, and clarity of form, rather than subjectivity, heightened emotion, and the uncanny. The aims of the artists in the Italian Renaissance (literally, the "rebirth" of classical culture) were rejected in the 16th and 17th centuries by the mannerist and baroque artists. Classicism was revived in the 18th-century movement known as neoclassicism (also called the Enlightenment). Important artistic figures include Samuel Johnson and Alexander Pope (English literature), Pierre Corneille and Jean Racine (French literature), and Franz Joseph Haydn and Wolfgang Amadeus Mozart (music). The 19th-century romantic movement in art was partly a reaction to perceived overreliance on reason and order in neoclassicism.

Classification, in biology, systematic arrangement of the world's organisms into categories based on their characteristics. This science, sometimes called taxonomy, is often aimed at establishing evolutionary relationships. The system of classification comprises 7 major categories. These are, from most to least inclusive: kingdom; phylum (called division in botany); class; order; family; genus; species. Traditionally, there were only 2 kingdoms, plants and animals. Today, however, most biologists would recognize 3 others: the Protista (1-celled organisms and some forms of algae), the Monera (bacteria and blue-green algae), and the Fungi (mushrooms and molds). The species is the basic unit of classification. As a rule of thumb, 2 animals belong to the same species if they are capable of mating to produce fertile offspring. *See also:* Biology.

Claudel, Paul (1868-1955), French dramatist, poet, and diplomat. Influenced by Arthur Rimbaud and intensely religious, he drew inspiration for his sensuous, lyrical verse from nature and Oriental thought.

Claude Lorrain (Claude Gelée; 1600-82), a founder of French romantic landscape painting who lived and worked mostly in Rome. His canvases usually show a biblical or classical scene dominated by an idyllically lit landscape (*The Expulsion of Hagar*, 1668; *The Trojan Women Setting Fire to the Greek Fleet*; *Seaport at Sunset*). His later works are almost visionary in their intensity and inspired such painters as Poussin and Turner.

Claudius, name of 2 Roman emperors. **Claudius I** (Tiberius Claudius Drusus Nero Germanicus; 10 B.C.-A.D. 54) reigned 41-54. A sickly nephew of the emperor Tiberius, he was a scholar and writer. He invaded Britain (A.D. 43), annexed Mauretania, Lycia, and Thrace (41-46), improved Rome's legal system, and encouraged colonization. He was poisoned by his second wife, Agrippina, Nero's mother. **Claudius II** (Marcus Aurelius Claudius Gothicus; 214-270 A.D.) reigned 268-70. An army officer, he succeeded Gallienus.
See also: Rome, Ancient.

Clausewitz, Karl von (1780-1831), Prussian general, strategist, and military historian. His book *On War* (1833) revolutionized military thinking after his death. Defining war as an extension of diplomacy, he urged the destruction of enemy forces, morale, and resources, and has thus been called the prophet of total war, although he favored defensive fighting.

Clausius, Rudolf Julius Emmanuel (1822-88), German theoretical physicist. He was first to state the second law of thermodynamics (1850), that heat never flows from a colder to a hotter body without work, and proposed the term *entropy* (1865). He also contributed to kinetic theory and the theory of electrolysis.
See also: Entropy; Thermodynamics.

Clavichord, keyboard musical instrument popular in the 16th to 18th centuries. The strings were struck with metal wedges (a piano uses felt hammers), and the sound was quiet and delicate.

Clay, 1 of 3 main types of earth, found in layers under the earth's crust and often at river mouths. Most clays consist of very small particles of hydrated aluminum silicates (kaolinites) that are usually produced by the weathering of rocks. Clay is easily malleable when wet and retains its shape when dried. If it is fired (baked) in a high-temperature oven or kiln it becomes extremely hard and, if first coated with a glaze, nonporous. Electrical insulators, sewage pipes, cement, kitchen tiles, chinaware, bricks, and paper manufacture all require clay. Clay is essential to the soil, holding moisture and preventing organic material from being washed away.

Clay, Cassius *See:* Ali, Muhammad.

Clay, Cassius Marcellus (1810-1903), U.S. abolitionist, politician, and statesman. Clay founded the antislavery journal *True American*, in Lexington, Ky., 1845. He was a founder of the Republican Party (1854), and U.S. ambassador to Russia (1861-62 and 1863-69).
See also: Abolitionism.

Clay, Henry (1777-1852), U.S. statesman. Clay helped to create the Compromise of 1850, an attempt to reconcile North and South in the pre-Civil War period. He served as secretary of state under President John Quincy Adams (1825-29), ran unsuccessfully as the Whig party candidate for president in 1832 and 1844, and was a U.S. senator, 1849-52.
See also: Civil War, U.S.

Clay, Lucius DuBignon (1897-1978), U.S. general assigned to govern the U.S. zone of West Germany (1947-49). He supervised the Berlin Airlift.

Clayton, John Middleton (1796-1856), politician who served 3 terms as U.S. senator from Delaware. His greatest achievement was the Clayton-Bulwer Treaty of 1850.

Clayton-Bulwer Treaty, agreement signed by the United States and Great Britain in 1850, giving the 2 countries an equal role in protecting a canal to be built through Central America, the 2 countries agreeing to maintain the

neutrality of the canal and the land on either side of it. John Clayton, U.S. secretary of state, and Sir Henry Bulwer (1801-72), British minister to the United States, negotiated the treaty, which was replaced in 1901 by the Hay-Pauncefote Treaty, giving the United States the exclusive right to build and manage the canal.
See also: Hay-Pauncefote Treaties.

Clearinghouse, institution or system for exchanging checks among banks for the purpose of collection. The clearinghouse allows the banks in each city to settle their accounts among themselves on a daily basis. When the banks are in different cities, the clearinghouse function is performed by the Federal Reserve Bank of the district.

Cleary, Beverly (1916-   ), U.S. author of humorous and realistic children's books. The character Henry Huggins was introduced in Cleary's first book (1950). Ramona Quimby first appeared as a major character in *Beezus and Ramona* (1955). These popular youngsters, who live in a middle-class suburb of Portland, Ore., appeared in many books. In 1975, Cleary received the Laura Ingalls Wilder Award for her contributions to children's literature. *Dear Mr. Henshaw* (1883) won the 1984 Newbery Medal. *A Girl from Yamhill* (1988) is her autobiography.

Cleaver, (Leroy) Eldridge (1935-98), U.S. black militant, a leader of the Black Panther party. His autobiographical *Soul on Ice* (1968) deals with his own experience of racial hatred and of the U.S. penal system.
See also: Black Panther Party; Black Power.

Cleft palate, congenital malformation in which the tissues that form the palate do not unite in the fetus, leaving a longitudinal gap in the upper jaw. It is often an accompaniment of harelip. The deformity needs surgical repair.

Cleisthenes (6th century B.C.), statesman of ancient Athens who instituted democratic reforms. The noble clan, Alcmaeonid, which Cleisthenes led, had a prophet persuade Cleomenes, king of Sparta, to overthrow Hippias, who had held complete power until 510 B.C. As a result, Cleisthenes was able to set up a democratic form of government, ending the political control of the noble clans.
See also: Athens; Greece, Ancient.

Clematis, genus of vines and free-standing plants whose flowers bear 4 sepals but no petals. They are best known as garden plants, but wild species include the *virgin's bower* of eastern states, whose seeds are buried in a fluffy ball called old-man's beard.

Clemenceau, Georges (1841-1929), French statesman and journalist. Known as "the Tiger," he was founder of the Third Republic and twice French premier (1906-9, 1917-20). He worked with Léon Gambetta (1870) for the overthrow of the Second Empire, supported the writer Emile Zola in the Dreyfus Affair, and headed the French delegation to the Paris Peace Conference at Versailles after World War I.
See also: World War I.

Clemens, Samuel Langhorne *See:* Twain, Mark.

Clement VII (1478?-1534), pope (1523-34), reigning ineffectively during a difficult time in European political and religious affairs. Clement was born in Florence, Italy, into the powerful Medici family. When the Holy Roman Empire and France struggled for dominance in Italy, Clement formed an alliance with France. Troops of the Holy Roman emperor Charles V sacked Rome in 1527 and captured Clement. In 1529 Clement accepted peace and recognized Charles as emperor. Because of these preoccupations, Clement vacillated in responding to the Protestant Reformation, which spread in Germany and Scandinavia. The Reformation took hold in England partly because of Clement's unwillingness to grant King Henry VIII of England an annulment of his marriage to Catherine of Aragón.

Clement VII (1342-94), one of the so-called antipopes. In 1309 Pope Clement V moved the seat of the papacy from Rome to Avignon, France, where it was subject to French control. In 1378 Pope Gregory XI returned the papacy to Rome, but died soon after the move. Urban VI was elected his successor, but he alienated the cardinals, who elected Robert of Geneva (Clement VII) pope in his stead. Clement acted as pope in Avignon, while Urban VI was pope in Rome. This period is known in Catholic history as the Great Schism. For 40 years (1378-1418) there were 2 rival lines of popes, until the Council of Constance settled the matter in favor of Rome. Since then, the Church has regarded the line of Avignon popes begun with Clement VII as illegitimate.

Clement VIII (1536-1605), pope (1592-1605). Clement fasted extensively, practiced devotions, and traveled on foot to Rome's pilgrimage churches. Reversing a papal policy, he allied himself with France instead of Spain and recognized Henry of Navarre, a Protestant convert who reverted to Catholicism, as King Henry IV of France.

Clemente, Roberto (Walker) (1934-72), Puerto Rican-born U.S. baseball player. A star outfielder for the Pittsburgh Pirates (1954-72), he amassed 3,000 hits with 240 home runs, compiled a .317 lifetime batting average, and was a 5-time National League batting champion. He was elected to the Baseball Hall of Fame in 1973, soon after his death in an airplane crash while helping Nicaraguan earthquake victims.

Clementi, Muzio (1752-1832), Italian composer and pianist, known as "the father of the piano." His compositions include more than 100 sonatas, as well as symphonies and his studies for the piano, *Gradus ad Parnassum* (1817). He enjoyed a successful concert career thoughout Europe. In London he became a partner in one of the first firms to manufacture pianos (1799).

Clement I, Saint, or Clement of Rome (d. c.101 A.D.), citizen of Rome, elected pope c.29 A.D. Third in succession to Saint Peter as bishop of Rome, he is most famous for a letter to the church in Corinth c.96 A.D., condemning pride and arrogance in the church. The letter, which, except for the scriptures, is the oldest surviving Christian text, clarified the order of succession from bishop to presbyter (elder) to deacon (assistant). His feast day is Nov. 23.

Clement of Alexandria (c.150-215), Titus Flavius Clemens, Greek theologian of the early Christian Church. His most important work is the trilogy *Exhortation of the Greeks*, the *Tutor*, and *Miscellanies*. In his work he attempted to merge Platonic and Christian ideas.

Cleopatra (69-30 B.C.), queen of Egypt, daughter of Ptolemy XI. When her father died (51 B.C.) she was supposed to share the throne with her young brother-husband, Ptolemy XII, but his advisers drove her out of Egypt (49 B.C.). She won the support of Julius Caesar (48 B.C.), who had come to Alexandria in pursuit of Pompey. She became his mistress, bearing him a son, Caesarion (later Ptolemy XIV). With Caesar's help she recovered her throne. The accidental death of Ptolemy XII was followed by her marriage to a younger brother, Ptolemy XIII, whom she later had murdered (44 B.C.). After the battle of Philippi, Mark Antony summoned her to Tarsus, where she made him her lover. They were married in 37 B.C., but the marriage was not legal in Rome, where she was feared and hated. Antony helped restore Ptolemaic power in Syria, and war with Octavian (later Emperor Augustus) became inevitable. In the sea and land battle at Actium (31 B.C.) the forces of Antony and Cleopatra were routed. Antony killed himself, and Cleopatra, fearing humiliation in Octavian's triumph in Rome, also committed suicide. *See also:* Antony, Marc; Caesar, (Gaius) Julius.

Cleopatra's needles, 2 large stone pillars called obelisks, originally erected in 1460 B.C. by Thutmose III before a sun temple at Heliopolis. Sent by Ismail Pasha as gifts (1878, 1880), one currently stands in Central Park, New York City, and the other on the Thames Embankment in London.

Clermont, first steamboat designed by U.S. engineer Robert Fulton. Fulton sailed the wood-burning boat up the Hudson River from New York City to Albany in 1807. Driven by a paddle-wheel, the ship averaged about 5 mi (8 km) per hour. It measured 142 ft (43 m) long and 14 ft (4.3 m) wide. *See also:* Fulton, Robert.

Cleveland (pop. 502,500), Ohio's largest city, situated on Lake Erie at the mouth of the Cuyahoga River. It is a major port and railway center and an important manufacturer of steel, automobile parts, chemicals, paints, plastics, precision machinery, petroleum products, trucks and tractors, machine tools, and electrical products. When the Ohio and Erie Canal was completed in 1832 with Cleveland as its terminus, the settlement began to grow rapidly. In 1851 the first railroad reached the city, which was established as a major shipping point. Cleveland was a center of the abolitionist movement, aiding escaping slaves on their way to Canada on the underground railway. During the Civil War the city's iron and petroleum industries mushroomed, and the organization of the Standard Oil Company by John D. Rockefeller (1870) made Cleveland the nation's leading oil center. The post-Civil War boom continued until the Great Depression of the 1930s, which saw the collapse of several financial empires. However, because of its industrial diversification, the city survived the depression decade relatively well. In 1967 Cleveland became the first major U.S. city to elect a black mayor, Carl B. Stokes. Surrounded by 15,000 acres (6,000 hectares) of scenic woodland, the central city contains over 2,500 acres (1,000 hectares) of park and recreation area, including Rockefeller Park, which contains the Cleveland Cultural Gardens, and Brookside Park, the site of the Cleveland Zoo. The Cleveland Natural History Museum has a renowned collection, as does the Cleveland Museum of Arts. There is also a unique health museum. Cleveland's universities and colleges include Case Western Reserve University, Cleveland-Marshall Law School, and Cleveland State University. The Cleveland Orchestra enjoys a national reputation for excellence. The city is also the home of the Cleveland Browns football team and the Cleveland Indians baseball team.

See also: Ohio.

Cleveland, (Stephen) Grover (1837-1908), 22nd and 24th president of the United States (1885-89; 1893-97), the only president to have served 2 non-consecutive terms. Cleveland was first Democratic chief executive after 24 years of Republicans.

Early life. In 1855, Cleveland moved to Buffalo, N.Y., where he worked in a local law office, gaining admittance to the bar in 1859. In 1881, after years in local politics, he was elected mayor of Buffalo on a reform ticket and won a reputation for honesty and hard work. He was elected governor of New York in 1882, and in 1884, after an extremely close race, he defeated Republican candidate James G. Blaine in the presidential election.

First term. As president, Cleveland worked to reform the civil service system and regulated public land sales, leases of Native American land, and railroad grants. In 1887 he began campaigning for lower tariffs. This was a major issue in the 1888 election, which Cleveland lost to Republican Benjamin Harrison, although Cleveland actually won more votes. In the election of 1892, Cleveland defeated Harrison by a comfortable margin.

Second term. Shortly after Cleveland's second inauguration, a severe economic depression broke out (the "panic of 1893"). By the summer, numerous railroad companies had failed, along with thousands of businesses and banks. Unemployment reached 4 million.

In 1894 Cleveland used federal troops to break a strike at the Pullman works in Illinois. In 1896, with Cleveland's popularity at its lowest ebb, the Democratic party nominated William Jennings Bryan for the presidency. Cleveland retired to Princeton, where he became a university trustee and occasional lecturer. In the remaining years of his life, he came to be regarded with respect as an honest president in an era when honest politicians were rare. But despite his attempts to root out corruption, he had failed to deal with

Grover Cleveland

22nd and 24th U.S. President

Born:	Caldwell, N.J.; Mar. 18, 1837
Terms:	Mar. 1885-Mar. 1889; Mar. 1893-Mar. 1897
Vice Presidents:	1st term, Thomas Andrews Hendricks;
	2nd term, Adlai Ewing Stevenson
Political Party:	Democratic
Spouse:	Frances Folsom Cleveland
Children:	5
Died:	Princeton, N.J.; June 24, 1908

the social problems of those years: unemployment and general labor and farmer discontent.

Cliburn, Van (Harvey Lavan Cliburn, Jr; 1934-   ), U.S. concert pianist. He became world famous after winning the International Tchaikovsky Piano Competition in Moscow in 1958. An international event of the same kind is now held annually in his name in the United States.

Click beetle, long-bodied, short-legged beetle (family Elateridae) that can throw itself over with a "click" if placed on its back. On the underside of the first segment of its thorax is a spine that rests in a groove in the second segment. When upside down, the beetle bends its head back, pulling the spine out of the groove. This is then thrust sharply back, making an audible click and throwing the beetle into the air. The larvae of click beetles are wire-worms, serious agricultural pests.

Cliff dwellers, prehistoric Native American people who built elaborate houses, some with hundreds of rooms, sheltered beneath overhanging cliffs in the southwestern United States. The earliest of these multistoried dwellings dates from about A.D. 1000. They were a peaceful agricultural people whose inaccessible communities protected them from roving tribes such as the Apaches. In the 16th century the Spanish found the settlements mysteriously abandoned. Archeologists classify the cliff dwellers as members of the pueblo culture, ancestors of the tribes that built the large pueblo villages on the plains. The ruins of the cliff dwellings, well preserved in the dry desert climate, are found in Mesa Verde National Park, Colo., and in national monuments in Arizona, New Mexico, and Utah.

Clifford, Clark McAdams (1906-), U.S. lawyer who served as a special adviser to presidents Harry S. Truman and John F. Kennedy and was secretary of defense in the cabinet of President Lyndon B. Johnson (1968-69).

Climate, sum of weather conditions, or the characteristic weather, of any area. Weather conditions include temperature, rainfall, sunshine, wind, humidity, and cloudiness. One method of studying climate is to use average figures, but these often conceal wide variations; for example, mean temperatures are of little value in regions of extreme cold or heat. Climatology was developed by the ancient Greeks. Around 500 B.C. Greek philosopher Parmenides suggested that 5 climatic zones encircle the earth: a tropical zone on either side of the equator, 2 temperate zones in the middle latitudes, and 2 cold zones around the poles. This classification was based on latitude, the most important factor affecting climate.
Long after the ancient Greeks, climatologists recognized that many factors besides latitude influence climate, for example, elevation, ocean currents, and variations in atmospheric pressure. In the early 1900s a German meteorologist, Vladimir Köppen, classified the world's climatic-zones, combining temperature and rainfall boundaries with vegetation boundaries. He suggested 5 basic regions: tropical rainy climates with no cool season, dry climates, middle latitude rainy climates, northern forest climates, and polar climates with no warm season. Many other classifications exist, and each has its uses, but none takes into account all the features of climate. Paleoclimatologists,

who study past climates through the record of rocks and fossils, have shown that climates have changed considerably during the earth's history. For example, coal seams in northern Canada show that swampy tropical forests once grew there. Several theories have been advanced to explain climatic change over time. The theory of continental drift suggests that the continents have moved in relation to the poles. Other theories include sunspots, variations in solar radiation, and changes in the earth's orbit or tilt. Climatologists have observed small changes in climate in the past 100 years. Their findings have raised speculation about our ability to influence climatic change.
See also: Weather.

Clingman's Dome, highest point in Tennessee, located in Great Smoky Mountains National Park. It rises 6,643 ft (2,025 m) on the Tennessee-North Carolina boundary about 35 mi (56 km) southeast of Knoxville. The peak was named for Thomas L. Clingman, U.S. senator from North Carolina, who helped develop the area, a popular resort region.
See also: Great Smoky Mountains.

Clinical psychology, scientific and applied branch of psychology concerned with the study, diagnosis, and treatment of individuals with emotional or behavioral disorders. The disorders which may be brief and minor or more prolonged and serious in nature, such as neuroses and psychoses, are diagnosed through testing and treated through psycho therapy. Research serves as a means of discovering or improving on the various methods of diagnosis and treatment.
See also: Psychology.

Clinton, De Witt (1769-1828), U.S. politician who promoted the building of the Erie Canal and the Champlain-Hudson Canal. As mayor of New York City (most of 1803-15) and governor of New York state (1817-21 and 1825-28), he set up important civic and political reforms and social relief programs for Roman Catholics, slaves, and the poor.
See also: New York.

Clinton, George (1739-1812), U.S. statesman and soldier, vice president (1805-12) under Thomas Jefferson and James Madison. Elected in 1777 as New York's first governor, Clinton was reelected for a record 6 consecutive terms. Originally, he opposed New York's ratification of the U.S. Constitution because he believed in states' rights. His nephew DeWitt Clinton also later served as governor of New York.
See also: New York.

Clinton, Sir Henry (1738-95), British general. He was appointed (1778) commander-in-chief of British forces during the American Revolution after distinguishing himself at Bunker Hill. He captured Charleston in 1780 but resigned in 1781. He was blamed for the British surrender at Yorktown in that year.
See also: Revolutionary War in America.

Clinton, William Jefferson (Bill), U.S. president born after World War II, the third-youngest president, and the first to take office post-Cold War. He was also the first Democratic president in 12 years, defeating Republican incumbent President George Bush and Ross Perot, an independent candidate and Texas businessman.Early life. Clinton was born William Jefferson Blythe IV on Aug. 19, 1946, in Hope, Arkansas. He was named after his father, who had recently died in a car accident. When Bill was 4, his mother Virginia married Roger Clinton, a car dealer, and shortly thereafter the family moved to Hot Springs, Arkansas. There Virginia and Roger had another son, Roger Jr., and Bill adopted his stepfathers surname.

As a young man, Bill earned frequent academic honors. He expressed an early interest in a political career, inspired particularly by a 1963 meeting with President John F. Kennedy. Clinton was 17 at the time, visiting Washington as a delegate to the American Legion Boys Nation.In 1964 Clinton entered Georgetown University in Washington, D.C., where he majored in international affairs and worked as an intern for Sen. J.W. Fulbright of Arkansas. Upon receipt of his degree, he spent two years as a Rhode Scholar at Oxford University before entering Yale Law School in 1970. Throughout his schooling, Clinton remained politically active, most notably helping to manage 1972 presidential candidate George McGoverns Texas campaign. While at Yale he also met fellow law student/future wife Hillary Rodham. They were married in 1975 and five years later had a daughter, Chelsea.Entering politics. Law degree in hand, Clinton returned to Arkansas to teach and plan his political career. In 1974 he made a bid for a seat in the U.S. House but was narrowly defeated. He won his first statewide election in 1976, when he became Arkansass attorney general. Two years later he was elected, at age 32, the youngest governor in Arkansas history.He adopted a liberal, activist agenda, increasing motor vehicle licensing fees to pay for a road-improvement project, and restricting powerful timber and utilities interests. Upset voters failed to reelect him to a second term in 1980. Clinton soon rebounded, however, to win the next four gubernatorial elections in Arkansas on more moderate platforms (1982, 1984, 1986, and 1990). Beginning in 1983, Clinton decided to concentrate on two main problems, education and the economy, rather than a wide range of issues. Under his leadership Arkansas increased teachers salaries, required teacher competency exams, and established a high school entrance test for students. In addition, he expanded health-care services for the poor, introduced welfare reform, and promoted economic growth through favorable tax policies. In 1991 Clinton was rated the most effective governor in the nation in a poll of his colleagues.In addition to his duties as governor, Clinton served as vice chairman of the National Governors Association in 1985, and as chairman of the NGA in 1986 and 87.

In 1990 and 91, he headed the Democratic Leadership Council, an organization of moderate Democrats.Presidential campaign. Clinton campaigned for and won the Democratic presidential nomination in 1992, weathering charges of marital infidelity, draft evasion, and marijuana use. At his request, Senator Al Gore of Tennessee, another moderate Democrat, was selected as his running mate against incumbents President Bush and Vice President Mondale. The two then took the campaign directly to the people, targeting middle-class and young voters, touring the country by bus, and answering questions on television talk shows.Clintons platform focused primarily on domestic issues, with an emphasis on the economy and the high unemployment rate. He proposed higher taxes for the wealthy, tax cuts for the middle class, job-training programs, and reductions in defense spending. Moreover, he pledged to cut the immense federal budget deficit in half in four years.

William Jefferson Clinton

42nd U.S. President
Born: Hope, Arkansas; Aug. 19, 1946
Term: Jan. 1993-
Vice President: Al Gore
Political Party: Democratic
Spouse: Hillary Rodham Clinton
Children: 1

On social issues Clinton supported freedom of choice on abortion, welfare payments limited to those who cannot find work, and universal health care. His strategy proved successful, and in November his ticket won 43% of the popular vote in addition to an electoral landslide.Presidency. With one-party control of both the House and the Senate, Clinton had hoped to act on his agenda quickly, and did appoint more women and minorities to his Cabinet than had any previous president. However, his first months in office saw a number of political setbacks: Clintons proposal to end the ban on homosexuals in the military met with with widespread opposition and had to be altered substantially. In addition, the president appeared indecisive in dealing with foreign crises in Bosnia, Somalia, and Haiti.

His popularity fell, then plummeted when he failed to cut middle-class taxes. In October of 1993 he sent to Congress a plan for sweeping reform of the health-care industry, but Congress chose not to act on it.On other matters, Clintons 1993 and 1994 budgets did help to reduce the federal budget deficit, and the unemployment rate declined after Clinton took office. The president won a major victory in November 1993, when Congress approved the North American Free Trade Agreement, NAFTA (designed to eliminate trade barriers between the U.S., Canada, and Mexico), and again in August of 1994, when Congress passed an anticrime bill he supported. Additionally, he fulfilled several campaign promises by signing into law the Family and Medical Leave Act, initiating handgun reform, raising taxes on the wealthy, and reducing them for the working poor.Decisive initiatives to check an Iraqi threat to Kuwait, to halt the development of nuclear arms in North Korea, to oust the military dictatorship in Haiti, and further the peace process in the Middle East briefly lifted Clintons poll popularity late in the year. Nonetheless, in November of 1994, the Democrats lost control of both the legislative and executive branches.

Presidential highlights in 1995 included Clintons trip to Russia in May to hold discussions with Russian President Boris Yeltsin. Also in May, Clinton successfully threatened Japan with tariff increases on their luxury automobiles if they did not loosen restrictions on auto imports. Japanese car companies agreed to work toward this demand. On December 3, 1995 Clinton formally authorized the first deployment of U.S. troops to Bosnia to perform NATOs peacekeeping duties for one year. In 1998 he admitted to having had a sexual relationship with Monica Lewinsky, a White House trainee. The affair undermined his authority.

Clipper ship, 19th-century sailing ship, the fastest ever built. Clippers evolved from the Baltimore clippers. They were built in the United States and later in Britain. They had a very large area of sail, relied on a good crew, and traded with China and Australia, where speed paid off. Two famous ships were Donald McKay's *Lightning* and the British *Cutty Sark* (now at Greenwich, England).

Clive, Robert, Baron Clive of Plassey (1725-74), British soldier and administrator, twice governor of Bengal, who established British power in India. He defeated both the French at Arcot (1751) and the Bengal nawab, Siraj-ud-Daula, at Plassey (1757), thus securing all of Bengal for the East India Company. He reformed administrative corruption in Bengal. Investigated by Parliament on the charge of dishonesty when in office, he was acquitted, but afterward committed suicide.

Clock, device to indicate or record the passage of time. Generally a clock relies on a source of regular oscillation, such as a swinging pendulum or an electric current. Christiaan Huygens invented what was probably the first pendulum clock in the mid-17th century. The electric clock, commonly found in the home, was invented in the 19th century, and the quartz clock, utilizing the vibrations of a quartz crystal, in the early 20th. The atomic clock, invented in 1948, is accurate to within 1 second in 3 million years. The most common way to display time has been the analogue, with clock hands sweeping over a face, in imitation of the sundial. The most recent type of display is the digital clock, which uses integrated circuits to show the time in changing figures.

Cloisonné, artistic process by which metal objects are decorated with enamel. Metal strips are soldered edgewise onto the surface of the object, creating compartments (*cloisons*) to be filled with colored enamel. When the object is heated, the enamel fuses with the surface. Originally a Persian technique, cloisonné was perfected by the Chinese, Japanese, and French.

Cloister, courtyard surrounded by vaulted and arcaded passageways supported by columns. Usually adjoining an abbey or church, the cloister served as a sheltered access to the surrounding buildings and was mainly used for recreation and exercise. An essential feature of Romanesque and Gothic churches and monasteries since the 11th century, cloisters are found throughout Europe.

Clone, cell or organism genetically identical to the cell or organism from which it has been derived. Clones are produced by asexual reproduction, for example through cell division in bacteria, cell budding in yeasts, or vegetative duplication. Monoclonal systems (systems derived from a single cell) are used for the production of diagnostics and medicines. In 1997 scientists succeeded in cloning a sheep. It is likely that the technique of cloning can be used on all mammals, including humans.
See also: Genetic engineering.

Closed shop, establishment where the employer accepts only members of a specified union as employees and continues to employ them only if they remain union members. The Taft-Hartley Act of 1947 forbids closed shops in industries involved in or affecting interstate commerce.

Clothing, one of humanity's most important needs, including the various garments, accessories, and ornaments people throughout the world wear for decoration and protection. People probably began to wear clothing more than 100,000 years ago. By the end of the Old Stone Age (25,000 years ago) the needle had been invented, enabling people to sew skins into clothes. They learned to make yarn from plants and animal fur and to weave yarn into cloth. The advent of sewing machines and other machinery about 200 years ago ushered in the clothing industry, now a major business in many countries.

Cloture, or closure, in parliamentary procedure, closing of debate to ensure an immediate vote on a measure before the legislative body. In most parliamentary bodies, members cannot debate a cloture motion, but the motion must receive more than a majority vote. The main purpose of cloture is to check the *filibuster*, endless debate by a minority of the members to keep a motion from being voted upon. In the U.S. Senate a 60% majority is needed to invoke cloture.

Cloud, visible collection of water droplets suspended in the atmosphere. Clouds whose lower surfaces touch the ground are usually called fog. The water droplets are very small, indeed of colloidal size; they must coagulate or grow before falling as rain or snow. There are 3 main cloud types. Cumulus (heap) clouds, formed by convection, and often mountain- or cauliflower-shaped, are found from about 2,000 ft (610 m) up as far as the tropopause, even temporarily into the stratosphere. Cirrus (hair) clouds are composed almost entirely of ice crystals. They appear feathery, and are found at altitudes above about 20,000 ft (6,100 m). Stratus (layer) clouds are low-lying, found between ground level and about 5,000 ft (1,524 m). Other types of cloud include cirrostratus, cirrocumulus, altocumulus, altostratus, cumulonimbus, stratocumulus, and nimbostratus.
See also: Weather.

Cloud chamber, Wilson *See:* Wilson cloud chamber.

Cloud seeding *See:* Rainmaking.

Clove (*Syzygium aromaticum* or *Eugenia caryophyllata*), tropical evergreen tree of the myrtle family; also, its dried, unopened flower. Originally grown in the Moluccas (Spice Islands), the Philippines, and islands nearby, cloves were first appreciated by the Chinese for perfuming the breath. They are now grown in the West Indies and Mauritius. Their main use nowadays is as flavoring and in medicine.

Clover, familiar small plant (genus *Trifolium*) that grows wild in lawns and pastures and along paths and roads. Some U.S. clovers are natives, others have been introduced from Europe. The red clover, a native of Europe, is the state plant of Vermont. Clover leaves are normally divided into 3 parts, although more divisions are known; 4-leafed clovers are said to bring good luck. Clover is grown as forage and for hay. It is particularly valuable because, like other members of the pea family, its root contains nitrogen-fixing bacteria, so it enriches the soil if plowed back in.

Clytemnestra

Clovis I (A.D. 466-511), Frankish king (481-511), founder of the Merovingian monarchy. He amassed a huge kingdom from the Rhine River to the Mediterranean, defeating the Romans at Soissons (486) and the Visigoths under Alaric II of Spain at Vouillé (507). He became a Christian c.498 and compiled the code of Salic law.
See also: Merovingian.

Clown, comedy figure of the pantomime and circus. Modern clowns possibly derived from the vice figures of medieval miracle plays and jesters in medieval courts. They later figured as harlequins in the commedia dell'arte; but their grotesque makeup, baggy clothes, and slapstick developed fully only in the 1800s. The best-known 20th-century American circus clown was Emmett Kelly.

Clubfoot, deformity in which there is an abnormal relationship of the foot to the ankle; most commonly the foot is turned inward and down.

Club moss, or ground pine, primitive plant of the order Lycopodiales with small mosslike leaves, related to ferns. Many club mosses have creeping or climbing stems covered with leaves. Their distribution is mainly tropical, but some live in the United States, where they are used for Christmas decorations. Some are used in the manufacture of medicines and of fireworks.

Clumber spaniel, short, heavy hunting dog originally bred in France but developed in England in the 1800s. The Clumber has long, straight, white hair, stands 16-18 in (41-46 cm) high, and weighs 55-70 lb (25-31.5 kg). Uncommon in the United States, the Clumber is a small game hunter and family dog.

Clyde, most important river of Scotland and one of Britain's major commercial waterways. It rises on the Lanarkshire-Dumfriesshire border in southwest Scotland and flows some 106 mi (171 km) to its estuary, the Firth of Clyde. Its upper valley, Clydesdale, is noted for its fruit and market garden crops. Near Lanark, at the Falls of Clyde, the river is harnessed for hydroelectricity. From Lanark on, its valley is occupied by heavy industry. At the head of navigation is the city-seaport of Glasgow, Scotland's chief commercial center. To the west, on the northern bank, is Clydebank, with large engineering interests and shipyards.
See also: Scotland.

Clymer, George (1739-1813), American revolutionary patriot and statesman. One of the first colonists to advocate separation from England, Clymer was one of the signers of the Declaration of Independence and a delegate to the Second Continental Congress. He served in the first House of Representatives 1789- 91.
See also: Revolutionary War in America.

Clytemnestra, in Greek mythology, daughter of Leda and Tyndareus, twin sister of Helen of Troy, wife of Agamemnon, and mother of 3 daughters and a son, Orestes. Clytemnestra, along with her lover, killed her husband after he had sacrificed one of their daughters to the gods. She and her lover were both then killed by her son to avenge the death of his father.
See also: Agamemnon; Mythology; Trojan War.

Cnut *See:* Canute.

Coagulant, any substance that causes or stimulates a liquid to change to a thickened curdlike or solidified state.

Coahuila, state in northern Mexico. Industries include livestock, agriculture, mining, and manufacturing. One of the original Mexican states, Coahuila included Texas until 1836.
See also: Mexico.

Coal, hard, black mineral, predominantly carbon, the compressed remains of tropical and subtropical plants, especially those of the carboniferous and Permian geological periods, burned as a fuel. With its by-products coke and coal tar, it is vital to many modern industries. Coal formation began when plant debris accumulated in swamps, partially decomposing and forming peat layers. A rise in sea level or land subsidence buried these layers below marine sediments, whose weight compressed the peat, transforming it under high-temperature conditions to coal; the greater the pressure, the harder the coal. Coals are classified according to their fixed-carbon content, which increases progressively as they are formed. Lignite, or brown coal, which weathers quickly, may ignite spontaneously, and has a low calorific value. Subbituminous coal is mainly used in generating stations; bituminous coal is the commonest type, used in generating stations and the home, and often converted into coke; anthracite is a lustrous coal that burns slowly and well and is the preferred domestic fuel.
Coal was burned in Glamorgen, Wales, in the 2nd millennium B.C. and was known in China and the Roman Empire around the time of Jesus. Coal mining was practiced throughout Europe and known to Native Americans by the 13th century. The first commercial coal mine in the United States was at Richmond, Va. (opened 1745), and anthracite was mined in Pennsylvania by 1790. The Industrial Revolution created a huge and increasing demand for coal. This slackened in the 20th century as coal faced competition from abundant oil and gas, but production is again increasing. Annual world output is about 3 billion tons, 500 million tons from the United States. World coal reserves are estimated conservatively at about 7 trillion tons, enough to meet demand for centuries at present consumption rates.
See also: Diamond.

Coalition, combination or alliance of political groups having mutual interests. In countries with parliamentary systems, governments may be composed of coalitions when no single party has a majority.

Coal oil *See:* Kerosene.

Coal tar, heavy, black, viscous liquid liberated during the distillation of coal, the source of a number of valuable chemicals. Light oil, phenol (or medium oil), heavy oil, and anthracene oil (asphalt) are used as fuels, solvents, preservatives, lubricants, and disinfectants. The chemical products that can be extracted include benzene, toluene, xylene, phenol, pyridene, naphthalene, and anthracene, on which are based several important chemical industries, particularly pharmaceuticals, dyes, and explosives. Coal tar itself is

commonly used for street-paving; coal-tar creosote is an important wood preservative.
See also: Coal.

Coanda, Henri Marie (1885-1972), Romanian-born French aeronautics engineer and inventor, who designed an aircraft based on the jet-propulsion system. It crashed in 1912. Coanda also developed a dish-shaped aircraft and invented a device able to convert salt water to fresh water using solar energy.

Coast Guard Academy, United States *See:* United States Coast Guard Academy.

Coast Guard, U.S., branch of the armed services supervised in peacetime by the Department of Transportation, in war by the navy. It helps to maintain law and safety wherever the United States has jurisdiction on the high seas and navigable inland waters. Formed in 1915 by a union of the Life Saving Service and the Revenue Cutter Service, it is charged with search and rescue operations, maintaining weather ships and navigational aids, including the Loran radio network, collecting meteorological and oceanographic data, ice-breaking in inland waters and patrolling the North Atlantic for icebergs, enforcing navigation and shipping laws and marine safety regulations for sailors and the construction and equipment of ships, and operating against smugglers. In wartime the coast guard assumes the regular duties of the navy.

Coast Ranges, string of mountain ranges along the Pacific coast of North America, running from Kodiak Island in Alaska to southern California. These include the Los Angeles Ranges and the California Coast Range (in southern California); the Klamath Mountains (northern California and southern Oregon); the Oregon Coast Ranges and the Olympic Mountains (Oregon and Washington); the Vancouver Range and the Queen Charlotte Islands (British Columbia); and the Kodiak, Kenai, Chugach, and St. Elias ranges and the Alexander Archipelago (Alaska). These mountains are of widely varying geological origin and composition, the highest peak being Canada's Mt. Logan (19,850 ft/6,050 m).

Coati (*Nasua nasua*), small, carnivorous mammal related to the raccoon. Its long tail is held vertically above its back. It ranges from Arizona to South America. Coatis live in small bands made up of females and young, the males being solitary except in the breeding seasons. They roam through the forest, feeding on small animals and fruit and climbing trees.

Coatsworth, Elizabeth (1893-1986), U.S. author best known for her children's books. She won the 1931 Newbery Medal for *The Cat Who Went to Heaven* (1930).

Coaxial cable, cable consisting of 2 conductors, one within the other, separated by an insulator. The inner is usually a small copper wire; the outer, usually copper braid. Coaxial cables are used in the transmission of TV, telephone, and telegraph signals.

Cobalt, chemical element, symbol Co; for physical constants see Periodic Table. Cobalt was discovered by Georg Brandt in 1735. Cobalt is a gray-white, lustrous, hard and brittle magnetic metal. It is alloyed with other elements to make powerful magnets and high speed cutting tools. Compounds of cobalt have been used for centuries to give a blue color to ceramic materials. Radioactive cobalt-60, an artificial isotope, is a powerful source of gamma rays and is used in the treatment of cancer.

Cobb, Ty(rus Raymond) (1886-1961), U.S. baseball player. Nicknamed "Georgia Peach," Cobb is considered one of the greatest players of all time. His lifetime average is the highest in major league baseball history (.367), he is second on the all time hit list (4,191), and third in career stolen bases (892). From 1905-1928 Cobb played outfield for the Detroit Tigers and the Philadelphia Athletics. He was among the first group of players inducted into the National Baseball Hall of Fame (1936).

Cobbett, William (1763-1835), British radical writer and reformer, best known for his book *Rural Rides* (1830), which portrayed the misery of rural workers. His *Weekly Political Register* (founded 1802) was the major reform newspaper of its day. He was elected to Parliament after the 1832 Reform Act.

Cobden, Richard (1804-65), British politician and reformer, leader of the Manchester School. A textile merchant, he was known as "the Apostle of Free Trade." With John Bright and Robert Peel, he founded the Anti-Corn-Law League (1838-39), and was its chief spokesman in Parliament (1841-46). In 2 pamphlets, *England, Ireland, and America* (1835) and *Russia* (1836), he surveyed international relations and argued against British interventionist policies.

Cobra, venomous snake (family Elapidae) that rears up and spreads the ribs of the neck to form a "hood" when alarmed. Cobras are found in Africa and southern Asia. The ringhals, or spitting cobra, of Africa defends itself by spitting venom over a distance of 10-12 ft (3-3.7 m). If venom enters the eye it can cause blindness. The king cobra (*Ophiophagus hannah*) is the longest of all poisonous snakes, reaching a length of 18 ft (5.5 m). The Egyptian (*Naja haja*) and Indian (*Naja naja*) cobras are the traditional snakes of the snake charmer. Like all snakes, they are deaf to airborne sounds and are reacting to the snake charmer's swaying movement, not to the music.

Coca (*Erythroxylon coca*), shrub whose leaves contain various alkaloids. Native to the Andes, it is cultivated in Sri Lanka, Java, and Taiwan. South American Indians chew the leaves mixed with lime, which releases the drug cocaine. Cocaine-free coca extracts are used in making cola drinks.
See also: Cocaine.

Cocaine, colorless or white crystalline alkaloid, member of a broad group of plant substances that includes nicotine, caffeine, and morphine. In nature, cocaine is found in significant quantities in the leaves of 2 species of the coca shrub that grow throughout the eastern highlands of the Andes in Ecuador, Peru, and Bolivia and along the Caribbean coast of South America. In medicine it is used as a local anesthetic. Cocaine is used as a "recreational" drug to produce euphoria and a feeling of energy. Such use is illegal in the United States although cocaine was legal for a long time (it was an ingredient in the early years of the Coca-Cola soft drink). The drug-induced euphoria is most pronounced shortly before the blood concentration has begun to fall, and it disappears several hours before the blood concentration returns to zero. Technically, cocaine is not addictive, as repeated use does not result in tolerance for it (i.e., repeating the same dose causing a diminishing response). There are withdrawal signs (particularly depression, which may be severe), but they are milder than withdrawal syndromes associated with opiates (e.g., heroin), barbiturates, or alcohol. On the other hand, cocaine is severely habit-forming. Chronic use of the drug can cause nervous system disorders and delusions, weight loss, and lessening of physical well-being. U.S. law classifies cocaine as a narcotic. During the 1980s and 1990s a cocaine-derivative, called crack, has become the drug of choice in many urban areas. *See also:* Drug abuse; Narcotic.

Cochise (1815-74), chief of the Chiricahua Apache tribe. Aroused by the unjust execution of relatives by soldiers, he began a violent campaign against European Americans in Arizona in 1861 and effectively drove them from the area. In 1862 he was driven back by troops to the Dragon Mountains, which he held until his capture by Gen. George Crook in 1871. He escaped but gave himself up when the Chiricahua Reservation was formed in 1872. After his death, his people were removed from the reservation.

Cochran, Jacqueline (1912-80), U.S. pilot. She obtained her pilot's license in 1932 after only 3 weeks' flying. First woman to fly in a Bendix transcontinental race (1934), she won it in 1938. She organized and headed the Women's Airforce Service Pilots (WASP) in World War II, was the first civilian woman to win the Distinguished Service Cross, and was the first woman to fly faster than sound.

Cockatiel, gray bird (*Nymphicus hollandicus*) found in Australia. It is about 12.5 in (32 cm) long, has a crown of feathers, a long tail, and a heavy beak.

Cockatoo, parrot with erectile crest (especially, genus *Kakatoe*). Its plumage is usually white, sometimes black, pink, or yellow. Cockatoos live in Australia and neighboring parts. They are good talkers.

Cockcroft, Sir John Douglas (1897-1967), English physicist who first "split the atom." With E.T.S. Walton, he built a particle accelerator and in 1932 initiated the first artificial nuclear reaction by bombarding lithium atoms with protons, producing alpha particles. For this work Cockcroft and Walton received the 1951 Nobel Prize for physics.
See also: Atom; Walton, Ernest Thomas Sinton.

Cocker spaniel, popular breed of dog in the United States, bred from the English spaniel. They weigh 22-28 lb (10-13 kg) and stand 15 in (38 cm) at the shoulder.

Cockle, bivalve mollusk (order Eulamel libranchia) with cupped shell ornamented with radiating grooves. Cockles live buried in mud or sand, in shallow water, and dig themselves in by means of a muscular foot that can be protruded between the shells. There are numerous species along the coasts of North America ranging in size from the 4-in (10.2-cm) giant Pacific egg cockle to 1/4-in (0.6-cm) cockles. The common cockle of Europe is edible.

Cocklebur, any of several weeds (genus *Xanthium*) of the composite family. This plant grows throughout Europe and parts of the United States. It has spiny burs that usually contain 2 seeds, 1 of which germinates a season before the other. The seedlings are poisonous to grazing animals.

Cock-of-the-rock, bird of genus *Rupicola*, of the cotingas family, native to South American forests. Cocks-of-the-rock have ornate orange or red plumage and helmetlike crests.

Cockroach, or roach, flat-bodied insect of the family Blattidae with long antennae and hardened forewings that protect the hindwings, as in the beetle. Cockroaches feed on fungi and on plant and animal remains but also come indoors to eat exposed food, book bindings, and even wood. Sizes range from 0.5 in (0.6 cm) to 3 in (7.6 cm). There are about 70 species in the United States. Some species can fly.

Cockscomb, tropical Asiatic flower (*Celosia argentea*) of the amaranth family. The cockscomb grows in tropical America, Asia, the East Indies, and the United States. The rooster's-comb-shaped flowers have been developed into varying shapes and colors.

Coconut palm (*Cocos nuerfera*), tropical tree. Its origin is obscure because coconuts can survive prolonged immersion in the sea, and they have been spread around the world by ocean currents. The height of the coconut palm ranges from 60 to 100 ft (18 to 30 m). The trunk, which often tilts over, bears a cluster of long fronds at the top. A single palm can produce over 400 nuts in the course of a year. The husk surrounding the "nut" (seed) is used for mats and ropes. The nut is at first filled with a jelly. This liquefies when the nut is about 7 months old to become "coconut milk." Over the next 2 to 3 months the liquid solidifies to a white flesh used to make desiccated coconut. Finally, when a year old, the fruit falls of its own accord. The nuts are then cut out and split in two, and the flesh is allowed to dry. Then called copra, it yields an oil used in margarine, synthetic rubber, soap, and other items. Coconut palm fronds are used for thatching, and the copra, without its oil, is used as cattle feed. The tree is also a source of wood.

Cocoon, protective covering enclosing the larvae or pupae of insects. The larva prepares the cocoon as a shelter. While inside the cocoon, the larva becomes a pupa, which in turn develops into an adult insect.

Cocteau, Jean (1889-1963), French author, artist, and film director. He first rose to fame with poetry, ballets such as *Parade* (1917), and the novel *Thomas l'Imposteur* (Thomas the Imposter; 1923). After overcoming opium addiction, he produced some of his most brilliant work, such as the play *Orphée* (1926) and *La Machine Infernale* (The Infernal Machine; 1934). Prolific in many fields, he also made several films, including *Le Sang d'un Poete* (The Blood of a Poet; 1932), *Beauty and the Beast* (1945), *Orpheus* (1949), and *Les Enfants Terribles* (1950).

Cod, bottom-feeding fish (family Gadidae) of the northern Atlantic and the Pacific. The record weight is 211 lb (95.7 kg) for an Atlantic cod (*Gadus morrhua*), but the usual range is 2 to 25 lb (0.9 to 11.3 kg). Females lay up to 6 million eggs at a time. Cod fishing has been important in Europe since the 16th century, and Europeans soon discovered the New England and Newfoundland "cod banks," which played an important part in the colonization of the new continent. The cod were salted, their livers yielding an important vitamin-rich oil (cod liver oil), and the swimbladder was used for isinglass, a very pure form of gelatin.

Code, set of laws or rules arranged systematically and put in writing. Legal codes have existed for perhaps as long as writing. One of the earliest known codes is that of Hammurabi, the king of Babylonia, 18th century B.C. Roman law was codified in the form of the Twelve Tables around 450 B.C. By A.D. 534 its principles had been refined into the Code of Justinian, which had an enormous influence on later European law. The code Napoléon, formulated in 1804, served as the basis for the legal system of France and its colonies, including Quebec and Louisiana. In communications, code is a set of symbols made to yield information via specified operations. An example is the Morse code in telegraphy, a system of short and long signals in combinations that indicate letters of the alphabet. Codes whose rules are not revealed are often used for secret messages. Decoding these messages is called cryptography.

Code Civil *See:* Code Napoléon.

Codeine, mild but addictive narcotic alkaloid, analgesic, and cough suppressant derived from opium. It also reduces bowel activity, causing constipation, and is used to cure diarrhea.
See also: Narcotic.

Code Napoléon, French legal code, officially the *Code Civil*. Napoleon I, as first consul, appointed a commission to devise a replacement for the confused and corrupt local systems formerly in force. The code, made up of 2,281 articles arranged in 3 books, was enacted in 1804 and, although much altered, is still in force today.

Codes and ciphers, set of characters or signals, with prearranged meanings as letters or numbers, used for secrecy and brevity in transmitting messages, especially in wartime.

Codling moth, or codlin moth, small, nocturnal moth (*Laspeyresia pomonella*) whose caterpillars live in apples and pears. Infestations of codling moths can cause the destruction of entire orchards.

Cod-liver oil, pale yellow substance obtained from the liver of cod and related fish. Cod-liver oil is rich in vitamins A and D, and was formerly used by people with deficiencies of these vitamins.

Cody, John Patrick Cardinal (1907-82), archbishop of Chicago 1965-82. Cody served on the Vatican staff in the 1930s. He was appointed archbishop of New Orleans in 1964, and became a cardinal in 1967.

Cody, William Frederick *See:* Buffalo Bill.

Coeducation, education of both sexes in the same schools and classes. While coeducation in the primary grades became common in Protestant Europe after the Reformation, it was not introduced at higher educational levels until much later. In 18th- and 19th-century America, any tendency toward a double system of secondary schooling was offset by prohibitive cost. Now the majority of accredited colleges and universities in the United States are coeducational.

Coelacanth, lunged, bony fish of the family Coelacanthidae. Coelacanths were thought to be extinct until 1938, when one species (*Latimeria chalumne*) was discovered live off the South African coast. They are about 5 ft (150 cm) long, with circular overlapping scales. They were known as predecessors of the amphibians until in 1997 it was discovered that lungfish are more closely related to amphibians than coelacanths are.

Coelenterate, phylum of primitive, invertebrate animals, now renamed the *Cnidaria* (the *C* is silent). It includes anemones, corals, jellyfish, the fresh-water hydra, and many others. The basic body form is a two-layered sac, with a mouth at one end surrounded by a ring of tentacles. Food is captured and poisoned by means of *nematocysts,* or "stinging cells," in the tentacles. Coelenterates exist in two forms. Anemones, corals, and hydra are *polyps,* which are anchored and tubular. Jellyfishes are *medusae,* or free-swimming.

Coelom, major body cavity in vertebrates and higher invertebrates. In vertebrates, the coelom is partitioned into the pericardial, pleural, and ab-dominal cavities, which house the stomach, liver, digestive tract, and other body organs.

Coercive Acts *See:* Intolerable Acts.

Coffee, evergreen shrub or tree (genus *Coffea*) from whose seeds the drink of the same name is made. The plant was first discovered in Ethiopia, where its fruit was used for wine and food before A.D. 1000 The hot drink made of ground and roasted coffee beans was first made in the Arabian peninsula in the 15th century. It reached Europe in the 17th century and then spread, with European settlers, to the Americas. The shrub is now grown in many hot, humid areas of Asia, the Americas, and Africa. The highest quality coffees are varieties of Arabian (*Coffea arabica*). Coffee of Liberian (*C. liberica*) and Congolese (*C. robusta*) origin are also commercially significant. Brazil is the world's largest coffee producer. Other major producing countries are Costa Rica, El Salvador, Guatemala, Honduras, Mexico, Colombia, Ecuador, Cameroon, Ethiopia, Ivory Coast, Uganda, India, and Indonesia. The red, cherry-like berries of the coffee plant generally contain 2 seeds per berry. These seeds are harvested, cleaned, and roasted. It is the heat of the roasting process that creates the flavor and aroma. The roasting also causes the formation of caffeine, a stimulant that may be harmful in large doses.

Coffee house, variety of commercial establishment that arose in London in the mid-17th century. Coffee houses became centers of business, cultural, political, and religious information exchange. The first English newspapers arose as broadsheets distributed in coffee houses. The institution died away in London in the 19th century, but cafes remain widespread in most European, Mediterranean, and Latin American countries.

Cohan, George M(ichael) (1878-1942), U.S. songwriter, actor, composer and producer of popular, patriotic musicals. He is best remembered for hits like "Give My Regards to Broadway," "You're a Grand Old Flag," "Yankee Doodle Dandy," and the popular World War I song "Over There."

Cohesion, attractive force holding the atoms or molecules of a single substance together. Cohesion is generally contrasted to adhesion, the attractive force between different substances.

Cohn, Ferdinand Julius (1828-98), German botanist, one of the founders of bacteriology. He also contributed to the understanding of heat production by plants.
See also: Botany.

Coin, piece of stamped metal, of a fixed value and weight, issued to serve as money. Until banknotes came into use, coins were the only form of money. The principal metals used in coinage are gold, silver, and copper. They were originally used in their pure state, but were later alloyed (combined) with other substances to make the coins cheaper and more resistant to wear. Coins have presented a constant temptation to engage in monetary trickery. From the time of the Romans, when rulers had large debts, they reduced the amount of precious metals in coins and passed them off on their creditors at the old value; this process is called debasement.
The first known coins were struck in Lydia, Asia Minor, in the 8th century B.C. These coins, called *staters* (a unit of weight), were made of a natural combination of gold and silver and ornamented with crude animal likenesses. The Greek island of Aegina issued better-made silver *staters* about 700 B.C., and the use of coins soon spread throughout the Mediterranean world. The Athenian silver *tetradrachma* was the main coin from the 6th to the 4th centuries B.C., when the coinage of Alexander the Great replaced it. The Chinese independently developed coins about the same time as the Greeks. The first Roman coins, made of bronze (an alloy of copper and tin), date from the 4th century B.C.; during later Roman times, silver and gold coins were used. During the early Middle Ages, only silver coins were struck in western Europe. The breakup of the Roman Empire decreased the volume of trade, and the use of money diminished. In the 12th and 13th centuries, Genoa and Venice led the commercial revival, and their gold coins became a leading international medium of exchange. In modern times, gold replaced silver throughout most of the world. All monies were defined in terms of gold and bore a definite and fixed relationship to the value of gold. World War I and the Great Depression caused this system to break down, and most nations now no longer use gold coins. In the United States, the early colonists used the Native Americans' *wampum*, shell beads formed into belts, as money. Many different European coins circulated in the American colonies, but their value fluctuated widely from place to place. The Massachusetts Bay Colony produced the first American coins in 1652. The first U.S. Mint was established at Philadelphia in 1792, and its first coins date from the following year. U.S. coins have existed in their present metallic state longer than any other

coins used today. Many different types of coins have been struck in the course of the history of the United States, and they are still legal tender (though their value to collectors naturally exceeds their face value). Gold coins were used until 1933, when the government discontinued their use in domestic and foreign commerce.

Coin collecting, or numismatics, popular hobby throughout the world. Collecting involves the acquisition of coins of any particular grouping. Coins may be considered desirable for various reasons, including origin, history, rarity, and value. They are commonly graded according to quality. Categories of quality include: poor (features are mostly obliterated); good (worn, but with features mostly visible); very good (evenly worn, but with clear details); very fine or uncirculated (in newly minted condition); proof (specially struck from a highly polished die).

Coke, form of amorphous carbon that is left when bituminous coal is burned in special furnaces to remove volatile constituents. In the United States coke is used primarily as a fuel in metallurgy, especially in blast furnaces to extract metal from ores.
See also: Carbon.

Coke oven gas, hydrogen and methane mixture produced when coal is heated to about 2000°F (1100°C) in an airtight chamber. Coke oven gas is burned as an industrial fuel and for home heating.

Colbert, Jean Baptiste (1619-83), French diplomat and finance superinten-dent. He became chief finance minister to King Louis XIV in 1661 and held that post for 22 years, supporting French industry and commerce and building a powerful navy.
See also: Louis.

Colchicum, poisonous flowering plant (*Colchicum autumnale*) of the lily family, also known as autumn crocus or meadow saffron. Found on the British Isles and in mid- to southern Europe, these plants have crocus-like flowers, whose autumnal blooms range from purple to white. From the underground stems a substance (colcherine) is extracted that is used in the treatment of rheumatism and gout.

Cold, common, viral infection of the mucous membrane of the nose and throat, marked by discharge of mucus, sneezing, and watering of the eyes. More than 100 specific viruses have been identified as causes of the common cold. There is no known cure, but symptoms can be treated. Drinking fluids prevents dehydration. Pain relievers can lower fever. Decongestants may shrink mucous membranes.

Cold-blooded animal, or poikilotherm, animal that cannot maintain a con-stant internal body temperature and therefore attains a temperature close to that of its environment, making it dangerously subject to climatic changes. Cold-blooded animals include fish, amphibians, and reptiles.

Cold sore, skin lesion, generally of the lips or nose, caused by the Herpes simplex virus. Often characterized by blisters filled with a clear liquid, cold

sores may be triggered by infections such as the common cold or pneumonia. The virus frequently becomes dormant, persisting in the skin between attacks.
See also: Herpes.

Cold War, expression used to characterize the conflict after World War II between the Western powers led by the United States and the Communist bloc led by the USSR. The term arose to describe conditions of hostility and military build-up short of actual armed conflict. The 2 largest wars during the Cold War era were in Korea in the 1950s and in Indochina in the 1960s and early 1970s. The period was also characterized by the division of Europe into antagonistic military blocs: the North Atlantic Treaty Organization (NATO) in the West, the Warsaw Pact in the East. Most analysts would argue that the upheavals in Eastern Europe and the USSR in 1989 led to the end of the Cold War.

Cole, Thomas (1801-48), English-born U.S. landscape painter. He studied painting at Pennsylvania Academy of Fine Arts and gained fame beginning in 1825 for his Hudson River Valley paintings. Some of his works which had moral themes included *The Course of Empire* (1839) and *The Voyage of Life* (1840).
See also: Hudson River School.

Coleman, William Thaddeus, Jr. (1920-   ), U.S. secretary of transportation 1975-77, the second African-American cabinet member in U.S. history.

Coleridge, Samuel Taylor (1772-1834), English poet, philosopher, and critic. His works include the poems "Kubla Khan," "Christabel," and "The Rime of the Ancient Mariner," all 3 of which were included in the volume *Lyrical Ballads* (1798), a collection Coleridge produced with William Wordsworth. The book is one of the major works of English Romanticism.

Colette (Sidonie Gabrielle Colette; 1873-1954), French author noted primarily for her sensual style and her themes of women, love and jealousy. Among her many novels are *Cheri* (1920), *The Ripening* (1923), *The Cat* (1933), and *Gigi* (1945).

Coleus, tropical plant (genus *Coleus)* of the mint family. Native to the African and Indian tropics, the coleus plant grows to a height of 3 ft (91 cm) and is cultivated as a houseplant.

Colfax, Schuyler (1823-85), vice president of the United States during the first term of President Ulysses S. Grant (1869-73). Colfax served 22 years in Congress, the last 6 of which as Speaker of the House.

Colic, acute pain focused in an internal organ, frequently the colon or other component of the digestive tract.

Coliseum *See:* Colosseum.

Colitis, disease characterized by inflammation of the colon (large intestine). Symptoms include abdominal pain, cramps, and diarrhea. If ulcers develop

in the walls of the intestine, the condition can become chronic, with fever and complications. Colitis sometimes follows attacks of dysentery, but causative microorganisms have not been traced. There is probably a psychosomatic component, anxiety bringing on attacks of the disease. In severe cases a section of the colon may have to be removed by surgery.
See also: Colon.

Collage, 20th-century art form in which various objects and materials are glued onto a canvas or board, sometimes covered with paint. The term comes from the French word for pasting. The earliest experiments with collage were done by Pablo Picasso and Georges Braque in 1910-11. The technique was further developed by Henri Matisse and by the Dadaists, particularly Kurt Schwitters, who made entire compositions consisting of ticket stubs and other evocative remnants of paper. Later artists, like Jasper Johns, created more elaborate collages of wood, metal, and fabric.

Collagen, major component of connective tissue, constituting 70% of its dry weight. Collagen is an insoluble protein, whose fibers form a mesh. Collagen is also present in bones.

Collarbone, or clavicle, horizontal bone that connects with the breastbone (*sternum*) and the shoulder blade (*scapula*) to support the shoulder and to hold the arm in proper position. It is present in upright-walking mammals and in bats.
See also: Bone.

Collard (*Brassica oreracea*), headless cabbage of the mustard family commonly grown in the southern United States. Both a summer and winter crop, the collard plant reaches 2-4 ft (60-120 cm), and is a dietary source of vitamins A and C.

Collective bargaining *See:* Labor movement; National Labor Relations Act.

Collective behavior, sociological term for human behavior in crowds and other large, unorganized, temporary groups. Instances of collective behavior include riots, panics, fashions, cults, and revolutionary movements. U.S. sociologists Robert E. Park and Ernest W. Burgess introduced the concept in their book *Introduction to the Science of Sociology* (1921).
See also: Group dynamics.

Collective farm, agricultural enterprise operated cooperatively. The farm's land and equipment may be owned by members of the cooperative group or by the government, which controls production. Stalin introduced collectivization to the USSR in 1929, and it has been widely used in Communist countries and in Israel.

Collectivism, political doctrine that places control of economic activity in the hands of the community or the government, as opposed to individuals, as in the case under capitalism. The term may cover a wide variety of economic systems and structures, but will typically exclude private ownership of major means of production and distribution.
See also: Communal society; Socialism.

College entrance examination, series of tests administered in the United States by 2 agencies, the College Entrance Examination Board (CEEB) and the American College Testing Program (ACT), to determine eligibility for college or university admission. The CEEB gives the Scholastic Aptitude Test (SAT) in 3 sections of multiple- choice questions: verbal, mathematical, and written English; and the Achievement Tests, 14 1-hour tests measuring knowledge in specific areas such as foreign language and science. The ACT examination has 2 parts: an academic test of English, mathematics, natural science, and social studies; and a Student Profile, information about personal goals and interests. Each university or college sets its own standards for score interpretation.

Collie, 2 types of sheepdog, rough-coated and smooth-coated, originating in Scotland in the 1600s and brought to the United States by British colonists a century later. The collie stands 2 ft (60 cm) at the shoulder and may be sable and white, blue, tan, or all white, though early breeds were black. There is also a miniature variety.

Collins, Michael (1930-), U.S. astronaut. A member of the astronaut program 1963-70, he was pilot of the *Columbia* command module on the Apollo 11 mission that landed Neil Armstrong and Edwin Aldrin, Jr. on the moon (1969). In 1971 Collins became director of the National Air and Space Museum in Washington, D.C.

Collins, (William) Wilkie (1824-89), English novelist, often considered the originator of the detective novel in English. His works include *The Woman in White* (1860) and *The Moonstone* (1868).

Collodi, Carlo (Carlo Lorenzini; 1826-90), Italian journalist and author of humorous adult fiction and moral children's stories, of which the best known is *The Adventures of Pinocchio* (1883).

Colloid, mixture in which particles of one substance are dispersed in another. Colloids are similar to solutions and suspensions. What determines the difference is the size of the particles of the substance that is distributed. In a solution, the particles are molecules. In a suspension, they are much larger, visible either with the naked eye or a microscope. A colloid has particles larger than molecules but too small to be seen with a normal microscope. Colloids can be categorized according to whether the substances mixed together are solids, liquids, or gases. For instance, a gas may be dispersed in a liquid to form foam. A liquid dispersed in another liquid forms an emulsion. A liquid dispersed in a solid is a gel.

Colobus, or guerza, genus of thumbless, long-tailed, African monkey of the family Cercopithecidae. The colobus is vegetarian, diurnal (active in the daytime), and lives in trees, though it may travel on the ground. Colobus species are divided by color and may be black and white, red, or olive. Young are white at birth. Colobus live in groups of 3 to 80. Some species are aggressively territorial.

Cologne (pop. 916,200), river port and industrial city in western Germany, on the Rhine River. Its products range from heavy machinery to toilet water

---

Colombia

Capital:	Bogota
Area:	440,831 sq mi
	(1,141,748 sq km)
Population:	38,581,000
Language:	Spanish
Government:	Presidential republic
Independent:	1819
Head of gov.:	President
Per capita:	U.S. $ 1910
Mon. unit:	1 Colombian peso =
	100 centavos

(eau de cologne). The prosperity of Cologne (Köln in German) dates from its membership in the Hanseatic League in the 15th century.
See also: Germany.

Colombia (Republic of), fourth largest country in South America. It extends over 440,831 sq mi (1,141,748 sq km) of the extreme northwest of South America, bounded on the northwest by Panama, on the northeast by Venezuela, on the southeast by Brazil, and on the south by Peru and Ecuador. It is the only South American country that has both an Atlantic and a Pacific coastline.
Land and climate. Nearly half of the country is mountainous; more than half is comparatively uninhabited lowland plain. There are 4 major regions. By far the most important is the Andean region, where 3 great ranges branch out northward from the Pasto knot near the Ecuadorian border: the western, central, and eastern Cordilleras. Some 80% of the population lives in the narrow mountain valleys and basins of this region. Between the central and eastern Cordilleras, the Magdalena (Colombia's chief river) flows for 1,000 mi (1,609 km) to the Caribbean at the port of Barranquilla. A third of the population lives in the eastern cordillera (mountain chain), where the seat of government has been located since Chibcha times. Bogotá, the capital and largest city of Colombia, stands on a plateau at an altitude of 8,661 ft (2,640 km). The Caribbean coastal lowlands are the home of about 17% of the population; the chief centers are the ports of Barranquilla, Cartagena, and Santa Marta. The rivers draining the Caribbean lowlands—the Magdalena, Cauca, San Jorge, and César—form a maze of swamps and lagoons.
The Pacific lowlands are a rainy, marshy littoral. Buenaventura and Tumaco are Colombia's chief Pacific ports. The Pacific lowlands and the eastern plains beyond the eastern Cordillera account for only 5% of the population. The northern section of the eastern region is part of the *Ilanos* (tropical grasslands) of northern South America; the southern section is almost impenetrable jungle.lthough most of Colombia lies in the north tropical zone, the climate varies with topography. An excessively high rainfall prevails in the Pacific lowlands. Altitude modifies the climate of the highlands: The semitropical *tierra caliente* (hot land) extends to about 3,000 ft (914 m), where it is succeeded by the *tierra templada* (temperate land) coffee belt (to

about 6,500 ft/2,000 m), the *tierra fria* (cold land) (6,500-10,000 ft/2,000-3,000 m) where grain and potatoes are grown, and the almost polar *páramos* (grazing lands) below the snowline. The vast eastern plains are subject to successive wet and dry seasons, while in the Caribbean lowlands a hot, dry climate predominates.

People. More than half of Colombians are mestizos (of mixed European and Native American ancestry); there are about 20% whites, with minorities of mulattoes, blacks, and Native Americans.

Economy. Colombia is a major world coffee producer. It also grows cotton, bananas, sugar, tobacco, cocoa, rice, sorghum, corn, wheat, and barley. The country has the largest coal reserve in Latin America and substantial reserves of uranium. Other resources include oil, gas, and precious metals. Transportation is hindered by mountain ranges, but cities are joined by road, rail, or river and an advanced air network. Tourism is becoming an important source of foreign exchange.

History. Chibcha Native Americans of the eastern cordilleras had a highly developed culture when the Spanish arrived in the early 16th century. Spain ruled the area until independence, which followed Simón Bolívar's Boyacá victory over Spanish colonial forces (1819). At the end of the 19th century thousands died in fighting between liberals and conservatives, Colombia's 2 main political parties. Another civil war between liberals and conservatives, with about 200,000 casualties, lasted from 1948 until 1958, when a democratic government was reestablished. In the mid-1980s the government began battling the large and well-organized drug cartels that traffic in cocaine, which is processed from coca grown in Peru. In 1989 the United States supplied military personnel to help combat the increasing related violence. At the end of the 1990s the situation had not changed.

Colombo (pop. 615,000), capital, chief port, and largest city of Sri Lanka (Ceylon), located on the southwest coast of the island, in the Indian Ocean. The city's harbor, built in 1875 and modernized in the 1950s, is one of the world's largest. Tea, cinnamon, rubber, and coconut products are the chief exports.
See also: Sri Lanka.

Colombo Plan, cooperative program for economic development in South and Southeast Asia, inaugurated in 1951 at Colombo, Ceylon (now Sri Lanka). The first participants were members of the British Commonwealth, joined by the United States, Japan, and several Southeast Asian countries.

Colon, large intestine from the cecum (the pouch into which the small intestine empties) to the rectum, about 60 in (1.5 m) long. The colon is divided into 4 segments: the ascending, transverse, descending, and the sigmoid, or pelvic.
See also: Intestine.

Colón (pop. 137,800), third largest city of Panama, established in 1850 at what is now the Atlantic terminus of the Panama Canal. Originally named Aspinwall, the city was renamed to honor Christopher Columbus in 1890. As a duty-free trade zone, Colón is an important commercial port and tourist center.
See also: Panama.

Colonialism   236

Colonialism, political and economic subordination of an area by a geo-
graphically removed parent country. The ruling country is more technologi-
cally advanced than the colony. Often the rulers and the colonial subjects are
of different races. Colonialism dates to the Phoenicians; Rome was the largest
ancient colonizer. As a vehicle for European expansion, modern colonialism
dates from c.1500. Colonialism may be both beneficial and detrimental:
Developing areas may receive technological and economic advances, but
may have a foreign culture forced upon them or have their resources
exploited by the occupying state.

Colonial period, American, nearly 170 formative years of settlement and
adventure before U.S. independence. The first colonies were established by
chartered trading companies, groups of commercial speculators who shared
the profits of the colony in return for putting up the capital necessary for its
establishment. The first permanent English settlement in America, at
Jamestown (1607), was the project of the London Company, which failed to
exploit its new colony of Virginia and surrendered its charter to the crown
in 1624. The Pilgrim settlement at Plymouth (1620) merged with the later
Puritan settlement at Boston, and the 2 were governed by the charter of the
Massachusetts Bay Company until 1691, when it, too, became a royal
province under an appointed governor. Connecticut (1662) and Rhode Island
(1663) were established by settlers from Massachusetts. New York, origi-
nally New Amsterdam, was founded by the Dutch West India Company in
1625 and captured by the English in 1664. Delaware, founded by a Swedish
company in 1638, later fell under the control of the Penn family. Under the
system of proprietorship, the crown also granted huge tracts of land to
individuals or groups. Of the 13 colonies, 7 were founded as proprietorships:
Maryland, New Hampshire, New Jersey, the Carolinas, Pennsylvania, and
Georgia. All except Pennsylvania and Maryland became royal provinces
before 1776.
Economic life. Despite rocky soil and a short growing season, many crops
were raised on the small farms of New England. Fishing employed 10,000
people by 1765, and some 300 vessels were engaged in whaling. Shipbuil-
ding was the main industry, though woolen textiles, leather goods, and iron
tools and utensils were also produced. In the 18th century the distillation of
rum from West Indian molasses became the second most important industry.
The Middle Atlantic colonies—New York, New Jersey, and Pennsylvania—
supplied New England and Europe with food and raw materials. Manufac-
tures consisted of textiles, paper, glass, and iron. In the 17th century an
important fur trade was carried on through the Iroquois country from Albany.
In the Plantation Provinces, from Maryland south to Georgia, production
became increasingly concentrated on great staple crops—tobacco, rice, and
indigo. By the 1770s tobacco exports were around 50 million pounds a year,
rice half a million. The forests of the Carolina uplands also furnished lumber
for shipbuilding and "naval stores" (pitch, tar, and turpentine), which were
vital for the British navy.
Scarcity of labor was a problem common to all the colonies, for the ease with
which land could be acquired meant that industrious colonists quickly
became landlords in their own right. One solution was the employment of
"indentured" servants who were obliged to serve for a fixed period of years,
in return for payment of their passage across the Atlantic or sometimes as a
punishment for political or religious offenses or crimes. From Virginia

southward, African slaves were employed. The first shipload arrived as early as 1619; by 1760 there were 400,000 blacks in the English colonies.

Social and cultural life. The major colonial cities were ports whose main connection with each other was by sea, since roads were very poor. For more prosperous city dwellers life differed little from what they had left behind in England. On the frontier, however, life was crude and hazardous. Hostility from Native Americans encouraged communal settlement, and stockades surrounded the early villages. Food was obtained by hunting and fishing, clothing was made from animal skins, and the log cabin was the standard dwelling. In the cities class distinctions were evident; however, on the frontier a rough democracy prevailed. There were many sects and religions, but toleration was achieved only gradually. The early colonists took an active interest in providing schooling, particularly in New England, where each town   maintained a school. In the Middle Colonies schools were run by religious organizations, while in the South private tutors were employed. For the poor, apprenticeship took the place of schooling. Nine colleges were founded in the colonial period. Established primarily for the training of ministers, the colleges at first taught theology and the classics; in the 18th century science, medicine, and modern languages were introduced. Over 50 newspapers were established in the colonial period. The first printing press went into operation in Massachusetts in 1639. Private and public subscription libraries were founded in the 18th century, and the American Philosophical Society (1743), led by Benjamin Franklin, strove to unite scientists and philosophic thinkers. In painting the 18th century produced artists whose reputation reached as far as Europe: John Singleton Copley, Benjamin West, Charles Wilson Peale, and Gilbert Stuart. Singing societies and chamber concerts were popular outside the Puritan areas, and the Moravians were noted for their performances of German church music.

Migration from countries other than England brought new cultural influences to the colonies. King Louis XIV's revocation of the Edict of Nantes (1685) compelled many French Protestants to flee to America, where they became prominent in trade and industry and brought French styles of dress, furnishing, and architecture to Boston, New York, and particularly Charleston. Germans, mostly peasant farmers, settled in Pennsylvania, the Shenandoah Valley, and the Piedmont region of Virginia and North Carolina. Scotch-Irish from Ulster also settled in Pennsylvania and the colonies to its south. By 1775 there were probably 200,000 Germans and 300,000 Scotch-Irish in America as well as Swiss, Welsh, and Dutch. Nevertheless, the English inheritance was predominant: English was the main language and also the basis of a shared literature, legal system, and political outlook. In the free and vigorous atmosphere of colonial America the British tradition of personal liberty was to culminate in revolution and independence.

Colony, area and people controlled by a foreign power. Types of colony defined by social or economic characteristics include settlement, trade, missionary, penal, and protectorate. Since World War II, the trend toward reorganization of empire has allowed many colonies to obtain independence or to be placed under the supervision of the United Nations' General Assembly or Trusteeship System.

Color, visual effect caused by the eye's ability to react differently to different wavelengths of light. Color is a sensation rather than a property of a thing.

An object that reflects light of a certain wavelength will appear to be a certain color. The 3 primary colors—red, blue, and yellow—can be combined to form all other colors. Two colors whose light, when combined, produces white, are called complementary. In white light, an object that reflects all wavelengths will appear white, while one that absorbs all wavelengths will appear black.

Colorado, state in the Rocky Mountain region of the United States; bordered by Wyoming in the north, Nebraska in the north and east, Kansas in the east, Oklahoma and New Mexico in the south, and Utah in the west.

Land and climate. Colorado has the highest mean elevation (c. 6,800 ft/2,100 m) of any state. The high plains of the east, part of the Great Plains, cover two-fifths of the state. The land here is extremely flat, but rises in the west to meet the edge of the Rocky Mountains, which cover the middle two-fifths of Colorado. The Continental Divide, the line of elevated land that separates west-ward-flowing and eastward-flowing waters, runs through the Colorado Rockies. The several ranges that make up the Rockies in Colorado are the tallest in the entire chain: over 50 peaks reach 14,000 ft (4,270 m) or more. These ranges include the Sawatch Range, which contains Mt. Elbert. The Colorado Plateau in the west covers about one-fifth of the state. It is an area of lower mountains, plateaus, and mesas.

The most famous of the state's many important rivers is the Colorado, which drains one-twelfth of the United States. Despite the important rivers, the uneven distribution of water within Colorado is a problem. The mountains are considerably cooler than the plains and plateaus, which are dry and sunny. Principal cities are Denver, Colorado Springs, and Pueblo.

Colorado

Capital:	Denver.
Statehood:	Aug. 1, 1876 (38th state)
Familiar name:	Centennial State
Area:	104,091 sq mi (269,595 sq km); ranks 8th
Population:	3,893,000 (1997; ranks 26th)
Elevation:	Highest—14,433 ft (4,399 m), Mt. Elbert.
	Lowest—3,350 ft (1,021 m), Arkansas River
Motto:	Nil sine Numine (Nothing without Providence)
State flower:	Rocky Mountain columbine
State bird:	Lark bunting
State tree:	Colorado blue spruce
State song:	"Where the Columbines Grow"

Economy. Major manufactured products are scientific instruments, processed foods, machinery, and printed materials. Livestock and livestock products dominate agriculture. The chief crops, grown mostly on irrigated land, are hay, wheat, and corn. Colorado has vast deposits of petroleum, coal, and natural gas. Tourism is also important, with spectacular mountain scenery and skiing the major attractions. More than a third of Colorado's land is owned by the U.S. government.

Government. Colorado is governed by the constitution of 1876. The state government is headed by a governor elected for a 4-year term. The state legislature consists of a senate, whose 35 members are elected for 4-year terms, and a house of representatives, whose 65 members serve 2-year terms. It is represented by 2 senators and 6 representatives in the U.S. Congress.

History. Traces of ancient Native American culture in Colorado are evident in the Mesa Verde and other cliff dwellings. In the 1600s Spanish explorers were the first Europeans to enter the region, which was claimed by Spain in 1706. After the Louisiana Purchase (1803), explorers like Zebulon Pike began to open up the territory. The trader William Bent built Bent's Fort, the first permanent European American settlement, in 1833. In the Mexican War (1846-48) the United States conquered further Colorado territory. The discovery of gold near Denver in 1858-59 brought a rush of prospectors. Congress created the Colorado Territory in 1861. In the 1880s, the discovery of rich silver ore in the Leadville area started a boom, but the rapid drop of silver prices in 1893 resulted in unemployment and labor problems. In 1906, the U.S. Mint in Denver began producing coins. During World War II the state prospered as military bases and a flourishing defense industry were established. The subsequent population growth increased Colorado's need for irrigation and water storage, which led to the development of several water projects, the most recent completed in 1985. Colorado's coal and petroleum industries expanded during the energy crisis of the 1970s, but since the end of the boom in the 1980s, the state has faced a sagging economy.

Colorado Desert, arid basin of Southeast California and northwest Mexico, 2,000 sq mi (5,180 sq km). Part of the Sonoran Desert, it is bounded by the Pacific Coastal Ranges, the Colorado River, and the Eagle and San Bernardino Mountains. Much of the Colorado Desert, including the Salton Sea and the Imperial Valley, is below sea level.

Colorado River, major U.S. river, rising in the Rocky Mountains of northern Colorado and flowing 1,450 mi (2,333 km) in a generally southwesternly direction to enter the Gulf of California. The river has formed many canyons, including the Grand Canyon, one of the world's largest.
See also: Hoover Dam.

Colorado Springs (pop. 215,200), city in central Colorado, second-largest in the state and seat of El Paso County. Situated at the base of Pikes Peak, Colorado Springs is a popular resort, as well as an industrial center manufacturing chemicals, tools, airplane parts, and plastics. The United States Air Force Academy is 7 mi (11.3 km) to the north.
See also: Colorado.

Color blindness, inability to tell certain colors apart. An inherited trait, color blindness is caused by a disorder of the cones in the retina of the eye. The

commonest form is a difficulty in distinguishing red from green. It is usually found in males. Total color blindness, which is rare, causes a person to see only black, white, and various shades of gray.
See also: Spectrum.

Colosseum, or Coliseum, oval amphitheater in Rome, built c.75-80 A.D., with seats for about 45,000 spectators on 4 tiers. Begun by the Flavian Emperor Vespasian and completed by his son Titus, the Colosseum was used for gladiatorial combat and other events up to the 5th century. Though damaged by earthquakes, much of it still stands.

Colossians, Epistle to the, book of the New Testament written by St. Paul to the Christians of Colossae in southwest Asia Minor. Like Ephesians, it deals with the doctrine of the body of Christ.
See also: Bible; New Testament.

Colossus of Rhodes, one of the Seven Wonders of the World, statue of Helios, the sun god, erected c.290-280 B.C. by the sculptor Chares of Lindos in the harbor of Rhodes. The statue, made of bronze and 100 ft (30 m) high, commemorated the island's successful defense against an invasion in 304 B.C. There is no truth to the medieval legend that the statue straddled the harbor. The Colossus broke off at the knee in an earthquake in 224 B.C. and lay in ruins until A.D. 672, when Arab raiders broke it up and sold it for scrap.
See also: Seven Wonders of the Ancient World.

Colt, Samuel (1814-62), U.S. inventor and industrialist who devised the revolver, a single-barreled pistol with a revolving multiple bullet chamber, in the early 1830s. His factories pioneered mass-production techniques and the use of interchangeable parts.
See also: Revolver.

Colter, John (1775-1813), U.S. trapper and guide, best known for his explorations of what is now Yellowstone National Park. He guided the 1803 Lewis and Clark Expedition and other treks up the Missouri River.

Coltrane, John (1926-67), U.S. musician and composer. A saxophonist, he was one of the leading artists of African-American jazz in the 1950s and 1960s, performing with such gifted players as Dizzy Gillespie, Miles Davis, and Thelonious Monk. In the early 1960s he formed his own group, which soon became the most innovative in U.S. music. As a saxophonist, Coltrane was known for his distinctive tone and superlative technique. As a composer, he introduced the "sheets of sound" style and explored the possibilities of modal compositions, based on unusual scales. In his later years, he was also famous for his encouragement of younger musicians.
See also: Jazz.

Coltsfoot, *(Tussilago farfara)*, wild plant of the daisy family Compositae native to Europe and Asia. Dandelion-like yellow blossoms appear in spring before leaves. Coltsfoot grows to 6-18 in (15-45 cm).

Colum, Padraic (1881-1972), Irish poet and dramatist associated with the Celtic renaissance and the Irish National Theater; cofounder of the *Irish*

Review (1911) and writer of several plays for Dublin's Abbey Theater including *The Fiddler's House* (1907) and *Thomas Muskerry* (1910). Colum moved to the United States in 1914 and was president of the Poetry Society of America. Other works are *Orpheus* (1929), *The Frenzied Prince* (1943), *Collected Poems* (1953), and *The Poet's Circuits* (1960).

Columbia (pop. 95,802), city in central Missouri, seat of Boone County. Settled in 1821 as a stopping point on Boone's Lick Trail, Columbia has become an important medical center. In addition to the Ellis Fischel State Cancer Hospital and the Boone County Hospital, it is the home of the University of Missouri.
See also: Missouri.

Columbia (pop. 99,300), capital and largest city of South Carolina; seat of Richland County. Columbia was purchased in 1786 by the South Carolina legislature as the site for the state capital, established there four years later. An industrial and agricultural center, Columbia produces textiles, lumber, corn, and cotton. The University of South Carolina and five other colleges are located in the city.
See also: South Carolina.

Columbia River, large river arising in the Canadian Rockies in southeast British Columbia, and flowing south into the northwest United States, where it turns west and forms the border between Oregon and Washington and empties into the Pacific Ocean. It is 1,150 m (1,850 km) long, and its volume is the largest of any North American river except the Mississippi.
See also: British Columbia.

Columbia University, one of the major private U.S. universities. Founded as King's College in 1754, it was renamed Columbia College in 1784 and became a university in 1896. Its schools and facilities, mostly in New York City, include important research institutes for international relations and schools of journalism, business, medicine, law, and social work.

Columbine, plant (genus *Aquilegia*) related to the buttercup, with tall, slender stems, lobed leaves, and intricate flowers.

Columbite, dense oxide mineral composed of manganese, niobium, and iron, general chemical formula $(Fe,Mn)Nb_2O_6$. The element tantalum sometimes wholly or partially replaces niobium. When the mineral contains more tantalum than niobium, it is called tantalite. Both are black, often iridescent, and are found in granite rocks called pegmatites.
See also: Niobium; Tantalum.

Columbium *See:* Niobium.

Columbus (pop. 644,000), capital and second-largest city of Ohio, seat of Franklin County. Columbus is an industrial center, producing aircraft and missile components, plastics, household appliances, and auto parts. It is also the site of Ohio State University.
See also: Ohio.

Columbus (pop. 243,072), second-largest city in Georgia, seat of Muscogee County. Situated on the Chattahoochee River in the western part of the state, Columbus is a cotton and textile center and an important industrial city.

Columbus, Christopher (Cristoforo Colombo; 1451-1506), commonly credited as the discoverer of America. Born in Genoa, Italy, he was the son of a wool weaver. An experienced sailor and student of navigation, Columbus was convinced that he could pioneer a new route to the treasures of the Far East by sailing West across the Atlantic. In 1484 he tried to win financial support for his plans from King John II of Portugal, but the king's advisers estimated the distance (surprisingly accurately) at 10,000 nautical miles, which would require a sailing time of 1 year, considered impossible. Columbus presented his plan to Queen Isabella and King Ferdinand of Spain, who, after years of negotiations, agreed to finance his voyage. Three small ships, the *Niña*, the *Pinta*, and the *Santa María*, were equipped with provisions for 1 year. With a crew of 90 men they set sail from Palos on Aug. 3, 1492. On Oct. 12, 1492, when the crew was on the verge of mutiny, Columbus landed on the east coast of one of the Bahama Islands, now called Watling Island. He spent the next 3 months sailing from one Caribbean island to another in search of the eastern Grand Khan, to whom he had a letter of introduction. He wrecked the Santa María and left 39 men in Hispaniola (now the Dominican Republic). On March 15, 1493, he returned to Spain and was welcomed with honors. In Sept. 1493 Columbus left again for the Caribbean with a fleet of 17 ships, this time intending to set up trading posts and colonies, still believing he had discovered India. He explored Puerto Rico. The men he had left in Hispaniola had been wiped out, so he established a colony further east, named it Isabela, left his brother Bartholomew in charge, and set off in search of the mainland of India. He explored Jamaica and a number of the Lesser Antilles and explored the coast of Cuba, which he thought was an extension of the mainland. He wanted to take 500 natives back to Spain as slaves, but 200 died during the voyage. In 1498 he embarked on a third voyage. He sailed farther south this time, explored Trinidad and reached the South American mainland at the mouth of the Orinoco River, mistaking it for a new continent south of India. When he reached Santo Domingo, he found that there had been bloody uprisings because the colonists had established free towns and divided much of the best land among themselves, and he was forced to make compromises in order to prevent a full-scale rebellion. The disorders continued, however, and Francisco de Bobadilla was sent by Spain to take over the government of the colony. He deposed the Columbus brothers, put them in chains, and shipped them back to Spain, where they were immediately released but remained in disgrace. In 1502, after promising King Ferdinand not to enslave the natives, Columbus set out on his fourth voyage. He sailed to Central America,explored Honduras, and coasted along Nicaragua and Costa Rica to Panama. His ships were worm-eaten and in such poor condition that he had to stop at Jamaica, where he and his crew were stranded for more than a year. Finally, he chartered a ship to bring him back to Spain, where he arrived a few days before the death of Queen Isabella in 1504. King Ferdinand refused to grant him the reinstatement as viceroy and governor. Rich, honored, but ill and cripple he died on May 20,1506

Column, in architecture, vertical structural support, usually cylindrical, consisting of a base, shaft, and capital. Columns support the entablature on which the roof rests. Apart from their utilitarian functions, columns are also decorative, the various types forming the classical orders of architecture. *See also:* Architecture.

Coma, state of unconsciousness from which a person cannot be roused by sensory stimulation. Body functions continue but may be impaired, depending on the cause of the coma. Poisoning, head injury, diabetes, and brain dysfunctions (including strokes) are the most common causes.

Comanche, native North Americans of the Southwest, closely related to the Shoshone. Brilliant horsemen and fierce warriors, they were dominant among the southern Great Plains peoples, ranging into Mexico and stubbornly defending the buffalo hunting grounds against white incursions until the 1870s. Some 3,000 Comanche still live in western Oklahoma.

Combine harvester, farm machine that cuts, threshes, and cleans grain. The latest, self- propelled models cut a swath 20 ft wide. Practically all kinds of grain, including rice, can be harvested by the combine, as can soybeans and other legumes. Combines were first developed in Michigan as long ago as the 1830s, but they came into widespread use only in the 1920s.

Combustion, rapid oxidation (or burning) of fuel in which heat and usually light are produced. In slow combustion (for instance, a glowing charcoal fire) the solid fuel may react directly with atmospheric oxygen; more commonly the fuel is first volatilized, and combustion occurs in the gas phase.

Comedy, literary work that aims primarily to amuse, often through ridicule, exaggeration, or satire of human nature and institutions, usually ending happily. Comedy was considered one of the two main dramatic categories in ancient Greece, the other being tragedy.

Comenius, John Amos (Jan Amos Komensk; 1592-1670), Czech educational reformer and Protestant theologian, last bishop of the old Moravian church (from 1632). *The Great Didactic* (1628-32) was his best-known work. He advocated teaching in the vernacular instead of in Latin and favored a universal system open to women as well as men. His *Visible World* (1658) was probably the first children's picture book.

Comet, astronomical body consisting of a small mass, mostly gas and dust, spread over a large volume, orbiting the sun in a highly elliptical path that may take it as much as 150,000 times as far from the sun as the earth is. The head of a comet is bright, probably composed of ice and frozen gases. As it nears the sun, particles and gases are cast off into a tail that may be as long as 100 million mi (160 million km). The tail always points away from the sun. Some comets are visible from the earth at regular intervals. The most famous of these is Halley's comet, which reappears about every 76 years. Its most recent appearance was in 1986. In the past, comets were superstitiously considered omens of doom. The appearance of Halley's comet in 1066 is recorded on the Bayeux tapestry. De Chéseaux's comet of 1744 showed six separate tails. In 1846 Biela's comet broke in two as it passed the sun. In

1910, shortly before the return of Halley's comet, another comet appeared that was so bright it was visible in daylight. The comet with the shortest periodicity is Encke, which orbits the sun every 3.3 years.
See also: Astronomy.

Comics, also known as comic strips, series of drawings, usually accompanied by captions or dialogue, telling a continuous story. The text, if any, is often conveyed by means of speech "balloons." The first comics were explicitly humorous, but the term is now applied to anything presented in the comic-strip style. Although comics may actually have originated with the English social satirists Thomas Rowlandson and George Cruikshank, they grew in popularity in the late 19th and early 20th century. At first devoted purely to farce and slapstick, the comics soon moved into the adventure market and then into science fiction, illustrated classics, social satire, and serious social criticism. Comics have added words to the American language and influenced dress habits. In 1954 the industry responded to criticism of the violence and horror by issuing a code for conduct.

Cominform (Communist Information Bureau), international organization set up in 1947 to coordinate among Communist parties in the Soviet Union, eastern Europe, and some capitalist countries. Essentially an agency of the Soviet government, it was disbanded by Nikita Khrushchev in 1956.
See also: Communism.

Comintern (Communist International), organization founded by the Russian Communist Party and composed of national Communist parties from all parts of the world. The Russian revolutionary leader V.I. Lenin called for the formation of a world revolutionary organization after the outbreak of World War I in 1914, but the first meeting of the Comintern was held only in 1919. Also known as the Third International (to distinguish it from the Second, or Socialist, International, a world organization of Social Democratic parties), the Comintern attempted during the 1920s to foster workers' revolution on a world scale. During the 1930s, however, it became essentially an organ of the Soviet government. Stalin dissolved it in 1943 as a gesture to his Western Allies during World War II.
See also: Communism.

Comitia, in ancient Rome, assemblies of people summoned in groups to vote on proposals presented by magistrates. Dating from c.500 B.C., comitia performed different functions during various periods of Roman history. The earliest such institution, the Comitia Curiata, confirmed the selection of Roman kings. Later comitia, such as the Comitia Centuriata (organized according to wealth) and Comitia Tributa (organized by tribe) voted on laws, established titles of authority, and judged criminals. By 100 A.D. the comitias' legislative and judicial powers had been abrogated.

Commager, Henry Steele (1902-), U.S. historian and educator, who taught American history at New York University, Columbia University, and Amherst College. His works include *Majority Rule and Minority Rights* (1943), *The American Mind* (1950), and *Freedom, Loyalty, Dissent* (1954). He was a major interpreter of U.S. history and an exponent of liberal democracy.

Commando, military unit trained for swift, guerrilla-like raids into enemy territory. The British army adopted the word and the practice after the Boer War (1899-1902), and battalion-strength units were organized during World War II. The U.S. army Special Forces and Ranger units are modeled after the British commandos.
See also: Guerrilla warfare.

Commedia dell'arte, form of Italian comedy that flourished in the 16th-18th centuries. Traveling professional actors (often wearing masks) improvised action and dialogue around outline plots with stock characters. The commedia had a lasting influence on the theater throughout Europe.

Commerce, U.S. Department of, executive department of the U.S. government responsible for commercial policies and programs, formed in 1913, when the former Department of Commerce and Labor (established 1903) was divided in 2. It is headed by the secretary of commerce, a member of the cabinet appointed by the president and confirmed by the Senate. The secretary is the president's chief adviser on federal policies affecting commerce and industry. Principal divisions of the department are: Office of Business Economics, Bureau of Foreign Commerce, Bureau of the Census, Business and Defense Services Administration, Coast and Geodetic Survey, and National Bureau of Standards.

Commercial art, general term for any of the visual arts used in business, especially advertising, such as designing, drawing, and lettering for illustrations and advertisements, design and preparation of posters, billboards, display cards, packages, etc. The commercial arts are often distinguished from the fine arts in that their basic aim is to sell a product or service. But a more significant difference is that the products of commercial art have to be able to be reproduced by such techniques as zinc, steel, and halftone engraving; rotogravure; lithography; etching; electrotyping; and photography.

Commercial paper, generic term for various business documents involving the payment of money. Such documents include drafts, promissory notes, and bills of exchange. In a strict sense, the term denotes a short-term promissory note issued by a corporation. The note is redeemable for its full value, plus interest, on a given date.

Commission, military, written order and oath of service granting an individual the rank and authority of an officer in the armed services. A commission is accepted voluntarily and need not be renewed, though it may be resigned if allowed by law.

Committee for State Security *See:* KGB.

Committee of the whole, committee including the entire membership of an organization. It is convened to discuss matters whose disposition is not delegated to a smaller group.

Committees of correspondence, locally organized groups that formed a communication and information network in the 13 American colonies before and during the Revolutionary War. Initially appointed by legislatures to correspond with colonial agents in England, they later played a major role in unifying the colonial independence struggle. It was the Committees of Correspondence that summoned the First Continental Congress in September 1774.

See also: Revolutionary War in America.

Committees of safety, organizations set up at the urging of the Second Continental Congress to aid in the American transition to self-rule. They arose during the period between the overthrow of colonial governments and the establishment of new state governments.

Commodity Credit Corporation (CCC), government-owned corporation within the U.S. Department of Agriculture. Its purpose is to stabilize, support, and protect farm prices and income, to maintain balanced agricultural supplies, and to assist in the orderly distribution of farm commodities.

See also: Agriculture, U.S. Department of.

Commodity exchange, formal market in which participants buy and sell contracts providing for the delivery of certain products at future dates. The world's major commodity exchanges are in New York, Chicago, and London. Prices set in these markets largely determine prices in other parts of the world. Commodities (metals, crops, livestock, etc.) tend to fluctuate in value depending on availability. Since contracts calling for future delivery set the price in advance, commodity exchanges allow for speculation in a rising market and hedging in a falling market.

Common carrier, person or company that transports people, goods, or messages for the public at large. Examples of common carriers are bus lines, railroads, airlines, express companies, telephone and telegraph companies, and pipelines.

Common Cause, national citizens' lobby, organized in 1970 by John W. Gardner, former secretary of Health, Education, and Welfare. Its purpose was to reform campaign financing to end political corruption, to improve the internal workings of the federal and state governments, and to protect the environment. With some 280,000 members, it monitors the work of Congress, recommends legislative reforms to its members, files lawsuits, and engages in lobbying at the federal, state, and local levels.

Commoner, Barry (1917-), U.S. biologist, ecologist, and environmentalist who warned against the environmental threats of technology and nuclear energy in such books as *The Closing Circle* (1971), *The Poverty of Power* (1976), and *The Politics of Energy* (1979). A democratic socialist, he has spoken out against the concentration of corporate power in the United States and in 1980 ran for the U.S. presidency as the candidate of the Citizens' party.

See also: Environmental pollution.

Common law, body of laws based on court decisions and customs. It is usually contrasted to statute law, which is made by legislatures. Common law grew out of English custom and became established mainly by the adherence of judges to precedents, or previous decisions—a principle known as *stare decisis* (stand on things as decided). The decisions of earlier judges became the law of later ones. As new conditions arose, the body of the common law was expanded, and outdated principles fell into disuse, even if never actually abolished. Thus experience, rather than theorizing, furnished the basis for the development of common law. The body and concept of common law passed from England to the United States (except the state of Louisiana, which made the Code Napoléon the basis of its law), Canada (except Quebec), and other areas of the world that have been ruled or influenced by England. No organized body of law existed in England prior to the Norman conquest in 1066, but the Normans brought many new principles and greatly expanded legal institutions. The term common law itself came into general use during the reign of Edward I (1272-1307), who was responsible for a great deal of new legislation. Since by its very nature common law is relatively inflexible and not subject to change or adaptation to suit the needs of a particular case, the system of equity developed to permit judges to resort to the general principles of justice when existing law was inadequate to resolve a case fairly. Eventually, equity was merged with the common law. During the Middle Ages, Italian jurists pioneered the rediscovery of the principles of Roman law. These doctrines were accepted by many European countries, in which they then displaced the customary or common law. But the English legal system withstood the attempts of advocates of Roman law to establish their doctrine. The fight to maintain the authority of the common law, led by great lawyers such as Edward Coke, became part of the constitutional struggle of the 17th century between Parliament and the kings.

When the English colonies in North America framed their legal systems after declaring their independence of the mother country, they either kept the English common law as a guide to judges or formally adopted its principles in their statutes and constitutions. There is no federal common law, though precedents in federal cases are very important in later decisions.

Common Market, European, officially the European Economic Community (EEC), an economic union of West European nations. After World War II, West European nations sought new forms of cooperation in order to revive their damaged economies. The first step was the foundation of the European Coal and Steel Community (ECSC), set up in 1952 by the six future members of the EEC. The Treaty of Rome, creating the EEC, was signed in 1957 by West Germany, France, Italy, Belgium, the Netherlands, and Luxembourg. In 1973 "The Six" were joined by Great Britain, Ireland, and Denmark, and in 1981 by Greece. Spain and Portugal joined in January 1986 and Switzerland, Finland and Austria in 1995. In 1967, the EEC was absorbed under the larger administration of the European Community (EC). Both the EEC and the EC are often referred to as the European Common Market. The main mechanism in the EEC is the customs union: the abolition of tariffs on trade among member nations and the creation of a common external tariff against non-member countries. The EEC has governed itself with an organizational structure carried over from the ECSC and continued in the EC, including a Council of Ministers, an Executive Commission, a   European Assembly, and a Court of Justice.
See also: European Community.

Commons, House of *See:* House of Commons.

Commonwealth, from the phrase "common wealth" (public good), form of government based on the power and consent of the people. In the United States, the states of Massachusetts, Pennsylvania, Virginia, and Kentucky were historically known as commonwealths, as is Puerto Rico. The federated states of Australia are known as the Commonwealth of Australia, and various other nations are associated with Britain in the Commonwealth of Nations. In English history, the Commonwealth is the period of republican government (1649-60) that followed the execution of Charles I.

Commonwealth Games, sports competition among amateur athletes from British Commonwealth countries, first held in Hamilton, Ontario, in 1930 under the name of British Empire Games. The games are held in a different Commonwealth city every four years. They include track and field events, badminton, swimming and diving, boxing, wrestling, and weightlifting.

Commonwealth of Nations, association of Britain and over 40 former colonies, now independent states, and their dependencies. Although not governed by a constitution or specific treaty, member states are linked by economic and cultural interests. The British monarch is recognized as the symbolic head of the commonwealth. Commonwealth prime ministers and other officials meet at periodic conferences and exchange views on international, economic, and political affairs of mutual interest. Member states range in size from Canada, Australia, and India to Tonga and Fiji. Ireland has withdrawn from the commonwealth.

Communal society, cooperative group formed on the basis of shared interests (e.g., religious or political) and emphasizing the needs of the community above those of the individual. Communal societies usually forbid private possession of land and often restrict members' contact with the rest of society. Examples of communal societies are collective farms (kibbutzim) in Israel and Hutterite groups in Montana, South Dakota, and Canada.

Commune, term for small, locally governed territorial districts in France and some other countries. The commune's government structure resembles that of a township in the United States and includes a mayor and a council. The term was originally used to designate towns in medieval western Europe that had gained self-government through rebellion, treaty, or charter.

Communication, flow of information from one point (the source) to another (the receiver). The term is also used to describe the act of transmitting or making known.

Communications satellite, artificial earth-orbiting object used to relay radio signals between points on earth. The orbits of most such satellites are above the equator at a height of 22,300 mi (35,900 km). At that altitude a satellite orbits the earth at the same rate as the earth turns; it thus remains over a fixed point on the surface. The satellite carries a number of transponders that receive radio beams from the earth and retransmit them. The satellite is powered by solar cells. Communications satellites carry television programs, telephone calls, and business data.

Communications Satellite Corporation (COMSAT), private corporation established by act of Congress in 1962, to develop satellite systems for relaying telephone, telegraph, and television transmissions. Comsat is the U.S. member and general manager of the International Telecommunications Satellite Consortium (Intelstat), formed in 1964 under the auspices of the United Nations. Comsat's first satellite, Early Bird, also known as Intelstat I, was launched in 1965.

Communion, in Christian churches, name for the sacrament of the Lord's Supper. Communion, from the Latin word for "participation," is a ritual repetition of the Last Supper before Christ's crucifixion, when he told his disciples, "Take, eat. This is my body... This is my blood... This do in remembrance of me." In most Christian churches, the rite of communion involves the eating of a wafer of unleavened bread and the drinking of wine. *See also:* Christianity.

Communism, ideal economic order in which property and the means of production are held in common in a classless society. Elements of communism are as old as the Golden Age described by Greek poets and philosophers as a time long ago when people shared all things equally and lived simply. Primitive forms of communism are also discernible in the communities of early Christians and in the teachings and practices of certain groups considered heretical in the Middle Ages. The Utopia of Thomas More (1478-1535) also exerted a powerful influence on Western culture and politics, adding to that body of writings which inspired attempts to create a more perfect society. But modern communism, as developed by Karl Marx and Friedrich Engels through their writings in the mid to late 19th century, is radically different from its predecessors. As set forth in their seminal work, the Communist Manifesto (1848), the economic progress that accompanied the rise of modern capitalism divided society into 2 hostile camps, the bourgeoisie, who controlled capital and the means of production, and the proletariat or working class, who must sell their labor in order to live. This division was not seen as static but rather as dynamic. It was, in fact, a conflict central to understanding historical events; the development of cultures and civilizations, and the evolution of society. Marx and Engels repeatedly pointed out in their writings that their argument was based upon a study and analysis of actual political and economic developments, especially contemporary events, and was not filtered through or distorted by metaphysical abstraction. They argued that their analyses and conclusions rested on a scientific basis and, according to their analyses, the destruction of the bourgeois social and economic order and the rise and spread of a communist order throughout the world was historically inevitable. These ideas were more fully developed in the succeeding decades culminating in Marx's major work, Das Kapital.

Marx and Engels were careful to distinguish communism from socialism. As Engels explained in the preface to the English edition of the Manifesto

(1888), they could not have called their work a Socialist Manifesto because the socialists were either followers of Utopian visionaries like Robert Owen or Charles Fourier, or mere "social quacks" trying to remedy specific working class grievances rather than undertake full-scale revolution.

Communist parties were founded to advance the practical and effective cause of the proletariat and achieve communism through political action based upon strict party discipline. V. I. Lenin's Bolshevik party originally split from its fellow communists by espousing the violent overthrow of established regimes. In 1917, it adopted the title of Communist Party, and, thanks to the success of the Russian Revolution, enjoyed nearly unchallenged authority over international communism until 1948, when Yugoslavia rejected Soviet influence. In the 1960s, China under Mao Tse Tung would create a deeper and much more serious rift among communists.

In the more than 70 years since the Russian Revolution, communist regimes have proliferated, particularly in the Third World. Politically, they have been characterized by one-party rule, corrupt and inefficient bureaucracies, brutal and repressive secret police organizations, forced labor camps, strict censorship and thought control, the systematic murder of political opponents and entire groups of people considered dangerous to the state or the party and numbering in the millions.

Economically, even the larger powers, the Soviet Union and the People's Republic of China, though they have succeeded in creating huge military establishments, have failed to provide for basic needs for their people, including food. Beginning in 1987, major communist regimes, led by the Soviet Union, openly admitted the failures of communism and have been looking to capitalist and pluralist systems in restructuring their governments, economies, and societies.

Communist Manifesto *See:* Communism; Marx, Karl.

Communist Party *See:* Communism.

Community, term used in the social sciences to designate a group of people within a larger society sharing similar customs, interests, characteristics or beliefs. Biologists define communities as ecological entities consisting of interdependent populations of flora (plants) and fauna (animals).

Community property, legal system of property ownership by husband and wife existing in several states in the United States. Under the system, any property acquired by either spouse after marriage, except by gift or inheritance, is considered as being owned by both. Generally, each spouse may dispose by will of only a part of his or her half of the community property and is powerless to affect the other's half. In case of divorce the property is divided.

Comoros, island-state in the Indian Ocean off the east coast of Africa, between Mozambique and Madagascar. Its area is 719 sq mi (1,862 sq km). A former French colony, Comoros declared independence in 1975 and was

Comoros

Capital:	Moroni
Area:	719 sq mi
	(1,862 sq km)
Population:	545,000
Language:	Arabic, French
Government:	Islamic republic
Independent:	1975
Head of gov.:	Prime minister
Per capita:	US $470
Mon. unit:	1 Comorian franc = 100
	centimes

declared a Federal and Islamic republic in 1978. In 1997 the overpopulated island of Anjouan wanted to secede.

Compact disc (CD), small plastic disc used for storage of recorded sound or other data. The disc has a transparent coating that protects the stored information and allows it to be read by a laser beam. In the music recording industry the compact disc has virtually replaced the long-playing record. There are various variants for different purposes, such as CD-i CD-e, CD-WORM, and CD-s.

Comparative psychology, branch of psychology concerned with the study of animal (including human) behavior at different stages of development to discern similarities and differences in species. A single activity (for example, mating) performed by different species may be investigated, or the behavioral pattern of 2 or more related species may be studied, either in their natural environment or in controlled surroundings. The principal behavioral patterns studied by comparative psychologists include communication, learning, migration, orientation, reproductive behavior, and social behavior.
See also: Psychology.

Compass, instrument used to indicate direction. Navigators on ships and aircraft use a compass to determine the direction in which they are heading. There are 2 main kinds of compasses: magnetic compasses and gyrocompasses. Magnetic compasses point to the magnetic north pole; adjustments must be made to determine the true north.
See also: Navigation.

Compass plant, or pilotweed, prairie plant (*Silphium laciniatum*) of the family Compositae. Its name comes from the tendency of its lower leaves to line up in a north-south direction. The compass plant has a tall stalk, up to 12 ft (3.5 m), covered with short, rough hairs and large solitary flowers.

Competency-based education, teaching programs requiring students to attain specified levels of achievement in designated courses or skills. Some programs focus on the fundamental skills of reading, writing, and mathematics, while others include such disciplines as science and social studies.

Compositae, largest family of flowering plants, including more than 20,000 species. Their characteristic feature is that what appears to be a single flower is actually a flower head made up of a large number of florets. Those in the center, closely packed and resembling the pile of a rug, are simple tubular flowers having both stamens (the male part) and pistils (the female part). Surrounding them is a ring of ray flowers, often mistaken for petals, which have flattened corollas and are sterile or bear only pistils.

Compound, in chemistry, any substance composed of atoms of more than one element chemically bonded to form a fixed structure with distinctive properties. Compounds may be separated into two groups: organic (containing carbon atoms) and inorganic (all other compounds). Any compound may be described by a chemical formula that indicates the composition of one of its molecules, the molecule being the smallest unit of that compound to have the characteristics of that compound. The chemical formula for water, for example, is H_2O, which indicates that a molecule of water is made up of two atoms of hydrogen and one atom of oxygen.
See also: Chemistry.

Compound eye, organ of vision consisting of many tiny, closely packed lenses. The number of lenses varies from fewer than 100 to more than 20,000, depending on species. Compound eyes differ from the camera-type eye of only one lens. They apparently produce "mosaics" of light and color rather than clear images. Members of the phylum Arthropoda (spiders, insects, crustaceans, etc.) have compound eyes.
See also: Insect.

Comprehensive Employment and Training Act   See: CETA

Compromise of 1850, attempt by the U.S. Congress to resolve North-South conflicts over whether slavery would be extended to new territories, in particular Texas and other lands taken from Mexico in the 1846-48 wars. The compromise included a package of measures sponsored by Stephen Douglas and Henry Clay. They failed to resolve the dispute.
See also: Clay, Henry; Slavery.

Compton, Arthur Holly (1892-1962), U.S. physicist, Nobel Prize winner for physics (1927), for his discovery of the *Compton effect* (x-rays increase in wavelengths when they collide with electrons). At the University of Chicago Compton also contributed to the development of the atomic bomb during World War II.
See also: Physics.

Compton-Burnett, Ivy (1892-1969), English novelist. Her many novels, including *Pastors and Masters* (1925), *Parents and Children* (1941), and *Mother and Son* (1955), often feature crime and violence in English upper middle-class society at the turn of the century.

Computer, automatic device capable of carrying out calculations according to a predetermined set of instructions. First developed in the 1940s, their technological development has been rapid. Computers have taken over routine commercial calculations and are used in scientific research and technology design. Computers are usually classified according to their mode of operation: analog, digital, or a combination of the 2.*Analog computers* use some measurable quantity to represent physically the calculation being carried out. They can perform simulations, such as the outcome of a missile launch or the effects of wind and rain on the flight of an aircraft.*Digital computers* (such as the personal computer) contain 4 basic units: an input/output device, an arithmetical unit to perform basic math operations, a memory, and a control unit to interpret instructions and supervise operations. The applications of digital computers include forecasting, management, and preparation. Computers in the 1990s are becoming faster, smaller, and more powerful. Engineers are working to make computers more sophisticated, user-friendly, and accessible to all aspects of life.

Computer graphics, use of a computer for drawing lines, graphs, designs, and pictures. With the proper programs, computers are capable of displaying shapes as they would look from any angle. This has revolutionized the process of drafting and has also given rise to new art forms.
See also: Computer.

Computerized axial tomography *See:* CAT.

COMSAT *See:* Communications Satellite Corporation.

Comstock Law, U.S. legislation, passed in 1873 and named for anti-vice crusader Anthony Comstock. The law prohibited the mailing of obscene materials, defined at one time to include information on birth control and abortion. Comstock personally was responsible for the destruction of tons of literature and pictures that he considered objectionable.
See also: Obscenity and pornography.

Comstock Lode, enormously rich vein of gold and silver discovered near what became Virginia City in Nevada during the late 1850s. The lode, which eventually earned over $500 million, was named after one of its many claimants, Henry Comstock. The Virginia City mines brought settlers to Nevada, establishing a boom town and overnight fortunes. The lode was abandoned by the turn of the century.

Comte, Auguste (1798-1857), French philosopher and sociologist. His best-known work is *The Course of Positive Philosophy* (1830-42), which introduced the philosophy that later came to be called positivism. Comte believed that human society had 3 phases of development, which he called theological, metaphysical, and positive. Society is ruled by rational science only when it reaches the last stage. Comte invented the term "sociology" and influenced such thinkers as John Stuart Mill and Herbert Spencer.
See also: Positivism.

Conakry (pop. 705,300), capital and largest city of Guinea in West Africa. Located on Tombo Island on the Atlantic coast, Conakry is a modern port and a commercial center.
See also: Guinea.

Conant, James Bryant (1893-1978), U.S. educator. As president of Harvard University (1933-53), he introduced national scholarships to attract students from all over the United States. Conant was chairman of the National Defense Research Committee (1941-46), American high commissioner for Germany (1953), and ambassador to West Germany (1955-57).

Concentration camp, prison for the detention of political or military suspects, frequently found in totalitarian countries and sometimes in democratic nations during time of war. Concentration camps differ sharply from other prisons in the absence of regular judicial proceedings and the fact that prisoners may be held indefinitely. Camps have often served to confine large segments of the population felt to be dangerous to the government. During World War II the United States placed several thousands of its Japanese-American citizens in camps until the end of the war. The most notorious concentration camps were those maintained by the Nazi regime in Germany before and during World War II. Jews and a minority of nationals from occupied countries performed hard manual labor in a semistarved state. Those unwanted or unfit to work were sent to extermination centers to be gassed and afterward burned in incinerators. Sadism and torture were practiced in these camps. More than 6 million men, women, and children died in the German concentration camps, of which the largest were at Auschwitz, Dachau, Buchenwald, and Belsen.
See also: Auschwitz; Belsen; Buchenwald; Dachau; Holocaust.

Concerto, musical composition in which unequal musical forces play in opposition to each other, usually 1 solo instrument against a large orchestra. The 3- movement orchestral form was elaborated by J.S. Bach out of the *concerto da camera*, a type of chamber music. George Friedrich Handel added the *cadenza* (improvised or written out musical interlude for the soloist) as a regular feature. Wolfgang Amadeus Mozart set the style for the modern concerto: The orchestra announces an opening subject with a *tutti* (a passage for full orchestra), then takes a subordinate position when the solo instrument enters, thus establishing the pattern of interchanges.

Conch, name once applied to all mollusks—hence the term "conchology"—but now restricted to certain marine gastropod mollusks with large spiral shells. The shells have been used by primitive people throughout the world as trumpets. Conches are also prized as ornaments and for their meat. They live in warm waters.

Concord (pop. 17,076), town in eastern Massachusetts situated on the Concord River 20 mi (32 km) northwest of Boston. Founded in 1635, Concord was the home of the minutemen and site of the Battle of Concord during the Revolutionary War. Ralph Waldo Emerson, Louisa May Alcott, and Nathaniel Hawthorne all lived there, and Henry Thoreau's Walden Pond is nearby.
See also: Massachusetts.

Concord (pop. 36,006), capital of and third largest city in New Hampshire; seat of Merrimack County. Dating back to 1659, when it was a plantation,

and incorporated under its present name in 1765, the historic city is situated on the Merrimack River 75 mi (121 km) northwest of Boston. The city is the financial and political hub of New Hampshire.
See also: New Hampshire.

Concord, Battle of, second engagement in the American Revolutionary War after the Battle of Lexington. Both were fought on April 19, 1775. The British, 700 strong, marched on Concord, Mass., to destroy military stores. The Americans retreated but returned on seeing smoke from burning supplies. Under Major John Buttrick, they met the British at North Bridge and routed them.
See also: Revolutionary War in America.

Concordat, treaty concluded between the pope and the secular government of a state to regulate religious affairs within the state and deal with such questions as the appointment of bishops and the status of church property. The most notable concordat was the Concordat of 1801 between Napoleon and Pope Pius VII which reestablished the Roman Catholic Church in France. The best-known recent concordat (1929) is the Lateran Treaty, arranged between Pius XI and Victor Emmanuel III of Italy which established Vatican City as a sovereign state.

Concrete, versatile structural building material made by mixing broken stone or gravel with sand, cement, and water. Initially moldable, the cement hardens into a solid mass. Concrete is often reinforced by enbedding steel bars in it to bear the tension. It is used for all building elements and for bridges, dams, canals, and highways, often as precast units.
See also: Cement.

Concussion, temporary malfunction of brain activity, often including unconsciousness, due to a blow to the head causing the brain to jolt against the inner skull, injuring the brain's outer surface. Treatment usually consists of rest and close observation.

Condé, Louis II de Bourbon, Prince de (1621-86), also called the Great Condé, an outstanding French general of the Thirty Years' War, related to the Bourbon royal family. He turned against Mazarin, led troops in the Fronde rebellion, and served with Spain; but was pardoned and fought for Louis XIV in the Dutch Wars.

Condensation, in physics, change of a substance from the gaseous (vapor) to the liquid state. Condensation occurs when warm air meets cold surfaces or mixes with cold air. Dew, fog, and clouds are the result of condensation of water vapor in the atmosphere.
See also: Physics.

Condensed-matter physics *See:* Solid-state physics.

Condominium, in real estate, individual ownership in property, such as an apartment, that is part of a larger complex owned in common. In the 1960s and 1970s, a sharp increase in condominiums occurred in the United States. A cooperative building differs from a condominium in that tenants do not

actually own their apartments; they hold shares in a corporation entitling them to a long-term "proprietary" lease.
See also: Real estate.

Condor, one of two species of vultures and the largest flying birds in existence. They have broad wings with a span of 10 ft (3 m) and weigh up to 25 lb (11 kg). The Andean condor (*Vultur gryphus*), the larger of the two, is still fairly common in the Andes, but the numbers of the California condor (*Gymnogyps californianus*) have been greatly reduced.

Condorcet, Marie Jean Antoine Nicolas de Caritat, marquis de(1743-94), French mathematician and philosopher. A brilliant thinker, he wrote biographies of Voltaire and Turgot, important essays on integral calculus and the theory of probability, and works in political science. He is best known for his *Sketch for a Historical Picture of the Progress of the Human Mind* (1795), which sets forth his belief in the perfectibility of mankind.

Cone, three-dimensional geometric figure whose base is a closed curve, such as a circle or an ellipse, and whose dimensional sides meet at a single point called the vertex.
See also: Geometry.

Conestoga wagon, large covered wagon used by North American pioneers. Originating about 1725 in Pennsylvania, it became the chief means of transporting settlers and freight across the Alleghenies until about 1850. It had big, broad-rimmed wheels and a canvas roof supported by wooden hoops, and was pulled by 4-6 horses.
See also: Pioneer life in America.

Confederate States of America, government formed by the Southern states that seceded from the United States of America between Dec. 1860 and May 1861. South Carolina was the first, followed by Mississippi, Florida, Alabama, Georgia, and Louisiana by the end of Jan. Texas joined them in Feb. and was followed in the spring by Virginia, Arkansas, North Carolina, and Tennessee. Rebels from Missouri and Kentucky (both of which remained in the Union) set up their own governments in exile under the Southern banner and brought the number of Confederate states equal to the original 13. The original 6 seceding states (later joined by Texas) called a constitutional convention for Feb. 4, 1861, at Montgomery, Ala., choosing Jefferson Davis and Alexander Stephens president and vice-president respectively. By Mar. 11 the convention had produced a permanent constitution modeled on that of the United States, but with several exceptions. Congress was forbidden to enact protective tariffs, to limit the spread of slavery, or to appropriate funds for "internal improvements" (except for navigation). Davis was inaugurated under the provisional constitution on Feb. 18, 1861. On Apr. 13, the expected war began with the bombardment of Fort Sumter. In Nov. Davis was elected president. His second inauguration took place at the new capital in Richmond, Va., on Feb. 22, 1862. He was the leader of approximately 9 million people—of whom about 3.5 million were slaves—at war with the nearly 23 million citizens of the Union. The strong states' rights orientation of the South conflicted with traditional wartime executive prerogatives, and the Confederate Congress and president

were at odds from the start. However, in common with the president, the main business of the Confederate Congress was the conduct of the war, and most of its legislation was designed to keep a wartime society functioning. The constitution had provisions for a Supreme Court, but these were never carried out. Throughout the war the Confederacy tried to gain diplomatic recognition, aid, and alliances in Europe, but it was difficult to gain recognition for a state based on slavery. The economic factors that had driven the North and South apart were also perhaps the most significant in determining the war's outcome. The South was primarily an agricultural economy; the North, an industrial one. The South lacked the heavy industry to equip an army and the transportation network to supply it. Further, one of its major markets had become the enemy, and its other main buyer and source of money and equipment, Great Britain, was often cut off by the remarkably effective blockade by the Union Navy. Munitions, guns, and domestic supplies grew desperately short as the war drew on. Many soldiers had to supply their own rifles. A relief program for soldiers' families was difficult to administer, and it was increasingly difficult to find the food to distribute. Medicine was particularly scarce. Currency inflation also became disastrous. The South's emphasis on states' rights and its long congressional battles with Northern states over appropriations had made the central government reluctant to levy taxes for what many at first believed would be a very short conflict. The government therefore began printing ruinous amounts of currency and "war bonds." Although realistic taxes were levied by 1863, inflation had gone too far, and the actual resources of the South were too badly depleted for the government ever to regain a reasonable financial position. Despite initial Confederate battlefield victories, the Union's superior numbers and resources eventually overwhelmed the South. That the war lasted as long as it did—some 4 years—is testimony to the South's strong military leadership. After the fall of Richmond, General Robert E. Lee, commander of the Confederate forces, surrendered on Apr. 9, 1865, at Appomattox Court House.
See also: Civil War, U.S.

Confederation of Canada, union of British colonies established by the British Parliament in the British North America Act of 1867. This act provided for the formation of the Dominion of Canada and served as its constitution. It defined a self-governing community within the British Empire, not an independent country, with 2 levels of government, provincial and national. The dominion, which initially consisted of New Brunswick, Nova Scotia, Ontario, and Quebec, eventually developed into the Canada of today.

Confession, in Christianity, admission of sin, an aspect of repentance. General confession may be made in a congregation; private confession may be made to God or to a priest. The latter form, a sacrament of the Roman Catholic and Eastern churches, is also observed in some Lutheran and Episcopalian churches.

Confirmation, rite of certain Christian churches, usually administered in adolescence. The candidates confirm the promises made at their baptism, and the bishop lays his hands on them, invoking the Holy Spirit upon them. In the Roman Catholic and Eastern churches confirmation is a sacrament.
See also: Christianity.

Conflict of interest, situation in which an employee, part owner, officer or director of an organization has a financial or other interest in another organization that could cause him or her to favor one at the expense of the other.

Confucianism, philosophy based on the thinking of Confucius, the great Chinese philosopher and moralist. Confucianism teaches a moral and social philosophy and code of behavior based on certain abstract qualities and strengths, such as love, peace, harmony, order, humanity, wisdom, courage, and fidelity, without appealing to any ultimate higher authority or God. Heaven is the highest state one can attain, although no actual God-personality exists. One arrives at this perfect state by cultivating virtues such as curiosity, knowledge, patience, and sincerity, and by developing a personality based on the harmony of emotions and the harmony between the self and the universe. Thus people take their place in the universal pattern of creation, and immortality is won by those whose good name lives after them. Confucianism also has a strong social and political message. It teaches that individuals must not only cultivate themselves but must also enrich other people's lives.
See also: Confucius.

Confucius (551-479 B.C.), Chinese philosopher and sage, founder of Confucianism, the great moral and religious system of China. He began teaching at age 20, gathering about him a group of disciples. During the next 30 years he evolved the code of "right living" that was the basis of his philosophy. The ruling prince of the state of Lu appointed him magistrate of the city of Chang-tu, where Confucius put his principles into effect with great success. But he fell out of favor with the succeeding prince and for 13 years wandered with his followers, vainly seeking a patron and someone he could train as his "model ruler." Confucius's sayings and the most reliable information about his life are preserved in the *Confucian Analects*, compiled by his disciples shortly after his death. Although Confucius takes his place beside Gautama Buddha, Jesus, and Mohammed as founder of one of the world's great religions, he differs from them in being a rationalist who takes no account of mysticism or spirituality. His philosophy of human relationships, based on the golden rule "What you do not wish done to yourself, do not do to others," is essentially an appeal to reason and humanity.

Congenital defect *See:* Birth defect.

Conglomerate, corporation that has expanded into the production and sale of products quite different from those with which it was initially involved. Thus, a company identified with the extraction of metals may become conglomerate by moving into retail food, automobile accessories, and motion pictures.

Congo, Republic of the Congo, formerly part of French Equatorial Africa. It lies on the equator, with Gabon and the Atlantic Ocean to the west and Zaire to the east.
Land. A low, treeless plain extends from the coast inland for about 40 mi (64 km). The land then rises to the mountainous area of the Mayombé Escarpment, with its series of sharp ridges, a region of dense tropical rain forest. To the north is a plateau covered with grassland. The Zaire (Congo) River basin in the northeast is an area of numerous rivers and dense, tropical

Congo-Brazzaville

Capital:	Brazzaville
Area:	132,047 sq mi
	(342,000 sq km)
Population:	2,658,000
Language:	French
Government:	Republic
Independent:	1960
Head of gov.:	Prime minister
Per capita:	US $680
Mon. unit:	1 CFA franc = 100
	centimes

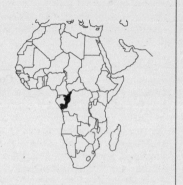

forests. The Zaire and its tributary, the Ubangi River, form most of the border between Congo and Zaire.

People. Some 60% of the population is rural, but there has been a major drift to the towns. Most people are Bantu speakers. French is the official language. The government has placed an emphasis on education, but the rate of illiteracy is still high.

Economy. Although the Congo has rich oil resources, a varied manufacturing sector, and ports providing it and its neighbors with vital outlets to the world market, it has had serious economic setbacks, mainly due to political instability and poor economic planning and management. The agricultural sector is underdeveloped.

History. The Congo was originally part of the Kingdom of the Kongo, a region first explored by the Portuguese in the 15th century and later broken up into smaller states and exploited by European slave traders. It became a French colony in 1891, an overseas territory of France in 1946, and an independent republic in 1960. Periodic civil strife from 1963 onward led to an army takeover in 1968. Following a presidential assassination in 1977 and subsequent martial law, the Congolese Labor Party, the sole legal party since 1970, confirmed a military head of state, Col. Denis Sassou-Nguesso, in 1979. Democratization in the early 1990s was accompanied by trouble and violence which eased off after a while. In 1997 the capital was largely destroyed as a result of the power struggle between Sassou-Nguesso (supported by Angolese troops) and the Congo government. Sessou-Nguesso ousted the democratically chosen president Pascal Lissouba (elected in 1992). Shortly afterwards, the country was closely involved in the power struggle in the neighboring country Congo (Kinshasa).

Congo (Kinshasa) *See:* Zaïre.

Congo River, or Zaire River, second-longest river in Africa. It flows north and west 2,700 mi (4,345 km) from its source in the Chambezi River, Zambia, to the Atlantic Ocean in western Zaire. In volume of water, it is second only to the Amazon. The Congo River was renamed the Zaire by Zaire's former President Mobutu in 1971.

Congregational Church, Protestant church that holds that each local congregation should have complete autonomy, though congregations may form loose associations. In the 16th century Robert Browne first stated Congregational doctrine. In the 17th century Congregationalists established churches in the New England colonies and founded Harvard and Yale universities. Most U.S. Congregationalists merged (1931) with the Christian Church and then with the Evangelical and Reformed Church (1957) to form the United Church of Christ.
See also: Protestantism.

Congressional Budget Office (CBO), agency of the U.S. Congress that provides information on the nation's economy, the federal budget, and federal programs to members of Congress. It prepares optional plans and studies their potential impact on the budget. It also prepares 5-year forecasts based upon existing federal policies of taxation and spending.

Congressional Record, printed daily account of the proceedings in the U.S. Congress. Initiated in 1873, the Congressional Record replaced other records of congressional activity dating from 1789. Because members of Congress may change their speeches before they appear in the Record, and because material other than speeches before Congress is printed there, the Congressional Record is not accurate as a transcript.

Congress of Industrial Organizations (CIO), association of industrial unions. Active from 1938 to 1955, it organized all workers in a plant into an industrial union (as opposed to a craft union, which focuses on one craft). The CIO organized both skilled and unskilled workers in steel, automotive, rubber, and other major industries. The CIO united with the American Federation of Labor (AFL) in 1955.
See also: American Federation of Labor and Congress of Industrial Organizations.

Congress of Racial Equality (CORE), U.S. interracial organization founded in 1942 by James Farmer to promote African American civil rights and liberties through nonviolent direct action projects. Its voter registration drives and "freedom rides" in the South led to civil rights legislation in the 1960s. In the 1970s CORE became more militant. By the 1980s it had virtually ceased to exist.

Congress of the Confederation, political body that operated the government of the United States from Mar. 1781 to Mar. 1789. It was established by the Articles of Confederation and replaced the Continental Congress. Upon adoption of the present constitution, the Congress of the U.S. replaced the Congress of the Confederation.
See also: Articles of Confederation.

Congress of the United States, legislative branch of the U.S. federal government. Congress consists of 2 houses: the Senate, composed of 2 members from each state, and the House of Representatives, in which seats are appointed to the states on the basis of population. House membership, which was 65 in 1789, has grown with the nation's population but is now permanently fixed at 435. Membership is in proportion to state population as determined every 10 years by the census, but every state has at least 1 representative. Each member of the House now represents about 470,000 people. The state legislatures have responsibility for drawing the boundaries of congressional districts, but in 1964 the Supreme Court intervened to order that congressional districts within each state be "substantially equal" in population. The whole House is elected every 2 years.

The Constitution grants the House special powers in 3 areas: impeaching federal officials (who are then tried by the Senate), originating all revenue bills, and electing the president if no candidate receives a majority in the Electoral College. The House is not a continuing body; it must organize itself anew when it meets for the first time in January following the election. The clerk of the House conducts the election of the speaker, who then takes office, swears in the other House members, and conducts the election of the other officers. The House adopts the rules of the new session, makes committee assignments, and begins work on a new round of legislation. The speaker is one of the most powerful figures in government, exercising an important influence over the course of legislation.

The U.S. Senate is composed of 100 members, 2 from each state. Since the Senate was created to represent the interests of the states, senators were elected by the state legislatures, rather than by popular vote, until 1913. The Senate is a continuing body; its members serve 6-year terms and only one-third of them are elected every 2 years. If a senator dies in office, the governor of the state names a replacement to serve until the next election. The Senate's advice and consent is necessary for appointments of all important government officials, including ambassadors and federal judges. The Senate also approves treaties, and the Foreign Relations Committee has become one of the most active in Congress, playing an important part in the conduct of foreign affairs. Since senators also represent much larger constituencies than do representatives, national and international issues generally play a larger role in Senate elections than in House contests. The Constitution provides that the vice-president shall preside over the Senate (he often delegates this duty to a senator), but the majority leader is usually the most powerful individual in the Senate. The Senate, being a smaller body than the House, allows much freer and more extensive debate, and many senators can attain considerable national stature.

For a bill (a proposed piece of legislation) to become law, the House and Senate must separately approve an identical text, which the president then must sign. If the latter vetoes (disapproves) a bill, Congress may repass it by two-thirds majority in each house. If the Senate and House versions of a bill differ, a committee is created to resolve the differences through compromise, and both houses vote on the new bill. Occasionally the House and Senate cannot agree, and the bill dies. Debate in the House is severely restricted because of the size of the body, but in the Senate, members may talk indefinitely and thus kill a bill unless cloture (closure of debate) is invoked by a two-thirds vote. Either house may separately pass a resolution on any subject, but such a resolution is not binding on the other house or on the president.

Congreve, William (1670-1729), English Restoration dramatist, known for his comedies of manners. Among his comedies are *The Old Bachelor* (1693), *Love for Love* (1695), and his masterpiece, *The Way of the World* (1700).

Conifer, any cone-bearing tree or shrub. Examples include the yews, pines, redwood, cypress, and araucarias. Conifers are found in the drier parts of the world, particularly in cold regions. They usually have needle- or scale-like leaves that reduce the loss of water from the plant. Except for the larches and bald cypress, conifers are evergreen, retaining their leaves all year round.

Conjunctivitis, inflammation of the conjunctiva of the eye (the mucous membrane that lines the inner surface of the eyelids); also called pink-eye. Viruses and allergies are the most common causes of this condition. Mixed or unidentifiable disease-causing microorganisms may be present, and irritation of the conjunctiva by wind, dust, smoke, and other types of air pollution is often responsible. Conjunctivitis may also accompany the common cold, infections involving skin rashes (especially measles), and irritation of the eye's cornea resulting from intense electric light, sunlamps, and reflections from snow.

Connally, John Bowden (1917-   ), U.S. secretary of the Navy (1961-63), governor of Texas (1963-69), U.S. secretary of the treasury (1971-72). Connally was seriously wounded while riding in John F. Kennedy's car when the president was assassinated in 1963. A Democrat throughout much of his career, Connally switched to the Republican party in 1973.

Connaught and Strathearn, Duke of (Arthur William Patrick Albert; 1850-1942), governor general of Canada (1911-16), son of Queen Victoria and Prince Albert of Great Britain. In 1874 he was made Duke of Connaught and Strathearn. He served as commander in chief of the British forces of the Mediterranean, 1907-09. As governor general of Canada he helped to inspire patriotism during the early years of World War I, and he reestablished the Canadian Patriotic Fund to help dependents of people serving in the Canadian armed forces.
See also: Canada.

Connecticut, state in the New England region of the United States; bordered by Massachusetts in the north, Rhode Island in the east, Long Island Sound in the south, and New York in the west.
Land and climate. The state is divided by the Connecticut River Valley into the western and eastern New England Uplands. The Taconic Mountains in the extreme northwest include Mt. Frissell. From these peaks the land slopes through rolling hills down to the coastal plain along Long Island Sound. The Connecticut River is the longest in New England. Connecticut's weather is moderate. Principal cities are Bridgeport, Hartford, New Haven, Waterbury, and Stamford.
Economy. Most of the state's prosperity comes from industry: Connecticut produces fabricated metal goods, electrical equipment, machinery, and, most importantly, transportation equipment. Groton is a national center for submarine production. Hartford is an important insurance center in the United States. Yale, founded in 1701, was the nation's third university.
Government. Under the constitution of 1965, the governor is elected for a 4-year term. The general assembly, elected every 2 years, consists of a senate of 36 members and a house of representatives of 177 members. Connecticut has no system of county government; the towns and cities are the units of

Connecticut

Capital:	Hartford
Statehood:	Jan. 9, 1788 (5th state)
Familiar names:	Constitution State, Nutmeg State
Area:	5,018 sq mi (12,997 sq km; ranks 48th)
Population:	3,270,000 (1997; ranks 27th)
Elevation:	Highest—2,380 ft (725 m), Mt. Frissell. Lowest—sea level
Motto:	Qui transtulit sustinet (He who transplanted still sustains)
State flower:	Mountain laurel
State bird:	American robin
State tree:	White oak
State song:	"Yankee Doodle"

local government in the state. Connecticut is represented by 2 senators and 6 representatives in the U.S. Congress.

History. In 1614 Adriaen Block, a Dutch explorer, discovered the Connecticut River. English colonists from Massachusetts established Connecticut's first permanent European settlement, Windsor, in 1633. In 1636 Hartford, Windsor, and Wethersfield formed an independent commonwealth, the Connecticut Colony. The colony adopted the Fundamental Orders, regarded by some as the first written constitution, in 1639. As one of the 13 original colonies, Connecticut took an active part in the American Revolution (1775-83). The state was a staunch supporter of the Union during the Civil War (1861-65), supplying 60,000 troops. Connecticut was an important industrial state by the late 19th century, thanks in part to the inventors who worked there, including Eli Whitney, who helped develop the system of mass production in the early 1800s. Except during the Great Depression of the 1930s, Connecticut has prospered throughout the 20th century, and it ranks among the top states in *per capita* income.

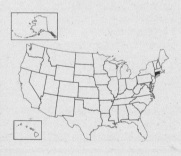

Connecticut River, longest river in New England. Rising in northern New Hampshire, the Connecticut flows south 407 mi (655 km) through Massachusetts and Connecticut before emptying into Long Island Sound. Discovered by Dutch explorers in 1614, the river is of great historical, agricultural, and industrial significance to the northeastern United States.

Connective tissue, basic tissue that constitutes the connective and supporting element of the body. Forms of connective tissue include fibrous bands, fat, blood, and bone. All forms of connective tissue consist of cells separated by a medium that has differentiated into matrix (amorphous elements) and fibers (formed elements). The matrix is a jellylike mass containing a variable number of fibers. Young cartilage is composed of a large number of cells surrounded by a firm matrix that contains a small number of fibers. Blood comprises a liquid matrix containing cells and fibers in a soluble form. The development of supporting tissue, such as cartilage and bone, results in cells being enclosed in a matrix that has a firm or hard composition.

Connelly, Marc(us Cook) (1890-1980), U.S. playwright, best known for his Pulitzer Prize-winning play *The Green Pastures* (1930). He collaborated with George S. Kaufman on several plays, including *Beggar on Horseback* (1924).

Connors, Jimmy (1952ᵉ   ), U.S. tennis player. He was the top-ranked player in the world through most of the 1970s. Known for his left-handed, two-fisted backhand, he won the U.S. Open (1974, 1976, 1978, 1982, 1983) and Wimbledon (1974, 1982).

Conquistadors, 16th-century military adventurers who founded Spain's empire in the Americas. Most famous among them were Hernán Cortes and Francisco Pizarro.

Conrad, Charles, Jr. (1930-), U.S. astronaut. In 1965 Conrad made an 8-day spaceflight in *Gemini 5* intended to prove that humans could endure weightlessness long enough to reach the moon and return. In 1970 Conrad was commander of the *Apollo 12* flight, which was the second moon landing.

Conrad, Joseph (1857-1924), English novelist of Polish birth. His years at sea, during which he acquired a remarkable command of the English language, provided backgrounds for many of his novels. His lasting concern was the individual in isolation, struggling against adversity, moral degradation, and the forces of nature. His early novels include *Almayer's Folly* (1895) and its powerful sequel *An Outcast of the Islands* (1896), both set in Borneo. *The Nigger of the "Narcissus"* (1897), *Lord Jim* (1900), and *Typhoon* (1903) are examples of his skill in creating atmosphere and character. The novella *Heart of Darkness* (1902) takes place on the Congo River, and the book Conrad considered his masterpiece, *Nostromo* (1904), is a story of revolution and corruption in South America.

Conrail, official nickname for Consolidated Rail Corp., a quasi-governmental U.S. organization created to take over 7 bankrupt railroads in the northeastern and northwestern regions, including the Penn Central, Erie & Lackawanna, Lehigh Valley, and Reading. Conrail began operations on April 1, 1976.

Conscientious objector, person opposed to war in any form or in the specific form it is then taking, who by reason of conscience and conviction refuses to bear arms in wartime. The United States requires either noncombat duty within the armed forces or alternative service in a socially useful category for those who, as conscientious objectors, refuse regular services. Many other countries recognize this status—including Great Britain, the

Commonwealth Nations, the Russian Federation, and many others in Europe and Latin America. Most require alternative noncombat service.
See also: Pacifism.

Conscription *See:* Draft, military.

Conservation, management and protection of the earth's natural resources to assure adequate supplies for future generations. Conservation aims to provide an environment free from pollution of air, water, and land, and to protect the welfare of plants, animals, and humans.

Conservatism, term for social and political philosophies or attitudes that stress traditional values and continuity of social institutions and that reject sudden radical change, while maintaining ideals of progress. It was first used in the early 19th century to describe the policies of the British Tory party. Modern conservative political parties include the British Conservative and Unionist Party, the Canadian Progressive-Conservative Party, and, in the United States, the Republican Party.

Conservative Party, one of the two major political parties in Great Britain. The second major political party is the Labor Party. The Conservative Party succeeded the Tory Party that appeared in the late 1600s. Benjamin Disraeli, a founder of the Conservative Party, strongly supported imperialism and advocated rights for the working class. In recent history, the Conservative Party has been in control of the British government since 1979. As head of the Conservative Party 1979-90, Margaret Thatcher became the first woman prime minister in British history. She was succeeded by Conservative John Major. At the general elections in 1997 the Conservative Party achieved the worst loss of seats since 1832. As a result, Major resigned as party leader.
See also: Disraeli, Benjamin.

Considérant, Victor Prosper (1808-93), French socialist. He promoted the doctrines of Charles Fourier, edited *La Phalange*, and published *Social Destiny* (1834-38) and *Principles of Socialism* (1847). He tried unsuccessfully to establish a communistic community in Texas (1855-57).

Conspiracy, in U.S. law, agreement between two or more people to commit an unlawful act. The act of conspiracy is in itself a crime; the unlawful act does not have to be committed. Conspiracy is punishable by fines or imprisonment.

Constable, John (1776-1837), English painter. He and J.M.W. Turner were England's 2 greatest landscapists. Believing that painting should be pursued scientifically, he explored techniques of rendering landscape from direct observation of nature under different effects of light and weather.

Constance Missal, one of the earliest books printed in Europe. Believed to be printed by the inventor of movable type, Johannes Gutenberg c.1450, Constance Missal was a book of masses for the German diocese of Constance.

Constanta (pop. 350,700), Romanian Black Sea seaport city. An industrial center with a modern harbor, Constanta exports petroleum and grain and is

Romania's primary Air and naval base Founded by the Greeks (7th century B.C.), Constanta became part of Romania in 1878.

Constantine (pop. 448,600), trading center in Algeria about 50 mi (80 km) from the Mediterranean Sea. A natural fortress, the city is on a plateau nearly surrounded by a steep gorge. Named for its patron, the Roman emperor Constantine the Great, it was built in A.D. 313 on the site of Cirta, a city destroyed by war.

Constantine, 2 kings of Greece. **Constantine I** (1868-1923) reigned 1913-17 and 1920-22. During World War I he opposed the Allies and was forced to abdicate the throne to his second son, Alexander. Brought back into power after Alexander's death, he abdicated again after the Greeks were defeated in a war with the Ottoman Empire. **Constantine II** (1940-) was king of Greece 1964-74. As a result of his unsuccessful attempt to overthrow the military junta ruling Greece at the time, Constantine II was forced into exile in Italy. In 1974 the Greek people voted to replace the monarchy with a republican form of government.
See also: Greece.

Constantine I, The Great (c.280-337), first Emperor of Rome to convert to Christianity. After his father, Constantius, died in 306, there was a struggle for the succession. In 312 on the eve of the decisive Battle of Milvian Bridge, near Rome, Constantine, who was already sympathetic to Christianity, is said to have seen a vision of a flaming cross in the sky. He won the battle and became emperor in the West, while his brother-in-law, Licinius, was emperor in the East. In 324 war broke out between them, and in 325 Licinius was killed. Constantine thus became the sole ruler of the Roman world. In 325 he convened the Council of Nicaea, which settled various disputes in church doctrine. He made Christianity the official religion of the empire and moved the capital to the city of Constantinople, named for him and dedicated to the Virgin Mary. Constantine reigned as an absolute ruler until his death.
See also: Christianity; Rome, Ancient.

Constantinople *See:* Istanbul.

Constellation, first U.S. Navy ship to capture a foreign warship. On Feb. 9, 1799, the *Constellation* captured the French frigate *L'Insurgente* during the 1798-1800 undeclared war between France and the United States.

Constellation, group of stars that appear to lie in the same area of the sky. Constellations figure prominently in the mythology and folklore of ancient civilizations. The Greeks, for instance, saw the shape of Orion the hunter, who, with a shield and club, is facing Taurus the bull. Many of the characters in adjoining constellations are related. Cepheus was the husband of Cassiopeia, whose daughter Andromeda was rescued from the sea monster Cetus by Perseus. Many of the star divisions and names were originated by the Greeks.

Constipation, decrease in the frequency of bowel actions from the norm for an individual; also increased hardness of stool. Often precipitated by inactivity or changed diet or environment, it is sometimes due to gastrointestinal tract disease.

Constitution, system of fundamental principles or rules for the government of a nation, society, labor union, or other group that establishes basic guidelines and a framework of orderly procedure. While most Western countries have written constitutions, it is important to distinguish between written and unwritten constitutions. The written constitution of the United States specifically catalogs the powers of the federal government and the rights of the citizens and states. Great Britain has an unwritten constitution in which common law and tradition play a greater part in the framework of the country's political and legal system than any single written document. There are also "hard" and "soft" constitutions. A "hard" constitution is difficult to alter, thus rendering it unresponsive to short-term political change. With a "soft" constitution alteration can be achieved relatively easily, for example, by a simple vote of the legislature. The constitution of the United States is a fairly "hard" document, since constitutional amendments require lengthy and involved procedures.

Constitutional law, U.S., section of the law that interprets and enforces the provisions of the U.S. Constitution. Although the Constitution, with its 7,000 words, launched the fledgling Union as a sovereign, democratic nation, it refrained from specifying too precisely the limits of governmental power or the roles of its institutions. A closer definition of these was left to history and experience. Constitutional law studies this historical development and pronounces on the contemporary status of its many concepts, concentrating on 3 topics: judicial review, the separation of powers, and the federal system. Judicial review deals with the powers of the U.S. courts—ultimately the Supreme Court—to pass judgment on the constitutionality of laws or specific acts of government. The U.S. Constitution did not provide for judicial review, but the Supreme Court has claimed, and exercised, the right to decide on constitutionality ever since Chief Justice John Marshall's famous decision in *Marbury* v. *Madison* (1803). His reasoning was simple: The Constitution is the supreme law of the land and it is the function of the courts to uphold the law; consequently, the courts are duty-bound to declare invalid any government law or action in conflict with the basic provisions of the Constitution. The Supreme Court exercises its power of review with restraint, and the burden of proof rests on the party challenging the law's constitutionality, not on the legislation. The Court assumes that the legislation does not enact measures intended to violate the Constitution.

The doctrine of separation of powers maintains that despotism is best prevented by dividing the powers of government among several branches that "check and balance" one another. The Constitution confers the legislative power upon Congress, the judicial authority upon the courts, and executive power upon the president. The federal system divides the powers of government between the national, or federal, government and the state administrators. The powers of the national government are enumerated in the Constitution, all other powers being reserved to the state governments. However, provisions like the clause that gives Congress the power to make all laws "necessary and proper" to carry out its Constitutional function and the right to regulate interstate commerce have greatly increased federal power.

Constitutional Union Party, U.S. political party formed from remnants of the Whig and American parties, active 1859-60. Its platform upheld the Constitution and the Union, while ignoring the slavery issue. As a result, the vote in 1860 was split and Lincoln was elected by the electoral college, the first President without a popular majority.

Constitution, USS, American frigate carrying 44 guns, known as "Old Ironsides." Launched in Boston in 1797, it served in the war with Tripoli and the War of 1812. In 1828 a plan to dismantle the warship provoked Oliver Wendell Holmes's poem "Old Ironsides." The *Constitution* was rebuilt, berthed in Boston, and opened to the public in 1934.

Constitution of the United States, supreme law of the nation. Written in Philadelphia in the summer of 1787, the Constitution was approved by the 55 delegates representing the 13 original states and went into effect on March 4, 1789, after ratification by the required 9 states. The actions of the virtually autonomous states and the failure of the country's first constitution, the Articles of Confederation, convinced the delegates that a strong executive and a powerful federal government were needed if the United States were to survive as a cohesive entity. The conflicting desires of large and small states resulted in a bicameral legislature, one house based on population size, the other house with an equal number of seats for each state. Most important was the eventual recognition by all stats that a strong central government would be needed if the United States was to be more than just a loose confederation. The states allayed their fears by constructing a separation of powers to limit governmental power. In 1791 a Bill of Rights to guarantee personal freedoms was added as the first 10 amendments to the Constitution. Only 16 amendments have been added since 1791.

Constructivism, artistic movement developed in Russia 1913-20 by Vladimir Tatlin, Naum (Pevsner) Gabo, and Antoine Pevsner. Partly influenced by cubism and futurism, it was related to technology and industrial materials. Gabo and Pevsner went into exile in 1921 when Soviet authorities moved against all modern art movements.